Philip Schaff

The Teaching of the twelve Apostles

Or, The oldest Church Manual

Philip Schaff

The Teaching of the twelve Apostles
Or, The oldest Church Manual

ISBN/EAN: 9783337162498

Printed in Europe, USA, Canada, Australia, Japan

Cover: Foto ©Lupo / pixelio.de

More available books at **www.hansebooks.com**

THE
Teaching of the Twelve Apostles

(ΔΙΔΑΧΗ ΤΩΝ ΔΩΔΕΚΑ ΑΠΟΣΤΟΛΩΝ)

OR, THE

OLDEST CHURCH MANUAL

THE DIDACHÈ AND KINDRED DOCUMENTS

IN THE ORIGINAL

WITH TRANSLATIONS AND DISCUSSIONS OF POST-APOSTOLIC TEACHING
BAPTISM WORSHIP AND DISCIPLINE

AND

WITH ILLUSTRATIONS AND FAC-SIMILES OF THE
JERUSALEM MANUSCRIPT

BY

PHILIP SCHAFF, D.D., LL.D.

PROFESSOR OF CHURCH HISTORY IN THE UNION THEOLOGICAL SEMINARY, NEW YORK

THIRD EDITION, REVISED AND ENLARGED

NEW YORK:
FUNK & WAGNALLS, Publishers
18 AND 20 ASTOR PLACE.

1890.

DOMINO REVERENDISSIMO AC DOCTISSIMO

Philotheo Bryennio, S.T.D.

METROPOLITANO NICOMEDIENSI

VIRO DE LITTERIS CHRISTIANIS OPTIME MERITO

CODICIS HIEROSOLYMITANI ATQUE EIUS LIBRI PRETIOSISSIMI
QUI INSCRIPTUS EST

Διδαχὴ τῶν δώδεκα Ἀποστόλων

INVENTORI EDITORI EXPLANATORI

HOC OPUS DEDICAT

PHILIPPUS SCHAFF

THEOLOGUS AMERICANUS

Occidens Orienti S.D.

*Εἷς Κύριος μία πίστις ἓν βάπτισμα εἷς Θεὸς καὶ
Πατὴρ πάντων ὁ ἐπὶ πάντων καὶ διὰ
πάντων καὶ ἐν πᾶσιν*

PREFACE TO THE THIRD EDITION.

QUITE unexpectedly I am called upon to prepare a third edition of this monograph. This is due to the uncommon interest which the *Didache* continues to excite as one of the few documents which connect the apostolic with the post-apostolic age, and shed light upon both. Already the *Didache* literature exceeds that on any of the so-called Apostolic Fathers. It was with considerable difficulty that I secured, soon after the discovery of the *Didache*, some fac-simile pages through friends in Constantinople; but now the whole document has been photographed, thanks to the kindness of the Greek Patriarch, Nicodemus of Jerusalem, and the American enterprise and zeal of the Rev. Dr. Hale, now in Iowa, Mr. Henry Gillman, United States Consul in Jerusalem, and the Johns Hopkins University of Baltimore. No such honor has been done yet to any other patristic work. The fac-simile proves the scholarly accuracy and conscientious care of Dr. Bryennios, whose edition and commentary will always remain in some respects the most remarkable. The only errors are the reading καθῆσαι in Chs. XII., 8, and XIII., 1, for καθῆσθαι, and κοσμοπλάνος in Ch. XVI., 4, for κοσμοπλανής (which is not so natural as the former).

The precious manuscript was in 1887 transferred from Constantinople to the Greek patriarchate of Jerusalem, where it properly belongs; and there, in the mother city of Christendom, the photographs have been taken.

The works on the *Didache* which appeared since the second edition in 1886 required the addition of a second Appendix—pp. 307–320. This completes the literature to date, without claiming to be exhaustive. A few minor corrections have been made in the text, the Index is enlarged, and the title page changed by putting the main title before "The Oldest Church Manual," which is explanatory. Otherwise the body of the book is unchanged.

I take great pleasure in acknowledging the efficient aid I received in the preparation of the second Appendix and the reading of the proof from my pupil and friend, Rev. Arthur C. McGiffert, who, after completing his theological studies in Europe and acquiring the degree of Doctor of Philosophy at Marburg, is now engaged in a new translation and commentary on the Church History of Eusebius for my "Library of the Nicene and Post-Nicene Fathers."

PHILIP SCHAFF.

January, 1889.

PREFACE TO THE SECOND EDITION.

THE call for a new edition gave me a welcome opportunity to make a number of corrections and improvements in the plates, and to add a supplement to the literature in an appendix (pp. 297 sqq.).

The *Didache* continues to engage the pens of biblical and historical scholars in Europe and America, and will continue to do so for some time to come. The last word on this important discovery has not yet been spoken. The *Didache* has secured a permanent place in every future collection of the Apostolic Fathers, in every future history of the New Testament Canon, of catechetical instruction, of primitive worship and discipline, and in Commentaries on the Gospel of Matthew.

So far there seems to be a growing unanimity on the views expressed in this book, and I have no reason to change them. I feel profoundly grateful for the favorable public notices and private letters of competent scholars at home and abroad.

P. S.

NEW YORK, *March* 23, 1886.

PREFACE TO THE FIRST EDITION.

As soon as I received a copy of the newly discovered *Teaching of the Twelve Apostles*, I determined, in justice to myself and to my readers, to prepare an independent supplement to the second volume of my revised *Church History*, which had appeared a few months before. Accordingly, during a visit to Europe last summer, I made a complete collection of the *Didache* literature, but could not put the material into shape before the fourth volume of that *History* was published. The delay has enabled me to use several important works which reached me while my own was passing through the hands of the printer.

PREFACE TO THE FIRST EDITION.

The *Didache* fills a gap between the Apostolic age and the Church of the second century, and sheds new light upon questions of doctrine, worship, and discipline. Herein lies its interest and significance.

My object is to explain this document in the light of its Apostolic antecedents and its post-Apostolic surroundings, and thus to furnish a contribution to the history of that mysterious transition period between A.D. 70 and 150.

The reader will find here, besides the discussions of the various topics, the full text of the *Didache* and kindred documents in the original with translations and notes, and a number of illustrations which give a unique interest to the volume.

To the Metropolitan of Nicomedia I desire to express my great obligation for the instruction derived from his admirable edition of the *Didache*, and for the special interest he has taken in my work. My thanks are due also to Professor Warfield, Dr. Crosby, and Mr. Arthur C. McGiffert for valuable contributions. The portrait of the discoverer is from a photograph taken several years ago by the photographer of the Sultan, which Dr. Bryennios himself has kindly sent me.* The baptismal pictures are reproduced, by permission, from Roller's work on the Roman Catacombs. The view of the Jerusalem Monastery and the fac-similes of the famous MS. which contains the *Didache*, I secured through the aid of my esteemed friends, Dr. Washburn, President of Robert College, Constantinople, and Professor Albert L. Long, of the same institution, which shines on the shores of the Bosphorus as a beacon-light of promise for the intellectual and spiritual regeneration of Turkey and the cradle-lands of Christianity.

THE AUTHOR.

NEW YORK, UNION THEOLOGICAL SEMINARY,
    May 21, 1885.

---

* I have just received a friendly letter from Dr. B., dated Nicomedia, April $\frac{11}{23}$, 1885, in which he expresses great satisfaction with advanced proofs I had sent him a few weeks ago, and gives me permission to dedicate my book to him.

CONTENTS.

THE OLDEST CHURCH MANUAL,
CALLED THE
TEACHING OF THE TWELVE APOSTLES.

		PAGE
CHAPTER I.	THE JERUSALEM MONASTERY	1
" II.	A PRECIOUS VOLUME	2
	(TWO FAC-SIMILES OF THE JERUSALEM MS., 6 AND 7.)	
" III.	PHILOTHEOS BRYENNIOS	8
" IV.	PUBLICATION OF THE DIDACHE	9
" V.	A LITERARY SENSATION	10
" VI.	VARIOUS ESTIMATES	12
" VII.	THE TITLE	14
" VIII.	AIM AND CONTENTS	16
" IX.	THE CATECHETICAL PART	17
" X.	THE TWO WAYS	18
" XI.	THE THEOLOGY OF THE DIDACHE	22
" XII.	THE RITUAL OF THE DIDACHE	26
" XIII.	THE LORD'S DAY AND THE CHRISTIAN WEEK	27
" XIV.	PRAYER AND FASTING	29
" XV.	BAPTISM IN THE DIDACHE	29
" XVI.	BAPTISM AND THE CATACOMBS	36
	(FOUR ILLUSTRATIONS.)	
" XVII.	IMMERSION AND POURING IN HISTORY	41
" XVIII.	THE AGAPE AND THE EUCHARIST	56
" XIX.	ECCLESIASTICAL ORGANIZATION	62
" XX.	APOSTOLIC AND POST-APOSTOLIC GOVERNMENT	64
" XXI.	APOSTLES AND PROPHETS	67
" XXII.	BISHOPS AND DEACONS	73
" XXIII.	THE END OF THE WORLD	75
" XXIV.	THE DIDACHE AND THE SCRIPTURES	78
" XXV.	THE STYLE AND VOCABULARY OF THE DIDACHE	95
" XXVI.	AUTHENTICITY OF THE DIDACHE	114
" XXVII.	TIME OF COMPOSITION	119
" XXVIII.	PLACE OF COMPOSITION	123
" XXIX.	AUTHORSHIP	125

CONTENTS.

CHAPTER XXX. THE APOSTOLICAL CHURCH ORDER, OR THE ECCLESIASTICAL CANONS OF THE HOLY APOSTLES...... 127
" XXXI. THE APOSTOLICAL CONSTITUTIONS............... 132
" XXXII. SUMMARY OF LESSONS FROM THE DIDACHE........ 138
" XXXIII. THE LITERATURE OF THE DIDACHE.............. 140

THE DOCUMENTS.

I. THE DIDACHE, GREEK AND ENGLISH, WITH COMMENTS.......... 161
II. A LATIN FRAGMENT OF THE DIDACHE, WITH A CRITICAL ESSAY... 219
III. THE EPISTLE OF BARNABAS, GREEK AND ENGLISH.... 227
IV. THE SHEPHERD OF HERMAS, GREEK AND ENGLISH.............. 234
V. THE APOSTOLICAL CHURCH ORDER, GREEK AND ENGLISH 237
VI. THE APOSTOLICAL CHURCH ORDER FROM THE COPTIC, ENGLISH... 249
VII. THE SEVENTH BOOK OF THE APOSTOLICAL CONSTITUTIONS, GREEK AND ENGLISH... 259
A LETTER AND COMMUNICATION FROM METROPOLITAN BRYENNIOS. 289

FIRST APPENDIX.

THE DIDACHE LITERATURE,
From May, 1885, till March, 1886............................. 297

SECOND APPENDIX.

THE DIDACHE LITERATURE,
From 1886 till 1888................................. 307
Alphabetical Index................................. 321

ILLUSTRATIONS.

PORTRAIT OF BRYENNIOS......................................*Frontispiece*
THE JERUSALEM MONASTERY OF THE MOST HOLY SEPULCHRE........... 1
FAC-SIMILE OF THE FIRST LINES OF THE DIDACHE.................... 6
FAC-SIMILE OF THE LAST PAGE OF THE JERUSALEM MANUSCRIPT........ 7
FOUR BAPTISMAL PICTURES FROM THE ROMAN CATACOMBS.....37, 38, 39, 40
AUTOGRAPH LETTER FROM BRYENNIOS............................ 296

THE JERUSALEM MONASTERY OF THE MOST HOLY SEPULCHRE IN STAMBUL.

The Library which contains the "Jerusalem Manuscript," is the small building shaded by the trees. The monks in front, one with the "Didache" in his hand, are looking towards the Golden Horn and Pera. The large new building in the background is a Greek National School.

THE

OLDEST CHURCH MANUAL

CALLED

"TEACHING OF THE TWELVE APOSTLES."

CHAPTER I.

The Jerusalem Monastery.

THE JERUSALEM MONASTERY OF THE MOST HOLY SEPULCHRE is an irregular mass of buildings in the Greek quarter of Constantinople, called "Phanar." It belongs to the Patriarch of Jerusalem, who resides there when on a visit to the capital of Turkey. In the same district are the church and residence of the Constantinopolitan patriarch, and the city residences of the chief metropolitans of his diocese. The Phanar surpasses the Moslem quarters in cleanliness and thrift, and its inhabitants, the Phanariotes, are largely employed as clerks and transcribers of documents.

Around the humble and lonely retreat of the Jerusalem Monastery and its surroundings cluster many historical associations. The mind wanders back to the "upper room" in Jerusalem, the first Pentecost, the mother church of Christendom, the last persecutor of the religion of the cross and its first protector, the turning-point of the relation of church and state, the founding of New Rome, the transfer of empire from the banks of the Tiber to the lovely shores of the Bosphorus, the doctrinal controversies on the Holy Trinity and Incarnation, the Œcumenical Councils, the conflict between the Patriarch and the Pope, the Filioque and the Primacy, the origin and progress of the great Schism, the wild romance of the Crusades, the downfall of Constantinople, the long sleep and oppression of the Eastern Church, the revival of letters and the Reformation in the West. We see the decline and approaching end of Turkish misrule, and look hopefully forward to the solution of the Eastern problem by a political and moral renovation which is slowly but surely progressing.

The Monastery of the Holy Sepulchre is a type of the Christian Orient; it is a shrine of venerable relics; it has the imploring beauty and eloquence of decay with signs of a better future. Some rich and patriotic Greeks in Constantinople have recently erected near the Monastery a magnificent building for national Greek education.* May a new Church of the Resurrection at no distant day rise out of the Monastery of the Sepulchre!

CHAPTER II.

A Precious Volume.

The Jerusalem Monastery possesses, like most convents, a library. It is preserved in a small stone chamber, erected for the purpose and detached from the other buildings. It receives scanty light through two strongly barred windows. Its entrance is adorned with holy pictures. It contains about a thousand bound volumes and "from four hundred to six hundred manuscripts," as the present superior, the archimandrite Polycarp, informed a recent visitor "with characteristic indefiniteness."

Among the books of this library was one of the rarest treasures of ancient Christian literature. It is a collection of manuscripts bound in one volume, covered with black leather, carefully written on well preserved parchment by the same hand, in small, neat, distinct letters, and numbering in all 120 leaves or 240 pages of small octavo (nearly 8 inches long by 6 wide). The book was transferred to Jerusalem in 1887. It embraces seven Greek documents as follows: †

---

* See picture of the Monastery, reproduced from a photograph, facing p. 1.

† The volume was first described by Bryennios in the Prolegomena to his ed. of the Clementine Epistles, 1875; and by Prof. Albert L. Long, of Constantinople, in the New York *Independent* for July 31, 1884. The *Didache* has since been photographed in Jerusalem and published by the Johns Hopkins University of Baltimore, 1887. See p. 310 *sq.*

1. A Synopsis of the Old and New Testaments in the Order of Books by St. Chrysostom (fol. 1–32).

The Synopsis, however, closes with the prophet Malachi, and omits the New Testament. Montfaucon had published such a work down to Nahum, in the sixth volume of his edition of Chrysostom, reprinted by Migne. Bryennios, in his edition of the *Didache*, has now supplied the textual variations to Migne, and the unpublished portions on Habakkuk, Zephaniah, Haggai, Zachariah, and Malachi.*

2. The Epistle of Barnabas (fol. 33–51ᵇ).

This is an additional copy to that found in the Codex Sinaiticus of the Bible, and published by Tischendorf, 1862. The older editions contain the first four chapters only in the Latin version. The value of the new MS. consists in a number of new readings which Bryennios communicated to Professor Hilgenfeld, of Jena, for his second edition (1877) †

3. The First Epistle of Clement of Rome to the Corinthians (fol. 51ᵇ med.—70ᵃ med.).

This is the only *complete* manuscript of that important document of the post-apostolic age; the only other MS. in the Codex Alexandrinus of the Bible, preserved in the British Museum, is defective towards the close.‡

4. The Second Epistle of Clement to the Corinthians (fol. 70ᵃ med.—76ᵃ med.).

Likewise the only *complete* copy. It contains the first Christian Homily extant, but it is not by Clement, although the discoverer considers it genuine.

They differ in the numeration of the MS.: Bryennios gives 456 as its number in the library; Long, from more recent examination, 446. Perhaps the former is a printing error, or the volumes of the library have been re-numbered.

* In the third Appendix to his Prolegomena, pp. ρϑ'-ρμζ'.

† The Jerusalem MS. is also utilized in the second edition of Barnabas by von Gebhardt and Harnack, Leipzig, 1878, and by Fr. X. Funk, in his ed. of *Opera Patrum Apost.* (the fifth of Hefele), Tübingen, 1878.

‡ Bryennios calls the new text of the Clementine Epistles " The Jerusalem MS." (Ἱεροσολυμικός), and is followed by Hilgenfeld, but von Gebhardt, Harnack, and Lightfoot designate it by the letter C (Constantinopolitanus) in distinction from A (Alexandrinus). In the case of the *Didache* there is no rival MS.

Documents 3 and 4 were published by Bryennios in 1875 to the great delight of Christian scholars.*

5. THE TEACHING (DIDACHE) OF THE TWELVE APOSTLES, on four leaves (fol. 76ᵃ med.—80).

By far the most valuable of the documents, although less than ten pages. It begins on the fourth line from the bottom of fol. 76ᵃ. The half page at the close of the *Did.* is left blank.

The following is a fac-simile of the title and first lines, which we obtained through the aid of influential friends in Constantinople:

Διδαχὴ τῶν δώδεκα ἀποστόλων.
Διδαχὴ κυρίου διὰ τῶν δώδεκα ἀποστόλων τοῖς ἔθνεσιν. ὁδοὶ δύο εἰσί, μία τῆς ζωῆς καὶ μία τοῦ θανάτου· διαφορὰ δὲ πολλὴ μεταξὺ τῶν δύο ὁδῶν. ἡ μὲν οὖν ὁδὸς τῆς ζωῆς ἐστιν αὕτη· πρῶτον, ἀγαπή—

[*Translation.*]

" Teaching of the Twelve Apostles.
Teaching of the Lord, through the Twelve Apostles, to the Gentiles. Two Ways there are: one of Life and one of Death; but there is a great difference between the two Ways. Now the Way of Life is this: first, Thou shalt love.."

6. THE SPURIOUS EPISTLE OF MARY OF CASSOBOLI † to the Bishop and Martyr Ignatius of Antioch (fol. 81–82ᵃ med.).

---

* Under the title, as translated into English: THE TWO EPISTLES OF OUR HOLY FATHER CLEMENT, BISHOP OF ROME, TO THE CORINTHIANS, *from a manuscript in the Library of the Most Holy Sepulchre in Phanar (ἐν Φαναρίῳ) of Constantinople; now for the first time published complete, with Prolegomena and Notes by* PHILOTHEOS BRYENNIOS, *Metropolitan of Serræ.* Constantinople, 1875. The new portions are given in full with valuable notes in Lightfoot's *Appendix* to his ed. of *S. Clement of Rome* (London, 1877). Von Gebhardt and Harnack have used the Constantinopolitan MS. in their second ed. of Clement (1876), and Funk in his ed. of the Ap. Fathers (1878). Comp. my *Church History,* II. 648 sqq. (revised ed.).

† *Μαρία Κασσοβόλων* or *Κασταβάλων.* See the different readings in Zahn's ed. of *Ignat.*, p. 174, and in Lightfoot's *S. Ignat.*, II. 719 sq.

Cassoboli or Cassobola is either Castabala,* a city of Cilicia, or more probably a small town in that province.† The Epistle is worthless.

7. TWELVE PSEUDO-IGNATIAN EPISTLES, beginning with a letter of Ignatius to Mary of Cassoboli and ending with that to the Romans (fol. 82ᵃ med.—120ᵃ).

The value of these Epistles consists in the new readings, which Bryennios generously furnished to Professor Funk of Tübingen for his edition of the Apostolic Fathers.‡

Near the middle of the left-hand page of the last leaf is the subscription of the copyist "Leon, notary and sinner," in the most contracted and abbreviated style of handwriting, with the date Tuesday, June 11, in the year of the world 6564 according to Byzantine reckoning, which is equivalent to A.D. 1056.§

Leon, probably an humble monk, did not dream that eight hundred years after his death the work of his hand would attract the liveliest interest of scholars of such nations and countries as he never heard of, or knew only as rude barbarians of the West.

"The hand that wrote doth moulder in the tomb;
The book abideth till the day of doom."

The following is a fac-simile of the last page of this remarkable volume, which contains the conclusion of the pseudo-Ignatian Epistle to the Romans, the subscription, and notes on the genealogy of Christ.

---

* Καστάβαλα. See Funk, *Patr. Ap.*, II. 46. † Lightfoot, *l. c.*, II. 720.

‡ Funk says (*Opera Patr. Apost.* Vol. II. p. xxx.): "*Philotheus Bryennius, metropolita Nicomediensis, vir de literis Christianis optime meritus, maxima cum liberalitate epistulas pseudoignatianas in usum meum accuratissime contulit.*" The longer Greek recension embraces the Epistles to Mary of Cassoboli, to the Trallians, the Magnesians, the Tarsians, the Philippians, the Philadelphians, the Smyrnæans, to Polycarp, to the Antiochians, to Heron (deacon of Antioch), to the Ephesians, and to the Romans (pp. 46–214). Funk gives pp. 214–217, the three additional letters of Ignatius to John the Evangelist and the Virgin Mary, with her response, which exist only in Latin. See also Lightfoot's *S. Ignatius*, II., 653–656.

§ The Greek Calendar of Constantinople estimates the Saviour's birth to have taken place 5508 years after the creation, according to the reckoning of the Septuagint. Deduct 5508 from 6564, and you have the date A.D. 1056.

[Greek manuscript text - not transcribable with confidence]

σὺν πολλοῖς καὶ ἄλλοις Κρόκος, τὸ ποθητὸν ὄνομα. Περὶ τῶν προσελθόντων ἀπὸ Συρίας εἰς Ῥώμην εἰς δόξαν Θεοῦ πιστεύω ὑμᾶς ἐπεγνωκέναι· οἷς καὶ δηλώσετε ἐγγύς με ὄντα· πάντες γάρ εἰσιν ἄξιοι Θεοῦ καὶ ὑμῶν· οὓς πρέπον ἐστὶν ὑμῖν κατὰ πάντα ἀναπαῦσαι. Ἔγραψα δὲ ὑμῖν ταῦτα τῇ πρὸ ἐννέα καλανδῶν Σεπτεμβρίων. Ἔρρωσθε εἰς τέλος ἐν ὑπομονῇ Ἰησοῦ Χριστοῦ.—

Ἐτελειώθη μηνὶ Ἰουνίῳ εἰς τὴν ιά, ἡμέραν Γ'. Ἰνδικτ. Θ', ἔτους ϛτϟξδ', χειρὶ Λέοντος νοταρίου καὶ ἀλείτου.

[*Translation*, including the remainder of the tenth chapter of the pseudo-Ignatian Epistle to the Romans.]

"(I write this to you from Smyrna through Ephesians worthy of happiness. But there is with me) Crocus, the beloved name, along with many others also. Concerning those coming from Syria unto Rome for the glory of God I believe you know them; and to them ye will announce that I am near. For they are all worthy of God and of you, and it is becoming that you should refresh them in every way. I have written these things unto you on the day before the 9th Kalends of September. Fare ye well until the end in the endurance of Jesus Christ."

[Subscription.]

"Finished in the month of June, upon the 11th (of the month), day 3d (of the week, *i.e.*, Tuesday), Indiction 9, of the year 6564. By the hand of Leon, notary and sinner."

The rest of the page is filled out by the same hand with notes on the genealogy of Joseph and Mary, following the authority of Julius Africanus and Eusebius, who reconcile Matthew and Luke by the theory that Matthew gives the royal descent of Joseph through Solomon, Luke the private descent of Joseph through Nathan. Bryennios has deciphered the MS. and prints it in legible Greek, in his edition of the *Didache*, p. ρμη'. It begins:

Ἰωσὴφ ὁ ἀνὴρ Μαρίας, ἐξ ἧς ἐγεννήθη ὁ Χριστός, ἐκ Λευιτικῆς φυλῆς κατάγεται, ὡς ὑπέδειξαν οἱ θεῖοι εὐαγγελισταί. Ἀλλ' ὁ μὲν Ματθαῖος ἐκ Δαβὶδ διὰ Σολομῶντος κατάγει τὸν Ἰωσήφ· ὁ δὲ Λουκᾶς διὰ Νάθαν, Σολομῶν δὲ καὶ Νάθαν υἱοὶ Δαβίδ.

CHAPTER III.

Philotheos Bryennios.

THE Jerusalem Manuscript was hidden from the knowledge of the world for eight hundred years. The library was examined by Bethmann in 1845, by M. Guigniant in 1856, and by the Bodleian librarian, Rev. H. O. Coxe, in 1858, but they failed to observe its chief treasure. The monks themselves were as ignorant of its contents and value, as the monks of Mount Sinai were of the still greater treasure of the Codex Sinaiticus. At last it was discovered in 1873, and a portion of it published (The Clementine Epistles) in 1875.

The happy discoverer and first editor is PHILOTHEOS BRYENNIOS, formerly Metropolitan of Serræ, an ancient see (Heraclea) of Macedonia, now Metropolitan of Nicomedia (Ismid). This was once the magnificent capital of Bithynia and the residence of the Emperor Diocletian, where the last and the most terrible persecution of the Church broke out (A.D. 303), and where Constantine the Great, the first Christian Emperor, was baptized and closed his life (337). Bryennios is next in rank to the Patriarch of Constantinople and the Bishop of Ephesus, and usually resides in Constantinople, in a narrow, unpainted, wooden house of four stories, opposite the entrance of the patriarchal church and a few steps from the Jerusalem Monastery.

He is probably the most learned prelate of the Greek Church at the present day. He was born in Constantinople (1833), studied in the patriarchal Seminary on the island of Chalce, and in three German Universities (Leipzig, Berlin and Munich). He attended the second of the Old Catholic Conferences at Bonn (in 1875). He is well versed in the patristic, especially Greek, and in modern German literature. He freely quotes, in his two books on the Clementine Epistles, and on the *Didache*, the writings of Bingham, Schröckh, Neander, Gieseler, Hefele, von Drey, Krabbe, Bunsen, Dressel, Schliemann, Bickell, Tischendorf, Hilgenfeld, Lagarde, Ueltzen, Funk, Probst, Kraus, Uhlhorn, Migne's *Patrologia*, Winer's *Biblisches Realwörterbuch*, and the writers in Herzog's *Real-*

Encyklopädie.* He was cordially welcomed by the scholars of the West, Catholic and Evangelical, to a permanent seat of honor in the republic of Christian learning. He may be called the Tischendorf of the Greek Church. The University of Edinburgh, at its tercentennial festival in 1884, justly conferred on him the honorary degree of Doctor of Divinity.

Bryennios is described as a tall, dignified, courteous Eastern prelate, in the prime of manhood, with a fine, intelligent and winning face, high forehead, black hair, long mustache and beard, dark and expressive eyes, great conversational power and personal magnetism. He was a prominent, though passive candidate for the vacant patriarchal chair, which, however, has been recently filled (1884) by a different man.†

CHAPTER IV.

Publication of the Didache.

BRYENNIOS seems to have paid no particular attention to the *Didache* when he announced its title, and nothing more, among the contents of the Jerusalem Manuscript.‡ But after the close of the Russo-Turkish war, in 1878, he examined it more carefully, and at last published the Greek text, with learned notes and Prolegomena, written in Greek, at the close of 1883, at Constantinople.§

---

* It is quite amusing to meet these names in Greek dress, as ὁ Σροίκχιος, ὁ Νέανδρος, ὁ Γισελέριος, ὁ Βικκέλλιος, ὁ Ἔφελος, ὁ Ἰλγεμφέλδος, ὁ Οὐλχόρνιος (ἐν τῇ Real-Encycl. τοῦ Herzog), etc.

† I learn from a friend in Constantinople (Feb. 10, 1885,) that "Bryennios is now in Nicomedia and not allowed to come to Constantinople," but that there is no truth in the newspaper rumor of a "rapprochement between the Greek and Roman Churches" under the new Patriarch.

‡ Nor could any other scholar infer its importance from the mere title. Bishop Lightfoot (in his *Appendix to S. Clement of Rome*, 1877, p. 231) simply said : "What may be the value of the *Doctrina Apostolorum* remains to be seen."

§ The title, translated into English, reads : TEACHING OF THE TWELVE APOSTLES. *From the Jerusalem Manuscript now for the first time published with Prolegomena and Notes, by Philotheos Bryennios, Metropolitan of*

Great as was his service to Christian literature by the publication of the Clementine Epistles, which were in part known before, that service was eclipsed by the publication of the *Didache*, which had entirely disappeared, with the exception of a few references to it among the Greek fathers.

CHAPTER V.

A Literary Sensation.

SELDOM has a book created so great a sensation in the theological world. Tischendorf's discovery of the Codex Sinaiticus of the Greek Bible, in the Convent of St. Catherine, at the foot of Mount Sinai, in 1859, after three journeys through the wilderness, is far more important, and has besides all the charm of a heroic romance. But the interest felt in "the find" of Bryennios was perhaps even more extensive, though less deep and lasting. The German divines fell upon the precious morsel with ravenous appetite. The first public notice of the *Didache* appeared in the "Allgemeine Zeitung" of Munich, January 25, 1884. A few days afterwards, Dr. Adolf Harnack, Professor of Church History in the University of Giessen, who had received an advance copy directly from the editor in Constantinople, published a notice with a German translation of the greater part (from Chs. VII.–XVI.) of the document.* This was only a forerunner of his able and learned book on the sub-

---

Nicomedia. Constantinople, 1883. The book has no preface, but was finished in December of that year, and therefore would, according to European fashion, bear the imprint of 1884. It contains 149 pages Prolegomena and 55 pages text with critical notes, to which are added indexes and corrigenda (p. 57-75). It is the only edition taken from the MS. itself, and the parent of all other editions. The MS. has since become almost inaccessible, but there is not the slightest ground for distrusting either the learning and ability, or the honesty of Bryennios; on the contrary, they are evident on every page of his edition.

* In the "Theologische Literaturzeitung" (of which he is the editor), Leipzig, Feb. 3, 1884. It was from this article that the first notice was sent to America, by Dr. Caspar René Gregory, in a communication to the New York "Independent" for Feb. 28, 1884, containing an English translation of the German version of Harnack.

ject which appeared in June of the same year.* Dr. Hilgenfeld, Professor in Jena, received likewise a copy directly from Bryennios, January 13, 1884,† and forthwith published the Greek text with critical emendations. ‡ Dr. Aug. Wünsche soon followed with an edition of the Greek text and German translation and brief notes, in May, 1884. Independently of these publications, Dr. Theodor Zahn, Professor in Erlangen, and one of the first patristic scholars of the age, made the *Didache* the subject of a thorough investigation in his "Supplementum Clementinum" (278-319), which appeared in June or July, 1884. § Bickell, of Innsbruck; Funk, of Tübingen; Krawutzcky, of Breslau,—three eminent Roman Catholic scholars,—Holtzmann, of Strassburg; Bonwetsch, of Dorpat, and many others, followed with reviews and discussions of special points in various German periodicals.

In England the first notice of the *Didache* appeared in the "Durham University Journal" for February, 1884, by Rev. A. Robertson, Principal of Hatfield Hall, Durham. Professor John Wordsworth, of Oxford, Archdeacon Farrar, of London, Professor A. Plummer, of Durham, and a number of other Episcopalians, appeared on the field with editions, translations and critical discussions in the "Guardian," the "Contemporary Review," the "Church Quarterly Review," etc. Prof. Hatch, of Oxford, delivered an interesting lecture on the subject (not yet published) in the Jerusalem Chamber, London. Bishop Lightfoot discussed the document briefly in the Church Congress at Carlisle (Sept., 1884). Rev. Mr. De Romestin (1884) and Canon Spence (1885) published the Greek text with an English version, notes and discussions.

---

* DIE LEHRE DER ZWÖLF APOSTEL *nebst Untersuchungen zur ältesten Geschichte der Kirchenverfassung und des Kirchenrechts.* With an Appendix by Oscar von Gebhardt, Leipzig, 1884. Text and translation with notes, 70 pages, Prolegomena, 294 pages.

† So he informs us in his "Zeitschrift für wissenschaftl. Theologie," 1885, No. I, p. 73.

‡ In the second ed. of his *Novum Testam. extra Canonem receptum.* Lips., 1884. Fasc. IV., 94-103.

§ Comp. also his critical notice of Harnack's book in the "Theol. Literaturblatt," Leipzig, for June 27 and July 11, 1884.

More extensive even than in any country of Europe was the interest with which the *Didache* was received in the United States. As soon as the first copies reached the Western hemisphere, the book was reprinted, translated and commented upon by theological professors and editors of religious newspapers of all denominations and sects. The first American edition, with the Greek text and notes, was prepared by Prof. Roswell D. Hitchcock, D.D., and Prof. Francis Brown, D.D., of Union Theological Seminary, New York, as early as March, 1884. Almost simultaneously appeared a translation by the Rev. C. C. Starbuck, with an introductory notice by Prof. Egbert C. Smyth, D.D., in the "Andover Review" for April, 1884. Since that time at least half a dozen other translations with or without the original were published; while a list of discussions and notices in the periodical press would fill several pages.

The document has also excited more or less attention in France, Holland, Switzerland, and the Scandinavian countries.

CHAPTER VI.

Various Estimates.

THE cause of this unusual attention to an anonymous book of no more than ten octavo pages, is obvious. The post-Apostolic age from the destruction of Jerusalem (A.D. 70) to the middle of the second century is the darkest, that is, the least known, in Church history. The newly discovered document promised a long-desired answer to many historical questions.

In Germany and on the Continent generally, where theology has a predominantly scientific and speculative character, the *Didache* was discussed with exhaustive learning and acumen as a contribution to historical information, with regard to its authorship, the time and place of composition, its precise text, its relation to cognate documents, as the Epistle of Barnabas, the Pastor Hermæ, the Judicium Petri, the Ecclesiastical Canons, and the Apostolical Constitutions.

In England, and especially in America, where theology is

more practical and more closely connected with Church life than in Germany, the *Didache* was welcomed in its bearing upon controverted points of doctrine, ritual and polity, and utilized for sectarian purposes.

Pædobaptists found in it a welcome argument for pouring or sprinkling, as a legitimate mode of baptism; Baptists pointed triumphantly to the requirement of immersion in living water as the rule, and to the absence of any allusion to infant baptism; while the *threefold* repetition of immersion and the requirement of previous fasting suited neither party. Episcopalians were pleased to find Bishops and Deacons (though no Deaconesses), but non-Episcopalians pointed to the implied identity of Bishops and Presbyters; while the travelling Apostles and Prophets puzzled the advocates of all forms of Church government. The friends of liturgical worship derived aid and comfort from the eucharistic prayers and the prescription to recite the Lord's Prayer three times a day; but free prayer is likewise sanctioned, and "the Prophets" are permitted to pray as long as they please after the eucharistic sacrifice with which the Agape was connected. Roman Catholic divines found traces of purgatory, and the daily sacrifice of the mass, but not a word about the Pope and an exclusive priesthood, or the worship of Saints and the Virgin, or any of the other distinctive features of the Papal system; while another Roman Catholic critic depreciates the *Didache* as a product of the Ebionite sect. Unitarians and Rationalists were pleased with the meagreness of the doctrinal teaching and the absence of the dogmas of the Trinity, Incarnation, depravity, atonement, etc.; but they overlooked the baptismal formula and the eucharistic prayers, and the fact that the roots of the Apostles' Creed are at least as old as the *Didache*, as is proven by the various ante-Nicene rules of faith. Millennarians and anti-Millennarians have alike appealed to the *Didache* with about equal plausibility.

We must look at the *Didache*, as on any other historical document, impartially and without any regard to sectarian issues. It is, in fact, neither Catholic nor Protestant, neither Episcopalian nor anti-Episcopalian, neither Baptist nor Pædo-

Baptist, neither Sacerdotal nor anti-Sacerdotal, neither Liturgical nor anti-Liturgical; yet it is both in part or in turn. It does not fit into any creed or ritual or Church polity or Church party of the present day; yet it presents one or more points of resemblance to Greek, Latin, and Protestant views and usages. It belongs, like the writings of the Apostolic Fathers, to a state of transition from divine inspiration to human teaching, from Apostolic freedom to churchly consolidation. This is just what we must expect, if history is a living process of growth. The *Didache* furnishes another proof of the infinite superiority of the New Testament over ecclesiastical literature. Interesting and important as it is, it dwindles into insignificance before the Sermon on the Mount, or the Gospel of John, or the Epistle to the Galatians, or even the Epistle of James, which it more nearly resembles.

The *Didache* claims no Apostolic authority; it is simply the summary of what the unknown author learned either from personal instruction or oral tradition to be the teaching of the Apostles, and what he honestly believed himself. It is anonymous, but not pseudonymous; post-Apostolic, but not pseudo-Apostolic. Its value is historical, and historical only. It furnishes us important information about the catechetical instruction and usages in the age and in the country where it was written, but not beyond. It takes its place among the genuine documents of the Apostolic Fathers so-called—Clement of Rome, Polycarp, Ignatius, Barnabas, Hermas. These writings fill the gap between the Apostles and the Church Fathers, from the close of the first to the middle of the second century; just as the Apocrypha of the Old Testament fill the gap between Malachi and John the Baptist.

CHAPTER VII.

The Title.

THE title of the *Didache* is borrowed from Acts, ii. 42, where it is said of the primitive disciples that " they continued steadfastly in *the Apostles' teaching* * and fellowship, in the breaking of bread and the prayers." It is to be understood in the same sense as in "the Apostles' Creed," of the contents, not of the form. The author does not claim to be an Apostle, but simply gives what he regards as a faithful summary of their teaching. The work is apocryphal, but no literary fraud. It differs in this respect very favorably from similar productions where the Apostles are introduced by name as speakers and made responsible for doctrines, canons and regulations, of which they never dreamed.

The manuscript of the *Didache* has two titles: "TEACHING OF THE TWELVE APOSTLES," † and a longer one, "TEACHING OF THE LORD THROUGH THE TWELVE APOSTLES TO THE GENTILES." ‡ The latter indicates the inspiring author as well as the inspired organs, and the persons to be taught. "The Gentiles" are the nations generally to whom the gospel is to be preached, Matt. xxviii. 19, and more particularly the heathen in course of preparation for baptism and church membership, or catechumens of Gentile descent, as distinct from Jewish candidates for baptism.§

Strictly speaking, however, the addition "to the Gentiles"

---

* τῇ διδαχῇ τῶν ἀποστόλων. The E. V. renders διδαχή by *doctrine*, the E. R. by *teaching*.

† Διδαχή τῶν δώδεκα Ἀποστόλων. This corresponds to the titles as given by Eusebius, Athanasius, Nicephorus, Rufinus, and Pseudo-Cyprian, except that they omit "twelve," and that Eusebius and Pseudo-Cyprian use the plural διδαχαί, *doctrinæ*, for the singular. The short title is probably an abridgement by the copyist. The Germans call it the *Zwölfapostellehre*.

‡ Διδαχή Κυρίου διὰ τῶν δώδεκα Ἀποστόλων τοῖς ἔθνεσιν. Zahn appropriately compares with this title 2 Peter, iii. 2 : ἡ τῶν ἀποστόλων ὑμῶν ἐντολὴ τοῦ κυρίου καὶ σωτῆρος.

§ So Bryennios, in his note, p. 3, τοῖς ἐξ ἐθνῶν προσιοῦσι καὶ βουλομένοις κατηχεῖσθαι τὸν τῆς εὐσεβείας λόγον· εἰς τὴν τούτων γὰρ κατήχησιν καὶ διδασκαλίαν φέρεσθαί μοι δοκεῖ πρώτιστα δὴ καὶ μάλιστα τὰ πρῶτα τῆς Διδ. κεφάλαια. Harnack (p. 27 sq.) objects to this natural interpretation as fatal to the integrity of the *Did.*, and understands ἔθνη to mean "Gentile *Christians*," as Rom. xi 13 ; Gal. ii. 12, 14 ; Eph. iii. 1, since the *Did.* is intended for Christians. True ; but for Christians in instructing Catechumens, to whom the doctrinal part, Ch. I.-VI., applies, before baptism is mentioned (Ch. VII). Athanasius says expressly that the *Did.* was used in the instruction of catechumens (τοῖς ἄρτι προσερχομένοις καὶ βουλομένοις κατηχεῖσθαι τὸν τῆς εὐσεβείας λόγον Ep. *Fest*. 89).

applies only to the first six chapters, or the *Didache* proper; while the remainder is intended for church members, or the congregations which administer the sacraments, elect ministers and exercise discipline. The division is clearly marked by the words with which the seventh chapter begins: "Having said all these things, baptize," that is, after all this preliminary instruction to the catechumens baptize them into the name of the Holy Trinity. Hence also the address: "My child," is only found in the first six chapters, namely, five times in Ch. III., once in Ch. IV., and "children" in Ch. V.*

CHAPTER VIII.

Aim and Contents of the Didache.

The *Didache* is a Church Manual or brief Directory of Apostolic teaching, worship and discipline, as understood by the author and taught and practised in the region where he lived.

It is intended for teachers and congregations. It serves its purpose admirably: it is theoretical and practical, short and comprehensive, and conveniently arranged in four parts.

The *Didache* is the oldest Manual of that kind. It was afterwards expanded in various modifications, and ultimately displaced by fuller manuals, especially by the pseudo-Clementine Constitutions, which correspond to a later development in doctrine and discipline. †

The work is very complete for its size, and covers the whole field of Christian life. It easily falls into four parts:

I. The doctrinal and catechetical part, setting forth the whole duty of the Christian. Chs. I.-VI.

---

* The same view is taken by Zahn (in his *Supplem. Clem.*, p. 286), and by Massebieau (*L'enseignement des douze apôtres*, p. 6), who says that the first part of the *Did.* (I.-VI.) is intended "*aux païens disposés à se convertir,*" the second "*aux fidèles.*"

† On the relation of the *Did.* to later documents. see below, Ch. XXX., and especially the learned discussions of Harnack, *Proleg.*, pp. 170-208, and Holtzmann, *Die Didache und ihre Nebenformen*, in the "*Jahrbücher für Protest. Theologie*," Leipzig, 1885, pp. 154-167.

II. The liturgical and devotional part, giving directions for Christian worship. Chs. VII.-X. and Ch. XIV.

III. The ecclesiastical and disciplinary part, concerning Church officers. Chs. XI.-XIII. and XV.

IV. The eschatological part, or the Christian's hope. Ch. XVI.*

CHAPTER IX.

The Catechetical Part, Chs. I.-VI.

THE Doctrinal and Moral part is a summary of practical religion as a guide of Christian conduct in the parabolic form of Two Ways, the Way of Life and the Way of Death. It corresponds to our Catechisms.

The first division, Chs. I.-IV., teaches the Way of Life, which consists in keeping the royal commandments of love to God and love to our neighbor. The second division, Chs. V.-VI., shows the Way of Death, or the way of sin. The lessons are given as exhortations to the learner, who is addressed as " my child."

The *Didache* begins thus :

"There are two Ways, one of Life and one of Death, but there is a great difference between the two Ways. The Way of Life then is this: First, thou shalt love God who made thee; secondly, thy neighbor as thyself; and whatsoever thou dost not wish to be done to thee, do not thou to another."

Then the Way of Life is set forth in brief sentences positively and negatively, with warnings against murder, adultery, theft, etc., according to the second part of the Decalogue (Chs. I.-IV.). The Way of Death is described by a list of sins

---

* Harnack, pp. 37-63, gives a much more minute analysis, but it is artificial and deserves in part the adverse criticism of Hilgenfeld and Holtzmann, although Harnack is right against Hilgenfeld in maintaining the unity and integrity of the *Didache*. He assumes three parts with many subdivisions: I. The Commandments of Christian Morals, which constitute the Christian character of the churches. Chs. I.-X. II. Directions concerning congregational life and intercourse. Ch. XI.-XV. III. Concluding exhortation to watchfulness. Ch. XVI. H. de Romestin makes only two parts: I. Rules of Christian morality, and the duties of individuals (I.-VI.); II. Duties of Christians as members of the Church (VII.-XVI.).

and sinners (Ch. V.). Then follow warnings against false teachers, and the eating of meat offered to idols (Ch. VI.).

The first part of the *Didache* is an echo of the Sermon on the Mount, as reported in Matthew, Chs. V.-VII., with some peculiar features derived from oral tradition; but the reminiscences from Matthew are far superior to the new matter.

CHAPTER X.

The Two Ways.

THE popular figure of the Two Ways was suggested by Jeremiah, xxi. 8: "Thus saith the Lord: Behold, I set before you the way of life, and the way of death;" by Moses, Deut. xxx. 15: "I have set before thee this day life and good, and death and evil;" and by the passage in the Sermon on the Mount which speaks of "the broad way that leadeth to destruction," and the "narrow way that leadeth unto life" (Matt. vii. 13, 14). Somewhat similar is also the saying of Elijah: "How long halt ye between two opinions? If Jehovah be God, follow him, but if Baal, then follow him" (1 Kings, xviii. 21).

Peter used this mode of teaching; for he speaks of "the way of truth," "the right way," "the way of righteousness," and contrasts it with "the way of Balaam."*

Here is, perhaps, the origin of the connection of the name of this Apostle with a lost apocryphal book mentioned by Rufinus † and Jerome ‡ under the double title, "The Two Ways" (*Duæ Viæ*), and "The Judgment of Peter" (*Judicium Petri*). This mysterious book has been identified by some with the "Apostolical Church Order," because Peter has there the last word among the speakers.§ But it is, probably,

---

* ὁδὸς τῆς ἀληθείας, εὐθεῖα ὁδός, ὁδὸς τοῦ Βαλαάμ (2 Pet. ii. 2, 15, 21).

† *Expos. in Symb. Apost.*, Ch XXXVIII.

‡ *De Viris ill.*, Ch. 1.

§ So Hilgenfeld (in the first ed. of his *Nov. Test. extra canonem receptum*, 1866, and in the second ed., 1884, Fasc. IV., p. 110). An anonymous identical with the *Didache*, that is, with its first part, which may appropriately be entitled, "The Two Ways." The name of Peter, however, does not occur in it, nor that of any other Apostle; and in the "Apostolical Church Order," which is an apocryphal expansion of the *Didache*, the sentence of the Two Ways is attributed to St. John. For in the estimate of the Eastern Church, where both originated, John had the charisma of teaching, Peter the charisma of governing; the former was the theologian, the latter the churchman, or ecclesiastic, among the Apostles. The hypothesis of the authorship of Peter is connected with the Western conception of his primacy, and occurs only in Latin writers.

The same teaching of the Two Ways we find with slight modifications in several post-Apostolic productions still extant.

The Epistle of Barnabas contrasts "the Way of *Light*," and "the Way of *Darkness*," the first under the control of the angels of God, the second under the control of the angels of Satan. He calls them ways of "teaching and authority," and thus seems to claim Apostolic origin for this method of instruction.* He describes the Way of Light as the way of love to God and man, and the Way of Darkness as "crooked and full of cursing," as "the way of eternal death with punishment in which are the things that destroy the soul, namely, idolatry, arrogance, hypocrisy, adultery, murder, magic, avarice," etc. The concluding part of Barnabas (Chs. XVIII.-XX.) furnishes a striking parallel to the first part of the *Didache*, so that either the one must be the source of the other, or both are derived from a common source. On this question able critics are divided.†

---

writer in the "Christian Remembrancer" for 1854, p. 293 sq., had previously made the same conjecture, but had also suggested the possible identity of the document with the old *Didache* known to Eusebius and Athanasius. See also Bickell, *Gesch. des Kirchenrechts* (1843), I. 65 and 96.

* Ch. XVIII.: ὁδοὶ δύο εἰσὶν διδαχῆς καὶ ἐξουσίας, ἥ τε τοῦ φωτὸς καὶ ἡ τοῦ σκότους.

† (1) The priority of Barnabas is advocated by Bryennios (who, in the 11th Chapter of his Prolegomena, prints the parallel sections, marking the difference by distinct type), Hilgenfeld, Harnack, Krawutzcky. (2) For the priority of the *Didache* are Zahn, Funk, Farrar, Potwin, Taylor. (3) For an older source of both: Holtzmann, Lightfoot, Massebieau, Warfield, McGiffert.

But the brevity, simplicity and terseness of the *Didache* seem to me to decide clearly in favor both of its priority and superiority. It is less figurative, more biblical, and more closely conformed to the Sermon on the Mount. The last chapters of Barnabas are an ill-arranged and confused expansion of the *Didache*, or some older document not known.*

---

* Here are the passages on the Two Ways in parallel columns; the identical words being printed in small capitals:

DIDACHE, Ch. I.

"THERE ARE TWO WAYS, one of life and one of death; AND THERE IS A GREAT DIFFERENCE BETWEEN THE TWO WAYS. ('Οδοί δύο είσί, μία τῆς ζωῆς καὶ μία τοῦ θανάτου· διαφορὰ δὲ πολλὴ μεταξὺ τῶν δύο ὁδῶν. Barn. omits μεταξύ.)

Now THE WAY of life IS THIS:—First, THOU SHALT LOVE God WHO MADE THEE (ἀγαπήσεις τὸν θεὸν τὸν ποιήσαντά σε)—

secondly, THY NEIGHBOR as thyself (τὸν πλησίον σου ὡς σεαυτόν); and all things whatsoever thou wouldest not have done to thee, do not thou to another."

EPISTLE OF BARNABAS, Chs. xviii., xix.

"But let us now pass to another kind of knowledge and teaching. THERE ARE TWO WAYS of teaching and of authority, the one of light and the other of darkness; AND THERE IS A GREAT DIFFERENCE BETWEEN THE TWO WAYS. For over the one have been appointed light-bringing angels of God, and over the other angels of Satan; and the One is Lord for ever and ever, and the other is prince of the present season of lawlessness. * * *

Ch. xix.—Now THE WAY of light is THIS: If any one wishes to travel to the appointed place he must be zealous in his works. The knowledge, then, which is given to us for walking in this way, is this: THOU SHALT LOVE Him WHO MADE THEE (ἀγαπήσεις τὸν σε ποιήσαντα); thou shalt fear Him who formed thee; thou shalt glorify Him who redeemed thee from death. Thou shalt be simple in heart and rich in spirit. Thou shalt not join thyself to those who walk in THE WAY OF DEATH.
* * * * *

Thou shalt love THY NEIGHBOR above thine own soul. (ἀγαπήσεις τὸν πλησίον σου ὑπὲρ τὴν ψυχήν σου.)" The MS. in the Cod. Sin. corrects it into ὡς ἑαυτόν.

The Shepherd of Hermas, with another variation, speaks of a "*straight* Way" and a "*crooked* Way." *

In the so-called "Apostolical Church Order," or "Ecclesiastical Canons of the Holy Apostles," which exist in Greek, Coptic and Syriac and probably date from the third century, if not from the close of the second,† St. John, as already remarked, introduces the Apostolic instructions with the distinction of the Two Ways in the very words of the *Didache*.‡

The "Apostolical Constitutions" from the fourth century repeat the same teaching in a still more expanded form and interwoven with many Scripture passages.

The general distinction of Two Ways for two modes of life with opposite issues is not confined to biblical and ecclesiastical literature. The Talmud speaks of Two Ways, the one leading to Paradise, the other to Gehenna. The familiar myth of Hercules told by Prodicus in Xenophon's

---

* The $ὀρϑὴ$ $ὁδός$ and the $στρεβλὴ$ $ὁδός$. *Mandat.* vi. 1 and 2 (in Funk's ed., I. 406). Hermas assigns two angels to man, an angel of righteousness and an angel of wickedness ($δυο$ $εἰσίν$ $ἄγγελοι$ $μετὰ$ $τοῦ$ $ἀνϑρώπου$, $εἰς$ $τῆς$ $δικαιοσύνης$, $καὶ$ $εἰς$ $τῆς$ $πονηρίας$); and he warns the reader to follow the former and to renounce the latter. Funk quotes a parallel passage from the "Testaments of the XII Patriarchs," iv. 20, which speaks of two spirits in man, the $πνεῦμα$ $τῆς$ $ἀληϑείας$ and the $πνεῦμα$ $τῆς$ $πλάνης$. See also Bryennios, Proleg.

† First published in Greek by Bickell, 1843, and also by Hilgenfeld (*l. c.* 111-121), Harnack (in his book on the *Didache*, pp. 225-237), and others.

‡   Didache, Ch. I.   Ap. Church Order, Ch. I.

Didache, Ch. I.	Ap. Church Order, Ch. I.
"There are Two Ways, one of Life and one of Death; but there is a great difference between the Two Ways. Now the Way of Life is this: First, Thou shalt love God who made thee; Secondly, thy neighbor as thyself."	"John said: "There are Two Ways, one of Life and one of Death; but there is a great difference between the Two Ways. Now the Way of Life is this: first, Thou shalt love God who made thee, from thy whole heart, and thou shalt glorify him who redeemed thee from death, which is the first commandment. Secondly, thou shalt love thy neighbor as thyself, which is the second commandment, on which hang the whole law and the prophets." (Matt. xxii. 40.)

Memorabilia represents the hero in his youth as standing between the Way of pleasure and disgrace and the arduous Way of virtue and glory.

But there is a great difference between the heathen and the Christian conception of the Two Ways, as there is between the Ways themselves. Love of glory was the motive power of heathen virtue; love to God and man is the soul of Christian life, which derives its inspiration from the redeeming love of Christ.

CHAPTER XI.

The Theology of the Didache.

THE prominent features of the catechetical part of the *Didache* are its prevailing moral tone, and the absence of the specific dogmas of the Church which were afterwards developed in the theological controversies with Ebionism, Gnosticism and other heresies. For every true dogma is the result of a conflict, and marks a victory of truth over error.

Christianity appears in the *Didache* as a pure and holy life based upon the teaching and example of Christ and on the Decalogue as explained by him in the Sermon on the Mount, and summed up in the royal law of love to God and man. The *Didache* agrees in this respect with the Epistle of James, the Epistle of Polycarp, and the writings of Justin Martyr (who, however, already branched out into philosophical speculation). The younger Pliny describes the Christians in Bithynia as scrupulously moral and conscientious worshippers of Christ. It was by the practical proof of virtue and piety more than by doctrines that the Christian religion conquered the heathen world. And to this day a living Christian is the best apology of Christianity.

Compared with the New Testament, the *Didache* is very poor and meagre. It echoes only the Synoptical Gospels, and even them only in part; it ignores, with the exception perhaps of a few faint allusions, the rich Johannean and Pauline teaching. It is behind the doctrinal contents of some other post-Apostolic writings. It has neither "the pastoral pathos of Clement of Rome, nor the mystic fire of Ignatius, nor the pietistic breath of Hermas." Not even the doctrine of one God is laid down as the foundation, nor is the commandment of the love of God expanded. *

But we must not infer too much from these omissions. Silence here implies no opposition, not even ignorance. We cannot suppose for a moment that the writer depreciated the commandments of the first table, because they are not mentioned in detail. In such a brief tract, not larger than the Epistle to the Galatians, many things had to be taken for granted. It is only one among other means of instruction and edification. The *Didache* expressly and repeatedly refers to the "Gospel" as the source and rule of Christian life (Chs. VIII. 2; XI. 3; XV. 3, 4). The baptismal formula implies the germ of the dogma of the Holy Trinity, and the eucharistic thanksgivings the germ of the doctrine of the atonement. We should also remember that the more mysterious parts of the Christian system were from fear of profanation concealed from the Catechumens by the Secret Discipline of the ancient Church; but some confession of faith, similar to the Apostles' Creed, was early required from the candidates for Baptism, and hence the chief facts of revelation therein contained must have been made known in the preceding catechetical instruction. The rules of faith which we find in the writings of Irenæus, Tertullian, Cyprian, Novatian, Origen, and other ante-Nicene writers, date in substance from the post-Apostolic, if not from the Apostolic age.†

A Roman Catholic critic unjustly charges the *Didache* with Ebionism, and puts its composition down to the second half of the second century.‡ In this case it would lose all its value as a

---

* See Zahn, *Supplementum Clementinum*, pp. 288 sq.

† They are collected in Schaff's *Creeds of Christendom*, II. 11–44.

‡ Dr. Krawutzcky, of Breslau: *Ueber die sog. Zwölfapostellehre, ihre hauptsächlichsten Quellen und ihre erste Aufnahme*, in the "Theologische Quartalschrift" of the Roman Catholic Faculty of Tübingen, 1884, No. IV. pp. 547-606. He says, p. 585: "*Die angegebenen Einzelheiten, wozu noch der wahrscheinliche Gebrauch des Evangeliums der Nazaräer und Ebioniten und Nichtgebrauch der paulinischen und johanneischen Schriften kommt,*

link in the regular chain of post-Apostolic Christianity. But the *Didache* shows no trace of the chief characteristics of this Judaizing heresy: the necessity of circumcision for salvation, the perpetual obligation of the whole ritual as well as moral law of Moses, the denial of the divinity of Christ, the intense hostility to Paul as an apostate and heretic, the restoration of the Jews, the millennial reign of Christ in Jerusalem. It has no affinity with the legalistic or Pharisaical Ebionism whose forerunners Paul opposes in his Epistle to the Galatians, nor with the theosophic or Essenic Ebionism, the germs of which Paul refutes in the second chapter of Colossians, and least of all with the wild speculations of the *pseudo-Clementine Homilies*, which date from the middle or end of the second century. The *Didache* calls the Pharisees "hypocrites" and opposes their days of fasting; it recognizes the Lord's Day instead of the Jewish Sabbath, and completely ignores circumcision and the ceremonial law.

Let us gather up the theological points expressed or implied in this little book.

God is the Creator (I. 2), the Almighty Ruler who made all

---

führen zu dem Ergebniss, dass der Verfasser der Zwölfapostellehre wahrscheinlich einer ebionitisierenden Richtung huldigte und somit an dem Aufschwunge, welchen die Sekte der Ebioniten gegen das Jahr 200 nahm, wohl nicht unbetheiligt war." He remarks in a note that the Clementine Homilies appeared about the same time; while the vulgar Ebionism was a little later represented by Symmachus, the translator of the Hebrew Scriptures. He also refers to Blastus and Theodotus in Rome about 192, and ventures on the conjecture that Theodotus of Byzantium (Euseb. V. 19 sq.), was probably the author of the *Didache*. He derives the quotations from an apocryphal Gospel, instead of the canonical Matthew. He even finds in it a direct opposition to the doctrine of the atonement, and to the sacrifice of the New Covenant. He construes the second ordinances of the Apostles spoken of in the second Irenæus-Fragment (ed. of Stieren I. 854) into an appointment of the *new* sacrifice ($\nu \dot{\varepsilon} \alpha \nu \ \pi \rho o \sigma \varphi o \rho \dot{\alpha} \nu \ \dot{\varepsilon} \nu \ \tau \tilde{\eta} \ \varkappa \alpha \iota \nu \tilde{\eta} \ \delta \iota \alpha \vartheta \dot{\eta} \varkappa \eta$) made against the Ebionites under the fresh impression of the fall of the temple with its Jewish sacrifices, and infers from the *omission* of this reference to the *new* covenant in the *Didache*, Ch. XIV., that it was written in opposition to that apostolic ordinance. But this is certainly very far fetched, and set aside by the fact that the *Didache* quotes the same passage as Irenæus from Malachi in proof of the *continuance* of the sacrifice. Hence another Roman Catholic scholar (Dr. Bickell, of Innsbruck) finds here the germ of the sacrifice of the mass. But he is equally mistaken.

things (X. 3). He is our Father in heaven (VIII. 2). No event can happen without him (III. 10). He is the Giver of all good gifts, temporal and spiritual, the author of our salvation, the object of prayer and praise (IX. and X.). To him belongs all glory forever, through Jesus Christ (VIII. 2; IX. 4; X. 4).

Christ is the Lord and Saviour (X. 2, 3), God's servant and God's son (IX. 2) and David's God (X. 6). He is the author of the gospel (VIII. 2; XV. 4). He is spiritually present in his Church, and will visibly come again to judgment (XVI. 1, 7, 8). Through him knowledge and eternal life have been made known to us (IX. 3; X. 2). He is the Jehovah of the Old Testament (XVI. 7).

The Holy Spirit is associated with the Father and the Son (VII. 1, 3). He prepares man for the call of God (IV. 10). He speaks through the Prophets, and the sin against the Spirit shall not be forgiven (XI. 7).

The Holy Trinity is implied in the baptismal formula, the strongest direct proof-text for this central doctrine (VII. 1, 3).

The Church is God's instrument in bringing on the Kingdom of Heaven which he prepared for her; he will deliver her from all evil and perfect her in his love (IX. 4; X. 5). All true Christians are one, though scattered over the world, and God, the head of the Church, will gather them all from the four winds into his Kingdom (X. 5).

Baptism and the Eucharist are sacred ordinances instituted by Christ, and to be perpetually observed VII. 1-4; IX., X., XIV.). The Lord's Day shall be kept holy as a day of worship and thanksgiving (XIV. 1). The Lord's Prayer should be repeated daily (VIII. 2), and Wednesday and Friday be given to fasting (VIII. 1). Reverence and gratitude are due to the ministers of Christ (XI. 1, 4; XII. 1; XIII. 1, 2).

There is to be at the end of time a resurrection of the dead and a general judgment at the glorious appearance of Christ (XVI).

Man is made in the image of God (V. 2), but sinful, and needs forgiveness (VIII. 2); he must confess his transgressions to receive pardon (IV. 14; XIV. 1, 2).

Man's whole duty is to love God and his neighbor, and to show this practically by abstaining from all sins of thought, word and deed, and by observing all the commandments (Ch.

I. 6), according to the Gospel (XI. 3), neither adding nor taking away (IV. 13). This is the Way of Life, but the way of sin is the Way of Death. There is no third way, no compromise between good and evil, between life and death.

It would be difficult to find more theology in the Epistle of James, which has nearly the same size. If this teaching be Ebionism, then Ebionism is no heresy. But the *Didache* and the Epistle of James antedate the Ebionitic heresy properly so called, which was a stunted and impoverished Christianity *in opposition* to Catholic and orthodox Christianity. They represent the early Jewish-Christian type of teaching, before the universalism and liberalism of the great Apostle of the Gentiles had penetrated the Church. They teach a plain, common sense Christianity, not dogmatical, but ethical, not very profound, but eminently practical, and even now best suited to the taste of many sincere and devout Christians. We cannot disregard it as long as the Epistle of James keeps its place in the canon of the New Testament.

CHAPTER XII.

The Ritualistic or Liturgical Part.

THE Second Part of the *Didache* is a Directory of Public Worship, Chs. VII.–X. and XIV. It corresponds to our Liturgies and Prayer Books. It treats first of the administration of Baptism, which is to follow the catechetical instruction and conversion of the Catechumen (Ch. VII.); then of Prayer and Fasting (Ch. VIII.), and last of the celebration of the Agape and Eucharist (Chs. IX., X. and XIV.).

We have here an important addition to our knowledge of ancient worship. The New Testament gives us neither a liturgy nor a ritual, but only the Lord's Prayer, the baptismal formula, and the words of institution of the holy communion. The liturgies which bear the names of St. Clement, St. Mark, and St. James, cannot be traced beyond the Nicene age, though they embody a common liturgical tradition which is much older, and explains their affinity in essentials.* The full text of the first Epistle of Clement to the Corinthians, as published by Bryennios from the Jerusalem MS. in 1875, made us acquainted with the oldest post-Apostolic prayer, which was probably used in the Roman congregation towards the close of the first century.† But the *Didache* contains three eucharistic prayers besides the Lord's Prayer.

CHAPTER XIII.

The Lord's Day and the Christian Week.

As to sacred seasons, the *Didache* bears witness to the celebration of the first day of the week, and gives it (after the Apocalypse) the significant name of the Lord's Day, or rather (with a unique pleonastic addition), " the Lord's Day of the Lord." ‡

On that day the congregations are directed to assemble, to break bread, to confess their sins, to give thanks, and to celebrate the sacrifice of the Eucharist. But before these acts of worship every dispute between the brethren should be settled, that their sacrifice may not be defiled (comp. Matt. v. 23, 24). This is the pure sacrifice which shall be offered in every place and time, as the Lord has spoken through the prophet (Mal. i. 11, 14).

No reading of Scripture is mentioned, but not excluded. The use of the Old Testament may be taken for granted; the New Testament canon was not yet completed. Justin Martyr, writing about the middle of the second century, adds to the prayers and the Eucharist the reading of the Memoirs of the Apostles (*i. e.*, the Canonical Gospels) and the Prophets, and a verbal instruction and exhortation by the "president" of the

---

* See *Church History*, III. 517 sqq.

† Chs. LIX.–LXI. See *Church History*, II. 228 sq.

‡ Ch. XIV. 1: $\varkappa υριαχὴ\ Κυρίου$. The earliest use of $\varkappa υριαχή$ as a noun. St. John first used it as an adjective, $\varkappa υριαχὴ\ ἡμέρα$, *Dominica dies*, Rev. i. 10.

congregation, as regular exercises of Christian worship on Sunday.*

The celebration of the first day of the week is based upon the fact of the resurrection of Christ, as the completion of the new creation and redemption, and is sanctioned by Apostolic practice.† Its general observance during the second century is established beyond a doubt by the concurrent testimonies of Pliny ("*stato die*"), Barnabas ("the eighth day," in distinction from the Jewish Sabbath), Ignatius ("the Lord's Day"), Justin Martyr, Melito, Irenæus, and Tertullian. ‡

Next to the first day of the week, the *Didache* gives a subordinate prominence to the fourth day (Wednesday), and the Preparation day (Friday), as days of fasting, in distinction from the second and fifth days which the Pharisees observed as fasts (Ch. VIII.).

Here, too, the testimony of the *Didache* foreshadows the custom of the second century, to observe Wednesday as the Day of the Betrayal, and Friday as the Day of the Crucifixion, by special prayer and half-fasting (*semijejunia*).

The Christian week was determined by the passion and resurrection of the Lord, as the two great events through which the salvation of the world was accomplished. They are to be commemorated from week to week, the Lord's Day by rejoicing and thanksgiving for the victory over sin, Wednesday and Friday by exercises of repentance. This was the idea and practice of the ante-Nicene Church.

Beyond these simple elements of the Christian week the *Didache* does not go. It shows no trace of annual church festivals, not even of Easter, although this certainly was already observed as the Christian Passover, in the days of Polycarp of Smyrna (d. 155), who had a controversy with Anicetus of Rome on the time and manner (not on the fact) of its observance. § This silence is one of the many indications of the antiquity of our document.

---

* Apol. I. c. LXVII.
† Acts, xx. 7; 1 Cor. xvi. 2; Rev. i. 10.
‡ See the details in *Church History*, II. 201 sqq.
§ Irenæus in Eusebius, *Hist. Eccl.* V. 24. See *Church History*, II. 213 sqq.

CHAPTER XIV.

Prayer and Fasting.

The *Didache* prescribes the recital of the Lord's Prayer three times a day, in imitation, no doubt, of the Jewish hours of devotion at nine, twelve, and three, and of the example of Daniel (VI. 10). Tertullian adds to them the morning and evening prayers (*ingressu lucis et noctis*), which need no special injunction.

The Lord's Prayer is given in the very words of Matthew (VI. 9–13), with slight alterations ("heaven" for "heavens," and "debt" for "debts"), and with the doxology (though not complete, "the kingdom" being omitted). This is the oldest authority for the use of the Lord's Prayer. The doxology no doubt passed from Jewish custom (comp. 1 Chr. xxix. 11) into the Christian Church at a very early day, and was afterwards inserted into the current text of the Gospel.

The *Didache* thus sanctions a form of prayer in the daily devotions, and gives besides three thanksgivings for the public celebration of the Eucharist, but with the express reservation of the right of free prayer to the Prophets. The prescription of the frequent repetition of the Lord's Prayer, however, and the apparent restriction of free prayer in public worship to the Prophets, indicate the beginning of liturgical bondage.

The prescription to fast before Baptism (in Ch. VII. 4) and on Wednesdays and Fridays (Ch. VIII.) goes beyond the New Testament, and interferes with evangelical freedom. The Lord condemns the hypocritical fasting of the Pharisees, but left no command as to stated days of fasting.

CHAPTER XV.

Baptism in the Didache.

The *Didache* knows only two sacraments, Baptism and the Eucharist. On the former it gives the following important and interesting directions, which have, in America, excited more attention than any other part of the book (Ch. VII.):

"As regards Baptism, baptize in this manner: Having first given all the preceding instruction [on the Way of Life and the Way of Death, Chs. I-VI], baptize into the name of the Father, and of the Son, and of the Holy Spirit, in living [running] water.

"But if thou hast not living water, baptize into (εἰς) other water; and if thou canst not in cold, [then] in warm [water].

"But if thou hast neither [neither running nor standing, neither cold nor warm water, in sufficient quantity for immersion], pour (ἔκχεον) water on the head three times, into the name of Father and Son and Holy Spirit."*

"But before Baptism let the baptizer and the candidate for Baptism fast, and any others who can; and thou shalt command him who is to be baptized to fast one or two days before."

It is instructive to compare with this chapter the next oldest description of Baptism by Justin Martyr, which is as follows: †

"As many as are persuaded and believe that the things taught and spoken by us are true, and promise to be able to live accordingly, are instructed to pray, and to entreat God with fasting for the remission of their past sins, while we at the same time pray and fast with them. Then they are brought by us to a place where there is water (ἔνθα ὕδωρ ἐστί), and are regenerated (ἀναγεννῶνται) in the same manner in which we ourselves were regenerated. For in the name (ἐπ' ὀνόματος) of the Father and Lord of the whole universe, and of our Saviour Jesus Christ, and of the Holy Spirit, they then receive the washing with water (τὸ ἐν τῷ ὕδατι τότε λουτρὸν ποιοῦνται). For Christ also said, 'Except ye be born again, ye shall not enter the kingdom of heaven.'" (John, iii. 5.)

From the baptismal directory of the *Didache* we may infer the following particulars:

1. Baptism shall take place after preceding instruction in the Way of Life and the Way of Death.‡

---

* The definite article in this passage is omitted by the carelessness of the writer or copyist. In the first paragraph the form is given correctly according to the text in Matthew.

† Apol. I. 61.

‡ The words ταῦτα πάντα προειπόντες refer, of course, to the preceding six chapters. No baptismal creed is implied. The Apostles' Creed was not yet shaped; but a shorter rule of faith may have been used with a promise of obedience to Christ. The Apost. Const. vii. 40 sqq. give a long form of the renunciation of Satan, and a confession of faith.

Nothing is said of Infant Baptism. The reference to instruction and the direction of fasting show that the writer has in view only the Baptism of catechumens, or adult believers. Christianity always begins by preaching the gospel to such as can hear, understand and believe. Baptism follows as a solemn act of introduction into fellowship with Christ and the privileges and duties of church-membership. Infant Baptism has no sense and would be worse than useless where there is no Christian family or Christian congregation to fulfil the conditions of Baptism and to guarantee a Christian nurture. Hence in the Apostolic and the whole ante-Nicene age to the time of Constantine Baptism of believing converts was the rule, and is to this day on every missionary field. Hence in the New Testament the baptized are addressed as people who have died and risen with Christ, and who have put on Christ. Baptism and conversion are almost used as synonymous terms.*

But for this very reason the silence of the *Didache* about Infant Baptism cannot be fairly used as an argument against it any more than the corresponding passages in the New Testament, which are addressed to adult believers. When Christianity is once established and organized, then comes in family religion with its duties and privileges. That Infant Baptism was practised in *Christian* families as early as the second century is evident from Tertullian, who opposed it as imprudent and dangerous, and from Origen, who approved it and speaks of it as an apostolic tradition.† *Compulsory* Infant Baptism, of course, was unknown even in the Nicene and post-Nicene age, and is a gross abuse, dating from the despotic reign of Justinian in close connection with the union of church and state.

2. Baptism must be administered into the triune name ($\varepsilon i\varsigma$ $\tau \dot{o}$ $\ddot{o}\nu o\mu a$) of the Father, and the Son, and the Holy Spirit. This is the prescribed form of Christ. (Matt. xxviii. 19.)

The shorter form "into the name of Jesus," is not mentioned.

---

* Comp. Acts ii. 38, 41; Rom. vi. 3, 4; Gal. iii. 27.

† *Ep. ad Rom. l. v. c.* 6; "*Ecclesia ab Apostolis traditionem suscepit, etiam parvulis baptismum dare.*" *Hom. XIV. in Luc.*: "*Parvuli baptizantur in remissionem peccatorum. Quorum peccatorum ? vel quo tempore peccaverunt ? . . . Quia per baptismi sacramentum nativitatis sordes deponuntur, propterea baptizantur et parvuli.*" See *Church History*, vol. ii. 258 sqq.

3. The normal and favorite mode of Baptism is threefold immersion* "in living water," *i.e.* fresh, running water, either in a stream or lake or fountain, as distinct from standing water in a pool or cistern. Immersion must be meant, otherwise there would be no difference between the first mode and the last which is aspersion or pouring. Besides it is the proper meaning of the Greek word here used. The preference for a river was naturally derived from our Saviour's Baptism in the Jordan. Justin Martyr, when he says that the converts were led to a place "where there is water," means probably a river; since water sufficient for pouring or sprinkling could be had in every house. The direction of the *Didache* receives confirmation from the baptismal pictures in the catacombs where the baptized stands ankle-deep or knee-deep or waist-deep in a stream and the baptizer on dry ground, extending his hand to perform the act. We shall return to this subject in the next chapter. Tertullian represents it as a matter of indifference whether Baptism take place in the sea, or in a lake, or a river, or in standing water,† but he insists on *trine* immersion.‡ This was the universal practice of the ancient Church, and is still continued in the East. It was deemed essential with reference to the Holy Trinity. Single immersion was considered heretical or incomplete, and is forbidden by the Apostolical Canons.§

After Constantine, when the Church was recognized by the secular government and could hold real estate, special Baptisteries were built in or near the churches for the more convenient performance of the rite in all kinds of weather and away from running streams.

---

* "Three times" is only mentioned in connection with pouring, but must, of course, be supplied in the normal form of immersion.

† *De Bapt.*, c. iv: "*Nulla distinctio est, mari quis an stagno, flumine an fonte, lacu an alveo diluatur.*"

‡ *Adv. Prax.* c. xxvi: "*Nec semel, sed ter, ad singula nomina in personas singulas tinguimur.*" *De cor. mil.* c. 3: "*Ter mergitamur,*" adding, however, "*amplius aliquid respondentes quam Dominus in evangelio determinavit.*" *De Bapt.* c. xiii: "*Lex tinguendi imposita est, et forma præscripta.*"

§ Can. 50: "If any Bishop or Presbyter does not perform the three immersions, but only one immersion, let him be deposed." In this point Protestant Baptists, who immerse but once, depart from the ancient practice on the ground that it has no Scripture authority.

4. While thus preference is given to immersion in living water, the *Didache* allows three exceptions:

(a) Baptism (by immersion) "into other water" (εἰς ἄλλο ὕδωρ), *i. e.* any other kind of (cold) water in pools or cisterns.

(b) Baptism (by immersion) in warm water (in the houses), when the health of the candidate or the inclemency of the climate or season may require it.

(c) Threefold aspersion of the head, where neither running nor standing, neither cold nor warm water is at hand in sufficient quantity for total or partial immersion. The aspersion of the head was the nearest substitute for total immersion, since the head is the chief part of man. There *can* be no Baptism without baptizing the head; but there *may* be valid Baptism without baptizing the rest of the body.

Here we have the oldest extant testimony for the validity of baptism by pouring or aspersion.. It is at least a hundred years older than the testimony of Cyprian. The passages quoted from Tertullian are not conclusive.* Bryennios would confine the exception to cases of sickness or to what is called "clinical Baptism."† But the *Didache* puts it simply on the ground of scarcity of water, so that healthy persons might likewise be thus baptized (*e. g.* if converted in a desert, or on a mountain, or in a prison, or in a catacomb).

We have, therefore, a right to infer that at the end of the first century there was no rigid uniformity in regard to the *mode* of Baptism and no scruple about the validity of aspersion or pouring, provided only the head was baptized into the triune name with the intention of baptizing. In the third century the exceptional aspersion was only allowed on the sick-bed, and even then it disqualified for the priesthood, at least in North Africa and the East, though not from any doubt of its validity, but from suspicion of the sincerity of the baptized. ‡

---

* *De Bapt.* cap. xii (where he teaches the necessity of Baptism for salvation); and *De Poen.* cap. vi. (where he mentions hypothetically *asperginem unam cuiuslibet aquæ*, "one single sprinkling of any water whatever," and uses "bathing" in the same sense as baptizing).

† *Baptismus clinicorum;* κλινικός, *bed-ridden* (from κλίνη, *couch;* κλίνειν, *to recline*).

‡ This is the reason assigned by the Council of Neo-Cæsarea in Cappado-

Novatianus in Rome was indeed baptized by aspersion when on the point of death, and was nevertheless ordained to the priesthood; but his defective Baptism was probably one of the reasons of his non-election to the See of Rome and an occasion for the subsequent schism which is attached to his name. Cyprian wrote a special tract in defence of clinical Baptism against those who denied its validity. "In the sacraments of salvation," he says, "where necessity compels and God gives permission, the divine thing, though outwardly abridged, bestows all that it implies on the believer." *

Thus explained, the directions of the *Didache* are perfectly clear and consistent with all the other information we have on Baptism in the ante-Nicene age. Trine immersion into the triune name was the rule, as it is to this day in all the Oriental churches; trine aspersion or pouring was the exception. The new thing which we learn is this, that in the post-Apostolic age a degree of freedom prevailed on the mode of Baptism, which was afterwards somewhat restricted.

From this fact we may reason (*a fortiori*) that the same freedom existed already in the Apostolic age. It cannot be supposed that the Twelve Apostles were less liberal than the writer of the *Didache*, who wrote as it were in their name.

It is astonishing how this testimony has been twisted and turned by certain writers in the sectarian interest. Some exclusive Immersionists, in order to get rid of the exception, have declared the *Didache* a literary forgery; while some zealous advocates of sprinkling, as the supposed original and Scriptural mode, have turned the exception into the rule, and substituted an imaginary difference between pouring in running water and pouring on dry ground for the real difference between immersion and pouring water on the head.

5. Baptism is to be preceded by fasting on the part of both

---

cia (c. 314), in its twelfth canon: "If any one has been baptized in sickness, inasmuch as his [profession of] faith was not of his own free choice but of necessity, he cannot be promoted to the priesthood, unless on account of his subsequent zeal and faithfulness, or because of lack of men."—See Fulton's *Index Canonum* (N. Y., 1883), p. 217.

* *Epist.* LXXVI. (al. LXIX.) cap. 12, *ad Magnum.*

the catechumen and the baptizer and some others who may join. The former is required to fast one or two days.

There is no such prescription in the New Testament. In the case of Christ fasting followed his Baptism (Matt. iv. 2.); and the three thousand pentecostal converts seem to have been baptized on the day of their conversion (Acts, ii. 38–40).

Fasting is likewise mentioned as customary in connection with Baptism by Justin Martyr and Tertullian, but not so definitely as in the *Didache*. The fasting of the baptizer probably soon went out of use.

6. Baptism is not represented as a clerical function, but the directions are addressed to all members of the congregation; while in the corresponding direction of the Apostolical Constitutions the Bishop or Presbyter is addressed,* and Ignatius restricts the right to baptize to the Bishop, or at all events requires his permission or presence. † Justin Martyr mentions no particular person. Tertullian, in his Montanistic opposition to a special priesthood, expressly gives the right even to laymen, when bishops, priests, or deacons are not at hand; for what is equally received can be equally given. ‡

7. No mention is made of exorcism, which preceded the act of Baptism, nor of the application of oil, salt or other material, which accompanied it as early as the second and third centuries. The silence is conclusive, not indeed against the use of these additions, but against their importance in the estimation of the writer and his age. It is another indication of the early date of the book.

---

* Book vii. 22: περὶ δὲ βαπτίσματος, ὦ ἐπίσκοπε ἢ πρεσβύτερε... οὕτως βαπτίσεις.

† *Ad Smyrn.* 8: οὐκ ἐξόν ἐστιν χωρὶς τοῦ ἐπισκόπου οὔτε βαπτίζειν οὔτε ἀγάπην ποιεῖν.

‡ *De Bapt.* xvii. The Roman Catholic and Lutheran churches allow lay-Baptism, even the Baptism by midwives in case of necessity, *i. e.* in danger of death and in absence of a minister. This concession is connected with the view that Baptism is (ordinarily) necessary to salvation. The Calvinistic churches reject this view, and consequently also lay-Baptism. The Baptists regard Baptism unnecessary for salvation, but enjoined upon adult believers; the Quakers discard it altogether.

CHAPTER XVI.

*The Didache and the Catacombs.**

THE oldest baptismal pictures in the Roman Catacombs may be traced to the close of the second century. They are rude and defaced and have no artistic merit, but considerable archæological value and furnish monumental evidence of the mode of Baptism which prevailed at that time. They are found on the walls of the Crypt of Lucina, the oldest part of the Catacomb of Pope St. Callistus (Calixtus) on the Via Appia, and in two of the six so-called "Chambers of the Sacraments" in that cemetery.†

The art of painting can only exhibit the beginning or the end of the act, not the entire process.‡ But as far as they go these pictures confirm the river-Baptism prescribed by the *Didache* as the normal form, in imitation of the typical Baptism in the Jordan. They all represent the baptized as standing in a stream, and the baptizer on dry ground; the former

---

* On this subject the reader is referred to the illustrated works on the Catacombs and early Christian art, by Commendatore DE ROSSI, GARRUCCI, ROLLER, NORTHCOTE & BROWNLOW, KRAUS, J. H. PARKER, VICTOR SCHULTZE, all of which are mentioned in my *Church Hist.* vol. ii. 266, 285 sq. Add to these WOLFORD NELSON COTE (then at Rome): *The Archæology of Baptism*, London (Yates and Alexander), 1876, which contains many illustrations; EGBERT C. SMYTH (Andover): *Baptism in the "Teaching" and in Early Christian Art*, in the "Andover Review" for May, 1884, p. 533 sqq., with photo-engravings from Garrucci. Comp. also an article (by the writer) on the same subject in the N. Y. "Independent" for March 5, 1885.

† Giovanni Battista de Rossi, the pioneer of modern Catacomb research, in the first volume of his monumental *Roma Sotteranea*, gives a full description of the *Cripte di Lucina nel cemetero di S. Callisto*, with 40 tables of illustrations. For a brief account, see Schultze, *Die Katakomben* (Leipzig, 1882), p. 310 sqq. He says of the ante-Nicene baptismal pictures (p. 136): "*Die Taufdarstellungen vorkonstantinischer Zeit, deren Zahl sich auf drei beläuft, zeigen sämmtlich erwachsene Täuflinge, in zwei Fällen Knaben, von etwa zwölf Jahren, im dritten Falle einen Jüngling. Der Act wird durch Untertauchen vollzogen.*" The age of the pictures, however, is disputed. The late J. H. Parker, of Oxford, went too far in denying that there are any religious pictures in the Catacombs *before* the age of Constantine.

‡ In some later pictures given from MSS. in Roman libraries by Cote, pp. 37, 40, 41, the water is unnaturally represented as a pyramid, within which the baptized person stands, entirely surrounded by the element.

is nude, the latter is more or less robed. These two facts prove that immersion (either total or partial) was intended; otherwise the standing with the feet in water would be an unmeaning superfluity, and the nudity an unjustifiable indecency.* Pouring is also confirmed in two of these pictures, but in connection with partial immersion, not without it. The illustrations will show this more plainly.†

The oldest of these pictures represents the baptized as coming up (after immersion) from the river which reaches over his knees, and joining hands with the baptizer, who is dressed in a tunic, and assists him in ascending the shore; while in the air hovers a dove with a twig in its mouth. It is usually understood to exhibit the Baptism of Christ in the Jordan as he comes out of the water.‡

---

* The unclothing of the candidate was a universal custom in the ancient Church and regarded as essential. Hence the baptisteries were commonly divided into two distinct apartments, the one for men, the other for women. See Bingham, *Antiquities*, Book XI. Ch. xi. Sect. 1-3. In cases of river-Baptism the two sexes were baptized at different times or in different parts of the river.

† The following cuts are taken, by permission, from Roller's great work, *Les Catacombs de Rome* (1881), vol. i. pp. 94, 95, 100, 101. See also the 14th Table in the first vol. of De Rossi's *Roma Sotter.*, and the second vol. of Garrucci's *Storia delle arte Christiana*. The pictures of Roller are not so artistic as those of Garrucci, but more true to the homely simplicity of the originals. Those of De Rossi are colored (chromo-lithographs).

‡ Matt. iii. 16, ἀνέβη ἀπὸ τοῦ ὕδατος, and Mark i. 10, ἐκ τοῦ ὕδατος.

Another representation, apparently of the same scene, differs from the former by giving a slight covering to the baptized person.

In a later fresco picture of the Baptism of Christ in the Catacomb of San Ponziano, outside of Rome, Christ stands undressed in the Jordan with the water up to the waist, and John the Baptist from a projecting rock places his hand upon the head of Christ to immerse him, while the dove descends directly from the open heaven.* In a mosaic at Ravenna (S.

Roller (i. 99) thus explains the picture; "*Jésus, moitié plongé dans l'eau du Jourdain, nu, sans attributes divins, sans rayonnement au front, comme un simple homme, et à qui le Baptiste tend la main pour le fair sortir du fleuve.*" *Le Catacombs de Rome*, vol. i. 99. Victor Schultze doubts this application, because of the nudity of Christ, and of the twig in the mouth of the dove, which he thinks points rather to Noah's dove, since Baptism is often compared to the salvation from the flood. He finds here the Baptism of a member of the family to which that sepulchral chamber belonged. (*Die Katakomben*, p. 313). But these objections have no weight. Christ is nearly always represented as unclothed in baptism, and sometimes a ministering angel stands on a cloud holding his dress. See the pictures in Cote, on pp. 32, 46, etc.

* See Cote, p. 32. On the opposite shore an angel is seen upon a cloud, holding Christ's robes, and below a hart looking fixedly at the water to symbolize the ardent desire of the catechumen for baptism. Cote gives several other pictures of Christ's baptism, pp. 33, 37, 39, 46.

Giovanni in Fonte) from the year 450, the same scene is represented, but John the Baptist completes the immersion by pouring water with his right hand from a shell upon the head of Christ.*

Two other pictures in the Catacomb of Pope Callistus (the two oldest next to the first given above) represent the Baptism of young catechumens by immersion of the feet supplemented by pouring or some action on the head.

In the first picture a naked boy of about twelve or fifteen years stands only ankle-deep in a stream; while the baptizer, wearing a toga and holding a roll in his left hand, lays his right hand on the head of the candidate—either pouring water, or ready to dip him, or blessing him after the ceremony. †

---

* Smyth, p. 543, figure 6. The picture shows on the right the river-god rising from the Jordan to worship Christ. In another fresco of Ravenna, in the Arian Baptistery now called "S. Maria in Cosmedin," given on p. 544, the Baptist places the hand on the head ready to dip, as in the Catacomb of San Ponziano just mentioned.

† On the meaning of this action of the baptizer the authorities are not agreed, in view probably of the indistinctness of the fresco. Garrucci (*Storia*, etc. vol. ii. p. 12; comp. his picture on Table V.) explains it as the rite of

In the second picture the boy stands likewise in the river naked, and is surrounded by sprays of water as in a shower-bath, or as Garrucci says, "he is entirely immersed in a cloud of water."* The sprays are thrown in streaks of greenish color with a brush around the body and above the head. The baptizer lays his right hand on the head of the baptized, while another man (whose figure is mutilated) in a sitting posture draws a fish from the water.

---

confirmation, which immediately followed baptism in the ancient Church. De Rossi describes the picture as a slight immersion and simultaneous affusion ("*battesimo effigiato per poca immersione e simultanea infusione dell' acqua.*") Roller (a Protestant) likewise sees in the picture a specimen of incomplete immersion (*Les Catac.* I. 131). In the Orient and Africa, he says, Baptism was "*une triple immersion et une triple emersion, accompagnée d'une triple confession de foi au Père, au Fils et au Saint Esprit,*" but in Rome, he thinks, the Christians were for a time satisfied "*d'une immersion moins complète.*" The proof for such a distinction is wanting. The Tiber afforded ample facility for full immersion. Baptisms, however, were also performed in fonts in the Catacombs. An artist, whom I consulted, takes still another view, namely that the baptizer is about to dip the boy. But there seems to be not water enough for full immersion. If experts differ, how shall a layman decide?

* *L. c.* ii. 13: "*Un giovanetto tutto ignudo, è immerso interamente in un nembo di acqua. Il quale bagno è rappresentato da grossi sprazzi di verdemare, gittati col penello attorno alla persona e fin disopra alla testa di lui.*" See the picture of this Baptism on Table VII. Garrucci's plates are an artistic improvement of the original. De Rossi (Tavola XVI.) shows in colors the streaks of paint thrown with a brush around the body and above the head of the baptized. He explains the picture as a specimen of abundant affusion. It is also reproduced in Cote's *Archæology of Baptism*, p. 34, and in Smith and Cheetham. *Christ. Antiq.* I. 168. Roller omits the fisherman on the shore, which we have reproduced from De Rossi.

From these pictorial representations we have a right to draw the inference that the immersion was as complete as the depth of the accessible stream or fount would admit, and that the defect, if any, was supplemented by pouring water on the head. The Baptism of the head is always the most essential and indispensable part of Baptism.*

In one of the catacombs, the cemetery of St. Pontianus, there is a baptismal fount supplied by a current of water, about three or four feet deep and six feet across, and approached by a flight of steps.† In the Ostrianum cemetery, not far from the church of St. Agnes on the Via Nomentana, is the traditional spot of St. Peter's Baptisms, called *Ad Nymphas S. Petri* or *Fons S. Petri*. ‡

River-Baptism gradually ceased when Baptisteries began to be built in the age of Constantine in or near the churches, with all the conveniences for the performance of the rite.§ They are very numerous, especially in Italy. They went out of use when immersion ceased in the West. The last is said to have been built at Pistoia, in Italy, A.D. 1337. ‖

CHAPTER XVII.

Immersion and Pouring in History.

THE baptismal question has various aspects: philological (classical and Hellenistic), exegetical, historical, dogmatic, ritualistic, and liturgical. The controversies connected with it refer to the subjects, the mode, and the effect of the sacrament.

---

* Pouring on the head while the candidate stands on *dry* ground, receives no aid from the Catacombs, but may have been applied in clinical Baptism.

† Padre Marchi, as quoted in Smith and Cheetham, i. 174.

‡ De Rossi, *Rom. S tt.* i. 189.

§ Βαπτιστήριον, φωτιστήριον, *baptisterium, domus illuminationis*, was the name for the whole building in which the Baptismal ceremonies were performed; κολυμβήθρα, *piscina* (with reference to *Ichthys*, the mystic name of Christ), or *lavacrum* was the fountain or pool wherein the candidates were immersed.

‖ Ccte, p. 152 sqq., gives a very full account of Baptisteries in the East, in Italy, France, Germany, and England.

We confine ourselves here to the history of the *mode* as connected with our subject.

The *Didache*, the Catacomb pictures, and the teaching of the fathers, Greek and Latin, are in essential harmony on this point, and thus confirm one another. They all bear witness to trine immersion as the rule, and affusion or pouring as the exception.

This view is supported by the best scholars, Greek, Latin, and Protestant. Let us hear the standard writers on the subject. We confine ourselves to Pædo-Baptist authorities.

1. On the GREEK side, Bryennios explains the *Didache* in accordance with the practice of his Church, and admits pouring only on two conditions, the scarcity of water (on which the *Didache* puts it) and the necessity of baptism *in periculo mortis* (which he adds).*

Another modern Greek scholar and Professor of Church History, the Archimandrite Philaret Bapheidos, in his *Church History*, published in 1884, describes the ancient mode as a threefold immersion (submersion) and emersion, or descent into and ascent from the water, and restricts aspersion to cases of sickness. †

To them we may add the statement of Dr. John Mason Neale, the greatest Anglican connoisseur of the Greek Church, to whom we are indebted for the best reproductions of Greek hymns. He states, with abundant proofs from ancient Rituals, that "the mode of administration of the sacrament is, throughout the whole East, by trine immersion, or at least, by trine

---

* In his notes on Ch. VII. he says: ἤγουν ἐὰν μήτε ψυχρὸν μήτε θερμὸν ὕδωρ ἔχῃς ἱκανὸν εἰς τὸ βαπτίσαι, καὶ ἀνάγκη ἐπιστῇ τοῦ βαπτίσματος, ἔκχεον, κτλ.

† "Τὸ βάπτισμα ἐγίνετο διὰ τριπλῆς καταδύσεως καὶ ἀναδύσεως εἰς τὸ ὄνομα τοῦ Πατρὸς καὶ τοῦ Υἱοῦ καὶ τοῦ ἁγίου Πνεύματος, ἐξαιρουμένου μόνον τοῦ βαπτίσματος τῶν κλινικῶν, τελουμένου διὰ ῥαντισμοῦ ἢ ἐπιχύσεως (aspersio)." See his Ἐκκλησιαστικὴ ἱστορία ἀπὸ τοῦ Κυρίου ἡμῶν Ἰησοῦ Χριστοῦ μέχρι τῶν καθ' ἡμᾶς χρόνων. Τόμος πρῶτος. Ἀρχαία ἐκκλησ. ἱστορία. A.D. 1–700. Constantinople, 1884. Bapheides is the successor of Bryennios as Professor in the Patriarchal Seminary at Chalce, near Constantinople, and dedicated his *Church History* to him. Their works are a welcome sign of a revival of learning in the Greek Church, and it is remarkable that both quote a large number of German Protestant authorities (as Gieseler, Neander, etc.), but very few Latin books.

affusion over the head, while the Catechumen is seated, or stands, in water up to the elbows." He adds: "All the Syrian forms prescribe or assume trine immersion."*

The Orthodox Church of Russia adopted from the beginning the same practice. The Longer Russian Catechism of Philaret defines baptism to be " trine immersion in water," and declares this " most essential." †

Dr. Washburn, President of Robert College in Constantinople (an American Protestant), in answer to a recent letter informs the writer: "As to the Baptism question the Orthodox authorities here declare that no Oriental Church not under Roman Catholic or Protestant influence knows any other Baptism than trine immersion. When hard pressed, they add, '*except in case of necessity*,' but I could not get them to acknowledge any other necessity than *lack of water*." He adds, however, that he knew "a distinguished orthodox priest, now dead, who always immersed the child *once* and then poured water twice on the head. From this it would appear that single immersion may be supplemented by double pouring."

As to the mode of Baptism prevailing among the various Christian sects in Syria, I learn from the two best informed American missionaries at Beirut, Drs. van Dyck and Henry H. Jessup, that it is " *immersion*, in *whole*, or in *part*, supplemented by pouring, if necessary," and "that the Greek Church insists upon trine immersion as essential to salvation, whether in the case of infants or adults; yet sometimes, in cases of necessity, they baptize by pouring the water three times upon the head." †

2. The archæologists and historians of the ROMAN CATHOLIC Church are likewise unanimous as to the practice of ancient

---

* *General Introduction* to his *A History of the Holy Eastern Church*, London, 1850, p. 949 sq.

† Schaff, *Creeds of Christendom*, ii, 491. Rev. Nicholas Bjerring (formerly a Russian priest) says of the Russian mode: "Baptism is always administered by *dipping* the infant or adult *three times* into the water." (*The Offices of the Oriental Church*, N. York, 1884, p. xiii.) The priest, taking the infant into one arm, and covering the mouth and nose with one hand, submerges him in the baptismal font. In Greece, as I was informed in Athens, the priest dips the child only up to the neck, and then supplements the act by *pouring* water over the head.

‡ See Dr. Jessup's letter in the N. Y. "Independent" for Feb. 18, 1886.

times. The Jesuit P. Raffaele Garrucci, who wrote the most elaborate and magnificent work on Ancient Christian Art, says that the most ancient and solemn rite was "to immerse the person in the water, and three times also the head, while the minister pronounced the three names;" but he rightly adds that in exceptional cases baptism was also performed by "infusion" or "aspersion," when a sufficient quantity of water for immersion was not on hand, or when the physical condition of the candidate would not admit it.*

In the Latin Church immersion continued till the thirteenth century, but with some freedom as to the repetition. Pope Gregory I. (in a letter to Leander of Seville) allowed the Spanish bishops to use single immersion, which prevailed there for a short period, but gave the preference to trine immersion, which, though not divinely commanded, was more expressive and ancient.† Thomas Aquinas (died 1274), the standard divine of the middle ages, allowed pouring water on the head as the seat of life and intelligence, but declared it safer to baptize by immersion.‡

From that time pouring gradually, though not universally, took the place of immersion on the Continent. A Council at

---

* *Storia della arte Christiana*, Prato, 1881, vol. i., P. I., p. 27 sq.: "*Antichissimo e solenne fu il rito d'immergere la persona nell' acqua, e tre volte anche il capo, al pronunziare del ministro i tre nomi. Non è pertanto da credere che altrimenti non si battezzasse giammai. Perocchè mancando al bisogna o la copia di acqua richiesta all' immersione, o la capacità della vasca, ovvero essendo la condizione del catecumeno tale che gli fosse pericoloso il tuffarsi interamente nelle acque, ovvero per alcun altro grave motivo supplivasi col battesimo detto di infusione od aspersione, versando o spargendo l'acqua sul capo di colui che si battezzava, stando egli or dentro una vasca che non bastava a riceverlo tutto, o fuori di essa e sulla terra asciutta.*"

† So also Peter the Lombard, "the Master of Sentences." Quoting from Gregory, he says (*Sentent.* Lib. iv. Dist. viii.): "*Pro vario ecclesiarum usu semel, vel ter, qui baptizatur immergitur.*" He makes no mention of pouring.

‡ *Summa Theol.*, Pars III. Quæst. LXVI. De Bapt. Art. 7: "*Si totum corpus aqua non possit perfundi propter aquæ paucitatem vel propter aliquam aliam causam, opportet caput perfundere, in quo manifestatur principium animalis vitæ.*" He also says that "by immersion the burial with Christ is more vividly represented; and therefore this is the most common and commendable way." His contemporary, Bonaventura, says, that "the way of dipping into water is the more common, and the fitter and safer."

Ravenna in the year 1311 declared the two modes equally valid. The general rubric of the baptismal service edited by order of Paul V. says: "Though baptism may be administered by affusion, or immersion, or aspersion, yet let the first or second mode which are more in use, be retained, agreeably to the usage of churches."

The ritual now in use in the Roman Catholic Church gives this direction: " Then the godfather or godmother, or both, holding the infant, the priest takes the baptismal water in a little vessel or jug, and pours the same three times upon the head of the infant in the form of the cross, and at the same time, he says, uttering the words once only, distinctly and attentively:

"N. I BAPTIZE THEE IN THE NAME OF THE FA✠THER— he pours firstly; AND OF THE ✠ SON—he pours a second time; AND OF THE HOLY ✠ GHOST—he pours a third time."

The Ritual, however, provides also first for immersion both of children and adults.*

3. Anglican authorities are equally pronounced on the historical question. William Wall, who wrote the best historical vindication of Infant Baptism against the Baptists, freely admits that in ancient times the "general and ordinary way was to baptize by immersion, or dipping the person, whether it were an infant, or grown man or woman, into the water." "This," he says, "is so plain and clear, by an infinite number of passages, that as one cannot but pity the weak endeavors of such Pædobaptists as would maintain the negative of it, so also we ought to disown and show a dislike of the profane scoffs which some people give to the English Antipædobap-

---

* *Pontificale Romanum Clementis VIII. ac Urbani VIII. jussu editum, inde vero a Benedicto XIV. recognitum et castigatum.* Mechliniæ, 1845. Pars Tertia, p. 805 (*Pro Baptismo Parvulorum*): "*Si baptizet per immersionem, Pontifex mitram retinens, surgit, et accipit infantem : et advertens ne lædatur, caute caput ejus immergit in aquam, et trina mersione baptizans, semel tantum dicit:*

N. EGO TE BAPTIZO IN NOMINE PA ✠ TRIS, ET FI ✠ LII, ET SPIRITUS ✠ SANCTI."

The same form is provided *pro Baptismo Adultorum*, p. 852. The Ritual prescribes also a form of conditional Baptism, in case of reasonable doubt whether Baptism has not already been performed : "*Si non es baptizatus, ego te baptizo,*" etc.

tists, merely for their use of dipping. It is one thing to maintain that *that* circumstance is not absolutely necessary to the essence of Baptism,—and another, to go about to represent it as ridiculous and foolish, or as shameful and indecent; when it was in all probability the way by which our blessed Saviour, and for certain was the most usual and ordinary way by which the ancient Christians did receive their Baptism. I shall not stay to produce the particular proofs of this;—many of the quotations which I brought for other purposes, and shall bring, do evince it. It is a great want of prudence, as well as of honesty, to refuse to grant to an adversary what is certainly true, and may be proved so: it creates a jealousy of all the rest that one says."*

Joseph Bingham, whose work on the *Antiquities of the Christian Church*, is still an authority, says : † " The ancients thought that immersion, or burying under water, did more lively represent the death and burial and resurrection of Christ, as well as our own death unto sin, and rising again unto righteousness; and the divesting or unclothing the person to be baptized did also represent the putting off the body of sin, in order to put on the new man, which is created in righteousness and true holiness. For which reason they observed the way of baptising all persons naked and divested, by a total immersion under water, except in some particular cases of great exigence, wherein they allowed of sprinkling, as in the case of clinic Baptism, or where there was a scarcity of water." . . . . Again ‡ : " Persons thus divested, or unclothed, were usually baptized by immersion, or dipping of their whole bodies under water, to represent the death and burial and resurrection of Christ together; and therewith to signify their own dying to sin, the

---

* *The History of Infant Baptism*, vol. ii. 297, of the 4th London ed., 1819. The first edition appeared 1705. The edition of Henry Cotton, Oxford, 1836, is in 4 vols., and includes John Gale's *Reflections*, and Wall's *Defe·ce* against this learned Baptist minister. There is also a Latin translation of this work, GUILIELMI WALLI *Historia Baptismi Infantum*, by Ludwig Schlosser, Bremen, 1748 and 1753. 2 vols.

† Book XI. Chapter XI. Sect. 1. The *Antiquities* were first published in 10 vols., 8vo, 1710–1722, and translated into Latin by Grischovius, Halle, 1724–1729 (*Origines Ecclesiasticæ*, etc.).

‡ Book XI. Chapter XI. Sect. 4.

destruction of its power, and their resurrection to a new life. There are a great many passages in the Epistles of St. Paul, which plainly refer to this custom." Bingham then quotes Rom. vi. 4; Col. ii. 12, and continues: "As this was the original Apostolic practice, so it continued to be the universal practice of the Church for many ages, upon the same symbolical reasons as it was first used by the Apostles." He adds the proofs from the Apostolical Constitutions, from Chrysostom, Ambrose, Cyril of Jerusalem, Epiphanius, etc.

Dean Stanley, in his *Lectures on the History of the Eastern Church*, while clearly expressing his own preference for sprinkling, gives the same view of the ancient mode.* "There can be no question," he says, "that the original form of Baptism—the very meaning of the word—was complete immersion in the deep baptismal waters; and that, for at least four centuries, any other form was either unknown, or regarded, unless in the case of dangerous illness, as an exceptional, almost a monstrous case. To this form the Eastern Church still rigidly adheres; and the most illustrious and venerable portion of it, that of the Byzantine Empire, absolutely repudiates and ignores any other mode of administration as essentially invalid. The Latin Church, on the other hand, doubtless in deference to the requirements of a Northern climate, to the change of manners, to the convenience of custom. has wholly altered the mode, preferring, as it would fairly say, mercy to sacrifice; and (with the two exceptions of the cathedral at Milan and the sect of the Baptists) a few drops of water are now the Western substitute for the threefold plunge into the rushing rivers, or the wide baptisteries of the East."

In his last work, Dean Stanley gave the following pictorial description, which applies to the multitudinous Baptisms in the period of Constantine, when the masses of the Roman population flocked into the Church: †

"Baptism was not only a bath, but a plunge—an entire submersion in the deep water, a leap as into the rolling sea or the rushing river, where for the moment the waves close over the

---

* New York ed. 1862, p. 117.
† *Christian Institutions*, New York, 1881, p. 9

bather's head, and he emerges again as from a momentary grave; or it was the shock of a shower-bath—the rush of water passed over the whole person from capacious vessels, so as to wrap the recipient as within the veil of a splashing cataract This was the part of the ceremony on which the Apostles laid so much stress. It seemed to them like a burial of the old former self and the rising up again of the new self. So St. Paul compared it to the Israelites passing through the roaring waves of the Red Sea, and St. Peter to the passing through the deep waters of the flood. 'We are buried,' said St. Paul, 'with Christ by Baptism into death, that, like as Christ was raised up from the dead by the glory of the Father, even so we also should walk in newness of life.' Baptism, as the entrance into the Christian society, was a complete change from the old superstitious restrictions of Judaism to the freedom and confidence of the Gospel; from the idolatries and profligacies of the old heathen world to the light and purity of Christianity. It was a change effected only by the same effort and struggle as that with which a strong swimmer or an adventurous diver throws himself into the stream and struggles with the waves, and comes up with increased energy out of the depths of the dark abyss." Stanley goes on to show the inseparable connection of baptismal immersion with the patristic conceptions of repentance, conversion, regeneration, which were almost identified. Hence the doctrine of the necessity of Baptism for salvation held by all the ancient fathers, and chiefly by the great and good St. Augustin. "All," says Stanley (p. 17), "who profess to go by the opinion of the ancients and the teaching of Augustin must be prepared to believe that immersion is essential to the efficacy of Baptism, that unbaptized infants must be lost forever, that baptized infants must receive the Eucharist, or be lost in like manner. For this, too, strange as it may seem, was yet a necessary consequence of the same materializing system."

We add the testimony of one of the most recent Anglican writers on the subject, Wharton B. Marriott: * "Triple im-

---

* In Smith and Cheetham's *Dictionary of Christian Antiquities*, vol. i. (1875), p. 161.

mersion, that is thrice dipping the head ($\kappa\alpha\vartheta\acute{\alpha}\pi\epsilon\rho$ $\H{\epsilon}\nu$ $\tau\iota\nu\iota$ $\tau\acute{\alpha}\varphi\omega$ $\tau\tilde{\omega}$ $\H{\upsilon}\delta\alpha\tau\iota$ $\kappa\alpha\tau\alpha\delta\upsilon\acute{o}\nu\tau\omega\nu$ $\dot{\eta}\mu\tilde{\omega}\nu$ $\tau\grave{\alpha}\varsigma$ $\kappa\epsilon\varphi\alpha\lambda\acute{\alpha}\varsigma$, St. Chrysostom *in Joan.* iii. 5, *Hom.* xxv.), while standing in the water, was the all but universal rule of the Church in early times. Of this we find proof in Africa, in Palestine, in Egypt, at Antioch and Constantinople, in Cappadocia. For the Roman usage Tertullian indirectly witnesses in the second century; St. Jerome in the fourth; Leo the Great in the fifth; and Pope Pelagius, and St. Gregory the Great in the sixth. . . . Lastly the Apostolical Canons, so called, alike in the Greek, the Coptic, and the Latin versions (*Can.* 42 al. 50), give special injunctions as to this observance, saying that any bishop or presbyter should be deposed who violated this rule." I have omitted the references to the proof passages. The same writer (p. 169) quotes from the Armenian order as follows: "While saying this, the priest *buries the child* (or Catechumen) *three times in the water*, as a figure of Christ's three days' burial. Then taking the child out of the water, *he thrice pours a handful of water on his head*, saying, 'As many of you as have been baptized into Christ, have put on Christ, Hallelujah!'"

4. Of GERMAN historians, I will quote only two, one who wrote before the discovery of the *Didache*, and another who wrote after it.

Neander says:* "In respect to the form of Baptism, it was in conformity with the original institution and the original import of the symbol, performed by immersion, as a sign of entire Baptism into the Holy Spirit, of being entirely penetrated by the same. It was only with the sick, where the necessity required it, that any exception was made; and in this case Baptism was administered by affusion or sprinkling. Many superstitious persons, clinging to the outward form, even imagined that such Baptism by sprinkling was not fully valid; and hence they distinguished those who had been so baptized from other Christians by the name of *Clinici*. The Bishop Cyprian strongly expressed himself against this delusion."

Dr. Adolph Harnack, of Giessen, the chief German writer

* *General History of the Christian Church.* Translation of Jos. Torrey, Boston ed. vol. i., p. 310. German ed. i. 534.

on the *Didache*, in reply to some questions of C. E. W. Dobbs, D.D., of Madison, Indiana, made the following statement on "the present state of opinion among German scholars" concerning the ancient mode of Baptism: *

"GIESSEN, Jan. 16th, 1885.
C. E. W. DOBBS, D.D.

Dear Sir: Referring to your three inquiries, I have the honor to reply:
1. *Baptizein* undoubtedly signifies immersion (*eintauchen*).
2. No proof can be found that it signifies anything else in the New Testament, and in the most ancient Christian literature. The suggestion regarding a 'sacred sense' is out of the question.†
3. There is no passage in the New Testament which suggests the supposition that any New Testament author attached to the word *baptizein* any other sense than *eintauchen—untertauchen*.‡
4. Up to the present moment, likewise, we possessed no certain proof from the period of the second century in favor of the fact that baptism by aspersion was then even facultatively administered; for Tertullian (*De Pœnit.*, 6, and *De Baptismo*, 12) is uncertain; and the age of those pictures upon which is represented a Baptism by aspersion is not certain.

'The Teaching of the Twelve Apostles,' however, has now instructed us that already in very early times, people in the Church took no offence when aspersion was put in the place of immersion, when any kind of outward circumstances might render immersion impossible or impracticable. [Then follows Chap. VII. of the 'Teaching,' quoted in full, emphasizing the clause Ἐὰν δὲ ἀμφότερα, etc.: 'if thou hast neither, pour water thrice upon the head,' etc.]

For details regarding the above you will please to consult my commentary on the passage. This much is lifted above all question—namely, that the author regarded as the essential element of the sacrament, not the immer-

---

* Published in the N. Y. "Independent" for February 9, 1885. The "Independent," of Feb. 28, 1884, gave the first notice in America on the publication of the *Didache* by translating Harnack's article from his "Theolog. Literaturzeitung," of February 3, 1884.

† By "sacred sense" Dr. Dobbs means that the Greek verb in the New Testament denotes "the application of water for sacred purposes, irrespective of mode,"—an opinion held by many Pœdobaptists in America and advanced as an argument against the Baptists. The most learned advocate of this view is the Rev. James W. Dale, who wrote no less than four volumes on the subject, namely, *Classic Baptism* (Philadelphia, 1867); *Judaic Baptism* (1871); *Johannic Baptism* (1872); *Christic and Patristic Baptism* (1874). He condensed the substance of these books shortly before his death (1881), in an ingenious article for the Schaff-Herzog *Encyclop.* vol. i. 196-198, which is preceded and followed by other articles representing the different opinions held in the baptismal controversy.

‡ This assertion may be disputed. See below, p. 55.

sion in water, but chiefly and alone the use of water. From this one is entitled to conclude that, from the beginning, in the Christian world immersion was the rule ; but that quite early the sacrament was considered to be complete when the water was applied, not in the form of a bath, but in the form of an aspersion (or pouring). But the rule was also certainly maintained that immersion was obligatory, if the outward conditions of such a performance were at hand.

With high regard, your obedient,

ADOLPH HARNACK."

5. The question now arises, when and how came the mode of pouring and sprinkling to take the place of immersion and emersion, as a rule. The change was gradual and confined to the Western churches. The Roman Church, as we have seen, backed by the authority of Thomas Aquinas, "the Angelic Doctor," took the lead in the thirteenth century, yet so as to retain in her Rituals the form for immersion as the older and better mode. The practice prevailed over the theory, and the exception became the rule.

It is remarkable that in the cold climate of England the old practice should have survived longer than in the Southern countries of Europe. Erasmus says : " With us " (on the Continent) " infants have the water poured on them, in England they are dipped." *

King Edward VI. and Queen Elizabeth were immersed. The first Prayer-Book of Edward VI. (1549), following the Office of Sarum, directs the priest to dip the child in the water thrice, "first, dypping the right side ; secondly, the left side ; the third time, dypping the face towards the fronte." In the second Prayer Book (1552), the priest is simply directed to dip the child discreetly and warily, and permission is given, for the first time in Great Britian, to substitute pouring if the godfathers and godmothers certify that the child is weak. During the reign of Elizabeth, says Dr. Wall. "many fond ladies and gentlewomen first, and then by degrees, the common people would obtain the favor of the priests to have their children pass for weak children too tender to endure dipping in the water." † The same writer traces the practice of sprinkling to

---

* *" Perfunduntur apud nos, merguntur apud Anglos."* Erasmus in the margin of 76th Ep. of Cyprian, quoted by Wall, ii. 303.

† *History of Infant Baptism*, vol. ii. 309.

the period of the Long Parliament and the Westminster Assembly.*

This change in England and other Protestant churches from immersion to pouring and from pouring to sprinkling was encouraged by the authority of Calvin, who declared the mode to be a matter of no importance, † and by the Westminister Assembly of Divines (1643–1652), which decided that pouring or sprinkling is " not only lawful but also sufficient." The Westminister Confession declares: " Dipping of the person into water is not necessary ; but Baptism is rightly administered by pouring or sprinkling water upon the person." ‡

But the Episcopal ritual retains the direction of immersion, although it admits sprinkling or pouring as equally valid. In the revision of the Prayer Book under Charles II. (1662) the mode is left to the judgment of the parents or godfathers, and the priest is ordered : " If the godfathers and godmothers shall certify him that the child may well endure it, to dip it in the water discreetly and warily ; but if they certify that the child is weak, it shall suffice to pour water upon it." The difference is only this: by the old rubric the minister was to dip unless there was good cause for exception in case of weakness ; by the new rubric he was to dip if it was certified that the child could endure it. The theory of the Anglican Church favors dipping, but the ruling practice is pouring. §

---

* Vol. ii. 311 : " And as for sprinkling properly called, it seems it was, at 1645, just then beginning, and used by very few. It must have begun in the disorderly times after 1641 ; for Mr. Blake had never used it, nor seen it used."

† *Instit.* IV. Ch. XV. § 19. He adds, however, that " the word *baptize* means to *immerse (mergere)*," and that " immersion was the practice of the ancient Church."

‡ Chapter XXVIII. 3. The proof passages quoted are Heb. ix. 10, 19–22; Acts, ii. 41 ; xvi. 33 ; Mark, vii. 4. On the Baptismal controversy in the W. Assembly, see Lightfoot's *Journal*, Aug. 7, 1644 ; *Works*, xiii. 299 sqq.

§ See Wall, *l. c.* II. 812. The *Prayer Book Interleaved* (London and Oxford, 1873, p. 185) states the facts thus : " Trine immersion was ordered in the rubric of 1549, following the Sarum Office. In 1552 single immersion only was enjoined. The indulgence of affusion for weak children was granted in 1549 and continued in 1552. In 1662 dipping remained the rule, but the proviso was then added. ' if they shall certify that the child may well endure it.' Trine immersion or affusion was the ancient rule." In the

On the Continent the change had taken place earlier. Yet the mode of Baptism was no point of controversy between Protestants and Catholics, nor between the Reformers and the Anabaptists. Luther gave decided preference to immersion, as more expressive.* The Lutheran and Reformed Confessions prescribe no particular mode. They condemn the Anabaptists for rebaptism and the rejection of Infant Baptism, (some also for teaching that infants may be saved without the sacrament), but not for practising immersion.† Nor was this practice general among the early Baptists themselves; on the contrary, the Mennonites baptize by sprinkling.‡ It was the English

preparation of the Reformed Service of Baptism under Edward VI. "much use was made of the previous labors of Bucer and Melanchthon in the 'Consultation' of Archbishop Hermann; and some ceremonies, which had the authority of that treatise, were retained in 1549, although afterwards discarded." Procter, *History of the Book of Common Prayer*, 11th ed., London, 1874, p. 371. The change in the revision under the Restoration Procter (p. 381, note 3) explains as a protest against the Baptists and the "the undue stress laid upon immersion." In the American editions of the Prayer Book the condition in the rubric is omitted, and the following substituted: "And then, naming it [the child] after them, *he shall dip it in the water discreetly, or shall pour water upon it*, saying," etc.

* See his *Sermon vom Sacr. der Taufe*, 1519, and his *Taufbüchlein*, 1523. Weimar ed. of Luther's *Works*, vol. II. 727.

† Thus *e. g.* the Augsburg Confession (1530) says, Art. IX.: "They condemn the Anabaptists who allow not the Baptism of children, and affirm that children are saved without Baptism (*pueros sine Baptismo salvos fieri*)." In the altered ed. of 1540, Melanchthon added "*et extra ecclesiam Christi*." But in the German edition he omitted the last clause, saying simply and more mildly: "*Derhalb werden die Wiedertäufer verworfen* [not, *verdammt*], *welche lehren, dass die Kindertauf nicht recht sei*" The Calvinistic Confessions make salvation to depend upon eternal election, not on the temporal act of Baptism, and the Second Scotch Confession, of 1580, expressly rejects, among the errors of the Pope, "his cruel judgment against infants departing without the sacrament," and "his absolute necessity of Baptism." Zwingli first advanced the opinion that all infants dying in infancy, as well as many adult heathen, are saved. Schaff, *Creeds of Christendom*, I. 378; III. 482.

‡ And so did also the first English Baptists who seceded from the Puritan emigrants and organized a congregation in Amsterdam. See Henry Martyn Dexter: *The Congregationalism of the Last Three Hundred Years* (N. York, 1880), p. 318, note 108: "Although a Baptist church, it is clear that they did not practise immersion. Aside from various circumstances which need not be dwelt upon to make this probable, it is made certain by the fact that when some of them subsequently applied for admission to a Mennonite church in Amsterdam which baptized by affusion, that church said, after questioning them as to their mode of Baptism, 'no difference was found

Baptists in the seventeenth century who first declared immersion essential and put it in their revision of the Westminster Confession.*

6. Let us now briefly sum up the results of this historical survey concerning the mode of Baptism.

(*a*) Trine immersion and emersion of the whole body was the general practice in the ancient Church, Greek and Latin, and continues to this day in all the Eastern churches and sects and in the orthodox State Church of Russia.

(*b*) Trine affusion or pouring was allowed and practised in all ancient churches as legitimate Baptism in cases of sickness or scarcity of water or other necessity.

(*c*) Single immersion has no proper authority in antiquity, as it was forbidden in the East, and only tolerated in the West as valid but incomplete.

(*d*) Affusion or pouring was used first only in exceptional cases, but came gradually into general use since the thirteenth century in the Latin Church, and then in all the Protestant churches, last in England, except among Baptists, who during the seventeenth century returned to the practice of immersion.

7. We will also state the bearing of the historical facts upon the parties at issue.

(*a*) The Pædobaptists are sustained by antiquity on the subject of Infant Baptism, but as regards the mode they can only plead the exceptional use, which they have turned into the

---

between them and us.'" John Smyth, the founder of the Arminian Baptists, baptized himself (hence called Se-Baptist), and then his followers, by affusion. Barclay, as quoted by Dexter, p. 318 sq., says that the practice of immersion "seems to have been introduced into England [*i. e.*, among the Baptists] 12 September, 1633." But in his *True Story of John Smyth the Se-Baptist* (Boston, 1881, p. 49), Dexter dates it from 1640 or 1641. The Baptists called it "a new Baptism," their opponents "a new crotchet." The Puritan Episcopalian Featly wrote a spicy book against the Baptists, with immersion pictures, *The Dippers Dipt*, London, 1644, 6th ed. 1651.

* The Baptist Confession of 1677 and 1688 declares: "Immersion, or dipping of the person in water, is necessary to the due administration of this ordinance." Schaff, *Creeds of Christendom*, vol. iii. 741. The New Hampshire Baptist Confession of 1833 defines Christian Baptism to be "the immersion in water of a believer into the name of the Father, and Son, and Holy Ghost." *Ibid.* iii., 747. The definition of the Free Will Baptist Confession of 1834 and 1868 is substantially the same. *Ibid.*, p. 755.

rule. They defend their position, first, by assuming that the terms *baptize* and *baptism* have in Hellenistic Greek a wider meaning than in classical Greek, so as to include the idea of washing and affusion;* secondly, by the general principle that the genius of Christianity in matters of form and ceremony allows freedom and adaptation to varied conditions, and that similar changes have taken place in the mode of celebrating the sacrament of the Lord's Supper. Water is necessary in Baptism, but the quality and quantity of water, and the mode of its application are unessential. Other arguments are inconclusive and should be abandoned.†

---

* The chief (and only applicable) passages adduced are Judith, xii. 7, (Sept. ἐβαπτίζετο ἐν τῇ παρεμβολῇ ἐπὶ τῆς πηγῆς τοῦ ὕδατος, "she *baptized*, *i.e.*, bathed herself in the camp at the fountain of water"); Sirach, xxxi. 25 ("being *baptized*, βαπτιζόμενος, from a dead body, what good will it do, if he wash it again;" compare the description of the ceremony, Num. xix. 11–22); Mark, vii. 4 (where it is said of the Jews that in returning from market, they do not eat, except "they *baptize*," *i.e.*, they wash themselves; and where Westcott and Hort, with some of the oldest authorities, read ῥαντίσωνται, *i e.*, *sprinkle themselves*, for the received text βαπτίσωνται, compare the passage Matt. xv. 2. "*wash* their hands," νίπτονται); Mark, vii. 4 (where in the same connection "*baptisms*, βαπτισμοί, of cups and pots and brazen vessels" are spoken of); Heb. vi. 2 ("the teaching of *Baptisms*," various kinds of Baptism); ix. 10 (διάφοροι βαπτισμοί, "divers washings," by immersion or bathing or pouring or sprinkling). The advocates of pouring appeal also to the tropical use of βαπτίζω, *to baptize in (with) the Holy Ghost, and in (with) fire* (Matt. iii. 11; Luke, iii. 16); and *to baptize* (*i. e.* to overwhelm) *with calamities* (Matt. xx. 22, 23; Mark, x. 38, 39; Luke, xii. 50 . Dr. Edw. Robinson in his *Lexicon of the N. T.* (p. 118) takes this view : "While in Greek writers, from Plato onwards, βαπτίζω is everywhere *to sink, to immerse, to overwhelm* [ships, animals, men], either wholly or *partially ;* yet in Hellenistic usage, and especially in reference to the rite of Baptism, it would seem to have expressed not always simply *immersion*, but the more general idea of *ablution* or *affusion*."

† It is often urged that the pentecostal Baptism of three thousand persons by total immersion (Acts, ii. 31; comp. iv. 4) was highly improbable in Jerusalem, where water is scarce and the winter torrent Kidron is dry in summer (I found it dry in the month of April, 1877). But immersion was certainly not impossible, since Jerusalem has several large public pools (Bethesda, Hezekiah, Upper and Lower Gihon) and many cisterns in private houses. The explorations of Captain Wilson (1864) and Captain Warren (1867) have shown that the water supply of the city, and especially of the temple, was very extensive and abundant. The Baptism of Christ in the Jordan and the illustrations of Baptism used in the New Testament (Rom. vi. 3, 4; Col.

(b) The Protestant Baptists can appeal to the usual meaning of the Greek word, and the testimony of antiquity for immersion, but not for *single* immersion, nor for their *exclusiveness*. They allow no exception at all, and would rather not baptize than baptize in any other way. The root of this difference is doctrinal. The Greek and Latin (we may also say, with some qualification, the Lutheran and Anglican) creeds teach baptismal regeneration and the (ordinary) necessity of Baptism for salvation; hence they admit even lay-baptism to insure salvation. Their chief Scripture authority are the words of Christ, John iii. 5 (understood of water-Baptism) and Mark xvi. 16 (ὁ πιστεύσας καὶ βαπτισθεὶς σωθήσεται). The Baptists, on the other hand—at least the Calvinistic or Regular Baptists—deny both these doctrines, and hold that Baptism is only a sign and seal (not a means) of conversion and regeneration, which must precede it and are therefore independent of it. They reason from the precedence of faith before Baptism (Mark xvi.16) and from the Pentecostal Baptism of converted adults (Acts ii. 38, 41).* They hold moreover that children dying in infancy are saved without Baptism (which would be inapplicable to them), and that adult believers are saved likewise if they die before immersion can be applied to them in the proper way.

The Baptists come nearest in this respect to the Quakers, who go a step further and dispense with the sacraments altogether, being contented with the inward operation of the Holy Spirit, who is not bound to any visible instrumentalities.

The Baptists and Quakers were the first organized Christian communities which detached salvation from ecclesiastical ordi-

---

ii. 12; 1 Cor. x. 2; 1 Pet. iii. 20, 21) are all in favor of immersion rather than sprinkling, as is freely admitted by the best exegetes, Catholic and Protestant, English and German. Comp. *e. g.* Meyer and Weiss on Rom. vi. 3, and Lightfoot on Col. ii. 12. Nothing can be gained by unnatural exegesis. The aggressiveness of the Baptists has driven Pædobaptists to the opposite extreme.

* On this point they might also quote Tertullian, who says, *De Pœn.* VI. " The Baptismal bath (*lavacrum*) is a seal of faith (*obsignatio fidei*). . . We are not washed (*abluimur*, baptized) *in order* that we *may* cease from sinning, but *because* we *have* ceased, since in heart we have been bathed already (*quoniam jam corde loti sumus*)."

nances, and taught the salvation of unbaptized infants and unbaptized but believing adults.

A settlement of the baptismal controversy will require 1) a full admission, on both sides, of the exegetical and historical facts; 2) a clearer understanding of the meaning and import of the sacrament and its precise relation to conversion and regeneration; 3) a larger infusion of the spirit of Christ which is the spirit of freedom.

CHAPTER XVIII.

The Agape and the Eucharist.

THE Lord's Supper is the second Sacrament of the Apostolic Church, which has ever since been observed and will be observed to the end of time, in remembrance of his dying love and sacrifice on the cross for the redemption of the world. "Eucharist," or "Thanksgiving," was the original name for the celebration of this ordinance, in connection with the Love-Feast or Agape. The *Didache*, in Chs. IX. and X., gives us the oldest elements of a eucharistic service, but without the words of institution or any directions as to particular forms and ceremonies and posture of the communicants. The whole has the character of utmost simplicity.

The Eucharist is again mentioned in the beginning of Ch. XIV. as a pure sacrifice to be offered on the Lord's Day, in fulfilment of the prophetic passage of Malachi (i. 11, 14), which was often used as early as the second century for the same purpose.

The following are the eucharistic prayers:

(Chap. IX.). "As regards the Eucharist, give thanks in this manner.
First for the Cup:
'We thank Thee, our Father, for the holy vine of David, thy servant, which Thou hast made known to us through Jesus, Thy servant [or, child]: to Thee be the glory for ever.'
And for the broken bread:
'We thank Thee, our Father, for the life and knowledge which Thou hast made known to us through Jesus, Thy servant: to Thee be the glory for ever. As this broken bread was scattered [in grains] upon the mountains, and

being gathered together became one, so let Thy church be gathered together from the ends of the earth into Thy Kingdom; for Thine is the glory and the power through Jesus Christ forever.'

But let no one eat or drink of your Eucharist except those who have been baptized into the name of the Lord, for respecting this the Lord has said, 'Give not that which is holy to dogs.'

(Chap. X.). "And after being filled, give thanks in this manner: 'We thank Thee, O Holy Father, for Thy holy name, which Thou hast enshrined in our hearts, and for the knowledge, and faith, and immortality which Thou madest known to us through Jesus, Thy servant: to Thee be the glory for ever. Thou, O Sovereign Almighty, didst create all things for the sake of Thy name, and gavest both food and drink to men for enjoyment, that they may give thanks to Thee. But to us Thou hast graciously given spiritual food and drink and life eternal through Thy servant. Before all things we thank Thee, that Thou art mighty: to Thee be the glory for ever Remember, O Lord, Thy Church to deliver her from every evil, and to make her perfect in Thy love; and do Thou gather her together from the four winds [the Church] sanctified for Thy Kingdom, which Thou didst prepare for her: for Thine is the power and the glory for ever. Let grace [Christ?] come, and let this world pass away. Hosanna to the God of David. If any one is holy, let him come; if any one is not, let him repent. Maran-atha! Amen.'

But permit the Prophets to give thanks as much as they wish."

In order to understand these prayers, we must remember that the primitive Eucharist embraced the Agape and the Communion proper.* The Agape was the perpetuation of the last Passover of our Lord, and culminated in the participation of his body and blood. The Jewish Passover meal consisted of five distinct acts:

(1) The head of the family or party (numbering no less than ten) asked a blessing on the feast and blessed and drank the

---

* See 1 Cor. xi. 20 sqq.; Jude, ver. 12. The *Did.* comprehends both in the word $εὐχαριστία$, Ignatius (*Ad Rom.* vii.; *Ad Smyrn.* vii. and viii.) in the word $ἀγάπη$. $Εὐχαριστία$ means the expression of gratitude in words (thanksgiving, 1 Cor. xiv. 16; 2 Cor. iv. 15; ix. 11, 12; Phil. iv. 6, etc.), or in act (thank-offering), or both united in the sacrament. The last is the early patristic usage (Justin Martyr, Clement of Alex., Origen). Sometimes it denotes the consecrated elements of bread and wine, sometimes the whole sacramental celebration with or without the Agape. The earliest eucharistic pictures represent chiefly the Agape or supper which preceded the actual Communion. Thus an Agape with bread and fish (referring to the miraculous feeding and the anagrammatic meaning of $ἰχθύς$) is painted in the very ancient crypt of Domitilla, which De Rossi traces to Flavia, the granddaughter of Vespasian. The bread and fish occur repeatedly in the Catacomb of St. Callistus. See Smith and Cheetham, vol. i. 626.

first cup of wine (always mixed with water). This is mentioned in Luke, xxii. 17, before the thanksgiving for the bread, ver. 19.

(2) The eating of the bitter herbs the first part of the Hallel (Ps. cxiii. and cxiv.) and the second cup. The father, at the request of the son (Ex. xii. 26), explained the meaning of the feast and gave an account of the sufferings of the Israelites and their deliverance from Egypt.

(3) The feast proper, that is, the eating of the unleavened loaves, the festal offerings, and the paschal lamb.

(4) The thanksgiving for the meal, and the blessing and drinking of the third cup.

(5) The singing of the remainder of the Hallel (Ps. cxv.–cxviii.), and the drinking of the fourth cup (occasionally a fifth cup, but no more).

No male was admitted to the passover unless he was circumcised, nor any man or woman who was ceremonially unclean.

The eucharistic cup which the Lord blessed and gave to the disciples, corresponds to the third paschal cup of thanksgiving which followed the breaking of the loaves and was made by Him, together with the broken bread, the sacrament of redemption by the sacrifice of his body and blood.

The Christian Agape was a much simpler feast than the Jewish Passover. Rich and poor, master and slave sat down together once a week on the same footing of brotherhood in Christ and partook of bread, fish and wine. Tertullian describes it as "a school of virtue rather than a banquet," and says, "as much is eaten as satisfies the cravings of hunger; as much is drunk as benefits the chaste." * But occasional excesses of intemperance occurred already in Apostolic congregations, as at Corinth, † and must have multiplied with the growth of the Church. Early in the second century the social Agape was separated from the Communion and held in the evening, the more solemn Communion in the morning; and afterwards the Agape was abandoned altogether, or changed into a charity for the poor.

---

* *Apol.* xxxix.: "*Editur quantum esurientes capiunt, bibitur quantum pudicis utile est . . . ut qui non tam cœnam cœnaverint quam disciplinam.*"

† 1 Cor. xi. 20–22.

In the *Didache* the two institutions seem to be as yet hardly distinguishable. It contains the three prayers of thanksgiving, given above, first for the cup, secondly. for the broken bread, thirdly for all God's mercies spiritual and temporal, with a prayer for the Church universal.*

Between the second and the third prayer is inserted a warning against the admission of unbaptized or unconverted persons, and the phrase, "*after being filled.*" The question arises: Does this phrase refer to the Communion,† or to the Agape. ‡ I think it must be applied to both, which were then inseparably connected, the Agape preceding, the Communion completing the Christian Passover. If referred to the Communion alone, the expression is too strong; if referred to the Agape alone, the Communion must be put after the third prayer. But the Communion is indicated before the third prayer by the warning: "Let no one eat or drink of your Eucharist except those who have been baptized," etc. And the author of the Apostolical Constitutions so understood it when he substituted for "after being filled," the phrase "after participation," or "communion." § Consequently the third thanksgiving must be a *post*-communion prayer.

This view, however, is not free from objections:

1. That the thanksgiving for the cup precedes the thanksgiving for the broken bread, and seems to be a preparatory blessing corresponding to the blessing of the first cup in the Passover. This is the reverse of the usual liturgical order, but had a precedent in Luke xxii. 17 (comp. 19). ‖

---

* These prayers are much enlarged in the *Apost. Constit.* vii. 9, 10.

† Bryennios, John Wordsworth, Harnack.

‡ Zahn (p. 293) rightly insists that $\dot{\epsilon}\mu\pi\lambda\eta\sigma\vartheta\tilde{\eta}\nu\alpha\iota$ implies the satisfaction of hunger and thirst by a regular meal (comp. John, vi. 12; Luke, i. 53; vi. 25; Acts, xiv. 17); for it is here not taken in a spiritual sense as in Rom. xv. 24.

§ Lib. vii. c. 26: $M\epsilon\tau\dot{\alpha}\ \delta\dot{\epsilon}\ \tau\dot{\eta}\nu\ \mu\epsilon\tau\dot{\alpha}\lambda\eta\psi\iota\nu\ o\tilde{v}\tau\omega\varsigma\ \epsilon\dot{v}\chi\alpha\rho\iota\sigma\tau\dot{\eta}\sigma\alpha\tau\epsilon.$ The warning of the *Did.*: "Give not that which is holy to the dogs" (Matt. vii. 6), is equivalent to the later liturgical formula, *holy things to holy persons* ($\tau\dot{\alpha}\ \tilde{\alpha}\gamma\iota\alpha\ \tau o\tilde{\iota}\varsigma\ \dot{\alpha}\gamma\dot{\iota}o\iota\varsigma$), which immediately preceded the distribution of the elements.

‖ Paul also mentions the cup first in 1 Cor. x. 16 and 21, but in the report of the institution, 1 Cor. xi. 23, he gives the usual order. So also the *Did.* in the warning at the close of Chap. ix. "Let no one eat or drink."

2. That the warning after the third prayer: "If any one be holy let him come, if any one be not holy let him repent," seems to be an invitation to the Communion. But as such an invitation with a warning is contained at the close of the second prayer, we must understand the second warning as an exhortation to catechumens to join the church.*

3. That there is no allusion to the atoning death of Christ—the central idea of the Eucharist. Very strange. But the *Didache* calls the Eucharist a sacrifice, shows the influence of John's Gospel (Chs. VI. and XVII.), and leaves room for additional prayers and exhortations by the Prophets.

The eucharistic service of the *Didache* indicates a mode of worship not far removed from the freedom of the Apostolic age. The fourteenth chapter of Paul's first Epistle to the Corinthians, written in the year 57, makes the impression—to use an American phrase—of a religious meeting "thrown open." Everybody who had a spiritual gift, whether it was the gift of tongues, or the gift of interpretation, or the gift of prophecy, or the gift of sober, didactic teaching, had a right to speak, to pray, and to sing; even women exercised their gifts (comp. 1 Cor. xi. 5). Hence the Apostle checks the excesses of this democratic enthusiasm and reminds the brethren that God is not a God "of confusion, but of peace," and that "all things should be done decently and in order" (1 Cor. xiv. 33, 40). It was especially the Glossolalia or the abrupt, broken, ejaculatory, ecstatic outburst of devotion in acts of prayer or song, which was liable to abuse and to produce confusion. Hence the Apostle gave the preference to prophesying, which was addressed to the congregation and tended directly to practical edification.

In the *Didache* we find no trace of the Glossolalia, and the worship is already regulated by a few short prayers, but it is not said who is to offer these prayers, nor is praying confined to these forms, on the contrary the "Prophets" are allowed to pray in addition as much as they please. A similar liberty was exercised, according to Justin Martyr, by the "President" (Bishop) of the congregation, who prayed according to his

* So Harnack (p. 36).

ability under the inspiration of the occasion."* The Montanists wished to revive or to perpetuate the liberty of prophesying by laymen as well as ministers, by women as well as men (like the Quakers in recent times), but the strong tendency to order and hierarchical consolidation triumphed over freedom and restricted the active part of worship to a clerical function according to prescribed and unalterable liturgical forms, which appear under various Apostolic and post-Apostolic names in the Nicene age. The Reformation of the sixteenth century revived the idea of the general priesthood of the laity, and recognized it in congregational singing and in responsive liturgies.

CHAPTER XIX.

Ecclesiastical Organization.

THE third Part of the *Didache* is a Directory of Church Polity and Discipline. It contains instructions to Christian congregations concerning various classes of ministers of the gospel, Chs. XI.–XIII and Ch. XV. The intervening fourteenth chapter treats of the observance of the Lord's Day and the sacrifice of the Eucharist; it interrupts the natural connection and belongs rather to the second or liturgical section of the book. With this exception the order of the *Didache* is remarkably clear and logical.

The *Didache* places us into the situation between the church polity of the Pastoral Epistles and the establishment of Episcopacy, or between St. Paul and Ignatius of Antioch. The Apostolic government was about to cease, and the Episcopal government had not yet taken its place. A secondary order of Apostles and Prophets were moving about and continued the missionary work of the primitive Apostles; while the government of the particular congregations remained in the hands of Presbyter-Bishops and Deacons, just as in Philippi

---

* *Apol.* I. lxvii: ὅση δύναμις αὐτῷ, *quantum potest, quantum facultatis eius est* See the notes of Otto, and comp. Tertullian's "*ex proprio ingenio,*" "*ex pectore,*" "*sine monitore.*"

and other congregations of Paul. Such a state of things we should expect between A.D. 70 and 110.

The organization of the Church in the *Didache* appears very free and elastic. There is no visible centre of unity, either at Jerusalem, or Antioch, or Ephesus, or Rome; which are not even mentioned. The author is silent about Peter, and knows nothing of his primacy or supremacy. No creed or rule of faith is required as a condition of membership or bond of union; but instruction in Christian morality after the pattern of the Sermon on the Mount precedes Baptism. The baptismal formula which includes some belief in the Trinity, and the eucharistic prayers which imply some belief in the atonement, are a near approach to a confession, but it is not formulated.*

Nevertheless there is a spiritual unity in the Church such as Paul had in view, Eph. iv. 3. All Christians are brethren in the Lord, though scattered over the earth: they believe in God as the author of all good, and in Jesus Christ as their Lord and Saviour; they are baptized into the triune name; they partake of the same Eucharist; they pray the Lord's Prayer; they abstain from the sins forbidden in the Decalogue and all other sins; they practise every Christian virtue, and keep the royal law of love to God and to our neighbor; they look hopefully and watchfully forward to the second coming of Christ and the resurrection of the righteous. The Church is to be perfected into that kingdom which God has prepared for her.

There is a strong feeling of Christian brotherhood running through the eucharistic prayers and the whole *Didache*.† Every wandering brother who shares the faith and hope

---

* Harnack, p. 90: "*Von einer formulirten regula fidei ist in der Διδαχή noch nicht die Rede; unzweifelhaft genügt dem Verfasser noch der Gebrauch der Abendmahlsgebete und der Taufformel, um den christlichen Charakter dessen, der auf den Namen 'Christ' Anspruch erhebt, festzustellen.*"

† G. Bonet-Maury (*La doctrine des douze apôtres*, Paris, 1884, p. 4), says: "*L'auteur a un vif sentiment de la solidarité de tous les membres dispersé de l'église universelle.*" This catholicity of feeling is incompatible with the bigotry of the Ebionitic sect, and a strong argument against Krawutzcky's hypothesis.

of the Church is to be hospitably received, without formal letters of recommendation. False prophets and corrupters are mentioned, but their errors are not described.

The solidarity and hospitality of the primitive Christians are acknowledged and ridiculed as a good-natured weakness by the heathen Lucian, the Voltaire of the second century, who had no conception of the irresistible attraction of the cross of Christ. But they were often abused, which made caution necessary. Hence the restriction of congregational hospitality to two or three days, and the requirement of labor from those who can perform it (xii. 3, 4).

CHAPTER XX.

Apostolic and Post-Apostolic Forms of Government.

It is interesting to compare the church polity and church officers of the *Didache* with the preceding and succeeding condition.

I. Let us first glance at the organization of the Apostolic churches. Christ himself founded the Church, appointed Apostles, and instituted two sacraments, Baptism for new converts, and the Lord's Supper for believers. Beyond this fundamental work he left the Church to the guidance of the Holy Spirit which he promised.

(1) In the Acts of the Apostles we find *Apostles*, *Prophets* and *Teachers* (xiii. 1), *Evangelists* (xxi. 8), *Presbyter-Bishops* or *Elders* (xi. 30; xiv. 23; xv. 2, 4, 6, 22, 23; xvi. 4; xx. 17, 28; xxi. 18; xxiii. 14; xxiv. 1; xxv. 15), and in Jerusalem also *Deacons*, under the name of *the Seven* (vi. 3; xxi. 8).

(2) In the Pauline Epistles, the following officers and functions are mentioned:

1 Cor. xii. 28: "first *Apostles*, secondly *Prophets*, thirdly *Teachers*, then miracles (powers, $\delta v \nu \acute{a} \mu \varepsilon \iota \varsigma$), then gifts of healing, helps, governments, divers kinds of tongues. Are all Apostles? are all Prophets? are all workers of miracles? have all gifts of healings? do all speak with tongues? do all

interpret?" Paul here unites officers and gifts together without strict regard to order or completeness. He omits Evangelists Bishops and Deacons (unless they are included in "Teachers" and in "helps and governments"), and the gifts of wisdom, of knowledge (ver. 8), of discerning of spirits (ver. 10), and love, the greatest of all gifts, described in Ch. XIII.

Eph. iv. 11: "And he gave some to be *Apostles;* and some *Prophets;* and some *Evangelists;* and some *Pastors* and *Teachers;* for the perfecting of the saints unto the work of ministering, unto the building up of the body of Christ." Here Evangelists are distinguished from Apostles and Prophets; Bishops and Deacons are not named; but probably included in Pastors and Teachers.

Phil. i. 1: "*Bishops* and *Deacons*" of the congregation at Philippi. The "Bishops" (mark the plural) must be Presbyters or Elders; for one congregation could not have more than one Bishop in the later diocesan sense.

In the Pastoral Epistles, Paul gives the qualifications of *Bishops* and *Deacons*, omitting the *Presbyters*, because they were identical with the Bishops, 1 Tim. iii. 2. 8, 12; Tit. i. 7; but the Presbyters are mentioned in 1 Tim. v. 1, 17, 19 and Tit. i. 5. Besides, "the work of an *Evangelist*" is spoken of in connection with Timothy, 2 Tim. iv. 3, and the "Presbytery," or body of Presbyters, 1 Tim. iv. 14 (comp. Acts, xxii. 5; Luke, xxii. 6).

(3) The Epistle to the Hebrews mentions the church officers in the aggregate, without specification of classes, under the name of *rulers* ($\dot{\eta}\gamma o \dot{\upsilon} \mu \varepsilon \nu o \iota$) who "speak the word of God." Ch. xiii. 7, 17, 24. The "Elders" in ch. xi. 2 is a title of dignity and equivalent to Fathers.

(4) The Catholic Epistles throw no light on church organization.

James mentions *Teachers* (iii. 1), and says that the *Elders* of the congregation should visit the sick to pray with them (v. 14).

Peter exhorts the *Elders*, as a "Fellow-Elder," to tend the flock of God (1 Pet. v. 1–4).

(5) The Apocalypse speaks of "holy *Apostles* and *Prophets*"

(xviii. 20), but also of false Apostles (ii. 2) and a false Prophetess (ver. 20). *Elders* are repeatedly mentioned in the visions (iv. 4, 10; v. 5, 6, 8, 11, 14; vii. 11, 13; xi. 16; xiv. 3; xix. 4), but not in the usual ecclesiastical sense. The *Angels* of the Seven Churches in Asia Minor are probably the representatives of the body of congregational officers.*

II. In the second and third centuries, we find a considerable change, first in the Ignatian Epistles (about 110), and then more fully developed in Irenæus (c. 180), Tertullian (200), and Cyprian (250). The clergy and laity are separated, and the former are clothed with a sacerdotal character after the precedent of the Levitical priesthood. The three orders (*ordines majores*) of the ministry appear, namely, *Bishops*, *Priests* (*Presbyters*), and *Deacons*, with a number of subordinate officers called the *minor* orders (Sub-deacons, Readers, Acolyths, Exorcists, etc.); while the Apostles, Prophets, and Evangelists disappear. The Bishops rise above the Presbyters from a local congregational to a diocesan position and become in the estimation of the Church successors of the Apostles (the Bishop of Rome, successor of Peter).

Among the Bishops again the occupants of the "Apostolic Sees" so called (Jerusalem, Antioch, Alexandria, Ephesus, Rome) rose in the Nicene age to the dignity of Metropolitans, and five of them (Jerusalem, Antioch, Alexandria, Rome, Constantinople or New Rome) to the higher dignity of Patriarchs; while the Bishop of Old Rome claimed a still higher dignity, a primacy of honor, and a supremacy of jurisdiction over the whole Church as the successor of Peter, and the vicar of Christ, —a claim, however, which the Oriental Church never conceded.†

III. The *Didache*, as already remarked, stands between the Apostolic organization of the first century and the Episcopal organization of the second, and fills the gap between the two. It mentions five officers, namely *Apostles*, *Prophets* and *Teachers*, for the church at large; and *Bishops* and *Deacons* for particular congregations.

---

* See my *Church History*, i. 497 sq., and *History of the Apostolic Church*, p. 537 sqq.

† See on these changes, *Church History*, ii. 121-154.

In the last respect it agrees with the Epistle of Clement of Rome. The Shepherd of Hermas likewise belongs to this transition period. He does not yet mention three orders, but Apostles, Prophets, Teachers, Bishops and Deacons.

The Irvingites might find new proof in the *Didache* for their church polity, which includes Apostles, Prophets, and Evangelists, but confines the number of Apostles to twelve.

CHAPTER XXI.

Apostles and Prophets.

LET us now consider the several gospel ministers of the *Didache*.

1. The APOSTLES spoken of in the eleventh chapter, are not the Twelve mentioned in the title, but their associates and successors in the work of Christianizing the world. They are travelling evangelists or missionaries who preached the Gospel from place to place in obedience to the great commission of Christ to his disciples. The word is used in a wider sense, corresponding to its etymology. The original Twelve were chosen with special reference to the twelve tribes of Israel. It was a typical number, as was also the number of the seven Deacons in Jerusalem. The spread of Christianity among the Gentiles required an extension of the Apostolate. First of all, Paul is the typical "Apostle of the Gentiles," and being directly called by the exalted Saviour, he stands on a par in authority with the Twelve. Next to him such men as Barnabas, James the Lord's Brother, Epaphras, Andronicus and Junias, Timothy, Titus, Mark, Luke, Silvanus, Apollos, are or may be called Apostles in a wider and secondary sense.*

---

* Comp. Acts xiv. 4, 14 (where Barnabas is certainly included in ἀποστόλοι); 1 Thess. ii. 6 (where Silvanus and Timothy seem to be included in the plural; both being mentioned with Paul in the inscription, i. 1); Rom. xvi. 7 (where Andronicus and Junias are called ἐπίσημοι ἐν τοῖς ἀποστόλοις "noted among the Apostles"; see the Commentaries); 1 Cor. xv. 5. 7 (τοῖς ἀποστόλοις, as distinct from the δώδεκα, ver. 5); 2 Cor. xi. 5; xii. 11. In the N. T. the term ἀπόστολος occurs 79 times (68 times in Luke and Paul),

Hence false "Apostles" are also spoken of, who counteracted the work of the genuine Apostles and sowed tares among the wheat.*

The Shepherd of Hermas speaks of "forty Apostles and Teachers." †

The Lord himself had, during his earthly ministry, set in motion such a secondary class of Apostles, in anticipation and authorization of Evangelists of future ages, by the mission of the *Seventy* who went out "two and two before his face into every city and place whither he himself was about to come." ‡ The instructions he gave to them, as well as to the Twelve, on a similar preparatory mission, help us very much to understand the state of things in the post-Apostolic age.

The love of Christ kindled an extraordinary missionary enthusiasm; and this alone can explain the rapid spread of Christianity throughout the Roman empire by purely moral means and in the face of formidable obstacles. Justin Martyr was a travelling Evangelist or peripatetic Teacher of Jews and Gentiles in different places. Eusebius has a special chapter on "Preaching Evangelists who were yet living in that age," *i. e.*, the age of Ignatius under the reign of Trajan. § He thus describes them:

> "They performed the office of Evangelists to those who had not yet heard the faith, whilst, with a noble ambition to proclaim Christ, they also delivered to them the books of the Holy Gospels. After laying the foundation

---

ἀποστολή 4 times (thrice in Paul and once in Luke). See Bishop Lightfoot's *Com. on Gal.* pp. 92–101, where he discusses at length the classical, Jewish, Apostolic, and ecclesiastical uses of the term.

* 2 Cor. xi. 13; Rev. ii. 2.

† *Sim.*: ix. 15. οἳ δέ μ' ἀπόστολοι καὶ διδάσκαλοι τοῦ κηρύγματος τοῦ υἱοῦ τοῦ Θεοῦ (*quadraginta apostoli et doctores prædicationis filii Dei*). Again in cap. 16 and ix. 25. The number forty has reference to the forty stones in the building of the tower, which is a figure of the Church. Comp. *Vis.* III. 5: λίθοι . . . εἰσιν οἱ ἀπόστολοι καὶ ἐπίσκοποι καὶ διδάσκαλοι καὶ διάκονοι.

‡ Luke, x. 1 sqq.; comp. Matt. x. 5 sqq.

§ περὶ τῶν εἰσέτι τότε διαπρεπόντων εὐαγγελιστῶν, *De Evangelii prædicatoribus qui adhuc ea ætate florebant, Hist. Eccl.* iii. 37. In the preceding ch. 36 he treats of Ignatius, in ch. 38 of Clement of Rome, in ch. 39 of Papias He means, therefore, the time from the close of the first and to the middle of the second century.

of the faith in foreign parts as the particular object of their mission, and after appointing others as shepherds of the flocks, and committing to these the care of those that had been recently introduced, they went again to other regions and nations, with the grace and coöperation of God. The holy Spirit also wrought many wonders as yet through them, so that as soon as the gospel was heard, men voluntarily in crowds, and eagerly, embraced the true faith with their whole minds. As it is impossible for us to give the numbers of the individuals that became Pastors or Evangelists during the first immediate succession from the Apostles in the churches throughout the world, we have only recorded those by name in our history, of whom we have received the traditional account as it is delivered in the various comments on the Apostolic doctrine still extant."

This description is the best commentary on the "Apostles" of the *Didache*.

These wandering Evangelists are to be received as the Lord, but are only allowed to remain a day or two in the Christian congregations. This was a measure of self-protection against imposition by clerical vagabonds. A true Apostle would not forget his duty to preach the gospel to the unconverted. False Apostles and false Prophets were known already in the Apostolic age, and predicted by Christ. Paul was tormented by Judaizing missionaries, who followed him everywhere, and tried to undermine his authority and work in Galatia, Corinth, Philippi, and elsewhere. The Apostle, according to the *Didache*, is entitled to his living, but if he asks for money he is a false prophet. Mercenary preachers have been a curse from the beginning in unbroken succession. How easily the simple-hearted Christians were imposed upon by selfish leaders, we learn from Lucian's "Peregrinus Proteus." *

In this connection the *Didache* directs that every Christian "who comes in the name of the Lord," shall receive hospitality for two or three days; but if he remains longer, he shall work, and if he refuses, he is a "Christ-trafficker;" *i. e.*, one who makes merchandise of his Christian profession, or uses the name of Christ for selfish ends, like Simon Magus.†

2. The PROPHETS are mentioned in close connection with

---

* See *Church History*, vol. ii., 93 sqq.

† Ch. XII. 5. $Χριστέμπορος$ is a post-apostolic word, but used also by Pseudo-Ignatius, Athanasius, Chrysostom, and Basil. The idea is the same as 1 Tim. vi. 5, "supposing that godliness is a way of gain."

the Apostles, but with this difference, that they were not sent as missionaries to the heathen, but instructors and comforters of converts, and might settle in a particular congregation. In this case they are to receive a regular maintenance, namely, all first fruits of the products of the wine-press and threshing-floor, of oxen and sheep, and of every possession. They are to be supported like the priests in the Jewish theocracy, "according to the commandment." * A congregation, however, may be without a Prophet, though not without Bishops and Deacons. There were, it seems, itinerant Prophets and stationary Prophets. In the absence of a Prophet the congregational offerings should be given to the poor.

The *Didache* shows a preference for the Prophets: they are mentioned fifteen times (the Apostles only three times); they are called "chief-priests," † and they alone are allowed the privilege to pray extempore as much as they please in public worship. But as there are false Apostles, so there are also false Prophets, and they must be judged by their fruits. Avarice is a sure sign of a false Prophet.

Paul gives the Prophets the preference over the Glossolalists, because prophecy was for the edification of the congregation, while the glossolalia was an abrupt, broken, ejaculatory, transcendental utterance of prayer and praise for the gratification of the individual, who spoke in an ecstatic condition of mind, and required interpretation into the ordinary language of common sense to benefit others. It seems to have passed away soon after the Apostolic age. ‡ It is not mentioned in the *Didache*.

A Prophet in the biblical sense is an inspired teacher and exhorter who reveals to men the secrets of God's will and word and the secrets of their own hearts for the purpose of conver-

---

* Ch. XIII. 5, 7. Probably with reference to the Mosaic law. The tithes are not yet mentioned.

† Ch. XIII. 3, $οἱ ἀρχιερεῖς ὑμῶν$, a title given to the heads of the twenty-four courses of priests and to the members of the Sanhedrin. This is the first intimation of the sacerdotal conception of the Christian ministry.

‡ On the glossolalia and the other charismata of the Apostolic Age, see *History of the Christian Church* (revised ed.), i., 230–242 and 436 sqq., and the commentators on Acts, ii. and 1 Cor. xii. and xiv.

sion and edification. As the word indicates, he is a spokesman or interpreter of God to men.* The predictive element does not necessarily enter into his office. Some of the greatest prophets among the Hebrews did not foretell future events, or only to a limited extent. In the New Testament all Apostles were inspired prophets, more especially John, the apocalyptic seer of the future conflicts and triumphs of the kingdom of Christ. Agabus was a Prophet from Jerusalem, who predicted at Antioch the famine, under Claudius Cæsar, A.D. 44 (Acts, xi. 28), and afterwards (in 58) at Cæsarea the captivity of Paul, when, like some of the Hebrew Prophets, he accompanied his word with a symbolic action by binding his own hands and feet with Paul's girdle (xxi. 10, 11). Barnabas, Simeon Niger, Lucius of Cyrene, Manæn, and Saul are called "Prophets and Teachers" of the church at Antioch, and through them the Holy Spirit appointed Barnabas and Saul for the missionary work among the Gentiles (Acts, xiii. 1–4). Nor was the prophetic gift confined to men. As in the Old Testament Miriam and Deborah were prophetesses, so the four unmarried daughters of Philip the Evangelist, prophesied (xxi. 9). Paul recognizes the same gift in women (1 Cor. xi. 4), but forbids its exercise in the public assembly (xiv. 34; 1 Tim. ii. 11, 12). In the Jewish dispensation the Prophets, since the time of Samuel, constituted one of the three orders of the theocracy, with the sacerdotal and royal order. In the New Testament, there is no trace of a prophetic order. The gift was distributed and exercised chiefly in expounding the deeper sense of the Scriptures and rousing the conscience and heart of the hearers.

The Prophets of the *Didache* are the successors of these earlier Prophets. The Shepherd of Hermas is a weak echo of Apostolic prophecy and is full of revelations. Justin Martyr and Irenæus testify to the continuance of the prophetic office in the Church. The Peregrinus of Lucian's satirical romance is represented as

---

* This is the usual classical meaning of προφήτης, *one who speaks for another*, especially *for a god ;* hence an *interpreter*. Thus Apollo is called the prophet of Zeus. In the Sept. it is the translation of *Nabi*. Aaron was the prophet of Moses (Ex. vii. 1).

a Prophet and a sort of Bishop, but was an impostor. Celsus mentions Prophets in Phœnicia and Palestine. Gradually the prophetic office disappeared before the episcopal, which would not tolerate a rival, and was better suited for the ordinary government of the Church. Montanism revived prophecy in an eccentric and fanatical shape with predictions of the approaching Millennium; but the Millennium did not appear, and the new prophecy was condemned and defeated by the episcopal hierarchy. In our days Irvingism made a similar attempt and met a similar fate. Prophecy, like all the other supernatural gifts of the Apostolic age, was necessary for the introduction, but not for the perpetuation, of Christianity. Yet in a wider sense there are prophets or enlightened teachers speaking with authority and power in almost every age of the Christian Church.

There is no trace of a Montanistic leaning in the *Didache*, as Hilgenfeld assumes. The chief doctrines of Montanism, concerning the Paraclet, the Millennium, the severe fasts, the female prophecy, the general priesthood of the laity, the opposition to the Catholic clergy, are nowhere alluded to. The book evidently ante-dates Montanism.

3. The term TEACHERS ($\delta\iota\delta\acute{a}\sigma\kappa\alpha\lambda o\iota$) seems to be used in a general way, and may apply alike to the Apostles and the Prophets, and also to the Bishops.* For teaching was one of the chief functions of their office. The church of Smyrna calls her Bishop Polycarp "an Apostolic and Prophetic Teacher."† But there were also many uninspired teachers without the prophetic gift, like Justin Martyr, Tatian,

---

* In Ch. XIII. 1, 2, $\pi\rho o\varphi\acute{\eta}\tau\eta\varsigma$ $\dot{a}\lambda\eta\vartheta\iota\nu\acute{o}\varsigma$ and $\delta\iota\delta\acute{a}\sigma\kappa\alpha\lambda o\varsigma$ $\dot{a}\lambda\eta\vartheta\iota\nu\acute{o}\varsigma$ seem to be identical. In Acts, xiii. 1, Barnabas, Saul, and others are called "Prophets and Teachers." Paul requires of the Bishop—*i. e.*, of the local Presbyter—that he be apt to teach ($\delta\iota\delta\alpha\kappa\tau\iota\kappa\acute{o}\varsigma$), 1 Tim. iii. 2. In 1 Cor. xii. 28 he puts the Teachers after the Prophets, in Eph. iv. 11 after the Evangelists and in connection with the Shepherds ($\tau o\grave{v}\varsigma$ $\delta\grave{e}$ $\pi o\iota\mu\acute{e}\nu\alpha\varsigma$ $\kappa\alpha\grave{\iota}$ $\delta\iota\delta\alpha\sigma\kappa\acute{a}\lambda o\upsilon\varsigma$). Hermas (*Sim.* ix. 15) connects "Apostles and Teachers." Zahn, *l. c.*, p. 300, understands by the Teachers of the *Didache*, members of the congregation.

† *Martyr. Polyc.* xvi. (ed. Funk i. 301): $\delta\iota\delta\acute{a}\sigma\kappa\alpha\lambda o\varsigma$ $\dot{a}\pi o\sigma\tau o\lambda\iota\kappa\acute{o}\varsigma$ $\kappa\alpha\grave{\iota}$ $\pi\rho o\varphi\eta\tau\iota\kappa\acute{o}\varsigma$, and at the same time $\dot{e}\pi\acute{\iota}\sigma\kappa o\pi o\varsigma$ $\tau\tilde{\eta}\varsigma$ $\dot{e}\nu$ $\Sigma\mu\acute{v}\rho\nu\eta$ $\kappa\alpha\vartheta o\lambda\iota\kappa\tilde{\eta}\varsigma$ $\dot{e}\kappa\kappa\lambda\eta\sigma\acute{\iota}\alpha\varsigma$.

Pantænus, and the teachers of the catechetical school at Alexandria, and other institutions of religious and theological instruction and preparation for church work.

CHAPTER XXII.

Bishops and Deacons.

THE local churches or individual congregations are ruled by Bishops and Deacons elected or appointed by the people.* They derive their authority not directly from the Holy Spirit, as the Apostles and Prophets, but through the medium of the Church. They are to be worthy of the Lord, meek and unselfish, truthful and of good report, and to be honored like the Prophets and Teachers (XV. 1, 2).

This is all we learn of the two classes of congregational officers. They are evidently the same with those mentioned in the Acts and the Pauline Epistles. The Bishops are the regular teachers and rulers who have the spiritual care of the flock; the Deacons are the helpers who attend to the temporalities of the Church, especially the care of the poor and the sick. Afterwards the Deaconate became a stepping-stone to the Presbyterate. Deaconesses are not mentioned in the *Didache*, but undoubtedly existed from Apostolic times, at least in Greek churches (comp. Rom. xvi. 1), for the care of the poor and sick and the exercise of hospitality and various offices of love among the female portion of the congregation. They were required by the strict separation of the sexes. The office continued in the Greek Church down to the twelfth century.

The Bishops of the *Didache* are identical with the Presby-

---

* Ch. XV. 1: χειροτονήσατε οὖν ἑαυτοῖς ἐπισκόπους καὶ διακόνους. Comp. Acts, xiv. 23; 2 Cor. viii. 19. The A. V. renders the word in Acts wrongly by "ordain," which is a later ecclesiastical sense. The R. V. corrects it: "When they had *appointed* for them elders in every church." The election of Bishops by the people continued to be the practice till the time of Cyprian, Ambrose, and Augustin, who were all so elected; but ordination was performed by other Bishops.

ters; hence the latter are not mentioned at all. This is a strong indication of its antiquity. It agrees with the usage in the New Testament, and differs from the usage of the second century, when Bishops, Priests and Deacons were distinguished as three separate orders.*

Bishops and Presbyters in the Acts and Epistles are not two distinct ranks or orders, but one and the same class of congregational officers. "Bishop" ($\dot{\epsilon}\pi\acute{\iota}\sigma\kappa o\pi o\varsigma$), *i.e.*, Overseer, Superintendent, was the title of municipal and financial officers in Greece and Egypt, and occurs in the Septuagint for several Hebrew words meaning "inspector," "taskmaster," "captain." The term "Presbyter" ($\pi\rho\epsilon\sigma\beta\acute{\upsilon}\tau\epsilon\rho o\varsigma$), or Elder, was used of the rulers of the Synagogue and corresponds to the Hebrew *seken*. It was originally a name of age and dignity (like "Senator," "Alderman"). Both titles were transferred to the rulers and teachers of the Apostolic churches, and used interchangeably. Hence the Ephesian "Presbyters" in Acts, xx. 17, are called "Bishops" in ver. 28; hence Bishops and Deacons alone are mentioned in the Epistle to the Philippians (ch. i. 1) and in the Pastoral Epistles. There were always several Presbyter-Bishops in one congregation (even the smallest), and constituted a college or board called "Presbytery," for the government of the Church, probably with a presiding officer elected by his colleagues and corresponding to the chief ruler of the Synagogue.

This same identity we find in the *Didache*, and also in the Epistle of Clement of Rome, which was written before the close of the first century. Clement mentions "Bishops and

---

* So also Bishop Lightfoot (on the *Did.* in "The Expositor," Jan. 1885, p. 71: "When our author wrote, Bishop still remained a synonym for 'Presbyter,' and the Episcopal office, properly so called, had not been constituted in the district in which he lived." This is, no doubt, the natural view sustained by the Pauline Epistles and by the Epistle of the Roman Clement. I cannot agree with Dr. Harnack (p. 142 sqq.) who labors to prove that the Bishops were originally identical with the *Deacons*, and that their office was purely administrative. He had previously advocated this theory in *Die Gesellschafts-verfassung der Christlichen Kirchen im Alterthum;* Giessen, 1883, p. 229 sqq. (An enlarged translation of Hatch's *Organization of the Early Christian Churches*, 1881.) Comp. the essays on the Christian Ministry by Sanday, Harnack, Harris, Milligan, and others, in "The Expositor," London, 1887.

Deacons" as congregational officers, enjoins obedience to "Presbyters" without mentioning "Bishops," and calls the office of the Corinthian "Presbyters" episcopal supervision (ἐπισκοπή).*

But these are the last instances of the New Testament use of the term "Bishop." In the Ignatian Epistles he is already clearly distinguished from the Presbyters, as representing a higher order, though not yet a diocesan, but simply as the head of a single church and of its board of Presbyters and Deacons. By and by as the Apostles, Prophets, and Evangelists disappeared, the Bishops absorbed all the higher offices and functions, and became in the estimation of the Church the successors of the Apostles; while the Presbyters became Priests, and the Deacons Levites in the new Christian Catholic hierarchy.

CHAPTER XXIII.

The End of the World.

THE *Didache* aptly closes with an exhortation to watchfulness and readiness for the coming of the Lord, as the goal of the Christian's hope. The sixteenth chapter is an echo of the eschatological discourses in the Synoptical Gospels, especially the twenty-fourth chapter of Matthew, with the exception of those features which especially refer to the destruction of Jerusalem and the Temple. The eucharistic prayers allude likewise to the end, when God will gather his Church from the four winds into his kingdom (ix. 4 and x. 5).

Christ prophetically described the downfall of the Jewish theocracy and the judgment of the world as analogous, though not synchronous events. The divine mind sees the end from the beginning. The prophet beholds the future as a panoramic vision in which distant scenes are brought into close

---

* *Ep. ad Cor.* chs. 42, 44 and 57. Comp. Rothe's *Anfänge der Christl. Kirche;* Bishop Lightfoot's *S. Clement of Rome,* and his essay on *The Christian Ministry* (Excursus to his *Com. on Philippians*); and the author's *Church History,* ii., 139 sq.

proximity. History is an ever-expanding fulfilment of prophecy. The downfall of Jerusalem is itself a type of the end of the world. The disciples asked about both, and Christ answered accordingly.

The Synoptical Gospels were written before A.D. 70, and hence contain no hint at the fulfilment, which could hardly have been avoided had they been written later.* The Epistles often allude to the parousia of the Lord as being near at hand, and hold it up as a stimulus to watchfulness, but wisely abstain from chronological predictions, since the Lord had expressly declared his own ignorance of the day and hour (Matt. xxiv. 37; Mark, xiii. 32). His ignorance was a voluntary self-limitation of his knowledge in the state of humiliation, or, as Lange calls it, "a holy unwillingness to know and to reflect prematurely upon the point of time of the parousia, thereby setting an example to the Church." It is an earnest warning against idle chronological curiosity. "It is not for you to know times or seasons which the Father hath set within his own authority" (Acts, i. 7). We cannot and ought not to know more on this subject than Christ himself knew or was willing to know when on earth, and what he refused to reveal even after his resurrection. All mathematical calculations and predictions concerning the Millennium and the end of the world, are a mere waste of learning and ingenuity, have failed and must fail. It is better for us be ignorant of the time of our own end that we may keep ourselves all the more in readiness to meet our Judge whenever he may call us to an account.†

The author of the *Didache* does not exceed these limits of Christian wisdom. He begins with the exhortation to watch and pray *because* we do not know the hour in which the Lord cometh (comp. Matt. xxv. 13). But he points out the premonitory symptoms, namely, the rise of false prophets and destroy-

---

* Comp. John, ii. 22: "When therefore he was raised from the dead, his disciples *remembered that he said this*," etc. Luke, xxiv. 6.

† Comp. Matt. xxiv. 33, 36, 43, 44; Acts, i. 7; Rom. xiii. 11, 12; 1 Cor. xv. 51; Phil. iv. 5; 1 Thess. v. 1, 2; James, v. 8; 1 John, ii. 18; 1 Pet. iv. 7; 2 Pet. iii. 10; Heb. x. 25; Rev. i. 3; iii 3; xvi. 15.

ers, the decay of love, the increase of lawlessness, persecution, and the appearance of the World-Deceiver* (or Anti-Christ), who will pretend to be the Son of God (Christ's antipode) and do signs and wonders and unheard-of iniquities. The race of men will be tried as by fire, but those who endure in their faith to the end shall be saved. Then the heavens will be opened (comp. Matt. xxiv. 30, 31), the trumpet will sound (comp. 1 Cor. xv. 52; 1 Thess. iv. 16, 17), the dead will rise, and the world will see the Lord coming upon the clouds of heaven with all his saints (comp. Zech. xiv. 8; Matt. xvi. 27; xxiv. 31; xxvi. 64). These events are, apparently, represented as simultaneous, "in a moment, in the twinkling of an eye" (1 Cor. xv. 52).

The resurrection here spoken of is restricted to the saints (xiv. 7). This may be understood in a chiliastic sense of the *first* resurrection ($\dot{\eta}$ $\dot{\alpha}\nu\dot{\alpha}\sigma\tau\alpha\sigma\iota\varsigma$ $\dot{\eta}$ $\pi\rho\dot{\omega}\tau\eta$, Rev. xx. 5); but the author of the *Didache* says nothing about a Millennium, and of a *general* resurrection after it. We have, therefore, no right to commit him either to the chiliastic or to the antichiliastic school, but the greater probability is that he was a Chiliast, like Barnabas, Papias, Justin Martyr, Irenæus, Tertullian, and the majority of ante-Nicene fathers before the great revolution under Constantine, when the Church from the condition of a persecuted sect was raised to power and dominion in this world, and the opinion came to prevail (through the influence chiefly of St. Augustin) that the Millennium was already established.†

---

* $\kappa o\sigma\mu o\pi\lambda\dot{\alpha}\nu o\varsigma$ (xvi. 4), a very significant word, used here for the first time, and retained by the author of the Apost. Const. viii. 32, with the addition $\dot{o}$ $\tau\tilde{\eta}\varsigma$ $\dot{\alpha}\lambda\eta\vartheta\epsilon\dot{\iota}\alpha\varsigma$ $\dot{\epsilon}\chi\vartheta\rho\dot{o}\varsigma$, $\dot{o}$ $\tau o\tilde{v}$ $\psi\epsilon\dot{v}\delta o\upsilon\varsigma$ $\pi\rho o\sigma\tau\dot{\alpha}\tau\eta\varsigma$. It was probably suggested by 2 John, ver. 7; $\pi o\lambda\lambda o\dot{\iota}$ $\pi\lambda\dot{\alpha}\nu o\iota$ (deceivers, impostors) $\dot{\epsilon}\xi\tilde{\eta}\lambda\vartheta o\nu$ $\epsilon\dot{\iota}\varsigma$ $\tau\dot{o}\nu$ $\kappa\dot{o}\sigma\mu o\nu$, Matt. xxvii. 63: $\dot{\epsilon}\kappa\epsilon\tilde{\iota}\nu o\varsigma$ $\dot{o}$ $\pi\lambda\dot{\alpha}\nu o\varsigma$, and Rev. xx. 3: $\ddot{\iota}\nu\alpha$ $\mu\dot{\eta}$ $\pi\lambda\alpha\nu\dot{\eta}\sigma\eta$ $\ddot{\epsilon}\tau\iota$ $\tau\dot{\alpha}$ $\ddot{\epsilon}\vartheta\nu\eta$, and ver. 10: $\dot{o}$ $\delta\iota\dot{\alpha}\beta o\lambda o\varsigma$ $\dot{o}$ $\pi\lambda\alpha\nu\tilde{\omega}\nu$ $\alpha\dot{v}\tau o\dot{v}\varsigma$. Comp. also Josephus, *De B. J.* ii. 13, 4: $\pi\lambda\dot{\alpha}\nu o\iota$ $\ddot{\alpha}\nu\vartheta\rho\omega\pi o\iota$ $\kappa\alpha\dot{\iota}$ $\dot{\alpha}\pi\alpha\tau\epsilon\tilde{\omega}\nu\tau\epsilon\varsigma$.

† See *Church History*, ii. 614 sqq. The indefiniteness of the *Didache* on this subject, as compared with the explicit chiliastic theory of Barnabas (ch. xv), is an additional argument in favor of the prior date of the *Didache*, and I cannot conceive how Harnack (p. 287 sq.) from a comparison of *Did.* XVI. 2 with Barnabas iv. 9 can come to the opposite conclusion. Dr. Craven (in the *Teaching of the Twelve Apostles*, printed in "The Journal of

CHAPTER XXIV.

*The Didache and the Scriptures.**

THE *Didache* will hereafter occupy an important position in the history of the New Testament Canon.

The Apostles quote the Old Testament usually according to the Greek version of the Septuagint, as they wrote in Greek and for Greek readers. But they quote very freely, in the fulness of the spirit of revelation, now from memory, now correcting the Septuagint from the Hebrew original, now adapting the text to the argument. They never quote from the Apocrypha, unless the allusion to the Book of Enoch in Jude, ver. 14, be considered an exception.

The Apostolic Fathers, who wrote between A.D. 90 and 150, deal as freely but far less wisely with the Old Testament, and use also indiscriminately the Apocrypha for homiletical and practical purposes. As to the New Testament, they still move in the element of living tradition and abound in reminiscences of Apostolic teaching. These reminiscences agree with the facts and doctrines, but very seldom with the precise words of the Gospels and Epistles. They give no quotations by name, except in a few cases. Barnabas quotes two passages from Matthew, without naming him.† Clement of Rome refers to

---

Christian Philosophy," N. Y., 1884, p. 78 sqq.) claims the *Didache* for the pre-millennian theory. "If the writer," he says, "believed in an earthly period of righteousness and blessedness, a *Millennium*, it must have been one which he regarded as subsequent to the Advent. On this point, there cannot be a rational doubt. Pre-millenarianism may not be affirmed in the document, but most certainly Post-millenarianism is impliedly denied." Dr. Hitchcock (p. 62) leaves the matter doubtful, and says: "The peculiar chiliasm of Barnabas, so unlike that of Papias, is best explained by supposing it to have come in between the *Teaching* and Papias."

* See the table of Scripture quotations in Bryennios, p. 57; the full discussion of Harnack, pp. 65–88; De Romestin, pp. 10–17, and the third Excursus of Spence, pp. 101–107. Zahn (p. 319) promises to discuss this subject in the First Part of his projected *History of the Canon.*

† In chap iv. from Matt. xxii. 14 (with the solemn quotation formula ὡς γέγραπται), and chap. v. from Matt. ix. 13. Barnabas furnishes also

Paul's (first) Epistle to the Corinthians and shows familiarity with Paul, James, and especially with the Epistle to the Hebrews, but gives only three quotations from the New Testament. * Ignatius echoes and exaggerates Pauline and Johannean ideas in his own fervent language. Polycarp's short Epistle to the Philippians " contains," as Westcott says,† "far more references to the New Testament than any other work of the first age ; and still, with one exception, ‡ all the phrases which he borrows are inwoven into the texture of his letter without any sign of quotation." Hermas, on the contrary, has no quotations from the Old or New Testament, and never mentions the Apostles by name, although he shows traces of a knowledge of Mark, James, and the Epistle to the Ephesians. Papias gives us valuable hints about the Gospels of Matthew and Mark, and faithfully collected the oral traditions about the Lord's Oracles, in five books (unfortunately lost), being of the opinion, as he says, that he "could not derive so much benefit from books as from the living and abiding voice." §

The next writer of importance who followed the Apostolic Fathers and was a younger contemporary of Polycarp and Papias, is Justin Martyr, who was born towards the close of the first or the beginning of the second century. He quotes very often from the Prophets and the Gospels, but very loosely, mostly from memory and without naming the Evangelists ; he never quotes from the Catholic Epistles and the Epistles of Paul ; the only book of the New Testament which he mentions expressly, is the Apocalypse of John. | With Irenæus, who

---

parallels to passages in Paul, Peter, and the Apocalypse, see *Church Hist.* ii. 674 sq. Comp. also Reuss, *History of the Canon*, transl. by David Hunter (1884), p. 22.

* See *Church History*, ii. 642, and Funk, *Patr. Ap.* i. 566–570.

† *History of the Canon*, p. 33. Funk (i. 573 sq.) counts six quotations of Polycarp from the O. T. and sixty-eight reminiscences from the New.

‡ Or rather two, namely, 1 John, iv. 3 and Matt. xxvi. 41, which are quoted in ch. vii., but the first not literally.

§ *Church Hist.* ii. 694 sq. It is a plausible conjecture that the pericope of the woman taken in adultery, John, vii. 53–viii. 11., was preserved by him.

| *Church History*, ii. 720.

flourished in the second half of the second century, begins the exact mode of quoting the New Testament Scriptures by name and from written copies, though free and loose quotations from memory never ceased among the fathers, and their children and children's children.

In view of these facts we must judge the relation of the *Didache* to the canon. It is essentially the same as that of the Apostolic Fathers, but it has more quotations from the Gospel of Matthew than any or all of them.

1. From the Old Testament two prophetic passages are quoted as Scripture, as follows :

MAL. I. 11, 14 (Sept.).	DIDACHE, XIV. 3.
Ἐν παντὶ τόπῳ θυμίαμα προσάγεται ἐπὶ τῷ ὀνόματί μου [Hebrew שְׁמִי] καὶ θυσία καθαρά. διότι μέγα τὸ ὄνομά μου ἐν τοῖς ἔθνεσι, λέγει Κύριος παντοκράτωρ... 14. διότι μέγας βασιλεὺς ἐγώ εἰμι, λέγει Κύριος παντοκράτωρ, καὶ τὸ ὄνομά μου ἐπιφανὲς ἐν τοῖς ἔθνεσιν.	Αὕτη γάρ ἐστιν ἡ ῥηθεῖσα ὑπὸ Κυρίου·* Ἐν παντὶ τόπῳ καὶ χρόνῳ προσφέρειν μοι θυσίαν καθαράν· ὅτι βασιλεὺς μέγας εἰμί, λέγει Κύριος, καὶ τὸ ὄνομά μου θαυμαστὸν ἐν τοῖς ἔθνεσι.
In every place incense shall be *offered* in [unto] my name, and *a pure sacrifice;* for great shall be *my name among the Gentiles, saith the Lord* Almighty.... 14. *For I am a great king, saith the Lord* Almighty, *and my name is* illustrious *among the Gentiles.*	For it is that which was spoken by the Lord,* "*In every place* and time *offer* me *a pure sacrifice; for I am a great king, saith the Lord, and my name is* wonderful *among the Gentiles.*"

---

* The *Did.* seems to refer "Lord" to Christ, as he is called "Lord" in the same chapter, ver. 1.

ZECH. XIV. 5.	DIDACHE, XVI. 7.
	Οὐ πάντων δέ, ἀλλ' ὡς ἐρρέθη·
Καὶ ἥξει Κύριος ὁ θεός μου, καὶ πάντες οἱ ἅγιοι μετ' αὐτοῦ.	Ἥξει ὁ Κύριος, καὶ πάντες οἱ ἅγιοι μετ' αὐτοῦ.
	Not, however, of all, but as was said:
And *the Lord*, my God, *shall come, and all the saints with Him*.	"*The Lord shall come, and all the saints with Him*."

The other allusions to the Old Testament are too vague to be considered as quotations. Two are to canonical books (comp. III. 8 with Isa. lxvi. 2; and IV. 13 with Deut. xii. 32), and five to apocryphal books, Tobit and Sirach.

The first two chapters of the *Didache* are largely based on the Decalogue as interpreted and deepened by Christ. The direction concerning the first fruits is derived from the Mosaic ordinance (Deut. xviii. 4), but there is no indication that the author considered the ceremonial law as binding upon Christians.

2. As to the New Testament, the *Didache* appeals chiefly, we may say exclusively, to the "Gospel," as the source of Apostolic teaching. The writer goes back to the fountain-head, the Lord himself, as is indicated by the larger title of the book. "Pray not as the hypocrites, but as *the Lord in his Gospel* has commanded." The Gospel is mentioned four or five times.[*] Once it is called "the Gospel of our Lord." The term is used in the general sense of the *one* Gospel, as in the N. T. without specification of one of the four records. The plural "Gospels" is never used any more than in the Gospels themselves. The word may refer to the oral Gospel, or to any of the written Gospels. In two passages a written Gospel seems to be meant (VIII. 2; XV. 4.), and apparently that of Matthew who has

---

[*] Ch. VIII. 2: ὡς ἐκέλευσεν ὁ Κύριος ἐν τῷ εὐαγγελίῳ αὐτοῦ. IX. 5: περὶ τούτου εἴρηκεν ὁ Κύριος. XI. 3: κατὰ τὸ δόγμα τοῦ εὐαγγελίου. XV. 3: ὡς ἔχετε ἐν τῷ εὐαγγελίῳ. XV 4: ὡς ἔχετε ἐν τῷ εὐαγγελίῳ τοῦ Κυρίου ἡμῶν.

the words there mentioned. It is true the *Didache* does not name any of the Evangelists nor any of the Apostles. But the reminiscences resemble our Greek Matthew so closely that it is difficult to avoid the conclusion that he had it before him.

Let us first compare the parallel passages. *

THE GOSPEL OF MATTHEW.	DIDACHE.
Ch. xxii. 37. Thou shalt love the Lord thy God... This is the great and first commandment... A second... thou shalt love thy neighbor as thyself.	Ch. I. 2. First, thou shalt love God who made thee; secondly, thy neighbor as thyself.
Ch. vii. 12. All things therefore whatsoever ye would that men should do unto you, even so do ye also unto them.	Ch. I. 2. All things whatsoever thou wouldest not should be done to thee, do thou also not to another. (Comp. Job, iv. 15.)
Ch. v. 44, 46. Love your enemies, and pray for them that persecute you.... For if ye love them that love you, what reward have ye?... Do not even the Gentiles the same? (Comp. Luke vi. 27, 28, 32.)	Ch. I. 3. Bless them that curse you, and pray for your enemies, but fast for them that persecute you. For what thanks is there if ye love them that love you? Do not even the Gentiles the same? But love ye them that hate you, and ye shall not have an enemy.
Ch. v. 39–41. Whosoever smiteth thee on thy right cheek, turn to him the other also. And if any man would go to law with thee, and take away thy coat, let him have thy cloke also. And whosoever shall compel thee to go	Ch. I. 4. If any one give you a blow on the right cheek, turn to him the other also, and thou shalt be perfect. If any one shall compel thee to go with him one mile, go with him twain. If any one take away thy cloak, give him thy coat

---

* I give the English version. The reader can easily compare the Greek in the document and the Greek Testament. See Harnack's list in Greek, p. 70 sqq.

one mile, go with him twain. (Comp. Luke, vi. 29.)

Matt. v. 42. Give to him that asketh thee.
[Luke, vi. 30. Give to every one that asketh thee; and ... ask ... not back.]

Matt. v. 26. Verily I say unto thee, thou shalt by no means come out thence, till thou have paid the last farthing.

Ch. v. 5. Blessed are the meek: for they shall inherit the earth.

Ch. xxviii. 19. Baptizing them into the name of the Father and of the Son and of the Holy Ghost.

Ch. vi. 16. When ye fast, be not, as the hypocrites, of a sad countenance; for they disfigure their faces, that they may be seen of men to fast.

Ch. vi. 5. When ye pray, ye shall not be as the hypocrites. . . .

Ch. vi. 9–13. After this manner therefore pray ye:

Our Father who art in the heavens ($\dot{\epsilon}\nu$ $\tau o\hat{\imath}s$ $o\dot{\upsilon}\rho a\nu o\hat{\imath}s$).
Hallowed be thy name.
Thy Kingdom come.
Thy will be done, as in heaven, so also on the earth ($\dot{\epsilon}\pi\dot{\imath}$ $\tau\hat{\eta}s$ $\gamma\hat{\eta}s$).

also. If any one take from thee what is thine, ask it not back, for neither canst thou.

Ch. I. 5. Give to every one that asketh of thee; and ask not back (for the Father wills that from our own blessings we should give to all).

Ch. I. 5. Being in distress he shall be examined concerning the things that he did, and he shall not come out thence till he have paid the last farthing.

Ch. III. 7. Be thou meek, for the meek shall inherit the earth.

Ch. VII. 1. Baptize ye into the name of the Father and of the Son and of the Holy Ghost, in living water.

Ch. VIII. 1. Let not your fasts be with the hypocrites; for they fast on the second and fifth days of the week.

Ch. VIII. 2. Neither pray ye as the hypocrites, but as the Lord commanded in his Gospel, after this manner pray ye:

Our Father, who art in heaven ($\dot{\epsilon}\nu$ $\tau\hat{\omega}$ $o\dot{\upsilon}\rho a\nu\hat{\omega}$).
Hallowed be thy name.
Thy kingdom come.
Thy will be done, as in heaven, so also on earth ($\dot{\epsilon}\pi\dot{\imath}$ $\gamma\hat{\eta}s$).

Give us this day our daily [needful] bread.	Give us to-day our daily [needful] bread.
And forgive us our debts (τὰ ὀφειλήματα), as we also have forgiven (ἀφήκαμεν) our debtors.	And forgive us our debt (τὴν ὀφειλήν), as we also forgive (ἀφίεμεν) our debtors.
And bring us not into temptation,	And bring us not into temptation,
But deliver us from the evil one [or, from evil].	But deliver us from the evil one [or, from evil].
[For thine is the kingdom (ἡ βασιλεία), and the power, and the glory, forever. Amen.]*	For thine is the power and the glory, for ever. *
	Pray thus thrice a day.
Ch. xxiv. 31. They [the angels] shall gather together his elect from the four winds, from one end of heaven to the other.	Ch. X. 5. Gather her [the church] together from the four winds.
	Ch. IX. 4. Let thy church be gathered together from the ends of the earth into Thy kingdom.
Ch. vii. 6. Give not that which is holy unto dogs.	Ch. IX. 5. The Lord hath said, "Give not that which is holy unto dogs."
Ch. xxv. 34. Inherit the kingdom prepared for you from the foundation of the world.	Ch. X. 5. Into thy kingdom which thou didst prepare for her [thy church].
Ch. xxi. 9, 15. Hosanna to the son of David.	Ch. X. 6. Hosanna to the God of David.
Ch. xii. 31. Every sin and	Ch. XI. 7. For every sin

---

* The *Didache* follows Matthew almost literally, and differs from Luke not only in fulness, but also in the details. Luke has τὸ καθ' ἡμέραν for σήμερον, and ἁμαρτίας for ὀφειλήματα. The doxology of the textus receptus is omitted in the oldest MSS. and versions, and by the critical editors, as also in the English version. It is, however, an appropriate conclusion, based on 1 Chr. xxix. 11. It passed into the text from liturgical and devotional use, of which the *Didache* furnishes here the earliest testimony. The omission of ἡ βασιλεία occurs also in Gregory of Nyssa, and in the Sahidic or Upper Egyptian version of Matthew.

blasphemy shall be forgiven unto men; but the blasphemy against the Spirit shall not be forgiven.

Ch. x. 10. For the laborer is worthy of his food.

[Luke, x. 7. The laborer is worthy of his hire.]

Ch. v. 23, 24. If therefore thou art offering thy gift at the altar... go thy way, first be reconciled to thy brother, and then come and offer thy gift.

Ch. xxiv. 42, 44. Watch therefore: for ye know not on what day your Lord cometh .... Be ye ready: for in an hour that ye think not the Son of Man cometh. [Luke, xii. 35.]

Ch. xxiv. 10, 11. And [many] shall deliver up one another and shall hate one another. And many false prophets shall arise and shall lead many astray. And because lawlessness shall be multiplied, the love of the many shall wax cold.

Ch. xxiv. 10, 13. And then shall many stumble ... but he that endureth to the end, the same shall be saved.

Ch. xxiv. 30, 31. And then shall appear the sign of the Son of Man in heaven ... and they shall see the Son of

shall be forgiven, but this sin shall not be forgiven.

Ch. XIII. 1, 2. But every true prophet ... is worthy of his food. Likewise a true teacher is himself worthy, like the laborer, of his food.

Ch. XIV. 2. Let no one who has a dispute with his fellow come together with you until they are reconciled, that your sacrifice may not be defiled.

Ch. XVI. 1. Watch for your life; let not your lamps be quenched, and let not your loins be loosed, but be ye ready; for ye know not the hour in which our Lord cometh.

Ch. XVI. 3, 4. For in the last days the false prophets and the corrupters shall be multiplied, and the sheep shall be turned into wolves, and love shall be turned into hate; for when lawlessness increaseth, they shall hate one another and persecute and deliver up.

Ch. XVI. 5. And many shall stumble and perish; but they that endure in their faith shall be saved from [or, under] the curse itself.

Ch. XVI. 6-8. And then shall appear the signs of the truth: first, a sign of an expansion (opening) in heaven;

Man coming on the clouds of heaven with power and great glory. And he shall send forth his angels with a great sound of a trumpet, and they shall gather together his elect from the four winds from one end of heaven to the other.

then a sign of sound of a trumpet; and third, a resurrection of the dead, but not of all ... Then shall the world see the Lord coming upon the clouds of heaven.

We have in all four literal or nearly literal quotations from Matthew, and about eighteen general references to Matthew with some sentences from Luke. How shall we account for this fact?

Harnack supposes that the *Didache* used the Gospel of Matthew enriched from that of Luke, and that this mixed product was probably the "Gospel according to the Egyptians."* But this was of Gnostic origin, and furnishes in the remaining fragments no parallel to the *Didache*, which breathes a different spirit. †

Krawutzcky, with more plausibility, in connection with his false hypothesis of its alleged Ebionism, conjectures that the *Didache* borrowed its quotations from the apocryphal "Gospel according to the Hebrews."‡ But, 1) This Gospel, as far as

---

* Page 79. He says that "many arguments might be furnished for this hypothesis," but he omits to state any.

† Lipsius, in his article on the *Apocryphal Gospels*, in Smith & Wace's *Dict. of Christian Biography*, vol. ii. (1880), p. 712, calls the Εὐαγγέλιον κατ' Αἰγυπτίους "a product of that pantheistic gnosis which we find among the Naassenes of the 'Philosophumena' and some other kindred sects." Hilgenfeld has collected the few fragments in his *Evang. secundum Hebræos*, etc. (*Nov. Test. extra can. rec.*, second ed. iv., 43–44), and finds in them (p. 48) "*pantheismum quendam in trinitate et in animæ natura cum ascetica mundi contemptione et matrimonii damnatione conjunctum.*" He assigns the Gospel of the Egyptians, with Volkmar, to c. 170–180. It is first quoted by Clement of Alex., Origen, and Hippolytus (*Philosoph.* v. 7).

‡ In his second article, already noticed, p. 23 sq. His reasons are, that the Gospel of the Hebrews was also called "*Evangelium Domini secundum duodecim Apostolos*" at the time of Origen (see *Hom. i. in Luc.* ad i. 1, and Jerome, *Adv. Pelag.* iii. 2), and that, like the *Didache* XV. 3, it condemns with unbiblical severity an offence against a brother as one of the greatest crimes, according to Jerome, *Ad. Ezek.* xviii. 7: "*In Evangelio quod juxta Hebræos Nazaræi legere consueverunt, inter maxima punitur crimina, qui fratris sui spiritum contristaverit.*"

known, is a post-canonical, Ebionitic adaptation of Matthew to the Aramaic-speaking Jewish-Christians in Palestine, with various omissions and additions, and seems to date from the later part of the second century, as it is not quoted before Clement of Alexandria and Origen; while the *Didache* belongs to an earlier stage of theological development, and shows no trace of Ebionism. 2) The *Didache*, while closely agreeing with our Greek Matthew, furnishes not a single parallel to the more than twenty original fragments which still remain of the Gospel according to the Hebrews.* This Gospel is the best among the Apocryphal Gospels, and owed its popularity to the erroneous opinion, propagated by the Ebionites, that it was identical with the lost Hebrew Matthew; but it certainly must have differed very considerably from our Greek Matthew, else Jerome would not have thought it worth while to translate it both into Greek and Latin.†

---

* These fragments are collected by Hilgenfeld, *Novum Test. extra canonem receptum*, Fasc. iv. 1-31 (ed. ii. 1884), and by Nicholson, *The Gospel according to the Hebrews. Its Fragments translated and annotated*, London, 1879. See also Lipsius, *Apocryphal Gospels*, in Smith & Wace's *Dict. of Christian Biography*, vol. ii. (1880), p. 709 sqq. The text from which Epiphanius quotes, omitted the chapters on the genealogy, birth and childhood of Christ; but the texts used by Cerinthus and Carpocrates had the genealogy, though carefully excluding what relates to the supernatural conception. The Lord's Baptism was also differently related. Lipsius infers from these and other discrepancies that there were different recensions of this Εὐαγγέλιον καθ' Ἑβραίους. He supposes that it was nearly related to Matthew's λόγια τοῦ Κυρίου, and to a later redaction of these λόγια made use of by Luke, and in the Ebionite circles of Palestine. Mangold, Drummond, E. A. Abbott, and Ezra Abbot agree that the Gospel of the Hebrews was written some time after the canonical Gospels and was unknown to Justin Martyr. See E. Abbot, *The Authorship of the Fourth Gospel* (1880), p. 98.

† *De viris ill.* c. ii: "*Evangelium quod appellatur ' Secundum Hebræos,' et a me nuper in Græcum Latinumque sermonem translatum est, quo et Origenes sæpe utitur, post resurrectionem Salvatoris refert.*" Then follows the story of the appearance of Christ to James who had sworn never to eat bread or to drink wine, after the last passover, till he should see the Lord risen from the dead. In cap. iii. Jerome relates that he had seen (a. 413) the *Hebrew Matthew* in the library of Pamphilus at Cæsarea; but this must have been either only another title of the same book on the supposition of its identity with the Hebrew Matthew (*In Matt.* xii. 18: "*quod vocatur a plerisque Matthæi authenticum*"), or a document differing from the copy which he

If the *Didache* had been based upon an heretical Gospel, whether Gnostic or Ebionitic, we could not account for its use in catechetical instruction by Athanasius, "the father of orthodoxy."

There remains therefore only the alternative that the author of the *Didache* drew from our Greek Matthew, or from the lost Hebrew *Logia*, which are supposed to have formed the basis of the former. But the parallel passages agree so closely, more so than similar quotations in the writings of the Apostolic Fathers and Justin Martyr, that it is almost certain that our canonical Matthew was the chief written source of the *Didache*.*

The Gospel of Mark, which originated in Rome, is never quoted or alluded to. This fact is rather unfavorable to the prevailing modern hypothesis of the priority of Mark, as the *Urevangelist*, but it may be accidental, as the author of the *Didache* lived in the East.

The use of the Gospel of Luke may be inferred from *Did.* I. 3, 4, 5, compared with Luke vi. 27–35, and from *Did.* XVI. 1, compared with Luke xii. 35, where the *Didache* follows Luke rather than Matthew.

Luke xii. 35.		Did. XVI. 1.	
Ἔστωσαν ὑμῶν αἱ ὀσφύες περιεζωσμέναι καὶ οἱ λύχνοι καιόμενοι, καὶ ὑμεῖς ὅμοιοι ἀνθρώποις προσδεχομένοις τὸν Κύριον ἑαυτῶν, κ. τ. λ.	Let your loins be girded about, and your lamps burning, and be yourselves like unto men looking for their Lord.	Watch over your life, let not your lamps be quenched, and let not your loins be loosed [for ye know not the hour in which our Lord cometh.]	Γρηγορεῖτε ὑπὲρ τῆς ζωῆς ὑμῶν· οἱ λύχνοι ὑμῶν μὴ σβεσθήτωσαν, καὶ αἱ ὀσφύες ὑμῶν μὴ ἐκλυέσθωσαν, ἀλλὰ γίνεσθε ἕτοιμοι· [οὐ γὰρ οἴδατε τὴν ὥραν ἐν ᾗ ὁ Κύριος ἡμῶν ἔρχεται.]

had previously (392) found among the Nazarenes at Beroea, in Syria, and from which he made his translation. See my *Church History*, i. 622 sqq.

* Dr. Brown (Hitchcock and Brown, second ed. p. lxxvi.) concludes that the author of the *Did.* "either knew two written Gospels [Matthew and Luke], or that he knew one of them (probably Matthew) and combined with it, in his citations from memory phrases from the oral tradition which must have been fresh and strong in his time, and that these phrases agree with that form of the tradition which the other of the two Evangelists here to be considered (probably Luke) crystallized in his Gospel." Dr. Farrar ("The Expositor," Aug. 1884, p. 84): "It is certain that the writer knew

The first word and the last clause are in substance taken from Matt. xxv. 13: "*Watch* therefore, *for ye know not* the day nor *the hour in which* the Son of Man *cometh* (γρηγορεῖτε οὖν, ὅτι οὐκ οἴδατε τὴν ἡμέραν οὐδὲ τὴν ὥραν ἐν ᾗ ὁ υἱὸς τοῦ ἀνθρώπου ἔρχεται). But the body of the sentence is from Luke, who alone of the Evangelists uses the plural λύχνοι and ὀσφύες. (Matthew uses λαμπάδες in the parable of the Ten Virgins, xxv. 1-8.)

An acquaintance with the Gospel of Luke may also be inferred from a knowledge of Acts, which was certainly written by the same author. The *Didache* (IX. 2, 3; X. 3, 4) calls Christ the servant or child (παῖς) of God, as Peter did in the early days of the Church; Acts, iii. 13, 26; iv. 27, 80. A striking resemblance exists between the following passages:

ACTS, IV. 32.	DID. IV. 8.
And not one of them said that aught of the things which he possessed was his own (ἴδιον εἶναι), but they had all things common.	Thou shalt share all things with thy brothers and shalt not say that they are thine own (ἴδια εἶναι); for if ye are fellow-sharers in imperishable things, how much more in perishable. (Comp. Rom. xv. 27.)

Whether the author of the *Didache* had any knowledge of the Gospel of John is affirmed by some,[*] denied by others.[†] He never quotes from it, but there are remarkable resemblances between the two which cannot be accidental. The resemblance is strongest between the eucharistic prayers and the Sarcerdotal Prayer of our Lord. In both God is addressed as "Holy Father" (Πάτερ ἅγιε, *Did.* X. 1 and John, xvii. 11), but nowhere else in the New Testament. The thanksgiving of the *Didache* for "*life* and *knowledge* and faith and *immortality made known* to us through Jesus" (IX. 2, 3; X. 2) is

the Gospel of St. Matthew; and we have here an important confirmation of the views of those who, following the church tradition, hold that this was the earliest of all the Gospels."

[*] Plummer (Master of University College, Durham) in "The Churchman," London, July, 1884, pp. 274, 275. Lightfoot, and Spence. Dr. Harnack (p. 79 sqq.) denies that the author of the *Didache* had the written Gospel of John before him, but fully admits and points out the striking connection of the eucharistic prayers (IX. and X.) with John, vi. and xvii.

[†] John Wordsworth (of Oxford), Farrar, Brown, Krawutzcky (?), Lipsius.

a response to the solemn declaration: "This is *life eternal* that they should *know* Thee, the only true God," and "*I made known* (ἐγνώρισα) unto them Thy name." The prayer for the unity of the Church, and such phrases as "*became one*" (ἐγένετο ἕν), the "*sanctified*" Church (τὴν ἁγιασθεῖσαν, sc. ἐκκλησίαν), "deliver her from *all evil*" (ἀπὸ παντὸς πονηροῦ), "*perfect her in Thy love*" (τελειῶσαι αὐτὴν ἐν τῇ ἀγάπῃ σου), remind one of similar petitions and words in the Sacerdotal Prayer (John, xvii. 11: ἵνα ὦσιν ἕν, v. 15: τηρήσῃς αὐτοὺς ἐκ τοῦ πονηροῦ; 17: ἁγίασον αὐτούς, 19: ἵνα ὦσιν καὶ αὐτοὶ ἡγιασμένοι, 23: ἵνα ὦσιν τετελειωμένοι εἰς ἕν).

In the same eucharistic prayers we cannot mistake some significant allusions to the mysterious discourse of our Lord on the bread of life after the miraculous feeding, in the sixth chapter of John. The sentence, "Thou gavest us spiritual food and drink and *eternal life* through thy child Jesus" (x. 3), is Johannean (comp. vi. 27: "the meat abideth unto *eternal life*, which the Son of Man shall give unto you," 32, 33: "the true bread out of heaven ... which giveth *life* unto the world;" 58: "he that eateth this bread shall live for ever"). The eucharistic prayers of the *Didache*, then, breathe a Johannean atmosphere and must have proceeded from a primitive circle of disciples controlled by the spirit and teaching of St. John.

Compare also the following passages, in which a correspondence of ideas and words is unmistakable.

JOHN, I. 14.

The Word *dwelt* (ἐσκήνωσεν) among us. Comp. xvii. 6: I manifested my *name* unto the men; v. 11, 26; Apoc. vii. 15; xxi. 3 (σκηνώσει μετ' αὐτῶν).

DIDACHE, X. 2.

We give thanks to Thee, *Holy Father*, for Thy holy *name*, which Thou hast caused *to dwell* (κατεσκήνωσας) in our hearts.

JOHN, xv. 1.

I am the true *vine* (ἡ ἄμπελος ἡ ἀληθινή), and my *Father* is the husbandman.

DIDACHE, IX. 2.

We give thanks to Thee, our *Father*, for the holy *vine* (ὑπὲρ τῆς ἁγίας ἀμπέλου) of Thy servant David which Thou hast made known through Thy servant Jesus.

JOHN, XV. 15.	DIDACHE, IX. 2, 3; X. 2.
All things that I heard from my Father I have *made known* (ἐγνώρισα) unto you. Comp. xvii. 26.	which Thou hast *made known* (ἐγνώρισας) to us through Thy servant Jesus.
1 JOHN, II. 5.	DIDACHE, X. 5.
In him verily hath *the love* of God been *perfected* (ἡ ἀγάπη τοῦ Θεοῦ τετελείωται). The very same Johannean phrase in iv. 12. Comp. also ver. 17, 18, and John, xvii. 23, quoted above.	Remember, O Lord, Thy Church to deliver her from all evil and to *perfect* her *in Thy love* (τελειῶσαι αὐτὴν ἐν τῇ ἀγάπῃ σου).
1 JOHN, II. 17.	DIDACHE, X. 6.
The world passeth away (ὁ κόσμος παράγεται). Comp. 1 Cor. vii. 31.	Let this world pass away (παρελθέτω ὁ κόσμος οὗτος).
1 JOHN, IV. 1.	DIDACHE, XI. 11.
Believe not every spirit, but *prove* (δοκιμάζετε) the spirits whether they are of God.	Every *approved* true (δεδοκιμασμένος ἀληθινὸς) prophet.
2 JOHN, 10.	DIDACHE, XI. 2.
If any one cometh unto you, and bringeth not this teaching (ταύτην τὴν διδαχήν), receive him not into your house, and give him no greeting.	But if the teacher himself turn and teach another teaching (ἄλλην διδαχήν) to destroy this, hearken not unto him.

The designation of God as the "Almighty" or "Sovereign Ruler" (παντοκράτωρ), in the eucharistic prayer, X. 2, is probably borrowed from the Apocalypse of John, in which it occurs nine times (i. 8; iv. 8; xi. 17; xv. 3; xvi. 7, 14; xix. 6, 15; xxi. 22); while elsewhere in the New Testament it occurs only once, 2 Cor. vi. 18, and there in a quotation from the Septuagint. The designation of Sunday as the Lord's Day (XIV. 1.), points likewise to the Apocalypse (i. 10.) The phrase "loving a lie" v. 2, occurs Rev. xxii. 15. The words: "If any one be holy" (X. 6), have some resemblance to Rev. xxii. 12, and the warning against additions to, and detractions from, the commandments of the Lord reminds one of the similar warning, Rev. xxii. 18, but may have been suggested by Deut. xii. 32.*

---

* These resemblances are remote, indeed, and Dr. Brown, p. lxxvii. denies that any traces of the Apocalypse are to be found in the *Didache*. So also

We conclude then that the writer of the *Didache* had some acquaintance with our fourth Gospel and the other Johannean writings, or at all events with the Johannean type of teaching. In the former case he would furnish the earliest, or one of the earliest, testimonies to the existence of that Gospel.

The *Didache* shows acquaintance with several Epistles of Paul (Romans, First Corinthians, Ephesians, and Thessalonians), and although it does not allude to his distinctive doctrines of sin and grace, justification by faith and evangelical freedom (as set forth in the Romans and Galatians), there is in it no trace whatever of the animus of the Ebionites who hated the Apostle of the Gentiles as an archheretic and abhorred his writings.*

The enumeration of vices in Chs. II. and III. reminds one of the fearful picture of heathen immorality, Rom. i. 28–32. The negative description of love to our neighbor in Ch. II. 2 has some resemblance to Rom. xiii. 9. The phrase "cleaving to that which is good" (v. 2, κολλώμενοι ἀγαθῷ) occurs only in Paul (Rom. xii. 9, κολλώμενοι τῷ ἀγαθῷ). The directions about the qualifications of Bishops and Deacons (xv. 1) presuppose the Pastoral Epistles. The passage about the "world-deceiver" and the reign of "lawlessness" (ἀνομία) in Ch. XVI. 4, points back to Paul's prophecy of the man of sin and the mystery of lawlessness (τὸ μυστήριον τῆς ἀνομίας),

---

Dr. Farrar (in "Expositor" Aug. 1884, p. 87). But considering the familiarity of the *Didache* with the Johannean vocabulary, the probability is in favor of the view advocated in the text.

* Harnack (p. 87) says: "*Paulinische Briefe sind in der Διδαχή nicht citirt; auch giebt es keine einzige Stelle, an welcher die Benutzung jener Briefe evident zu nennen wäre;*" but he points to several verbal coincidences, as εἰδωλόθυτον (VI. 3); μαρὰν ἀθά (X. 6); μυστήριον ἐκκλησίας (XI. 11); ἐργαζέσθω καὶ φαγέτω (XII. 3); προφῆται καὶ διδάσκαλοι (XIII. 1, 2), and the doctrine of the Antichrist and the parousia (XVI. 4–8). Bishop Lightfoot asserts, without going into details: "With St. Paul's Epistles the writer shows an acquaintance. Coincidences with four of these—Romans, 1 Corinthians, Ephesians and 2 Thessalonians—indicate a free use of the Apostle's writings." Canon Spence positively asserts (p. 105) that the author "was acquainted with the Epistles to the Thessalonians, the Romans, the Corinthians and the Ephesians." But I can find no trace of Second Corinthians. Farrar thinks that acquaintance with Romans and Thessalonians is probable, but cannot be positively proven.

which will precede the advent of the Lord. We may also point to the following passages which are more or less parallel.

Rom. xv. 27. If ye Gentiles have been partakers of their spiritual things, they owe it to them also to minister unto them in carnal things. Comp. 1 Cor. ix. 11, 14; Gal. vi. 6.	*Did.* IV. 5. If ye are fellow-partakers in imperishable things, how much more in perishable.
1 Thess. v. 22. Abstain from every form (or, appearance) of evil.	*Did.* III. 1. My child, flee from all evil, and from all that is like unto it.
Eph. vi. 5. Bondmen, be obedient unto them that according to the flesh are your masters, with fear and trembling, in singleness of your heart, as unto Christ. (Col. iii. 22.)	*Did.* IV. 11. Bondmen, be subject to your masters as to the image of God (ὡς τύπῳ θεοῦ) in reverence (or, modesty) and fear.

The Didachographer seems to have known also the Epistle to the Hebrews, if we are to infer as much from a few faint allusions, as the expression "evil conscience" (XIV. 1; comp. Heb. x. 22), and the exhortation to attend public worship (XIV. 1; Heb. x. 25), and to honor the ministers of Christ (XV. 1, 2; Heb. xiii. 7).

Of the Catholic Epistles one passage is reproduced nearly literally from the first Epistle of Peter.

1 PETER, II. 11.	DIDACHE, I. 4.
παρακαλῶ .... ἀπέχεσθαι τῶν σαρκικῶν ἐπιθυμιῶν αἵτινες στρατεύονται κατὰ τῆς ψυχῆς." (Comp. Tit. ii. 12.)	ἀπέχου τῶν σαρκικῶν καὶ σωματικῶν [probably an error of the copyist for κοσμικῶν] ἐπιθυμιῶν.

The allusions to the Johannean Epistles have already been mentioned. With Jude the *Didache* has in common the term κυριότης (IV. 1 of Jude 8), which, however, occurs also twice in Paul (Eph. i. 21; Cor. i. 16), and once 2 Pet. ii. 10.

It is remarkable that the writer of the *Didache* furnishes no verbal parallel to the Epistle of James, although he is evidently most in sympathy with the conservative spirit and Jewish-Christian stand-point of the first Bishop of Jerusalem. They agree in emphasizing works rather than faith, in making use of the Sapiential literature of the Hebrews, in requiring public confession of sin (IV. 14 and XIV. 1; comp. Jas. v. 16), and in the warning against double-mindedness and doubtfulness in prayer (IV. 4; comp. Jas. i. 5, 8; iv. 8.)

SCRIPTURE QUOTATIONS AND ALLUSIONS IN THE *DIDACHE*.

I. Quotations from the Old Testament.

SCRIPTURE.	DIDACHE.
Zech. xiv. 5.	XVI. 7.
Mal. i. 11, 14.	XIV. 3.

II. Allusions to the Old Testament.

Scripture	Didache
Ex. xviii. 20. Deut. xxxi. 29.	I. 1.
Ex. xx. 13–17. Deut. v. 17–21.	II.
Num. xviii. 12, 13, 15, 30. Deut. xviii. 3, 4. Ezek. xliv. 30. Neh. x. 35–37.	XIII.
Deut. xii. 32.	IV. 13.
Job, iv. 10.	IV. 6.
Isa. lxvi. 2, 5.	III. 8.
Jer. xxi. 8.	I. 1.
Dan. iv. 27.	IV. 6.

III. Quotations from, and Allusions to, the Old Testament Apocrypha.

Scripture	Didache
Tobit, iv. 7.	IV. 6–8.
" " 15.	I. 2.
Ecclus. (Sirach) ii. 4.	III. 10.
" iv. 5.	IV. 8.
" " 31.	IV. 5.

IV. Quotations and Reminiscences from the New Testament.

Scripture	Didache
Matt. v. 5.	III. 7.
" " 23, 24.	XIV. 2.
" " 25, 26	I. 5.
" " 39–41 (Luke, vi. 29, 30).	I. 4.
" " 44–46 (Luke, vi. 27).	I. 3.
" vi. 5.	VIII. 2.
" " 1, 5.	XV. 4.
" " 9–13.	VIII. 2.
" " 16.	VIII. 1.
" vii. 6.	IX. 5.
" " 12.	I. 2.
" x. 9, 10 (comp. Luke, ix. 1–6; x. 4–7.)	XIII. 1, 2.
" xii. 31.	XI. 7.
" xviii. 15, 17.	XV. 3.
" xxi. 9.	X. 6.
" xxii. 37–39.	I. 2.

SCRIPTURE.	DIDACHE.
Matt. xxiv. 10-14.	XVI. 4, 5.
" " 30, 31.	XVI. 6, 8.
" " 31, 35.	XVI. 1.
" " ' 42, 44.	X. 5.
" " xv. 34.	X. 5.
" xxviii. 19, 20.	VII. 1.
Luke, vi. 27-30.	I. 3, 4, 5.
" xii. 35.	XVI. 1.

V. ALLUSIONS AND PARALLELS TO THE NEW TESTAMENT.

Acts, iv. 32.	IV. 8.
Rom. xv. 27.	IV. 8.
1 Cor. xv. 52.	XVI. 6.
1 Cor. xvi. 22 (Maranatha).	X. 6.
Eph. vi. 5, 9.	IV. 10, 11.
1 Thess. iv. 16, 17.	XVI. 4-8.
" v. 22.	III. 1.
2 Thess. ii. 8-10.	XVI. 4.
Heb. x. 22 ($\sigma v \varepsilon i \delta \eta \sigma i s$ $\pi o v \eta \rho \alpha$).	XIV. 1.
" x. 25.	XIV. 1.
" xiii. 7.	XV. 1, 2.
1 Pet. ii. 11. (Tit. ii. 12.)	I. 4.
Rev. i. 8, etc. ($\pi \alpha v \tau o \kappa \rho \alpha' \tau \omega \rho$).	X. 3.
Rev. i. 10 ($\kappa v \rho \iota \alpha \kappa \eta'$).	XIV. 1.
Rev. xxii. 15.	V. 2.

CHAPTER XXV.

*The Style and Vocabulary of the Didache.**

THE *Didache* is written in Hellenistic Greek, like the New Testament.† It is the common Macedonian or Alexandrian dialect with a strong infusion of a Hebrew soul and a Christian spirit. It differs on the one hand from the Septuagint,

---

* This subject has been specially investigated by American scholars, Dr. Isaac H. Hall, in the "Journal of Christian Philosophy," N. York, 1884, pp. 51-67 ; Prof. Lemuel S. Potwin, in the " Bibliotheca Sacra," for October, 1884, pp. 800-817, and Dr. Hitchcock, in his notes to the second ed. 1885. They give lists of the peculiar words of the *Didache*. Bryennios, *Proleg.* § 13, and Brown, pp. ci.-civ. describe the orthographic peculiarities of the Jerusalem MS. Brown gives also tables of textual variations and emendations, pp. cvi.-cxv.

† On the idiom of the New Testament and its evidential value, see the first chapter (pp. 1-81) of my *Companion to the Greek Testament*, N. York, revised edition, 1885.

the Jewish Apocrypha and the writings of Philo and Josephus by the deeper Christian meaning of words and phrases; and, on the other hand, from the post-Apostolic and patristic writings, first by the absence of technical ecclesiastical, and dogmatic terms,* and secondly by the presence of Hebraisms, which disappeared in later ecclesiastical writers, except in Scripture quotations.

Such Hebraisms are: "not all" (οὐ πᾶς, *lo kol*, the negative belonging to πᾶς and merely denying the universality) for "no one" (οὐδείς); "to accept the person" (πρόσωπον λαμβάνειν, *nasa panim*) for "to favor," "to be partial;" the designation of Friday as "Preparation day" (παρασκευή); "day and night" for "night and day." There are also traces of Hebrew parallelism, both antithetic and synthetic, *e. g.*:

> "Thou shalt not exalt thyself,
> Nor shalt thou give presumption to thy soul.
> Thou shalt not be joined to the lofty,
> But with the just and lowly shalt thou converse" (III. 9).

> "Thou shalt not desire division,
> But shalt make peace between those at strife" (IV. 3).

> "Thou shalt not forsake the commandments of the Lord,
> But shalt keep what thou hast received" (IV. 13).

> "In church thou shalt confess thy transgressions,
> And shalt not come to thy prayer with an evil conscience" (IV. 14)

> "Let not your lamps be quenched,
> And let not your loins be loosed" (XVI. 1).

> "The sheep shall be turned into wolves,
> And love shall be turned into hate" (XVI. 3).

> "Then shall the race of men come into the fire of testing,
> And many shall be offended and perish" (XVI. 5).

The style is simple, natural, terse, sententious, and popular. The vocabulary is redolent of the Synoptic Gospel tradition, and the words of the Saviour in the sixth and seventeenth chapters of John. It is essentially the same as that of the

---

* Or by the use of old terms with a different meaning, *e. g.*, the verb χειροτονεῖν has in the *Did.* XV. 1, the biblical sense *to elect, to appoint* (comp. Acts, xiv. 23; 2 Cor. viii. 19), but in the Apost. Const. and Canons it means *to ordain*.

New Testament; 504 words out of 552 being identical. The new words are either derived from the Septuagint, or the classics, or are modifications and compounds of apostolic words, and betray familiarity with apostolic ideas.*

Altogether the Didachographer, as to the linguistic form of his composition, shows himself a congenial contemporary, or direct successor of the Evangelists and Apostles.

One of my students, Mr. Arthur C. McGiffert, † has paid very careful and minute attention to the vocabulary of the *Didache* and has prepared, at my request, the following summary and tables which are more complete and accurate than any heretofore published.

The *Didache* contains 2,190 words. Its vocabulary comprises 552 words. Of the whole number 504 are New Testament words, 497 are classical, and 479 occur in the LXX. 16 occur for the first time in the *Didache*, but are found in later writers. 1 occurs only in the *Didache*. 14 occur in the New Testament with a different meaning.

On comparing the parallel chapters xviii.-xx. of the Epistle of Barnabas we find that these three chapters contain 625 words. Their vocabulary comprises 259 words; of which 239 are found in the classics, 238 in the LXX., 237 in the New Testament, and 211 in the *Didache*. Two words, πρόγλωσσος (XIX. 8), *of hasty tongue*, and φωτάγογος (XVIII. 1), *giving light, a light bringer*, occur for the first time in Barnabas, one of which, πρόγλωσσος, is a *hapax legomenon*, occurring only in Barnabas. None are peculiar to the *Didache* and Barnabas. Three are peculiar to the *Didache*, Barnabas, and the Apost. Const.

διγνώμων (*Didache*, II. 4; Barnabas, xix. 7; Apost. Const. ii. 6), *double-minded.*

διπλοκαρδία (*Didache*, V. 1; Barnabas, xx. 1; Apost. Const. vii. 18), *duplicity.*

---

* As κοσμοπλάνος, χριστέμπορος, and the much disputed ἐκπέτασις. See the notes *in loc.*, and the Tables below. There is only one absolute απαξ λεγόμενον, and this is perhaps a writing error, προσεξομολογησάμενοι for προεξομολ.

† Of Ashtabula, Ohio, a member of the graduating class (1885) in the Union Theol. Seminary.

πανθαμάρτητος (*Didache*, V. 2; Barnabas, xx. 2; Apost. Const. vii. 18), *a universal sinner.*

One is peculiar to the *Didache*, Barnabas, the Apost. Const. and the Apost. Canons.

ἀνταποδότης (*Didache*, IV. 7; Barnabas, xix. 11; Apost. Const. vii. 12; Apost. Canons, § 13), *a recompenser.*

Of the *Didache* the vocabulary comprises 25⅛ per cent. of the whole number of words; of the three chapters of the Epistle of Barnabas, 41½ per cent. The discrepancy is to be accounted for by the greater length of the *Didache*, which contains necessarily a larger percentage of common and therefore repeated words.

Of the *Didache*, about 90 per cent. of the vocabulary is classical; of Barnabas, 92¼ per cent. Of the *Didache*, 86¾ per cent. of the vocabulary belongs to the LXX.; of Barnabas, 91 $\frac{1}{10}$ per cent. Of the *Didache*, 91½ per cent. of the vocabulary is New Testament; of Barnabas, 91½ per cent. The agreement of the *Didache* and of Barnabas with reference to their percentage of New Testament words is remarkable. The agreement with reference to classical words is almost as close. But with reference to LXX. words there is quite a discrepancy, the vocabulary of Barnabas being much closer to that of the LXX. than the vocabulary of the *Didache* is. This may at least suggest an argument against the Egyptian authorship of the *Didache*.

We append six lists:

I. Words which do not occur in the New Testament. Total, 48.

II. Words which do not occur in the New Testament but are found in the classics. Total, 30.

III. Words which do not occur in the New Testament but are found in the LXX. Total, 17.

IV. Words which occur for the first time in the Didache but are found in later writings. Total, 16.

V. Words which occur only in the Didache. Total, 1.

VI. New Testament words not used in the New Testament sense. Total, 14.*

---

* The writer has used Tischendorf's edition of the LXX.; Migne's edition of the Apost. Const.; Von Gebhardt, Harnack and Zahn's edition of the Apostolic Fathers, and the Apost. Canons as given by Harnack in his *Lehre der zwölf Apostel*, pp. 225-237.

I.

WORDS NOT FOUND IN THE NEW TESTAMENT.

Total, 48.

ἀθάνατος, Did. IV. 8, *imperishable.*
αἰσχρολόγος, III. 3, *foul-mouthed.*
ἀμφιβολία, XIV. 2, *a controversy.*
ἀνταποδύτης, IV. 7, *a recompenser.*
αὐθάδεια, V. 1, *self-will.*
γόγγυσος, III. 6, *a murmurer.*
διαφορά, I. 1, *difference.*
διγλωσσία, II. 4, *doubleness of tongue.*
δίγλωσσος, II. 4, *double-tongued.*
διγνώμων, II. 4, *double-minded.*
διπλοκαρδία, V. 1, *duplicity.*
διψυχέω, IV. 4, *to hesitate.*
ἐκπέτασις, XVI. 6, *a spreading out,* or *an opening.*
ἐνδέω, IV. 8 ; V. 2, *to be in want.*
ἐπαοιδός, III. 4, *an enchanter.*
ἐριστικός, III. 2, *contentious.*
ζηλοτυπία, V. 1, *jealousy.*
θερμός, VII. 2, *warm.*
θράσος, III. 9, *over-boldness.*
θρασύτης, V. 1, *over-boldness.*
θυμικός, III. 2, *passionate.*
ἱδρόω, I. 6, *to sweat.*
κακοήθης, II. 6, *malicious.*
κοσμοπλάνος, XVI. 4, *the world-deceiver.*
κυριακὴ Κυρίου, XIV. 1, *the Lord's day of the Lord.*
μαθηματικός, III. 4, *an astrologer.*
μακρόθυμος, III. 8, *long-suffering.*
μῖσος, XVI. 3, *hate.*
μνησικακέω, II. 3, *to bear malice.*
οἰωνοσκόπος, III. 4, *an omen watcher.*
παιδοφθορέω, II. 2, *to corrupt boys.*
πανθαμάρτητος, V. 2, *a universal sinner.*
παρόδιος, XII. 2, *a traveller.*
περικαθαίρω, III. 4, *to use purifications.*

100 WORDS NOT IN NEW TESTAMENT BUT IN THE CLASSICS.

ποθέω, IV. 3, *to desire.*
πονέω, V. 2, *to labor.*
πονηρόφρων, III. 6, *evil-minded.*
ποτόν, X. 3 (twice), *drink.*
προνηστεύω, VII. 4, *to fast beforehand.*
προσεξομολογέω, XIV. 1, *to confess.*
πυκνῶς, XVI. 2, *often.*
σιτία, XIII. 5, *a baking of bread.*
συσπάω, IV. 5, *to draw in.*
τετράς, VIII. 1, *the fourth.*
ὑψηλόφθαλμος, III. 3, *lofty-eyed.*
φαρμακεύω, II. 2, *to use sorcery.*
φθορεύς, V. 2 ; XVI. 3, *a corrupter, a destroyer.*
χριστέμπορος, XII. 5, *one who makes gain out of Christ.*

II.

WORDS NOT IN THE NEW TESTAMENT BUT IN THE CLASSICS.

Total 30, of which 16 are LXX. words.

ἀθάνατος, IV. 8, *imperishable.*
    In Homer, Hesiod, *et al.* ; in the LXX. ; in the Apost. Canons, §13 ; found neither in Barnabas nor in the Apost. Const. The New Testament has ἄφθαρτος, ἀφθαρσία, and ἀθανασία.

ἀμφιβολία, XIV. 2, *a misunderstanding,* or *a controversy.*
    Occurs in classic Greek in a somewhat different sense: (1) *The state of mutual attack* (Hdt.). (2) *Ambiguity* (Aristotle, Sophocles). In Plutarch it is used in the sense of *doubtfulness.* The Apost. Const. vii. 30 (parallel passage) omit the word. The New Testament has ἔρις, *contention,* and μομφή, *complaint,* Col. iii. 13, πρός τινα ἔχῃ μομφήν.

αὐθάδεια, V. 1, *self-will.*
    In Plato, Aristotle, *et al.* ; in Barnabas xx. 1 ; in the Apost. Const. vii. 18. The New Testament has αὐθάδης. αὐθάδεια occurs in some old editions of the LXX. in Isa. xxiv. 8, but the best editions omit it.

διαφορά I. 1, *difference.*
    In Hdt. and Thuc. ; in the LXX. ; in Barnabas, xviii. 1 ; in

the Apost. Canons, §4; in Basil and later Fathers. The Apost. Const. vii. 1 (parallel passage) have τὸ διάφορον. The New Testament has διάφορος (adj.), but uses the nouns διαστολή and διαίρεσις.

δίγλωσσος, II. 4. *double-tongued.*

In Thucydides it is found with the meaning *speaking two languages;* hence, in Plutarch, as substantive, meaning *interpreter.* In the LXX. it has the meaning *double-tongued, deceitful;* Prov. xi. 13, etc; so in the Apost. Const. ii. 6; vii. 4; and in the Apost. Canons, §6. Barnabas, xix. 7 (parallel passage), has γλωσσώδης. The New Testament has δίλογος; 1 Tim. iii. 8.

ἐνδέω, IV. 8; V. 2, *to be in want.*

In Plato, Euripides, *et al.;* in the LXX.; in the Apost. Const. vii. 12; and in the Apost. Canons, §13. The New Testament has ἐνδεής, Acts, iv. 34.

ἐπαοιδός, III. 4, *an enchanter.*

In the form ἐπῳδός occurs in Plato, Æsch., Euripides, *et al.*, also in the LXX.; Ex. vii. 11, 22, etc. Ἐπαοιδός is found in the Apost. Canons, §10. The Apost. Const. vii. 6, have instead ἐπᾴδων. Barnabas omits the word. The New Testament has μαγεία (Acts, viii. 11), μαγεύω (Acts, viii. 9), and μάγος (Acts, xiii. 6, 8).

ἐριστικός, III. 2, *contentious.*

In Aristotle, Euripides, *et al.;* in the Apost. Canons, §7. Barnabas and the Apost. Const. (parallel passages) omit the word. The New Testament has ἐρίζω and ἔρις.

ζηλοτυπία, V. 1, *jealousy.*

It is found in Æschines in the bad sense *jealousy;* also in the LXX.; Num. v. 15, etc.; and in the Apost. Const. vii. 18. The New Testament has ζηλόω and ζῆλος in both the good and bad senses; so the LXX. also. The New Testament has also ζηλωτής, *a zealot.*

θερμός, VII. 2, *warm.*

In Homer, Hdt., *et al.;* in the LXX.; omitted in the Apost. Const., parallel passage. The New Testament has θερμαίνομαι, Mark, xiv. 54, and θέρμη, Acts, xxviii. 3.

θράσος, III. 9, *over-boldness*.

In classical usage (1) in the good sense *boldness*, (2) in the bad sense *over-boldness*. In the LXX. in the good sense. Occurs in the Apost. Const. vii. 8. The New Testament has θάρσος in the good sense *courage*, but it occurs only once (Acts, xxviii. 15).

θρασύτης, V. 1, *over-boldness*.

In Thucydides, *et al.*, in the bad sense. In the Apost. Const. vii. 18; and in Barnabas, xx. 1; in Theodoret, Chrysostom and other Fathers.

θυμικός, III. 2, *passionate*.

In the classics in both the good and bad senses; (1) *high-spirited* (Aristotle), (2) *passionate* (Plato, *et al.*). The Apost. Const. vii. 7, and the Apost. Canons, § 7, have instead θυμώδης, with the same meaning. The New Testament has θυμός and θυμόω.

ἱδρόω, I. 6, *to sweat*.

In Homer, Aristotle, *et al.* The Apost. Const. omit the word in the parallel passage. The New Testament has the noun ἱδρώς, Luke, xxii. 44.

κακοήθης, II. 6, *malicious*.

In Aristotle, Demosthenes, *et al.;* in the Apost. Const. vii. 5; and in the Apost. Canons, § 6. The New Testament has κακοηθεία (or κακοηθία according to Westcott and Hort), *malice*, Rom. i. 29.

μαθηματικός,, III. 4, *an astrologer*.

In Aristotle, *a mathematician*. In Plutarch it has the meaning *astronomical*, and in later times came to mean *an astrologer*, e. g., Sextus Empiricus (225 A.D.), and Porphyry (263 A.D.). Occurs in the Apost. Canons, § 10. The Apost. Const. vii. 6, have instead, μαθήματα πονηρά.

μαθηματική occurs in Socrates (380 A.D.) with the meaning *astrology*, and so this meaning attaches to the word in the later church councils.

The Latin *mathematici* is used of astrologers in Tacitus, Juvenal, and Tertullian; *mathematica* of astrology in Suetonius. The Latin word may, perhaps, explain the later Greek.

μῖσος, XVI. 3, *hate*.

In Plato, Euripides, *et al.;* in the LXX.; in the Apost. Const. vii. 32; in Clem. Alex., Chrysostom, Gregory Nyssa, etc. The New Testament has μισέω.

μνησικακέω, II. 3, *to bear malice, to be revengeful*.

In Herodotus, Demosthenes, *et al.* In Barnabas, xix. 4; in the Apost. Const. vii. 4; in the Apost. Canons, § 6; in the LXX.; in later writings.

οἰωνοσκόπος, III. 4, *an omen-watcher*.

In Euripides; in the Apost. Const. vii. 6; in the Apost. Canons, § 10; not in the LXX., which has οἰωνίζω, οἰώνισμα, οἰωνισμός, and οἰωνός. The Greek versions of Theodotion (c. 160 A.D.) and Symmachus (c. 200 A.D.) have οἰωνοσκόπος in Isa. xlvii. 12.

πάροδιος, XII. 2, *a traveller*.

Occurs in Hyperides (c. 335 B. C.) but in a different sense. *by* or *on the way*, of a wall *upon the street*. In Plutarch it is used of windows, *looking upon the street*. It is found in Basil and in Hesychius as an adjective in the sense of *common, proverbial* with λόγος and ῥῆμα.

The classical word for "traveller" is παροδίτης. The LXX. have πάροδος in the same sense; while in the New Testament πάροδος means *a way* (1 Cor. xvi. 7).

The Apost. Const. omit παρόδιος in the parallel passage.

The *Didache* therefore seems to stand alone in its use of παρόδιος in the sense of *a traveller*.

περικαθαίρω, III. 4, *to purify* or *to use purifications*.

In classical usage the word has no reference to religious rites. It occurs in Plato with τὴν στήλην, and in Aristotle with τὰ δίκτυα. In the LXX. it is used of "making a son pass through the fire," Deut. xviii. 10, from which the sense of the word in the *Didache* seems to be derived. It is also used in Josh. v. 4, of "circumcision." Occurs in the Apost. Canons, § 10. The Apost. Const. vii. 6 have περικαθαίρων τὸν υἱόν, which illustrates this passage and implies that the use of περικαθαίρω by itself with the meaning which it has in the *Didache* was uncommon. The New Testament has περικάθαρμα, *an outcast* (1 Cor.

iv. 13); and καθαίρω with the meanings (1) *to prune a tree* (John, xv. 2), (2) *to purify from sin* (Heb. x. 2).

ποθέω, IV. 3, *to desire.*

In Pindar, Herodotus, Plato, *et al.*; in the LXX. The New Testament has ἐπιποθέω, and ἐπιθυμέω. The Apost. Const. vii. 10, the Apost. Canons, § 13, and Barnabas, xix. 12, read ποιήσεις σχίσματα, which favors an emendation of the text in this place.

πονέω, V. 2, *to labor.*

Occurs in the classics in two senses, (1) *to labor,* (2) *to afflict, to distress;* occurs in the LXX., in Barnabas xx. 2, and in the Apost. Const. vii. 18. The New Testament has πόνος, meaning (1) *work* (Col. iv. 13), (2) *distress* (Rev. xvi. 10).

ποτόν, X. 3, (twice) *drink; that which one drinks.*

In Homer, Æschylus, Sophocles, *et al.*, in the same sense; in the LXX. twice (Job, xv. 16; Lev. xi. 34). ὁ ποτός, occurs in Porphyry of *a watering of horses* (see Sophocles' Lexicon). The New Testament has πότος (classical), *a drinking together, a drinking bout* (1 Pet. iv. 3). The Apost. Const. vii. 26 (parallel passage) omit the word.

προνηστεύω, VII. 4, *to fast beforehand.*

In Herodotus and Hippocrates. Apparently does not occur in later ecclesiastical Greek. The Apost. Const. vii. 22 have νηστεύω. The New Testament has νηστεύω and νηστεία, both of which occur in the classics, in the LXX. and in ecclesiastical Greek (Basil, Chrysostom, etc.).

πυκνῶς, XVI. 2, *often.*

Occurs in Aristophanes. Homer has πυκινῶς. The Apost. Const. vii. 31 omit the passage. The New Testament has the adjective πυκνός, and πυκνά and πυκνότερον as adverbs. The LXX. have πυκνός and πυκνότερον but not πυκνῶς.

συσπάω, IV. 5, *to draw together,* or *to draw in.*

In Aristophanes, Plato, *et al.*, with the meaning *to draw together;* so in Lucian (c. 160 A.D.) with δακτύλους. Occurs in Barnabas, xix. 9, and in the Apost. Canons, § 13, but the Apost. Const. have instead συστέλλων.

τετράς, VIII. 1, *the fourth*, i. e., *the fourth day of the week*.
In classical usage it has the meanings, (1) for τετρακτύς (a) *the sum of the first four numbers*, (b) *a quaternion*; (2) *the fourth day of the month* (Homer, Hesiod, etc.), (3) *a space of four days* (Hippocrates).
The LXX. have the word of *the fourth day of the month*. τετράς is used of the "fourth day of the week" in later writers (Clem. Alex.; Ignatius *Philipp.* § 13 interpol.; the Apost. Const. v. 14; vii. 23, etc).
The New Testament has τέταρτος, τεταρταῖος and τετράδιον, but not of "the fourth day of the week."

φαρμακεύω, II 2, *to use sorcery*.
In Hdt. in the same sense; in the LXX.; in the Apost. Const. vii. 3, and in the Apost. Canons, § 6. The New Testament has φαρμακεία, *sorcery*, φαρμακός, *a sorcerer*.

φθορεύς? V. 2; XVI. 3, *a corrupter, destroyer*.
This is probably a post-classical word, but is read by Brunck in Sophocles Fr. 155 (according to Liddell and Scott). It occurs in Plutarch and in Anthemius (570 A. D.), also in Barnabas, xx. 2, and in the Apost. Const. vii. 18. The New Testament has φθείρω, φθορά and φθαρτός, which are found also in the LXX.

III.

WORDS NOT IN THE NEW TESTAMENT BUT IN THE LXX.

Total, 17, of which 16 are classical words.

ἀθάνατος, IV. 8, *imperishable*.
Wisdom, i. 15; Sirach, xvii. 30.
διαφορά, I. 1, *difference*.
Wisdom, vii. 20.
δίγλωσσος, II. 4, *double-tongued, deceitful*.
Prov. xi. 13; Sirach, v. 9, 14; vi. 1; xxviii. 13.
ἐνδέω, IV. 8; V. 2, *to be in want*.
Deut. viii. 9; xv. 8; Prov. xxviii. 27.
ἐπαοιδός, III. 4, *an enchanter*.
Ex. vii. 11, 22, etc.; Lev. xix. 31, etc.

ζηλοτυπία, V. 1, *jealousy.*
  Num. v. 15, etc.
θερμός, VII. 2, *warm.*
  Josh. ix. 18; Job, xxxvii. 16, and often.
θράσος, III. 9, *over-boldness.*
  Ezek. xix. 7; Wisdom, xii. 17.
μακρόθυμος, III. 8, *long-suffering.*
  Ex. xxxiv. 6; Psa. lxxxv. 15, and often. In the Apost. Const. vii. 8; in the Apost. Canons, § 11; in Chrysostom, etc. The New Testament has μακροθυμέω, μακροθυμία and μακροθύμως. μακρόθυμος is not a classical word.
μῖσος, XVI. 3, *hate.*
  2 Sam. xiii. 15, and often.
μνησικακέω, II. 3, *to bear malice, to be revengeful.*
  Joel, iii. 4, *to repay evil;* Gen. l. 15, *to hate,* and so often with the same general meaning.
περικαθαίρω, III. 4, *to purify* or *to use purifications.*
  Deut. xviii. 10, of "making a son pass through the fire." Josh. v. 4, of "circumcision."
ποθέω, IV. 3, *to desire.*
  Prov. vii. 15; Wisdom, iv. 2, etc.
πονέω, V. 2, *to labor.*
  Isa. xix. 10; 1 Kings, xxii. 8, and often; but not with the meaning *to labor.* When used transitively it has the meanings *to afflict, to distress;* when used intransitively, *to suffer, to endure,* etc.
ποτόν, X. 3 (twice), *drink; that which one drinks.*
  Job, xv. 16; Lev. xi. 34.
τετράς, VIII. 1, *the fourth,* i. e. *the fourth day of the week.*
  Hag. ii. 1, 10, 18, etc., of "the fourth day of the month."
φαρμακεύω, II. 2, *to use sorcery.*
  In the active voice in 2 Macc. x. 13. In the passive in Psa. lxiii. 6; 2 Chron. xxxiii. 6.

IV.

WORDS WHICH OCCUR FOR THE FIRST TIME IN THE DIDACHE BUT ARE FOUND IN LATER WRITINGS.

Total, 16.

αἰσχρολόγος, III. 3, *foul-mouthed.*
  Occurs in Pollux (c. 180 A.D.), in the Apost. Const. vii. 6, and in the Apost. Canons, § 9. The New Testament has αἰσχρολογία and αἰσχρότης.

ἀνταποδότης, IV. 7, *a recompenser.*
  Occurs in Barnabas, xix. 11, in the Apost. Const. vii. 12, and in the Apost. Canons, § 13. The New Testament has ἀνταποδίδωμι, ἀνταπόδομα and ἀνταπόδοσις.

γόγγυσος, III. 6, *a murmurer.*
  Occurs in the Apost. Const. vii. 7; and in the Apost. Canons, § 11; also in Theodoret and in Arcadius. The New Testament has γογγυστής in the same sense (Jude, 16), also γογγύζω and γογγυσμός.

διγλωσσία, II. 4, *doubleness of tongue.*
  Found in Barnabas, xix. 7, and in the older editions of Barn. xix. 8. But the latest editions omit it in the latter passage and read instead παγὶς γὰρ τὸ στόμα θανάτου. Occurs in the Apost. Canons, § 6. The Apost. Const. vii. 4, have παγίς γὰρ ἰσχυρὰ ἀνδρὶ τὰ ἴδια χείλη.

διγνώμων, II. 4, *double-minded.*
  Occurs in Barnabas, xix. 7, and in the Apost. Const. ii. 6. The Apost. Const. vii. 4 (parallel passage) and the Apost. Canons, § 6, have instead δίγνωμος. The New Testament has δίψυχος.

διπλοκαρδία, V. 1, *double-heartedness, duplicity.*
  Occurs in Barnabas, xx. 1, and in the Apost. Const. vii. 18. Sophocles compares διπλῇ ψυχῇ in Hippolytus (Ox. ed. page 60).

διψυχέω, IV. 4, *to hesitate, to doubt.*
  Occurs in Barnabas, xix. 5, in the Apost. Canons, § 13, and in the Apost. Const. vii. 11; also in Clement of Rome,

First Epistle, § 23; in Hermas, *Vision* ii. 2; and in Cyril of Alexandria *In Johan.* vi. The New Testament has δίψυχος.

ἐκπέτασις, XVI. 6, *a spreading out*, or *an opening*.

The word occurs in Plutarch (*De Sera Numinis Vindicta*, xxiii., Hackett's edition) with the meaning *a spreading out, an expansion*. The Apost. Const. vii. 32 (parallel passage) have τότε φανήσεται τὸ σημεῖον τοῦ υἱοῦ τοῦ ἀνθρώπου ἐν τῷ οὐρανῷ. The verb ἐκπετάννυμι in the classics means *to spread out*. The LXX. have ἐκπετάζω with the same meaning in Job, xxvi. 9, where God "spreads out a cloud over his throne."

κοσμοπλάνος, XVI. 4, *the world-deceiver*.

Occurs in the Apost. Const. vii. 32. πλάνος (which in the classics means *a wanderer*) is used in the New Testament of *a deceiver*. For the meaning of κοσμοπλάνος compare Rev. xii. 9.

κυριακή, XIV. 1, *the Lord's day*.

Occurs as a noun in Ignatius, Gregory Nazianzen, etc., and in the Apost. Const. often. The Apost. Const. vii. 30 have τὴν ἀναστάσιμον τοῦ κυρίου ἡμέραν τὴν κυριακὴν φαμεν. The New Testament has the adjective, in 1 Cor. xi. 20, of *the Lord's Supper*, and in Rev. i. 10, of *the Lord's day*.

παιδοφθορέω II. 2, *to corrupt boys*.

Occurs in Barnabas, xix. 4, in the Apost. Const. vii. 2; and in the Apost. Canons, § 6; also in Justin Martyr, *Dial. c. Trypho*, § 95, and in Clement of Alexandria, *Cohortatio ad Gentes* (Migne, i. 225), *Pedagogus II.* (Migne, i. 504), etc. The classical word is παιδεραστέω, which is found in Plato.

πανθαμάρτητος, V. 2, *a universal sinner, a sinner in everything*.

Occurs in Barnabas, xx. 2, and in the Apost. Const. vii. 18. The formation of the adjective is peculiar; classic Greek having the adjective ἁμαρτήτικος but not ἁμάρτητος.

πονηρόφρων, III. 6, *evil-minded*.

Occurs in the Apost. Const. vii. 7, in the Apost. Canons, § 11, and, apparently, nowhere else.

σιτία, XIII. 5, *a baking of bread, a batch.*
: Occurs in the *Apophthegmata Patrum* (c. 500 A.D.). The Apost. Const. vii. 29 (parallel passage) have instead ἀρτῶν θερμῶν. The classics and the New Testament have σιτίον and σῖτος, *grain,* and ἄρτος, *bread.* The LXX. have ἄρτος and σῖτος, and ἄρτος is found also in Justin Martyr, Chrysostom, etc.

ὑψηλόφθαλμος, III. 3, *lofty-eyed,* or *wanton-eyed.*
: Occurs elsewhere only in the Apost. Canons, § 9.
: The Apost. Const. vii. 6 have instead ῥιψόφθαλμος which suggests the meaning *wanton-eyed* or *of leering eyes,* for ὑψηλόφθαλμος in the *Didache,* and this meaning accords best with μοιχεῖαι, *adulteries,* which follows.
: The same section of the Apost. Const. has also ὑψηλόφρων, *haughty,* and the LXX. have ὑψηλοκάρδιος, *haughty.* But this can hardly be the meaning of ὑψηλόφθαλμος in the *Didache.*

χριστέμπορος, XII, 5, *one who makes gain out of Christ.*
: The word is not found again until about 800 A.D. It occurs in Athanasius (d. 373 A.D.), in Basil (d. 379), in Gregory Naz. (d. 390 or 391), in Chrysostom (d. 407), and in the Ignatian Epistles (interpolated), *Ad Trall.* vi. and *Ad Magn.* vi. (date 300–400 A.D. ?).
: χριστεμπορεία occurs in Theodoret (d. 457).

V.

WORD FOUND ONLY IN THE DIDACHE, ABSOLUTE HAPAX LEGOMENON.

προσεξομολογέω, XIV. 1, *to confess.*
: προσομολογέω and ὁμολογέω are classical, and ὁμολογέω and ἐξομολογέω are found in the LXX., in the New Testament, and in ecclesiastical writers. The Apost. Const. vii. 30 (parallel passage) have ἐξομολογέομαι.
: Hilgenfeld and von Gebhardt (followed by Harnack in a note, page 54) prefer προεξομολογέω.

VI.

LIST OF NEW TESTAMENT WORDS NOT USED IN THE NEW TESTAMENT SENSE.

Total, 14.

αἰσχύνη, IV. 11, *modesty*.

In the New Testament in a bad sense only; subjectively, *the feeling of shame;* objectively, *a shameful deed*. In classical usage (1) subjectively, *shame for an ill-deed; the sense of honor*. (2) Objectively, *disgrace, dishonor*.

Occurs in the parallel passage in Barnabas, xix. 7. In the Apost. Const. vii. 13, προσοχή occurs instead. In later ecclesiastical Greek (Gregory Nyssa and Theodoret) it is employed in the bad sense.

ἀνταπόδομα, V. 2, *revenge*.

In the New Testament it means *a recompense* (1) of good, Luke, xiv. 12, (2) of evil, Rom. xi. 9. The sense of the word in Rom. xi. 9 approaches that in the *Didache*, but is not identical with it, the subjectivity which inheres in the word *revenge* (a word which exactly translates ἀνταπόδομα in the *Didache*) being wanting in Rom. xi. 9.

In the LXX. ἀνταπόδομα is used for גְּמוּל, *recompense*. The word is not classical.

δίκη, I. 5, *account* or *trial*.

δώσει δίκην, *shall give account* (Hitchcock and Brown, et al.); *shall submit to trial* (Orris). In the New Testament δίκη means (1) *judgment, sentence,* (2) *punishment*. In the classics the nearest approach to the sense of the word in this passage is in Hdt., Thuc., and Xen., where διδόναι δίκας occasionally means *to submit to trial;* the ordinary meaning of διδόναι δίκην being *to inflict* or *to suffer punishment*.

εἰρηνεύω, IV. 3, *to reconcile*.

In the New Testament used intransitively only, *to be at peace; to live in peace*. So in the classics. But in Babrius (c. 50

NEW TEST. WORDS NOT USED IN NEW TEST. SENSE. 111

B.C.) and in Dio Cassius (c. 180 A.D.) the transitive sense *to reconcile, to make peace* occurs. So in Barnabas xix. 12, in the Apost. Const. vii. 10, and in the Apost. Canons, § 13.

ἐκλύομαι, XVI. 1, *to be loosed.*

In the New Testament with the meaning *to be wearied, to be faint.* The phrase ὀσφύες ἐκλυέσθωσαν seems to be peculiar to the *Didache.* The Apost. Const. vii. 31 have ὀσφύες περιεζωσμέναι, which is a New Testament phrase.

εὐχαριστία, IX. 1, 5, *the Eucharist.*

In the New Testament with the meanings (1) *gratitude,* (2) *thanksgiving,* the expression of gratitude. In the classics *gratitude.* The word is used of "the Lord's Supper" in Ignatius (c. 115 A.D.) *Ephesians,* xiii. ; *Smyrnœans,* viii., etc. ; in Justin Martyr *First Apology,* § 66 ; *Dialogue with Trypho,* § 117 ; in Irenæus, iv. 8, 5 ; in Clem. Alex. ; in Origen ; in the Apost. Const., etc.

ζηλωτής, III. 2, *jealous.*

In the New Testament in the good sense of *zeal.* So in classical usage. ζηλόω and ζῆλος, however, are used in the classics and in the New Testament both in the good and in the bad sense. The word occurs in the Apost. Const. vii. 6, and in the Apost. Canons, § 7 (parallel passages).

κατασκηνόω, X. 2, *to cause to dwell.*

In the New Testament always intransitive, *to lodge, to dwell.* So in the classics. In the LXX. it is used transitively for the Hebrew הָרְבִיץ in Psa. xxii. 1 ; for שַׁכֵּן in Num. xiv. 30 ; and for הִשְׁכִּין in Psa. vii. 6, etc. The *Didache* therefore agrees with the LXX. in its use of this word, which is found also in the Apost. Const. vii. 26 in the same sense. *

---

* κυριότης, IV. 1, is included in this list by Hitchcock and Brown, who translate *that which pertaineth to the Lord.* But other translators (Harnack, Orris, Starbuck, Spence) read *Lordship, Sovereignty of the Lord,* etc., which is the New Testament sense of the word (Eph. i. 21 ; Col. i. 16 ; 2 Peter, ii. 10 ; Jude, 8) and the more literal rendering. The Apost. Const. vii. 9, however, favor Hitchcock and Brown's rendering, as they read ὅπου γὰρ ἡ περὶ θεοῦ διδασκαλία ἐκεῖ ὁ θεὸς πάρεστιν. But the Apost. Canons, § 12, read as does the *Didache.*

λύτρωσις, IV. 6, *a ransom.*
>   Occurs three times in the New Testament: Luke, ii. 38, "looking for (προσδεχομένοις λύτρωσιν) the *redemption* of Israel."
>   Luke, i. 68, "hath wrought *redemption* (ἐποίησεν λύτρωσιν) for his people."
>   Heb. ix. 12, "having obtained eternal *redemption* (λύτρωσιν εὑράμενος)." It is used therefore in the New Testament only of the *deliverance* or *redemption* itself. It occurs in the LXX. in the sense of *a redeeming, ransoming.* The word is not classical but occurs in Plutarch (Arat. 11) where it is rendered *ransoming* by Liddell and Scott.
>   Cremer (*Biblico-Theological Lexicon of New Testament Greek*) says "λύτρωσις literally denotes not the ransom but the *act of freeing or releasing; deliverance.* In Biblical Greek=*redemption, deliverance.*" λύτρον in the New Testament, in the LXX., and in the classics denotes *the means of loosing, that which is paid for the liberation* of anyone, *the ransom.*
>   In the *Didache* λύτρωσις is used quite anomalously of *the ransom paid*, as the synonym of the New Testament λύτρον. The Apost. Canons, § 13, agree with the *Didache.* It is significant that the Apost. Const. vii. 12 (parallel passage), read διὰ τῶν χειρῶν σου δός, ἵνα ἐργάσῃ εἰς λύτρωσιν ἁμαρτιῶν σου, using λύτρωσις in the sense of *remission*, for the New Testament ἄφεσις.
>   In Barnabas, xix. 10, we have διὰ τῶν χειρῶν σου ἐργάσῃ εἰς λύτρον ἁμαρτιῶν σου, where λύτρον is used after εἰς instead of the more exact λύτρωσις.

We can only say, therefore, that the *Didache* and its parallels use these two words in a very loose and careless way.

παρεκτός, VI. 1, *apart from.*
>   The word is rendered *apart from* by Hitchcock and Brown, and by Spence; *aside from* by Starbuck; *aloof from* by Orris; *anders als* by Harnack.
>   It occurs three times in the New Testament (Matt. v. 32; Acts, xxvi. 29; 2 Cor. xi. 28) and possibly a fourth time in Matt. xix. 9. According to Meyer it means always

NEW TEST. WORDS NOT USED IN NEW TEST. SENSE.

"*beside* in the sense of *exception.*" It is rendered in a different way each time by the English versions, but never has the meaning which it has in the *Didache*. The word does not occur in the classics, in the LXX., in Barnabas, nor in the Apost. Const.

συνοχή, I. 5, *arrest* or *confinement.*

Occurs but twice in the New Testament (Luke, xxi. 25; 2 Cor. ii. 4) with the meaning *distress, anguish*. In the classics it means *a being held together* in many different connections, and in Manetho [300 B.C., *Poet. Works*, I. 313] it is used of *imprisonment*. It occurs four times in the LXX., twice of a *siege* (Jer. lii. 5; Micah v. 1) where it translates the Hebrew מָצוֹר. The passage is omitted in the Apost. Const.

ὑπερεῖδον (second aorist of ὑπεροράω), XV. 2, *to despise.*

Occurs but once in the New Testament (Acts, xvii. 30) where it means *to overlook, to bear with*. In the classics it means both *to overlook* and *to despise*. In the LXX. it has frequently the meaning *to despise* (Tobit, iv. 8; Wisdom, xix. 21; Sirach, ii. 10, etc.). The Apost. Const. vii. 31 read ὑμεῖς δὲ τιμᾶτε τούτους, etc.

ὕψος, V. 1, *haughtiness.*

In the New Testament it means (1) *height*, of material elevation only; (2) *elevation* or *dignity* of a Christian, Jas. i. 9. In the classics it has the meanings (1) *height;* (2) Metaph. *the top, summit*. The Apost Const. vii. 18, have instead ὑψηλοφροσύνη. Barnabas, xx. 1 has ὕψος δυνάμεως.

φθορά, II. 2, *abortion; ἐν φθορᾷ, by abortion.*

In the New Testament the word means *corruption*, both physical and spiritual, and also *moral corruptness, depravity*. In the classics it means *destruction, decay*, etc. The meaning *abortion* appears only in ecclesiastical Greek; in Barnabas, xix. 5; in the Apost. Const. vii. 3, in the Apost. Canons, § 6, and in Clement of Alexandria.

8

CHAPTER XXVI.

Authenticity of the Didache.*

The *Didache* is no modern or ancient forgery, but has every internal evidence of very great antiquity and genuineness. It serves no party purpose, and disappoints all parties. "No one," says Bishop Lightfoot, "could or would have forged it." The existence of the Jerusalem MS. is placed beyond all doubt by a number of witnesses and the fac-similes which we published, pp. 5 and 6; and the conjecture that Bryennios wrote it, is not only contemptible but absurd. The forger, then, must have been Leo "the sinner," who wrote the MS. in 1056, or some older sinner from whom he copied. But it can be proven that the *Didache* is identical, at least in substance, with a book of that name which was known to the early fathers, and then disappeared for centuries.

Clement of Alexandria (who died about 216) gives us the first clear trace of the book, though without naming it. He quotes, in his *Stromata*, which were written between 201 and 203, a passage from it, as a passage of "Scripture" ($\gamma\rho\alpha\phi\eta$), and therefore regards it as an inspired book in a wider sense, like the Epistle of Barnabas and the Pastor of Hermas, which he used frequently, with a great want of critical discernment between the Apostolic and post-Apostolic writings.† He

---

* Bryennios discusses the authenticity in the fifth section (§ ε´) of his *Prolegomena*, Harnack in his *Prolegomena*, pp. 6–11, and Zahn in his *Supplementum Clementinum*, p. 279 sqq.; Comp. also Hitchcock and Brown, second ed. p. xxiii. sqq.

† *Strom.* lib. I. cap. 20 (in Migne's ed. I., col. 817):

Οὗτος κλέπτης ὑπὸ τῆς γραφῆς εἴρηται· φησὶ γοῦν, "Υἱὲ, μὴ γίνου ψεύστης· ὁδηγεῖ γὰρ τὸ ψεῦσμα πρὸς τὴν κλοπήν." (Such a one is called a thief *by the Scripture*; at least it says: "Son, become not a liar; for lying leads to theft.")

Didache, c. III. 5.

Τέκνον μου, μὴ γίνου ψεύστης· ἐπειδὴ ὁδηγεῖ τὸ ψεῦσμα εἰς τὴν κλοπήν. (My child, become not a liar; since lying leads to theft.)

The quotation (probably from memory) agrees with the passage in the seems moreover to refer to the *Didache* when he speaks of the doctrine of the Two Ways as being proposed by *the Apostles* (in the *Didache?*) as well as by the Gospel and the Prophets.* At the close of his *Pædagogue*, he gives himself a sort of Apostolic instruction for Neophytes based upon the Mosaic Decalogue and the two royal commandments of love, and this instruction corresponds in general with the teaching of the Two Ways in our document.† Clement also uses the term "Vine of David," which occurs nowhere else than in the *Didache*." ‡

Perhaps we may go still further back to Irenæus who flourished about twenty years earlier. In the second of the Fragments discovered by Pfaff, Irenæus speaks of "Second Ordinances (or Constitutions) of the Apostles," § which may possibly mean the *Didache*, as a secondary Apostolic, or post-Apostolic production. He says: "Those who have followed *the Second Ordinances of the Apostles* know that the Lord has established a new offering in the New Covenant, according to the word of Malachi the prophet" (Mal. i. 11, 14). The same passage of Malachi is quoted in the *Did.* (XIV. 3) for the same purpose, and was often used in the second century

---

Did. except that it reads υἱὲ for τέκνον μου, γάρ for ἐπειδή, and πρός for εἰς. Paul de Lagarde first directed attention to this quotation, in his *Reliquiæ juris ecclesiastici antiquissimæ*, Lips. 1856, but traced it to the Apost. Church Order, as the *Didache* was not yet discovered.

* *Strom.* lib. v. cap. 5 (in Migne's ed., vol. ii. col. 54): δύο ὁδοὺς ὑποτιθεμένου τοῦ εὐαγγελίου [cf. Matt. vii. 13, 14] καὶ τῶν ἀποστόλων [cf. our Διδαχὴ τῶν ἀποστ.] ὁμοίως τοῖς προφήταις ἅπασι [Jer. xxi. 8]. He then refers also to the myth of Prodicus on virtue and vice (Xenophon's *Memorab.* ii. 1, 21 sq.), and to the teaching of Pythagoras.

† *Pæd.* Lib. iii. cap. 12 ; ed. Migne i. col. 665 sqq. (ed. Potter, p. 304, sqq.). Krawutzcky in the "Theol. Quartalschrift", of Tübingen for 1884, p. 588 sqq., ingeniously, but unsuccessfully, tries to show that Clement, while acquainted with the *Didache*, was not quite satisfied with it, and that his quotation in *Strom.* i. 20 is probably from a shorter and older book of Peter on the *Two Ways*.

‡ ἡ ἄμπελος Δαβίδ. *Quis dives salvus*, cap. 29 ; comp. *Did.* IX. 2.

§ δεύτεραι τῶν ἀποστόλων διατάξεις. *Opera*, ed. Stieren, i. 854 sq.; Harvey's ed. ii. 500. Harvey (i. clxxii.) considers the Fragment genuine. Διατάξεις is the Greek word for the Latin *Constitutiones*. Rothe's elaborate argument that it means the institution of the Episcopate is a failure The context shows that it refers to the Eucharist. See *Church Hist.* ii. 137.

with reference to the sacrifice of the Eucharist.* Possibly the lost treatise of Irenæus on *Apostolic Preaching* or on the subject of *Teaching* was a comment on the *Didache*.†

Origen, the pupil of Clement, uses likewise the designation of Christ as "the Vine of David," and quotes a passage of the *Didache* (III. 10) and Barnabas as "divine Scripture." ‡

Eusebius, the historian (d. 340), who was familiar with the entire ante-Nicene literature, is the first to mention the book by its name, "*The so-called Teachings of the Apostles.*" He uses the plural and omits the number twelve. § The addition "so-called" (which occurs again in Athanasius) qualifies the Apostolic origin as being only indirect in the sense in which we speak of the "so-called Apostles' Creed." Eusebius puts the *Didache* last among the ecclesiastical but uncanonical and spurious books (ἐν τοῖς νόθοις), and in the same category with "The Acts of Paul," "The Shepherd of Hermas," "The Apocalypse of Peter," "The Epistle of Barnabas;" *i. e.*, with writings which were publicly used in some churches, but which he himself as an historian with good reason did not find sufficiently authenticated and intrinsically important enough to entitle them to a place among the "Homologumena," or even among the seven "Antilegomena," which are now parts of the New Testament canon.

Athanasius, Bishop of Alexandria (d. 373), in like manner mentions the "*Teaching so called of the Apostles*" ‖ (together with the Wisdom of Solomon, the Wisdom of Sirach, Esther, Judith, Tobit, and the Shepherd) among the books which

---

* Krawutzcky's hypothesis that the *Did.* was written in *opposition* to these *Ordinances* is utterly baseless. See above, p. 24 note.

† A plausible conjecture of Bryennios accepted by J. Rendel Harris (in the "Journal of Christian Philosophy," April, 1884, p. 35).

‡ *Hom. VI. in Lib. Jud.; De Princ.* III. 2, 7. These two references have been found by Bornemann and Potwin, but the second is from Barnabas. See First Append., p. 304.

§ Τῶν Ἀποστόλων αἱ λεγόμεναι Διδαχαί. Π. Ε. iii. 25. Rufinus, in his translation, substitutes for the plural the singular, *Doctrina quæ dicitur Apostolorum.* The *Apost. Const.* are called both Διάταξις and Διατάξεις τῶν Ἀπ., as Bryennios remarks.

‖ Διδαχὴ καλουμένη τῶν ἀποστόλων.

are not canonical, but useful for the instruction of catechumens.*

Rufinus, Presbyter of Aquileia and translator of Eusebius (d. 410), repeats this statement of Athanasius, but with two differences: he substitutes the books of the Maccabees for the book of Esther, and a little book, "The Two Ways," or "The Judgment of Peter," or "according to Peter," for the "Teaching of the Apostles." † Jerome (d. 419) likewise mentions Peter's "Judgment" among five apocryphal books ascribed to that Apostle. ‡ This was probably the same with the first six chapters of our *Didache*, or, possibly, an older source of it. § The name of Peter was probably used in a representative sense as he stood at the head of the Twelve, especially from the Roman point of view.

In a work, *De Aleatoribus*, falsely ascribed to Cyprian, there

---

* He calls them βιβλία οὐ κανονιζόμενα μέν, τετυπωμένα δε παρὰ τῶν πατέρων ἀναγινώσκεσθαι τοῖς ἄρτι προσερχομένοις καὶ βουλομένοις κατηχεῖσθαι τὸν τῆς εὐσεβείας λόγον, "books not canonized, but appointed by the fathers to be read to those that are just coming to us and desire to be instructed in the doctrine of godliness." *Epistola Fest.* 39, in *Opera* ed. Bened. I. 2, 963; in Migne's ed. ii. col. 1437. The Ep. is from the year 367.

† *Comment. in Symb. Apost.* c. 38 (*Opera*, ed. Migne, col. 374): "*Sciendum tamen est, quod et alii libri sunt, qui non canonici, sed ecclesiastici a majoribus appellati sunt.*" Then after mentioning the Apocrypha of the O. T. he continues: "*in Novo Testamento libellus qui dicitur 'Pastoris' sive 'Hermes'* (al. '*Hermatis*'); [*et*] *qui appellatur 'Duæ Viæ,' vel 'Judicium Petri.'*" The bracketed *et* before *qui* (omitted by Migne) is a conjecture of Credner. The older editions read *Judicium secundum Petrum*, and one MS. *secundum Petri*, which would imply a *primum Judicium Petri*, but is probably a mere error (*secundum* for *judicium*).

‡ *De viris illustr.* c. 1. He mentions, besides the two canonical Epistles of Peter, the following books ascribed to him: "*Libri e quibus unus 'Actorum' ejus inscribitur, alius 'Evangelii,' tertius 'Prædicationis,' quartus 'Apocalypseos,' quintus 'Judicii,' inter apocryphas Scripturas repudiantur.*"

§ Grabe (1711, *Spicileg.* i. 56) identified the *Duæ Viæ* or *Judicium Petri* with the *Prædicatio Petri* (κήρυγμα, abridged κρια, misunderstood for κρίμα), Hilgenfeld with the Apost. Church Order in which Peter gives the hierarchical instruction. Krawutzcky with an earlier (lost) document between Barnabas and the Church Order, Zahn, Harnack, and nearly all English and American writers with the *Didache*. Hilgenfeld explains the title *Judicium Petri* from 2 Pet. ii. 2 sq., and from the *Judicium Herculis* described by Prodicus in Xenophon (*l. c.* fv. 90).

is a quotation from a book called the "Doctrines of the Apostles" ("*in Doctrinis Apostolorum*"), but it bears only a very remote resemblance to a few passages in the *Didache*.*

The last mention of the "Teaching of the Apostles" from personal knowledge was made in the ninth century by Nicephorus, Patriarch of Constantinople (d. A.D. 828), who speaks of such a book as among the Apocrypha of the New Testament, and as consisting of two hundred lines ($\sigma\tau\iota\chi o\iota$).† It turns out that the MS. discovered by Bryennios numbers two hundred and three lines. ‡

After this notice the *Didache* disappeared from history till its recovery in 1873, or rather its publication in 1883. § The sub-

---

* See Bryennios, p. κη', and Harnack, p. 20 sq.

† Nicephorus gives a list of all the books of the O. and N. T., and nine Apocrypha of the N. T., with the number of $\sigma\tau\iota\chi o\iota$, and as the fifth among these Apocrypha he mentions (between the Gospel of Thomas and the Epistles of Clement, Ignatius, Polycarp and Hermas) the

$$\Delta\iota\delta\alpha\chi\eta\ \dot{\alpha}\pi o\sigma\tau o\lambda\omega\nu\ \sigma\tau\iota\chi o\iota\ \varsigma'$$

The canon of Nicephorus is fully discussed by Credner, *Zur Geschichte des Kanons* (Halle, 1847) p. 97 sqq., and printed pp. 117–122. See NICEPHORI *Opera*, ed. Migne (1865, in "Patrol. Gr." Tom. C. p. 1058 sq.), and also the fifth ed. of Westcott's *Hist. of the Can.* pp. 560–62.

‡ Bryennios assumes the substantial identity of the verse-measure of Leon's MS. with that of the text of Nicephorus. The verse-measure of antiquity was an average hexameter (about 15 syllables), but it varied according to the size of the page or the column. See the article *Stichometry* by J. Rendel Harris in Schaff Herzog, " Rel. Encycl.," iii. 2244 sqq. According to Harnack (p. 13, note 22), the *Did.* numbers 10,700 letters, *i. e.*, 305 stichoi, counting 35 letters to a stichos. Gordon ("Modern Review," 1884, p. 455) throws doubt on the value of the inference from Nicephorus. "This measurement," he says, 'so far from favoring the identity of the two, is an argument against it. Nicephorus fixes the combined length of the two Epistles of Clement at 2,600 lines ; they occupy in the *Jerusalem Manuscript* 1,120 lines (See Bryennios' Clement, p. 142, n. 4). What then, on this calculation, should be the length, in the *Jerusalem Manuscript*, of Nicephorus' 200-line tractate ? Not 203, but only some 86 lines. This would imply a very much shorter document than either the Greek or the Syriac *Teaching*. To suit the requirements of our Greek document the estimate in Nicephorus' stichometry would have to be increased to 455 lines, instead of 200."

§ Bryennios quotes two later authors who mention the *Did.*, namely Joannes Zonaras (c. 1120) and Matthæus Blastares (c. 1335), but they had no personal knowledge of it, and confounded it with the Apostolical Constitutions of Pseudo-Clement.

stance of it had passed into other books, the "Ecclesiastical Canons" and the "Apostolical Constitutions," which superseded it as a separate work.

Dr. Oscar von Gebhardt has recently (1884) ascertained the existence of an old Latin translation of the *Didache* and published a fragment of it, containing, with sundry variations, the substance of the first two chapters, and beginning: "*Viæ duæ sunt in seculo, vitæ et mortis, lucis et tenebrarum.*" It must be either a free translation of the *Did.* conformed to Barnabas and Hermas, or derived from an older source of all these books. It is too small to form a definite conclusion. The MS. dates from the tenth century, and was formerly in the convent library of Melk in Austria, but has unfortunately disappeared; the remaining fragment was copied by the librarian, Bernhard Pez, together with the sermon of Boniface *De abrenunciatione in baptismate.*[*]

Harnack conjectures that the Waldenses were acquainted with this translation and borrowed from it their institution of Apostles or travelling Evangelists.[†] But it is far more probable that they derived it directly from the tenth chapter of Matthew and the mission of the Seventy in the tenth chapter of Luke.

CHAPTER XXVII.

Time of Composition.

THE *Didache* has the marks of the highest antiquity and is one of the oldest, if not the very oldest, of the post-Apostolic writings. There is nothing in it which could not have been written between A.D. 70 and 100.

This is evident, negatively, from the absence of allusion to facts, movements, customs and institutions known throughout Christendom from the middle or beginning of the second century. No mention is made of a New Testament canon, or any

---

[*] *Texte u. Untersuch.* 1884, or Harnack, pp. 275-286. See below, Doc. II., and the Excursus of Dr. Warfield.

[†] See his Excursus on *the Didache and the Waldenses*, pp. 269-274.

book except "the Gospel;" there is no trace of a baptismal creed, or church festival (as Easter), or formulated dogma, or specific heresy, either Ebionism or Gnosticism, which were already rampant in the age of Trajan and Hadrian.* The *Didache* is entirely uncontroversial.

Still more conclusive are the positive indications of antiquity. The *Didache* presents Christian teaching and Christian institutions in primitive, childlike simplicity.† The Church appears in a state of orphanage, immediately after the death of its founders. Apostles still continue, but are of a lower grade and as it were dying out. The Prophets are the chief teachers and not yet superseded by the Bishops. Nor had the Presbyters taken the place of the primitive Bishops, but both are still identical. Of the supernatural gifts ($\chi\alpha\rho\iota\sigma\mu\alpha\tau\alpha$) prophecy was flourishing, but the glossolalia and the power of miracles had disappeared. The Agape and the Eucharist are one feast; while from the beginning of the second century they were separated. There is no class distinction of clergy and laity, no mention of ordination, of three orders, of sacerdotal functions. Only two sacraments are mentioned. Discretionary freedom is allowed in the mode of administering Baptism, and room is left for the extemporaneous exercise of the gift of prayer in public worship, which had not yet assumed a settled order. No reading of Scripture lessons is even mentioned.

---

* Hilgenfeld and Bonet-Maury find in the *Didache* allusions to the Montanistic prophecy, and the former also to Gnosticism by an arbitrary emendation of the text ($\kappa o\sigma\mu\iota\kappa\tilde{\omega}\nu$ for $\kappa o\sigma\mu\iota\kappa\acute{o}\nu$, and $\mu\nu\tilde{\omega}\nu$ for $\pi o\iota\tilde{\omega}\nu$ Ch. XI. 11). But this is certainly an error. The *Did.* ante-dates the Montanistic revival of prophecy and martyr-enthusiasm in opposition to the episcopal hierarchy and its secularizing tendency, and ignores all the characteristic features of that movement. See p. 72, and Brown, in H. and B. p. xciii sqq.

† As Bishop Lightfoot well expresses it: "There is an archaic simplicity, I had almost said a childishness, in its practical directions which is only consistent with the early infancy of a church." Dr. Caspari, of Christiania, a first-class judge of ancient Christian documents, received the same impression. I quote from a private letter (June 21, 1884): "*Mit neutestamentlich-evangelischem Maassstab gemessen steht sie [die Did.] nicht hoch, und repräsentirt so recht die νηπιότης der ersten nachapostolischen Zeit, zumal ihrer judenchristlichen Kreise.*"

The eucharistic thanksgivings are much shorter and simpler than those in the ancient liturgies. The sixteenth chapter moves in the eschatological atmosphere of the Synoptical Gospels; and the whole book reflects the Jewish Christian stage of the Church in the land of its birth under the living power of the one Gospel of the Lord.

The antiquity is confirmed by the close affinity of the style and vocabulary to the writings of the New Testament, as distinct both from classical and from patristic Greek.*

Let us reason back from the end of the second century when it was certainly known and used.

The *Didache* is older than Clement of Alexandria, c. 200, who already quoted it as "Scripture," regarding it as semi-Apostolic and semi-inspired. It cannot have been a new book then to be so highly esteemed.

It is older than Irenæus, c. 180, and Justin Martyr, c. 140, who opposed the full-grown Gnostic heresy, and present a more advanced state of doctrinal development and ecclesiastical organization.

It is older than the Epistle of Barnabas, which was certainly written before 120, probably before 100; † for Barnabas presents in the last chapters (which are wanting in the Latin version) a verbose and confused expansion of the first chapters of the *Didache* or some other similar document; while the *Didache* has all the marks of originality: brevity, simplicity and uniformity of style. ‡

It is older than the Shepherd of Hermas, whether composed

---

* See Ch. XXV. p. 94 sqq.

† On the different dates assigned to Barnabas, see *Church History*, vol. ii. 678.

‡ See above, p. 20. I am unable to understand how such learned and acute writers as Bryennios, Hilgenfeld, Harnack, and Krawutzcky can be of the opposite opinion. The priority of the *Didache* is strongly advocated by Zahn, Funk, Langen, Farrar, E. L. Hicks, Potwin, Hitchcock and Brown (second ed. p. xxxvi. sqq), De Romestin, Spence, and nearly all English and American writers on the subject. The only other possible view is that suggested by Lightfoot, Massebieau, Holtzmann, Lipsius, and Warfield, that both Barnabas and the writer of the *Did.* drew from a common source which is lost. But until this is found we must assume that the *Did.* is the source of Barnabas, or at all events the older of the two.

under Bishop Pius of Rome, 139–154, or much earlier at the time of Presbyter-Bishop Clement, 92–100: for in its brief parallel sections, Hermas is likewise an enlargement of the simpler statements of the *Didache*.*

It is older than the oldest recension of the Ignatian Epistles, which dates from the first quarter of the second century: for Ignatius enforces with great earnestness the Episcopal office as a distinct order of the ministry superior to the Presbyterate, and opposes Gnostic docetism; while the *Didache* still identifies the Episcopate with the Presbyterate, and specifies no heresy. .

This would bring us to the threshold of the Apostolic century.

Yet we cannot well go far back of the year 100. For the *Didache*, in the eschatological chapter, makes no allusion to the destruction of Jerusalem as an impending event. And it is not likely that any writer should have undertaken to give a summary of the "Teaching of the Twelve Apostles," while one or more of them were still alive. James, Peter, and Paul, it is true, had suffered martyrdom before the destruction of Jerusalem; but John lived to the reign of Trajan, which began A.D. 98.

We may therefore assign the *Didache* with some confidence to the closing years of the first century, say between A.D. 90 and 100.

In the Jerusalem MS. our document follows the Clementine Epistles and precedes the Ignatian Epistles. This nearly indicates, whether intentionally or not, the probable date of its composition.

The views of scholars still vary considerably, but seem to incline with increasing unanimity to a very early date. Bry-

---

* Hermas is probably younger than Barnabas, and hence still younger than the *Did*. The views on the date of Hermas differ very much. See *Church Hist*. ii. 687 sq. Zahn, while favoring the priority of the *Did*. over Barnabas, maintains its posteriority to Hermas, whom he assigns (with Caspari, Alzog, and Salmon) to the age of Clement of Rome or the reign of Domitian. But this early date cannot be maintained, since Hort has proven that Hermas made use of Theodotion's translation of Daniel.

ennios, on account of the supposed priority of Barnabas and Hermas, puts the *Didache* down to between A.D. 120–160; Harnack, for the same reason, to 120–165; Hilgenfeld and Bonet-Maury, who find in it anti-Montanistic features, assign its present shape to 160–190, and Krawutzcky traces it to Ebionitic origin at the close of the second century. But nearly all the other writers, especially the English and American scholars, favor an earlier date: Zahn between 80 and 120;* Hitchcock and Brown between 100 and 120; Farrar, 100; Lightfoot, 80–100; Funk, Langen, Massebieau, Potwin, Sadler, De Romestin, Spence, assign it more or less confidently to the last quarter of the first century; Bestmann goes back to 70–79; and Sabatier even to *c.* 50.

CHAPTER XXVIII.

Place of Composition.

THE majority of scholars assign the *Didache* to Alexandria in Egypt,† a minority to Palestine or Syria. ‡

Some city of Asia Minor, § or of Greece, ‖ or even Rome, ¶ has also been conjectured, but without response.

The choice is between Egypt and Syria including Palestine.

For Alexandria speaks the fact that there the *Didache* seems to have been first known and quoted (by Clement of Alexandria), and used for catechetical instruction (according to Athanasius). The kindred Epistle of Barnabas and the Apostolical Church Order are probably likewise of Egyptian origin.**

---

* Zahn puts the Ep. of Clement c. 96, Hermas 97–100, Ignatius 110, Barnabas 120–125.

† Bryennios, Zahn, Harnack, Bonet-Maury (p. 35), Farrar, Lightfoot (not confidently), De Romestin, Hitchcock and Brown.

‡ Caspari, Langen, Krawutzcky, Spence, Bestmann.

§ Hilgenfeld.

‖ Canon Wordsworth mentions Corinth, Athens, and Philippi; Hayman (in the "Dublin Review" for January, 1885), the region of Thessalonica.

¶ Massebieau, p. 17.

** Harnack and Bonet Maury (p. 35) argue also from the omission of the

But there is an insuperable objection to Egypt in the allusion, in one of the eucharistic prayers, to the broken bread which was "scattered (in grains) over the *mountains*." * This is entirely inapplicable to the valley of the Nile and to the bare rocks on the border of the desert. Of less weight is the provision for exceptional baptism in *warm* water (Ch. VII. 2), which seems to point to a cold climate.

On the other hand, nothing can be said against, and much in favor of, Southern or Northern Syria as the fatherland of the *Didache*, provided we put its composition, as we must, *before* the Ignatian Epistles and the establishment of Episcopacy in Syria, as a separate order of the ministry.

Some considerations point strongly to Palestine and even to Jerusalem: the constant use of the Gospel of Matthew, which originated in that country; the affinity with the theology and practical genius of James, whose letter hails from the capital of the theocracy; and the approval of the community of goods (comp. IV. 8 with Acts, iv. 32), which seems to have been confined to that city. The church of Jerusalem was indeed dispersed to Pella in the Decapolis during the Jewish war, but it was reconstructed afterwards and continued its existence down to the second and more complete destruction of the city under Hadrian, when its continuity was again interrupted. The *Didache* is not unworthy of the mother church of Christendom, where once all the twelve Apostles lived and labored, where the first Christian Council was held, and where James the brother of the Lord spent his public life as the last connecting link between the old and new dispensation and suffered martyrdom for his faith in Christ. That church was never much influenced by Paul's teaching and kept him at a respectful distance. This would well agree with the spirit of the *Didache*.

But nearly as much may be said for Antioch, the Northern

βασιλεία in the doxology of the Lord's Prayer, VIII. 1, and in the Sahidic version of the Gospels; but Gregory of Nyssa omits it likewise.

* IX. 4: ὥσπερ ἦν τοῦτο τὸ κλάσμα διεσκορπισμένον ἐπάνω τῶν ὀρέων. The last three words are significantly omitted in a similar eucharistic prayer ascribed to Athanasius and quoted in my notes *ad loc.*

capital of Syria, the mother church of Gentile Christianity, where the Christian name was first given to the disciples, where Jews and Gentiles first mingled into one community, and where the two nationalities first came into conflict with each other about the question of circumcision and the yoke of the ceremonial law. There, as well as in Jerusalem, all the conditions (except the community of goods) were given for such a Jewish-Christian Irenicum as the *Didache*. The book must have been well known in Syria, for there it was expanded and superseded by the Pseudo-Clementine Constitutions and Canons, which are certainly of Syrian origin.

CHAPTER XXIX.

Authorship.

THE author modestly concealed his name and gives no clue to his identification. But he was certainly a Jewish Christian, and probably a companion and pupil of the Apostles. He belongs to the school of Matthew and James; he emphasizes the legal and moral element in Christianity, but is fully pervaded at the same time by the spirit of charity, meekness, gentleness and generosity which animates the Gospel. He shows no influence of the ideas and doctrines of Paul, which had hardly reached the Jewish congregations, and never fully pervaded them. The few probable allusions to his Epistles refer to matters of common agreement. Yet he is no more opposed to Paul than either Matthew or James. He may be said to be ante-Pauline (as to spirit, not as to time), but not anti-Pauline.* He gives the teaching of the *Twelve Apostles*

---

* This is the opinion of Dr. Sadler in "The Guardian" for June 4, 1884 (I quote from the article of E. V. in the "British Quarterly Review" for April, 1885, p. 339). It is as far as a fair interpretation allows us to go. Canon Churton, in the same paper, is certainly wrong when he stigmatizes the *Didache* as "distinctly anti-Pauline and heretical," pervaded by a "Sadducean tendency" (*sic!*), and "evading the doctrines of the cross," like the of Israel, but with no more intention of denying the authority of the Apostle of the Gentiles than the author of the Apocalypse when he speaks of the "*Twelve Apostles*" of the Lamb (xxi. 14). His style and phraseology are Hebraistic. He calls the Prophets "high priests." He refers to the first fruits of the produce, and to the Jewish fasts on Tuesday and Thursday. He calls Friday "Preparation day." He is acquainted with the Old Testament and the Jewish Apocrypha (The Book of Ecclesiasticus and Tobit). He abstains from all polemics against the Jewish religion, and thereby differs strongly from the author of the Epistle of Barnabas. He enjoins the recital of the Lord's Prayer three times a day, in evident imitation of the Jewish hours of prayer. He abhors the eating of meat offered to the gods as a contamination with idolatry, and adheres to the compromise measures of the Council of Jerusalem, over which James presided. He even seems to recommend the bearing of the whole yoke of the law as a way to perfection, but he is far from requiring it or casting reflection upon the more liberal Gentile Christians. The whole sum of religion consists for him in perfect love to God and to our fellow-men as commanded in the Gospel, or in what James calls "the perfect law of liberty" (i. 25).

It does not follow, however, that the *Didache* was written exclusively for Jews; on the contrary, it is, according to the title, intended for "the nations" in the same sense in which the Gospel is to be preached to "all nations," according to the Lord's command in Matthew (xxviii. 19).

Beyond this we cannot safely go. The real author will probably remain unknown as much as the author of the Epistle to the Hebrews, which is of the order of Melchisedek, "without father, without mother, without genealogy, having neither beginning of days nor end of life."

In conclusion, we mention two conjectures as to authorship, which have been proposed by the most recent writers on the

---

false apostles and deceitful workers who transformed themselves into Apostles of Christ. Such a book would have been denounced and abhorred by Eusebius and Athanasius instead of being allowed to be used for catechetical instruction.

Didache, and which are about equally ingenious and plausible, but alike destitute of solid foundation.

Canon Spence* assigns the authorship to Bishop Symeon of Jerusalem, the son of Cleopas, the nephew of Joseph and cousin of our Lord, who, according to Hegesippus in Eusebius, succeeded James the Lord's brother after his martyrdom, and ruled the Pella community in the Decapolis from about 69 to 106. He wrote the *Didache* between 80 and 90 as a manual for the instruction of the surrounding heathens.

Dr. Bestmann† goes further back, to the momentous collision between Paul and Peter at Antioch before the church, and the reaction of Jewish conservatism under the lead of James of Jerusalem. Soon after the destruction of the city the *Didache* was issued as a Manifesto and Ultimatum of the Jewish section of the Antiochian Church, but was rejected by the Gentile portion, which issued the Epistle of Barnabas as a counter-Manifesto. This Epistle shows that God had already, through the Prophets, and then through Christ, abolished the law as an outward ordinance, that the unbelieving Jews have no claim to the Old Testament, and that it is only an allegory of Christianity. The opposition, however, was softened by the Appendix of the Two Ways, which was added to Barnabas for the purpose of exhibiting the harmony of the Jewish and Hellenic sections of the Church in the fundamental moral principles and practices of Christianity.

CHAPTER XXX.

The Apostolical Church Order, or the Ecclesiastical Canons of the Holy Apostles.

WITH the progress of ecclesiasticism, the change of customs, the increase of legislation, and the power of the clergy the *Didache* underwent various modifications and adaptations, and was ultimately superseded.

---

* Excursus ii., p 95 sqq.
† In his *Geschichte der christlichen Sitte*, Theil ii., Nördlingen, 1885, pp. 136–153.

It was long felt that the Pseudo-Clementine *Apostolical Constitutions and Canons*, of the fourth century, presuppose an older and simpler document free from sacerdotal and hierarchical interpolations. This was found at last in the *Didache*, but not at once. There is an intervening link, which probably dates from Egypt in the third century.*

This is the so-called APOSTOLICAL CHURCH ORDER,† or ECCLESIASTICAL CONSTITUTIONS AND CANONS OF THE APOSTLES, also quoted as EPITOME, or APOSTOLICAL CANONS, ‡ but not to be confounded with the Canons at the end of the eighth book of the Apostolical Constitutions. It is the great law book of the churches of Egypt.

It was first made known at the close of the seventeenth century in Æthiopic and Arabic texts, but excited little attention.§

Professor Bickell, of Marburg, an eminent historian of church law, discovered a Greek MS. at Vienna and published it with a German translation in 1843 under the title *Ordinatio ecclesiastica Apostolorum* or *Apostolische Kirchenordnung*.‖ He

---

* The argument which Lagarde drew from the quotation of Clement of Alexandria in favor of an earlier origin, in the second century, is now worthless, as that quotation is made from *the Didache*.

† *Apostolische Kirchenordnung.* Under this title it is usually quoted by German writers, as Bickell, Harnack, Krawutzcky, Holtzmann.

‡ A title preferred for brevity's sake by English and American writers.

§ The Æthiopic text was published by Hiob Ludolf at Frankfort in 1691, with a Latin version, in his *Commentary on Æthiopic History*, p. 314 sqq., The Arabic text was described by Assemani, and by Grabe in his *Essay upon Two Arabic MSS.*, in the Bodleian Library, 1711.

‖ In the first volume of his *Geschichte des Kirchenrechts*, Giessen, 1843, Part I. pp. 107-132. (The second part of the first vol. was published after his death by Dr. Röstell at Frankfort, 1849.) The title of the document in the Vienna MS. is Αἱ διαταγαὶ αἱ διὰ Κλήμεντος καὶ κανόνες ἐκκλησιαστικοὶ τῶν ἁγίων ἀποστόλων. But the name of Clement does not appear in this document, and is probably an error of the copyist who transferred it from the Apost. Constitutions, an abridgement of which is found in the same codex. Johann Wilhelm Bickell, like his friend Vilmar, was an evangelical Lutheran high-churchman. He says: (Preface, p. viii.):
"*Obgleich dem Glauben der evangelischen Kirche in welcher ich geboren bin aus voller Ueberzeugung zugethan, weiss ich mich doch von aller Parteilichkeit gegen die catholische Kirche frei. Ebenso ist mir nichts mehr*

directed attention to the close resemblance between this book and the appendix to Barnabas and the Seventh Book of the Pseudo-Clementine Apostolical Constitutions, and significantly hinted at its possible relationship to the *Didache*, then not yet discovered.*

The Greek text was again published with improvements and various readings from a Syriac MS. by the learned Orientalist, Paul de Lagarde (1856),† by Cardinal Pitra

verhasst als das Bestreben, die Geschichte nach einem im Voraus gebildeten System zu constrairen." His son, Georg Bickell, is a convert to the Roman Catholic church, and Professor in the University of Innsbruck. He finds in the *Didache* the germs of purgatory and the sacrifice of the mass. See Ch. XXXIII. on the Lit.

* *Ibid.*, p. 65, note 18, and p. 96, note 14. This conjecture is worth quoting as it has since been substantially verified, as well as the later conjecture of Krawutzcky. *" Ob die Didachen der Apostel,"* says Bickell, p. 96, *" deren bereits Eusebius gedenkt, mit unserer Schrift (Apost. Kirchenordnung) identisch sind, bleibt ebenso ungewiss als die Frage ob darunter die Apost. Const. in ihrer ursprünglichen Gestalt, oder in einem Ausgage zu verstehen seien. Man könnte allenfalls für die erstere Ansicht geltend machen, dass der Ausdruck Didache in unserer Kirchenordnung C. 5 vorkommt (vergl. auch Ap. Gesch. ii. 42 und Barnab. c. 18); ferner dass in der Stelle des Eusebius unmittelbar vor den Didachen der Apostel der Brief des Barnabas erwähnt wird, der mit dem ersten Theil unserer Kirchenordnung grosse Aehnlichkeit hat; dass der Umfang welchen die Didache der Apostel nach Nicephorus haben soll (200 Stichen oder Zeilen), welcher zu den Apost. Const. gar nicht passt, mit der Grösse unserer Kirchenordnung wohl übereinstimmen dürfte; endlich dass neben den Didachen in einem Oxforder griechischen Manuscript (s. oben S. 66 Not. 18) die Didaskalie des Clemens als hiervon verschieden erwähnt wird, unter der Didaskalie des Clemens aber recht wohl die sechs ersten Bücher der Apost. Const. verstanden seyn können, welche auch in den morgenländischen Sammlungen neben unserer Kirchenordnung als die durch Clemens besorgte Didaskalie der Apostel aufgenommen ist. Dieses alles sind indessen keine sichere Argumente, da der Inhalt dieser Didache bei keinem der erwähnten Schriftsteller näher angegeben ist. Gegen die Identität der erwähnten Didache und unserer Kirchenordnung kann der Umstand angeführt werden, dass gerade der wichtigste Theil der letzteren, abgesehen von der Einleitung, nicht in Didachen oder Lehren, sondern in eigentlichen Geboten or Verordnungen der Apostel besteht; so wie dass die Stelle aus den 'doctrinis apostolorum' in der Schrift 'de aleatoribus' (s. oben S. 66 Not. 18) zwar nicht in den Apost. Const., aber auch nicht in unserer Kirchenordnung steht."*

† *Reliquæ juris ecclesiastici antiquissimæ Syriace.* Lips. 1856. *Reliquæ juris ecclesiastici Græce.* Lips. 1856 (pp. 77-86).

(1864),* by Hilgenfeld (1866 and 1884),† by Bryennios (1883), ‡ and by Harnack (1884). §

The same book was issued in the Memphitic dialect, with an English translation by Henry Tattam (Archdeacon of Bedford), in 1848, from a MS. procured in Egypt by the Duke of Northumberland, which is beautifully written in Coptic and Arabic, ‖ and again in the Thebaic dialect of Egypt by Lagarde (1883). ¶

In this interesting document portions of the first six chapters of the *Didache* are literally put into the mouth of the several Apostles who are introduced in a sort of dramatic dialogue as speakers after the fashion of the legend of the Apostles' Creed. John, with his charisma of theological insight,

---

* *Juris ecclesiastici Græcorum historia et monumenta.* Tom. i. Romæ 1864 (pp. 75–86). Pitra used in addition to the Vienna MS. a Cod. Ottoboniensis gr. in the Vatican Library, dating from the fourteenth century, abridged and entitled ἐπιτομὴ ὅρων τῶν ἁγίων ἀποστόλων καθολικῆς παραδόσεως. It presents the same passages and omissions as the Syriac MS. used by Lagarde. "Epitome" is therefore an improper title for the whole.

† *Novum Testamentum extra canonem receptum*, ed. i., Fasc. iv., pp. 93–106; ed. altera, aucta et emend. Lips. 1884, Fasc. iv., 111–121, under the title *Duæ Viæ vel Judicium Petri*. Hilgenfeld still defends the identity of these documents, instead of identifying the *Duæ Viæ* with the *Didache*.

‡ In his ed. of the *Did.* § θ' under the title 'Ἐπιτομή.

§ In his *Die Lehre der zwölf Apostel*, pp. 225–237. He had previously (in the second ed. of Barnabas, 1878) directed attention to a new Greek MS. discovered by O. von Gebhardt in the Synodical Library at Moscow, which contains chs. iv.–xiv. Comp. his *Die Quellen der sogen. apost. Kirchenordnung*, Leipz. 1886. We give the text below with an English version as Doc. V.

‖ *The Apostolical Constitutions, or Canons of the Apostles in Coptic. With an English Translation.* London (printed for the Oriental Translation Fund), 1848. 214 pages. The first book, pp. 1–30, corresponds to the *Didache*. The dialect of the original is the Memphitic of Lower Egypt. But it is itself a translation from the Sahidic or Thebaic version, which was made directly from the Greek. Tattam had in his possession a defective Sahidic MS. with which he compared the Memphitic. See below, Doc. VI.

¶ *Ægyptiaca.* Gotting. 1883. The Thebaic MS. is from the year 1006, and is in the British Museum (*Orient.* 1320). Lightfoot had directed attention to it in his *Appendix to S. Clement of Rome*, Lond. 1877, pp. 466–468. "It is," he says, "of large 4to or small folio size, written on parchment, and was recently acquired from Sir C. A. Murray's collection. It consists of two parts, apparently in the same handwriting, but with separate paginations. At the end is the date . . . the year 722 of Diocletian, or A.D. 1006."

takes the lead in moral precepts; Peter, with the charisma of government, lays down the ecclesiastical laws. A curious feature is that Martha and Mary are likewise introduced as speakers, though only with a few enigmatic words, which seem to refer to the exclusion of deaconesses from all part in the distribution of the elements of the Lord's Supper.* Peter and Cephas are distinguished as two persons.† Bartholomew and Nathanael are also distinguished; but only one James is mentioned; while Matthias, who was elected in the place of Judas, is omitted, and Paul is ignored, although in the Apostolical Constitutions he figures as one of the speakers. The introductory salutation is taken from the Epistle of Barnabas, cap. i.

The last 17 canons (from 14–30) have nothing to do with the *Didache*, and contain directions about the qualifications of Bishops, Presbyters, Deacons, Readers. Widows and Deaconesses, and the duties of the laity, which evidently presuppose a more developed stage of ecclesiastical organization than the one of the *Didache*. There is also an approach to clerical celibacy. Peter (who was himself married) says of the Bishop (can. 16): "It is good if he be unmarried; if not, he should be the husband of one wife (comp. 1 Tim. iii. 2); a man of learning and capable of expounding the Scripture; if unlearned, he should be meek and full of charity to all." Peter concludes the colloquy with the exhortation: "This, my brethren, we request you, not as if we had authority to compel any one, but because we have a charge from the Lord to keep the commandments, nothing taking from, or adding to them, in the name of our Lord, to whom be the glory forever. Amen."

According to the careful investigation of Harnack, this

---

* Can. 26 in Harnack (p. 236), can. 30 and 31 in Bickell (p. 130). See Bickell's note. Harnack (p. 215, note) is disposed to derive this feature from the apocryphal Gospel of the Egyptians, and refers to the Coptic book "Pistis Sophia," where the Lord converses with Mary (namely, Mary Magdalene, who is identified with the sister of Martha).

† Clement of Alexandria (Euseb. i. 12) likewise distinguished Cephas whom Paul censured at Antioch (Gal. ii. 11), from the Apostle Peter (to save his character), but made him one of the seventy disciples. See Zahn, *Supplem. Clem.* p. 68 sq.

Apostolical Church Order is a mechanical and unskilful compilation from four or five older documents, the *Didache*, the Epistle of Barnabas, and two other writings, one from the end of the second, the other from the beginning of the third century. The compiler added the fictitious dress and distributed the matter among the different Apostles. Harnack assigns the composition to Egypt, at the beginning of the fourth century before the establishment of the imperial church, and several decades before the Apostolical Constitutions.*

CHAPTER XXXI.

The Apostolical Constitutions.

A SECOND expansion of the *Didache*, far more important and successful than the *Ecclesiastical Canons*, is the seventh Book of the Pseudo-Clementine *Apostolical Constitutions and Canons*, from the beginning or middle of the fourth century.†

---

* *L. c.*, p. 218. He gives as an argument that the term ἐπαρχίαι in the ecclesiastical sense is not used before A.D. 300. Bickell assigns the Canons to the beginning of the third century, Hilgenfeld and Lagarde, who identify it with the *Duæ Viæ* or *Judicium Petri*, to the end of the second (H. wrongly to Asia Minor, an account of the prominence given to John), Böhmer to a still earlier date (160), but Pitra, Krawutzcky, and Bryennios to the fourth century, Pitra as late as c. 381.

† Ed. princeps in Greek by Francis Turrian, Venice, 1563, and of the Latin interpretation by Bovius, Venice, 1563; then in Greek and Latin by Cotelier, *Patres Apost.*; also in Mansi's *Concilia;* Harduin's *Conc.;* Migne's *Patrol.* tom. i. 509 sqq. (a reprint of Cotelier, Gr and Lat.) Best critical editions of the Greek text only by Ueltzen (Rostock, 1853), and Paul de Lagarde (Lipsiæ et Londoni. 1862). English translation by William Whiston (a very able and learned, but eccentric divine and mathematician, professor at Cambridge, expelled for Arianism, d. 1742), in "Primitive Christianity revived," London, 1712, second vol. (*The Constitutions of the Apostles, by Clement, Greek and English*). In a third volume he tried to prove that these Constitutions "are the most sacred of the canonical books of the New Test." His translation, as amended by James Donaldson, is published in Clark's "Ante-Nicene Library," vol. xvii. (Edinb. 1870). The seventh Book from ch i.–xxxii., which runs parallel with the *Did.*, has also been reprinted by Bryennios in his Prolegomena (§ Σ', σελ. λζ'–ν', from Ueltzen's text), and by Harnack (pp. 178-192, from Lagarde's text, with comparative critical notes).

THE APOSTOLICAL CONSTITUTIONS. 138

This work, consisting of eight books, is a complete manual of catechetical instruction, public worship, and church discipline for the use of the clergy. It is, as to its form, a literary fiction, and professes to be a bequest of all the Apostles, handed down through the Roman Bishop Clement, the pupil of Paul and successor to Peter.* It begins with the words: "The Apostles and Elders to all who among the nations have believed in the Lord Jesus Christ. Grace and peace from Almighty God, through our Lord Jesus Christ, be multiplied unto you in the acknowledgment of Him." In the eighth book the individual Apostles are introduced by name with their ordinances;† while in the other books they speak as a body. It has long since been proven to be pseudo-Apostolical, and hence has no authority; but as an historical document it is very important and valuable. It is a mirror of the moral and religious condition of the Church in the third and fourth centuries.‡ It abounds in repetitions and Scripture quotations often arbitrarily selected. The tone is very pious and churchly. The style is diffuse and contrasts unfavorably with the terse sententiousness of the *Didache.*

The Constitutions consist of three parts, which are mechanically thrown together by the compiler of the last part.

So also in Doc. VII. of this book. For the literature on the Apost. Const. and Can. see *Church History* ii. 183 sqq.

* The first editors, Turrian and Bovius, had no doubt of its Apostolic origin, and Whiston even believed that Christ himself had given these instructions during the forty days between the resurrection and ascension. But Baronius pronounced the Constitutions apocryphal, or at all events interpolated, and Daillé (*De Pseudepigraphis Apostolicis s. Libris octo Constit. Ap. apocryph. libri iii.* Harderv. 1653) proved the forgery, which, however, must not be judged according to the modern standard of literary honesty. See Bickell, i. 69 sq.

† In the order given vi. 14: Peter and Andrew; James and John, sons of Zebedee; Philip and Bartholomew; Thomas and Matthew; James the son of Alphæus, and Lebbæus (Thaddæus); Simon the Canaæan and Matthias; James the Brother of the Lord and Bishop of Jerusalem; and Paul, the teacher of the Gentiles, the chosen vessel. The order is the same as in Matt. x. 2, except that Matthias is substituted for Judas Iscariot, and James the Brother of the Lord, and Paul are added.

‡ Von Drey and Krawutzcky call the first part of the seventh book a *Sittenspiegel.*

1. The first six books are often mentioned under the separate name of *Didascalia* or *Catholic Didascalia*.* They exist separately in Syriac, Æthiopic and Arabic MSS., and conclude with a doxology and Amen. The first book contains a system of morals for the laity; the second the duties of the clergy, Bishops, Priests and Deacons; the third treats of widows, of Baptism and Ordination; the fourth, of the care of orphans, of charity to the poor, of the duties of parents and children, of servants and masters; the fifth, of the imitation of Christ in suffering, of Stephen the first martyr, of fasts and feasts and the great passover week; the sixth, of schisms and heresies, of matrimony and celibacy, of the ritual laws and observances.

2. The seventh book, of which we shall speak presently, repeats the principles and maxims of Christian morality, treats of ordinations, and gives long forms of prayer.

3. The eighth book treats of spiritual gifts and ordinations, of first fruits and tithes, and contains a number of liturgical prayers. At the close are added 85 Apostolical Canons; the last of them gives a list of the canonical books of the Old and New Testaments including two Epistles of Clement of Rome, and "the Constitutions dedicated to you the Bishops by me Clement, in eight books." This is the first reference to the compilation.

The work is evidently a gradual growth of traditions and usages of the first three centuries. It originated in Syria, at all events in the East (for Peter and Rome are not made prominent), and assumed its present collected shape in the beginning of the fourth century, or during the Nicene age. The first six books agree in many passages with the larger Greek recension of the Ignatian Epistles.† Archbishop Ussher suggested that the two compilations are the product of the same author. Dr. Harnack, the latest investigator of the intricate question, takes the same view, and by a critical analysis and comparison comes to the conclusion that Pseudo-Clement, *alias* Pseudo-Ignatius, was a Eusebian or semi-Arian, and rather worldly-minded, anti-

---

* In i. 1; ii. 39; vi. 14, 18.

† Bickell gives a list of resemblances in his *Geschichte des Kirchenrechts*, i. 58 sq. See also Zahn, *Ignatius von Antiochien*, p. 144 sqq.

ascetic Bishop of Syria, a friend of the Emperor Constantius, between 340 and 360, that he enlarged and adapted the *Didascalia* of the third, and the *Didache* of the second century, as well as the Ignatian Epistles, to his own views of morals, worship and discipline, and clothed them with Apostolic authority.*

The Apostolical Constitutions were condemned by the Trullan Synod (Concilium Quinisextum), A.D. 692, because of heretical (semi-Arian) interpolations, but the 85 Canons of the Apostles were sanctioned as genuine and valid. Patriarch Photius, of Constantinople, the most learned divine of the ninth century, mentions this censure but passes a more favorable judgment.† The book continued to be highly esteemed and used in the Oriental churches as the chief basis for ecclesiastical legislation, but was little known in the West, which acknowledged only 50 of the Apostolical Canons.‡ The Constitutions were for the ancient Greek church what the Decretals of Pseudo-Isidor became for the Roman church in the dark ages.

We must now consider more particularly the relation of the *Constitutions* to the *Didache*. This is confined to the first 32 chapters of the seventh book. Here the *Didache* is embodied almost word for word, but with significant omissions, alterations and additions, which betray a later age. The agreement, as far as it goes, is a strong support for the purity of our text of the *Didache*.

The moral part of the *Didache* (I.-VI.) is almost wholly retained, but interwoven with Scripture passages and examples. The right to baptize (Ch. VII.) is confined to the clergy, and the act surrounded with additions of holy oil and perfume. Long prayers and confessions are put into the mouth of the catechumens, and a close line of distinction is drawn between two parts of public worship, one for the catechumens, and one

---

* See his book on the *Didache*, pp. 246–268. Holtzmann accepts this result, but Zahn and Funk dissent, though differing again among themselves. Zahn charges Pseudo-Ignatius with semi-Arianism (herein agreeing with Harnack), Funk with Appollinarianism. Lightfoot (*S. Ignat.* i. 258): "He leans to the side of Arianism, though without definitely crossing the border."

† *Biblioth.* cod. 112, 113. ‡ See Bickell, *l. c.* i. 71–86.

for the baptized. The eucharistic prayers of Chs. IX. and X. are greatly enlarged, and a full liturgical service is substituted for the free prayers of the Prophets. The phrase " after being filled " (X. 1), which refers to the Agape in connection with the Eucharist, is changed into " after participation " in the sacramental elements. The chapters on the wandering Apostles and inspired Prophets (XI. and XII.) are entirely omitted. Presbyters are inserted between the Bishops and Deacons (XV.) as a separate order, and Bishops are no more local officers, but diocesans and successors of the Apostles. In the eschatalogical chapter (XVI.) a general resurrection is substituted for the particular resurrection of the saints. The Bishops are designated "Chief Priests," the Presbyters "Priests" (ἱερεῖς), the Deacons "Levites;" tithes are exacted in support of the clergy; the clergy are separated from the laity, and the whole Jewish hierarchy is reproduced on Christian soil. In short, the *Constitutions* are an adaptation of the simple post-Apostolic Christianity of the *Didache* to the sacerdotal and hierarchical ecclesiasticism of the Nicene age.

The *Didache* was thus superseded by a more complete and timely Church Manual, and disappeared. As soon as it was rediscovered, scholars recognized it with great delight as the source of the Seventh Book of the Apostolical Constitutions.

But there was one dissenting voice from an unexpected quarter. Two years before the publication of the *Didache*, a Roman Catholic scholar, Dr. Krawutzcky, of Breslau, had made an ingenious attempt to reconstruct, from the Seventh Book of the Constitutions, the Apostolic Church Order, and the Epistle of Barnabas, an older and simpler document which is mentioned by Rufinus and Jerome under the title, "The Two Ways," or "The Judgment of Peter." His restoration turns out to agree essentially with the first or catechetical part of the *Didache*, and does great credit to his critical sagacity.*

---

† " *Ueber das altkirchliche Unterrichtsbuch* '*Die zwei Wege oder die Entscheidung des Petrus,*'" in the Tübingen " Theolog. Quartalschrift " (Rom. Cath.) for 1882. Heft III. pp. 359-445. The restoration of what he regards as the original text is given from p. 433-445. Harnack states the results of Krawutzcky (he always inadvertently omits the c of his name), and calls his

But since the discovery he refuses to acknowledge the result. He is not satisfied with the theology of the *Didache*, because it does not come up to the orthodox churchmanship of Peter, and he assigns it, as we have already seen, to an Ebionitizing source, after 150.* He assumes that the author of the *Didache*, besides the Old Testament and the apocryphal Gospel according to the Hebrews, made use of Barnabas, and especially of a much better book on " The Two Ways," which was issued under the high authority of Peter (hence also called " The Judgment of Peter ") and which was quoted as Scripture by Clement of Alexandria, but is now lost. The *Didache* had also a polemical reference to the " Second Ordinances of the Apostles " concerning the establishment of the eucharistic sacrifice. The Latin fragment of the *Doctrina Apostolorum* is probably a different recension of the *Didache*, likewise based upon " The Two Ways," with the use of Barnabas.

But this is an airy hypothesis. Until that mysterious "Judgment of Peter" is found by some future Bryennios, it is safe to believe that the "Teaching of the Twelve Apostles," now happily recovered from the dust of ages, is or includes that very book on "The Two Ways" or "The Judgment of Peter," spoken of by Rufinus and Jerome; and that it is the book which Clement of Alexandria quoted as Scripture which was placed among the New Testament Apocrypha by Eusebius, which was used in orthodox churches as a manual of catechetical instruction at the time of Athanasius, and which was enlarged, adapted and superseded by the Syrian compilation of the Apostolical Constitutions, wherein it has been laid imbedded until, in 1883, it was brought to light in its original simplicity and integrity.

---

essay "a critical masterpiece such as there are but few in the history of literary criticism " (p. 208). Brown (in the second ed. of H. and B) gives the restoration in English as "a brilliant example of legitimate and successful higher criticism," and indicates by distinct type the divergences from the actual *Teaching*. pp. lxix.-lxxiv. Neither Harnack nor Brown could anticipate the second paper of Krawutzcky.

* See his essay in the same Tübingen Quarterly for 1884, No. IV. 547–606, which we have noticed on p. 23 sq., and p. 86. In a private letter to the author, Aug. 25, 1885, Dr. Kr. somewhat modifies his view, and hence I put the date back from 200 to 150.

CHAPTER XXXII.

Lessons of the Didache.

THE *Didache* has no more authority than any other post-Apostolic writing. The truths it contains and the duties it enjoins are independently known to us from the Scriptures, and are binding upon us as revelations of Christ and his Apostles. It is not free from superstitious notions and mechanical practices which are foreign to Apostolic wisdom and freedom. Its value is historical and historical only, but this is very considerable, and exceeds that of any known post-Apostolic document. It touches upon a greater variety of topics than any of the Apostolic Fathers, so-called, and gives us a clearer insight into the condition of the Church in the transition period between A. D. 70 and 150.

The following is a summary of the lessons of the *Didache* as regards the state of Christianity in that part of the East where the author resided.

1. Catechetical instruction was required as a preparation for church membership.

2. That instruction was chiefly moral and practical, and based upon the Decalogue and the Sermon on the Mount. No doubt, it included also the main facts in the life of Christ; for the document assumes throughout faith in Christ as our Lord and Saviour, and repeatedly refers to his Gospel.

3. The moral code was of the highest order, far above that of any other religion or school of philosophy. It was summed up in the two royal commandments of supreme love to God and love to our neighbor, as explained by the teaching and example of Christ. It emphasized purity, gentleness, humility, and charity. The superior morality of Christianity in theory and practice carried in it the guarantee of its ultimate victory.

4. Baptism was the rite of initiation into church membership, and was usually administered by trine immersion in a river (in imitation of Christ's Baptism in the Jordan), but with a margin for freedom as to the quality of water and the mode of its application; and threefold aspersion of the head

was allowed as legitimate Baptism in case of scarcity of the element. Fasting before the act was required, but no oil, salt, or exorcism, or any other material or ceremony is mentioned.

5. The Eucharist was celebrated every Lord's Day in connection with the Agape (as at Corinth in the time of Paul), and consisted of a fraternal meal, thanksgivings and free prayers for the temporal and spiritual mercies of God in Christ. It was regarded as the Christian sacrifice of thanksgiving to be offered everywhere and to the end of time, according to the prophecy of Malachi.

6. There were no other sacraments but these two. At least none is even hinted at.

7. The Lord's Prayer with the doxology was repeated three times a day. This, together with the Eucharistic prayers, constituted the primitive liturgy; but freedom was given to the Prophets to pray from the heart in public worship.

8. The first day of the week was celebrated as the Lord's Day (in commemoration of his resurrection), by public worship and the Eucharist; and Wednesday and Friday were observed as days of fasting (in commemoration of the Passion).

9. The Church at large was extended and governed by travelling Apostles (or Evangelists), who carried the Gospel to unknown parts, and by Prophets either itinerant or stationary, who instructed, comforted and revived the converts; while the local congregations were governed by Bishops (or Presbyters) and Deacons, elected and supported by the Christian people.

10. Several books of the New Testament, especially the Gospel of Matthew, were more or less known, and their authority recognized, but there was as yet no settled canon of the Scriptures, and the quotations and reminiscences were more from living teaching than from written books.

11. Outside of the Gospel tradition nothing of any importance was known concerning Christ and the Apostles. The *Didache* mentions only one extra-canonical sentence, of uncertain authorship (I. 6.), possibly a reported saying of our Lord, but it adds nothing of consequence to the twenty-three

sentences which tradition ascribes to Him.* As Bishop Lightfoot says, "All the evangelical matter, so far as we can trace it, is found within the four corners of our canonical Gospels."

12. Christians are to live in prayerful expectation of the glorious coming of Christ and to keep themselves always in readiness for it.

These lessons are important, and yet very meagre when compared with the overflowing fulness and unfathomable depth of the real teaching of Christ through the Apostles in our Gospels and Epistles. Genius does not often propagate itself: Socrates, Plato, Alexander the Great, Charlemagne, Luther, Calvin, Shakespeare, Cromwell, Goethe, left no successors. Periods of great excitement and creative power are followed by periods of repose or decline. The intellectual inferiority of the Apostolic Fathers, even Clement, Ignatius, and Polycarp, need not surprise us. The Apostles' spirit and temper are there, but the Apostolic genius and inspiration are gone. The post-Apostolic writings are only a faint echo of the Gospels and Epistles, the last rays of the setting sun of a glorious day. The Church had to descend from the Tabor heights of transfiguration to the plain of every-day life and conflict.

The *Didache* makes no exception. It adds—and this is its best lesson—one more irrefutable argument for the infinite superiority of the New Testament over all ecclesiastical literature,—a superiority which can only be rationally explained by the fact of Divine inspiration.

CHAPTER XXXIII.

The Didache Literature.

Comp. the two Appendices, pp. 297-318.

THE literature on the *Didache*, considering the short time which has elapsed since its first publication in December, 1883,

---

* These have been collected by Fabricius, Grabe, Anger, Westcott, and in my *Church Hist.* (revised ed.) vol. i. 162-167. The only one of real importance and great beauty, is guaranteed as authentic by the authority of St. Paul, Acts xx. 35.

or we may say (as far as actual knowledge in the West is concerned) since February, 1884, is unusually large. Germany, England, and America have run a race of honorable rivalry in editions, translations, and comments, and given proof of the solidarity of the republic of Christian letters from the distant East to the limits of the West. The *Didache* has travelled in its mission on the wings of the printing-press from the Jerusalem Monastery, "ἐπὶ τὸ τέρμα τῆς δύσεως," to the extreme end of the West, as Clement of Rome, in a far narrower sense, says of Paul's journeys.

I furnished, a few months ago, for the second edition of Drs. Hitchcock and Brown, a *Digest of the Didache Literature* which covers thirteen pages (65-77). The list I now offer is partly abridged, partly enlarged, and differently arranged. I have omitted the articles in weekly newspapers, which are too numerous to mention, and mostly short, ephemeral and inaccessible (though some of them are of exceptional interest, as notably those in the London "Guardian" and the New York "Independent"); but I have added, on the other hand, a number of important titles which have reached me only within the last weeks, after the greater part of this monograph was in type. The principal works have been referred to already in the preceding chapters, but it will be convenient for the reader to have them all collected here with a summary of their contents. The list does not pretend to be complete, but it is far more complete than any yet published.

I.—Editio Princeps, Constantinople.

Bryennios, Philotheos (Metropolitan of Nicomedia and D.D. from Edinburgh University, 1884): Διδαχὴ | τῶν | δώδεκα Ἀποστόλων | ἐκ τοῦ ἱεροσολυμιτικοῦ χειρογραφου | νῦν πρῶτον ἐκδιδομένη | μετὰ προλεγομένων καὶ σημειώσεων | . . . ὑπὸ | Φιλοθέου Βρυεννίου | μητροπολίτου Νικομηδείας. | ἐν Κωνσταντινοπόλει | 1883. (Teaching of the Twelve Apostles, *from the Jerusalem manuscript, now published for the first time, with Prolegomena and Notes, together with a collation and unpublished part of the Synopsis of the Old Testament by John Chrysostom, from the same manuscript. By* Philotheos Bryennios, *Metropolitan of Nicomedia.* Constantinople, printed by S. I. Boutyra, 1883. The title page has also a motto from Clemens Alex., *Strom.* lib. vi. p. 647 ; "We must not ignorantly condemn what is said on account of him who says it . . . but we must examine it to see if it keep by the truth." εἰ τῆς ἀληθείας ἔχεται.

This is a careful transcript (with a few textual emendations) of the Jerusalem MS., the only one known to exist, and never copied since.* It is therefore the parent of all other editions. There can be no doubt of its accuracy. Br. is an expert in reading old Greek MSS., and thoroughly at home in biblical and patristic literature. Seldom has an *editio princeps* of any book appeared with such thorough preparation and such a just estimate of its value. The work contains 149 pages Prolegomena and 55 pages text with notes, to which are added indexes and corrigenda (pp. 57-75). The first part of the Prolegomena is devoted to the *Didache* itself ; the second part contains corrections and additions to the Epistles of Clemens Rom. and Barnabas, Chrysostom's Synopsis of the Old Testament, and other matter from the Jerusalem (Constantinopolitan) MS. Br. assigns the *Did.* to a Jewish convert, A.D. 120-160 (much too late), illustrates it by ample quotations from Scripture and early ecclesiastical writers, and discusses its relation to Barnabas, Hermas, the Ecclesiastical Canons, and the Apostolical Constitutions. He covers nearly the whole ground, answering many questions and raising new ones. In a conversation with Prof. Edmund A. Grosvenor, of Robert College, Constantinople, published in the New York "Independent" for Oct. 16, 1884, Bryennios expressed his view on the value of the *Teaching* to the effect that the first six chapters, which enforce duties and prohibit sins and crimes, must be regarded as coming from the Lord through the Apostles, and therefore as binding, but that the last ten chapters, which consist mainly of liturgical and ecclesiastical ordinances, "have no authority whatever, except so far as the writer happens to be correct in his injunctions." How far he was correct in these injunctions, the Bishop says we cannot know. He went on to say : "Christ did not formulate a system. He gave only a faith ; and the Apostles did hardly more." . . . "There is all the difference between the two parts, of inspiration on the one side, and of human compilation and contrivance on the other."

Comp. an article of BRYENNIOS, περὶ τῆς Διδαχῆς τ. δώδ. ἀποστ. in the 'Ἐκκλησιαστικὴ Ἀλήθεια, Constant. 1884, 10 (22) νοεμ. p. 51ᵇ–57ᵇ ; a brief letter in the "Andover Review" for June, 1884, pp. 662-663 ; and his autobiographical sketch at the close of this book. Also Prof. EDMUND A. GROSVENOR : *An interview with Bishop Bryennios*, in the "Andover Review" for Nov. 1884, pp. 515-516, and his sketch of Br. in the "Century Monthly Magazine," N. York, for May, 1885, pp. 167-171 ; PHILIP SCHAFF : *Philotheos Bryennios* in "The Independent" for April 16, 1885, and in "Harper's Weekly" for April 25, 1885.

BAPHEIDES, PHILARETOS (successor of Bryennios as Professor in the Patriarchal Seminary at Chalce) : a review of the ed. of Bryennios in the 'Ἐκκλησιαστικὴ Ἀλήθεια, Constant., Jan. ½, 1884.

He is inclined to date the *Did.* at about the year 100. This I learn from the "Theol. Literaturzeitung" for Feb. 23, 1884 (No. IV. fol. 104).

---

* See p. 310 for a notice of the fac-simile edition of Harris,

II.—German Editions, Translations, and Discussions.

BESTMANN, DR. H. J.: *Geschichte der christlichen Sitte.* Theil. II. Nördlingen, 1885, pp. 136-153.

The *Did.* was written at Antioch soon after the destruction of Jerusalem and issued as a church programme by the Jewish-Christian (Petrine) party with the view to gain the Gentile-Christian (Pauline) party (comp. Gal. ii.) to their conservatism, but was answered by the Hellenic brethren in the Epistle of Barnabas with a vigorous protest against Judaism, yet with an appended Irenicum in matters of practical morality. (*Geistreich*, but not *stichhaltig*.)—In a notice of Harnack, in Luthardt's "Theol. Literaturblatt" for Jan. 8, 1885 (col. 53-55), Bestmann denies that the *Did.* favors an ascetic tendency which ultimately produced the monastic system. "The yoke of the Lord" (vi. 2) is not celibacy, as Ha. holds, but the ceremonial law.

BICKELL, GEORG (Dr. and Prof. in the R. Cath. University of Innsbruck): *Die neuentdeckte "Lehre der Apostel" und die Liturgie.* In the "Zeitschrift für Kathol. Theologie." Innsbruck, 1884, Jahrgang VIII. Heft II. pp. 400-412.

Dr. B. (a convert to the Roman Cath. Church) regards the *Didache* as the source of the "Apostolic Church Order" (first edited in Greek by his father who was a Protestant), and of the seventh book of the "Apost. Constitutions," and puts it at the beginning of the second century, if not earlier. He finds in it the doctrine of purgatory (Ch. I. 5; comp. Matt. v. 26), of the dis-. tinction between good works commanded and good works recommended (Ch. VI 2), and of the sacrifice of the mass (Chs. IX., X., XIV.). In his article *Liturgie*, in the R. C. "Real-Encyclopædie der Christl. Alterthümer," ed. by F. X. Kraus, Freiburg i. B. 1885, p. 310 sqq., Bickell assigns the *Did.* to the end of the first century. It is not yet touched by Pauline and Johannean ideas (?), and is the source of Barnabas. The eucharistic prayers agree closely with the eulogiæ of the Jewish Paschal Ritual, and enable us to reconstruct the liturgy as it stood between the founding of the Church and the age of Justin Martyr. The thanksgivings in Chs. IX. and X. give the oldest forms of the ante-communion and post-communion prayers.

BIELENSTEIN, Pastor Dr. A.: *Warum enthält die Διδαχὴ τῶν δώ- δεκα ἀποστόλων nichts Lehrhaftes?* Riga (Russia), 1885. Reprinted from the "*Mittheilungen und Nachrichten für die Evang. Kirche in Russland*," for Feb. and March, 1885. 8 pp. Reviewed by Dr. Th. Zahn in Luthardt's "Theolog. Literaturblatt," Leipzig, for April 3, 1885, col. 123 sq.

I know this brochure only from the brief notice of Zahn, who agrees with its answer to the question why the *Did.* contains no doctrines. It is on account of its fragmentary character and immediate practical object in cate-chetical instruction. The words ταῦτα πάντα προειπόντες in vii. 1 refer to a brief address, introductory to the baptismal act, not to a long preceding instruction. The first six chapters point to the negative and positive baptismal vow (the ἀποταγή and συνταγή), which was no doubt connected with Baptism from the beginning.

BONWETSCH, G. N. (Prof. in Dorpat): *Die Prophetie im apost. und nach-apost. Zeitalter, in* Luthardt's "Zeitschrift," Leipz., 1884, Heft VIII. pp. 408-423; Heft IX. 460 sqq.

He puts the *Didache* between 100 and 125, and explains the prophetic office.

CASSEL, PAUL: Notice in "Sunem," No. 25, 1884.

FRIEDBERG, DR. EMIL (Prof. in Leipzig, author of *Lehrbuch des katholischen und evangelischen Kirchenrechts*, secd. ed. Leipz. 1884): *Die älteste Ordnung der christlichen Kirche*, in the "Zeitschrift für Kirchenrecht," xix. 4 (1884), pp. 408–425. (I could not procure this essay, which is probably important.)

FUNK, F. X. (Dr. and R. Cath. Prof. of Ch. Hist. in Tübingen): *Die Doctrina Apostolorum*. In the "Theol. Quartalschrift," Tübingen, 1884, No. III. pp. 381–402.

German translation and discussion. F. assigns the *Did.* to the first century and before Barnabas, and regards it as the oldest post-Apostolic book. He traces it to Egypt. In the same Quarterly for 1885, No. 1. pp. 159–167, Dr. Funk criticizes the editions of Hilgenfeld, Wünsche, and Harnack. He rejects Hilgenfeld's view of the Montanistic bias of the *Did.* He maintains against Harnack the priority of the *Did.* over Barn. and Hermas, denies the identity of Pseudo-Clement and Pseudo-Ignatius, and the semi-Arianism of the Apost. Const., and charges Ha. with several blunders. He says nothing about Krawutzcky's first paper, but notices it in the "Lit. Rundschau," Freiburg, Oct. 1884.

HARNACK, ADOLF (Dr. and Prof. of Church History in Giessen): *Die Lehre der zwölf Apostel nebst Untersuchungen zur ältesten Geschichte der Kirchenverfassung und des Kirchenrechts* (including an appendix by Oscar von Gebhardt). In "Texte und Untersuchungen zur Geschichte der altchristl. Literatur," herausgeg. von Oscar von Gebhardt und Ad. Harnack. Band II. Heft I., 1884 (July). Leipzig (J. C. Hinrichs'sche Buchhandlung).

The Gr. text and Germ. trans. with notes, pages 70; Prolegomena, pages 294. The most elaborate work on the *Didache*. The author directed early attention to it in Germany, and gave a translation of Chaps. VII.–XVI. in the "Theol. Literaturzeitung" for February 3, 1884. He maintains that the *Did.* was composed in Egypt between A.D. 120 and 165; that the author made use of Barnabas and Hermas; that one and the same writer interpolated the *Apostolical Constitutions* and the Ignatian Epistles, so that Pseudo-Clement and Pseudo-Ignatius are identical; and that this literary forger was a Syrian bishop of the semi-Arian party during the reign of Constantius. Comp. also "Theol. Literaturzeitung" ix. (1884) 2, 44; 3, 49–55; 14, 343–344; and Harnack's letter on the baptismal question in the New York "Independent" for February 19, 1885, and printed in this book on p. 50.

HILGENFELD, ADOLF (Dr. and Prof. in Jena): *Novum Test. extra canonem receptum. Fasc. iv. ed. ii. aucta et emendata.* Lips. (T. O. Weigel) 1884, pp. 87–121.

The Greek text with critical notes and conjectural readings. The same volume contains the fragments of the Gospel according to the Hebrews, the Preaching and Acts of Peter and Paul, the Apocalypse of Peter, the *Didascalia Apost.*, the *Duæ Viæ* or *Judicium Petri*. HILGENFELD wrote also a notice of the *Didache* in his "Zeitschrift für wissenschaftl. Theologie," Leipzig, 1884, pp. 366–371, a more elaborate one in the same periodical for 1885, Erstes Heft, pp. 73–102. He regards the *Did.* as a link between the Ep. of Barnabas (c. xviii.

—xx.) and the seventh book of the Apost. Const. (i.-xxi.), and assumes that it is in its present shape a later adaptation of the original doctrine of the *Duœ Viœ* to the use of Montanism after the middle of the second century. He defends this view at length against Harnack, who maintains the unity and integrity of the treatise (see his notice of Hilgenfeld in the "Theol. Lit. Ztg." for 1884, No. 14, col. 342).

HOLTZMANN, H. (Dr. and Prof. in Strassburg): *Die Didache und ihre Nebenformen*, in the "Jahrbücher für Protest. Theologie" (Leipzig) for 1885, Heft I. pp. 154-167.

A critical discussion of the relation of the *Didache* to Barnabas, Hermas, the Ecclesiastical Canons of the Ap., and the seventh Book of the Apost. Constitutions. H. accepts Harnack's view of the identity of Pseudo-Ignatius and Pseudo-Clement, who was a semi-Arian clergyman and made use of the *Didache* und the Ecclesiast. Canons, but he differs from him as regards the relation of the *Didache* to the cognate documents. He regards the *Didache* and Barnabas as two co-ordinate recensions of the allegory of the Two Ways or the Judicium Petri, which is lost. He also briefly reviewed Harnack's book, very favorably, in the "Deutsche Literaturzeitung," Berlin, Oct. 4, 1884, p. 1452, but without adding anything new.

KRAWUTZCKY, ADAM (Dr. and Rom. Cath. Subregens in Breslau): *Ueber die sog. Zwölfapostellehre, ihre hauptsächlichsten Quellen und ihre erste Aufnahme*, in the "Theol. Quartalschrift," Tübingen, 1884, No. IV., pp. 547-606.

Kr. derives the *Didache* from the Gospel of the Hebrews, from the *Duœ Viœ* or *Judicium Petri* (Rufinus. *In Symb. Apost.* c. xxxviii., and Jerome, *De viris ill.* c. i.), from the Ep. of Barnabas (chs. xviii.-xx.), and the Pastor of Hermas, and assigns it to an Ebionite heretic after the middle of the second century. This novel view, if proven, would materially diminish the value of the *Didache*. In a previous article in the same Quarterly (1882, No. III., pp. 433-445), Dr. Kr. had made a critical attempt to reconstruct, from the *Apost. Church Order*, the Seventh Book of the *Apost. Constitutions*, and the Ep. of Barnabas, the lost book, *Judicium Petri*, but declines now to accept the *Didache* as this original, although the results of his sagacious restoration agree substantially with the *Didache* as since published. He thinks that the seventh book of the *Ap. Const.* and the Latin *Doctrina Apost.*, a fragment of which was published by von Gebhardt, were rectifications of the *Didache*.

LANGEN, JOSEPH (Dr. and Old Catholic Professor in Bonn): *Das älteste christliche Kirchenbuch*, in von Sybel's "Historische Zeitschrift," München and Leipzig. 1885, Zweites Heft, pp. 193-214.

The most important discovery since that of the *Philosophumena* in 1842. Bryennios has already finally disposed of several questions and suggested others. The *Didache* presupposes a state of the Church in the first century rather than in the second. It is older than the Ecclesiast. Canons, older than Hermas, older than Barnabas (written during the reign of Nerva), and proceeded probably from the Jewish Christian Church of Jerusalem about A.D. 90, for the promotion of missions among the heathen. (I had reached similar conclusions before I saw this short but judicious paper of Dr.

Langen, who is well known by his *History of the Roman Church*, to Leo I., 1881, and from Leo I. to Nicolas I., 1885, 2 vols.; his History of the *Trinitarian Controversy*, between the Greek and Latin churches, 1876, etc.).

LIPSIUS, RICHARD ADELBERT (Dr. and Prof. of Theol. in Jena): (1) A review of Bryennios' ed. in the "Deutsche Literaturzeitung," ed. by M. Rödiger, Berlin. Jahrgang V. No. 40 (Oct. 4, 1884), p. 1449-'51.

The *Did.* goes far back to the first half of the second century, but is probably a composite production. The recension of the Two Ways is older than any hitherto known. The eucharistic section is "*grossentheils uralt*," but the baptismal direction about pouring water instead of immersion excites suspicion as a later interpolation. (No reason is given.) L. regrets that Bryennios did not use Lagarde's ed. of the Syriac $διδασκαλία$, which seems to be the basis of the first six books of the Apost. Const.

(2) In his more recent notice of Harnack's book, in Zarncke's "Liter. Centralblatt," Jan. 24, 1885, No. V. (signed Ψ), Lipsius agrees with Harnack in his view of the age between 140-165, but doubts the Egyptian origin, and denies the use of the Gospel of John in the eucharistic prayers. The "vine of David" (ix. 2), has nothing to do with John xv. 1, but is the Church consecrated by the blood of the Son of David ("*die durch das Bundes-Blut des Davidssohnes geweihte ἐκκλησία*"). He incidentally rejects Krawutzcky's recent hypothesis as quite unfortunate ("*ganz unglücklich*").

(3) In a notice of Zahn's *Suppl. Clem.* in the same paper, No. VIII. (Feb. 14, 1885, p. 233), Lipsius agrees with Zahn against Harnack, that the *Did* is independent of Barnabas, but supposes that both drew from an older source, an unknown catechetical book on the Two Ways. He thinks that the *Did.* will long occupy the attention of scholars.

LUTHARDT, C. E. (Dr. and Prof. of Theol. in Leipzig): "Zeitschrift für kirchliche Wissenschaft und kirchliches Leben." Leipzig, 1884. Heft III., 139-141. Reprint of the Greek text.

NIRSCHL, J.: Review of Bryennios in "Lit. Handweiser" (R. C.), Mainz, 1884 No. 13.

PETERSEN (Pastor in Rellingen): *Die Lehre der zwölf Apostel. Mittheilungen über den handschriftlichen Fund des Metropoliten Philotheos Bryennios und Bemerkungen zu demselben.* Flensburg, 1884, 15 pages.

WÜNSCHE, AUG. (Lic. Dr.): *Lehre der zwölf Apostel. Nach der Ausgabe des Metropoliten Philotheos Bryennios. Mit Beifügung des Urtextes, nebst Einleitung und Noten ins Deutsche übertragen.* Leipzig (Otto Schulze), 1884, 34 pages. The second edition of the same year is slightly improved, but not enlarged.

ZAHN, THEOD. (Prof. of Theol. in Erlangen): *Forschungen zur Geschichte des N. T.-lichen Kanons und der altkirchl. Lit.* Erlangen (Deichert), 1884, Theil III. (*Supplementum Clementinum*), pp. 278-319. Comp. also his review of Harnack's work in Luthardt's "Theologisches Literaturblatt," Nos. 26 and 28, Leipzig, June 27 and July 11, 1884.

Dr. Zahn, one of the best patristic scholars of the age, assigns to the *Did.* its historic position in the post-Apostolic literature as originating in Egypt between A.D. 80-130. In the review of Harnack (which is unjustly unfavor able), he suggests several plausible emendations of the text and explains difficult passages (as the μυστήριον κοσμικόν, ch. xi.), in substantial agreement with Bryennios against Harnack.

ZÖCKLER, O. (Dr. and Prof. of Theol. in Greifswald): *Die L. der 12 Ap.* In his "Evang. Kirchenzeitung," Greifswald, 1884, Nos. 18 and 33.

III.—ENGLISH EDITIONS, TRANSLATIONS, AND DISCUSSIONS.

ADDIS, W. E.: notice of several editions of the *Did.* (by Bryennios, Wünsche, Harnack, Farrar, Hitchcock and Brown, and Hilgenfeld), in "The Dublin Review" (Rom. Cath.) for Oct. 1884, pp. 442–450.

A. speaks enthusiastically of the interest and importance of this discovery. He prefers the *Did.* "to all other remains of the age which followed that of the Apostles." It is marvellously complete, and gives a perfectly accurate picture of the ecclesiastical discipline and constitution of the first half of the second century. It is a compendium of Apostolic teaching, a "Summa" accepted by Christians in A.D. 140, but represents a state of things which had died out in the greater part of the Church. It was probably written in Egypt. It may be compared to the cathedral of St. Magnus in the capital of the Orkneys, which witnesses at this day the survival of the Norman architecture in that remote district long after it had ceased in England. The reviewer speaks highly of Harnack's book (he seems not to have seen Bryiennios'), and of Farrar's translation.

DE ROMESTIN, H., M.A. (Incumbent of Freeland, and Rural Dean): *The Teaching of the Twelve Apostles* (Διδ. τ. δώδ. Ἀπ.). *The Greek Text with Introduction, Translation, Notes, and Illustrative Passages.* Parker & Co., Oxford and London, 1884 (Oct.), 118 pages.

A very neat and handy little book for the use of students (in uniform style with Heurtley's *De Fide et Symbolo*, Waterland's *Athanasian Creed*, *The Canons of the Church*, St. Gregory's *Pastoral Rule*, etc.). It contains, after a brief introduction, the illustrative passages from Scripture, Barnabas, Hermas, the Ecclesiastical Canons, and Apostolical Constitutions, the *Didache*, in Greek and English with a few notes, and an index of the most noticeable words and phrases which occur in the *Did.* The writer has mostly used Bryennios and Harnack, but puts the book much earlier. "It may well be the oldest Christian writing after the books of the New Testament, perhaps even earlier than most of them" (p. 6). As to the locality, he hesitates between Asia Minor and Egypt.

FARRAR, DR. FREDERIC W. (Archdeacon of Westminster). *The Teaching of the Apostles.* In "The Contemporary Review" for May, 1884 (London), pp. 698–706. Two articles by the same in "The Expositor," ed. by Rev. Samuel Cox, London (Hodder and Stoughton), May, 1884, pp. 374–392, and August, 1884, pp. 81–91.

In "The Cont. Rev.," Dr. Farrar gives a translation with brief notes. In the first article of "The Expos.," he discusses the character and age of the *Didache*, which he assigns to about A.D. 100, prior to the Ep. of Barnabas and the Pastor of Hermas. In the second article, he treats of the bearing of

"The Teaching" on the Canon, and shows that the author was, like James, much influenced by the Sapiential literature of the Hebrews, that he certainly knew the Gospel of Matthew, probably also Luke, and possibly some other writings of the New Testament, as Romans and Thessalonians, though there is no positive evidence that he was acquainted either with Paul or John. "The object of the writer," he concludes (p. 89), "was very limited, and if he wrote either as a member of some small community or in some remote district, it is quite possible that Gospels and Epistles which were current in Italy, Egypt, and in Asia Minor, might not yet have fallen into his hands. The dissemination of all the sacred books was perhaps less rapid than we sometimes imagine, and we have abundant evidence that some of them only won their way slowly into general recognition."

GORDON, ALEXANDER: *Teaching of the Twelve Apostles*, in the "Modern Review" for July, 1884, pp. 446-480, with a postscript in the Oct. No. pp. 563-769.

The $\Delta\iota\delta$. τ. $\mathrm{A}\pi o\delta\tau$. spoken of by Athanasius must have been a much shorter treatise answering to the measurement of Nicephorus, but was probably the basis of the Jerusalem MS. of Leo. The germ of the work is the third pentecostal sermon of Peter, Acts, ii. 40-42: "Be ye saved from this *crooked* [*crookedness* is used by Barnabas of the Way of Death] generation. Then they that received his word were *baptized* . . . And they were steadfastly adhering to the *teaching of the Apostles*," etc. The *Did.* is younger than the Barnabas Ep. proper, but older than the Barnabas Appendix on the Two Ways (chs. xvii.-xx.); younger than Hermas, who is opposed to a stated maintenance of the Prophets, while the Didachographer "with his shrewd sense" corrects him. The *Didache* then is a compilation which Gordon thus stratifies: "First comes the Two Ways antithesis, in its simplest form, as in the *Epitome;* on the one hand, the two-fold precept, Love God and thy neighbor, this being the finger-post of the Way of Life; on the other hand, a negative rendering of the golden rule, Do *not* to another what thou wouldst *not* wish for thyself, this being the finger-post of the Way of Death. Secondly comes, from the Sermon on the Mount, and from the *Shepherd* as corrected, a commentary on the Way of Life. Thirdly, the parallel with the *Epitome* is resumed, in the words: 'Now a second commandment of the teaching;' and it is remarkable that what the *Epitome* gives as its expanded comment on the *negative* precept, is here presented as an alternative Version of the Way of Life. Fourthly, yet another of comment on the Way of Life is given, containing the rules about education and slaves, etc., unknown to the *Epitome;* at the close is a marked sign of late workmanship, $\dot{\varepsilon}\nu\ \dot{\varepsilon}\varkappa\varkappa\lambda\eta\sigma i\alpha$ for 'in church.' Lastly comes an account of the Way of Death, the prototype of that in the Barnabas appendix, unless we prefer to consider it as derived by both *Teaching* and Appendix from a common document." The second part or "the churchmanship section" is likewise a compilation, but older than the Apost. Const. with some traces of Western and probably of Ebionitic origin. It will be seen from this abstract that Gordon somewhat anticipated the views of Krawutzcky's second paper.

HAYMAN, Rev. H., D.D. (R. C.), in the "Dublin Review," No. XXV. Jan.,

1885, pp. 91-106. He divides the *Did.*, like Hilgenfeld (without naming him), in two parts at Ch. VII., but assigns it to the region of Thessalonica, where the Epistles to the Thessalonians were known.

H., E. L. [Rev. Edward Lee Hicks, Rector of Tenny Compton, late Fellow and Tutor of Corpus Christi College, Oxford]: Art. in the "Guardian" for June 25th, 1884.

An elaborate comparison, sentence by sentence, of the *Didache* with Barnabas, showing his inferiority in clearness of thought, vigor of language, and lucidity of arrangement, and his indebtedness to the *Didache* as the earlier document.

Lightfoot, J. B. (Bishop of Durham), a brief but suggestive notice in a paper on *Results of recent Historical and Topographical Research upon the Old and New Testament Scriptures*, read at the Carlisle Church Congress, Sept.-Oct., 1884. Published in the "Official Report," pp. 230-232, and reprinted as revised in "The Expositor," Jan., 1885, pp. 1-11.

He dates the *Didache* "with most English and some German critics, somewhere between A.D. 80-110," and assigns it, "with some probability," to Alexandria. He says: "Its interest and importance have far exceeded our highest expectations . . . Its chief value consists in the light it throws on the condition of the infant church. Remembering that the whole work occupies a little more than six octavo pages, we are surprised at the amount of testimony—certainly much more than we had any right to expect—which it bears to the Canon of the New Testament."

Plummer, Rev. Alfred, D.D. (Master of University College, Durham), in "The Churchman," London, for July, 1884, pp. 274, 275.

A valuable note showing the connection of the *Did.* with the writings of St. John.

Robertson, Rev. A., in the "Durham University Journal," for February, 1884, gave the first notice of the *Did.* in England.

Spence, Canon (Vicar of S. Pancras, London): *The Teaching of the Twelve Apostles; Διδαχη τῶν δώδεκα Ἀποστόλων. A translation with Notes and Excursus Illustrative of the " Teaching," and the Greek Text.* London (James Nisbet & Co.), 1885. pp. 183.

Translation with notes first, the Greek text at the end. Nine Excursuses on the early history of the *Did.*, the source and authorship (which is ascribed, p. 95, to Bishop Symeon of Jerusalem, the successor of James), its testimony to the Canon, the Apostles, Prophets, Bishops and Deacons, and a timely sermon on "The Old Paths," preached, June 22, 1881, by the Canon in St. Paul's Cathedral. He calls the *Did.* "A writing immeasurably inferior in heart-moving eloquence to the Epistle of St. James, and yet full of beauty and dignity," which "possesses a charm peculiarly its own, giving us a unique picture of the Christian society of the first days, with its special dangers and sublime hopes and sacramental safeguards, with its leaders and teachers still sharing in those spiritual gifts which . . . had not yet exhausted their divine influence" (p. 100).

Taylor, Rev. C.: *A lately discovered document, possibly of the first century, entitled " The Teaching of the Twelve Apostles, with illustrations from the Talmud.* Two Lectures delivered (not yet published) at the Royal Institution, London, after Easter, 1885. See p. 316.

V., E. [EDMUND VENABLES, Canon of Lincoln Cathedral]: *The Teachings of the Apostles,* in "The British Quarterly Review" for April, 1885, London (Hodder and Stoughton), pp. 333–370.

An elaborate review of Bryennios, Hilgenfeld, Harnack, Wünsche, De Romestin, Spence, and Lightfoot, concurring in Lightfoot's conclusions as to the value, character, time and place of composition. He regards (p. 369) the *Did.* as "the most remarkable addition to our knowledge of the sub-Apostolic age made since the publication of the *editio princeps* of St. Clement in 1633, the value of which cannot be too highly estimated. If its revelations are startling and unexpected, such as are calculated to disturb preconceived views on some points of considerable importance, it all the more deserves, and we are sure will receive, patient investigation and unprejudiced consideration from all who deserve the name of theologians and scholars. If it should turn out that it will compel us to give up some cherished convictions and accept some unwelcome conclusions, we may be thankful to be delivered from error, even at the cost of some pain. The full bearing of the discovery is as yet by no means fully appreciated. Much has yet to be done in studying it in connection with the remains of the contemporary Christian literature, scanty and fragmentary, alas! but still most precious." The author thinks that the *Did.* was written by a Jewish Christian of the milder and more conciliatory type, probably a Hellenist, possibly in Egypt, before the close of the first century. It is older than Barnabas and Hermas. The original source of all may have been an *oral* tradition on the *Two Ways,* used in catechetical instruction, quoted from memory. (This reminds one of Gieseler's *Traditions-Hypothese* for the solution of the Synoptical Gospel problem.)

"WESTMINSTER REVIEW" (ultra-liberal) for Jan., 1885, pp. 206–209.

A brief notice of several books on the *Did.,* which the writer thinks is very much over-estimated. It is "a sort of church catechism, intensely Jewish." The doctrine of the Two Ways is traced to "the duplex organization of the human brain" and the dualism of Ormazd and Ahriman. "Jesus of Nazareth was ever harping (sic!) on the same Jewish theme." The "golden rule had long been the property of mankind before Christians were heard of" (but only in its *negative* form).

WORDSWORTH, JOHN (Prof. of Theol. at Oxford): *Christian Life, Ritual, and Discipline at the Close of the first Century.* In "The Guardian," London, March 19, 1884. Supplement.

J. W. gives a summary of the contents of each chapter, with a version of the more important passages, and brief notes. He assigns the book to the last years of the first century or the beginning of the second, and suggests "some church of Greece or Macedonia" (Corinth, or Athens, or Philippi), as the place of composition.—Several articles by various Anglican writers appeared on the *Did.* in subsequent numbers of the "Guardian" for 1884. Among these must be mentioned those of Dr. Sadler (June 4th) and E. L. H. (June 25th). See II.

Brief notices by anonymous writers in "The Church Quarterly Review" (London) for April, 1884, pp. 213-217; in "The Foreign Church Chronicle and Review" (Rivingtons, London), for June 2, 1884, pp. 92-98 and 112-116 (translation and notice); by BOASE in the "The Academy," April 19, 1884; Prof. STOKES in "The Contemp. Rev.," April, 1884; May, 1885; etc.

IV.—AMERICAN EDITIONS AND WORKS.

BRYENNIOS MANUSCRIPT, *Three pages of the, reproduced by Photography for the Johns Hopkins University*, Baltimore. Publication Agency of the Johns Hopkins University, April, 1885. [Superseded; see p. 31 .]

Only 125 copies were printed. Preface by President D. C. Gilman three pages of photographs procured by Rev. Charles R. Hale, D.D., Baltimore, through official letters of introduction to the Patriarch of Jerusalem, Jan. 31, 1885, and three pages of explanation by Prof. J. Rendel Harris. The photographs include parts of Barnabas and Clement, the beginning of the *Did.*, catalogue of Old Testament Books, and last page of the Jerusalem MS. Prof. Harris states that he has verified by calculation the scribe's statement that the proper number of the Indiction is 9 in the first nine months of the year 1056, and that the eleventh of June was a Tuesday in that year.

CRAVEN, REV. DR. E. R. (of Newark, N. J.): article in "Journal of Christian Philosophy." See "*Teaching*" etc.

FITZGERALD, J.: *Teaching of the Twelve Apostles.* New York (John B. Alden), 1884.

The Greek text and English translation, and an introductory note of two pages, dated April 2, 1884.

GARDINER, DR. FREDERIC (Prof. in the Berkely Divinity School, Middletown, Ct.), and Mr. C. C. CAMP: *The recently discovered Apostolic Manuscript.*

A translation, published first in the New York "Churchman," March 29, 1884, and separately as a pamphlet, New York (James Pott & Co), 1884 (26 small pages).

HALL, E. EDWIN: *Teaching of the Twelve Apostles.* In "The New Englander," vol. vii. July, 1884, pp. 544-560.

A Comparison with the Coptic Canons, as translated in Bunsen's *Hippolytus and his Age*, vol. ii.

HALL, ISAAC H., and NAPIER, JOHN T.: Translation in "Sunday School Times," Philadelphia, 1884, April 5 and 12.

The translation (as Dr. H. Clay Trumbull, ed. of the "S S. Times," informed me by letter, April 16, 1885) is the joint production of the two gentlemen named; each having taken one-half, and both going over the whole together. See also Dr. Hall's art. in the "Journal of Christian Philosophy," quoted sub "*Teaching;*" and his review of Hitchcock and Brown, and Spence in the "Independent," for April 16, 1885.

HITCHCOCK, ROSWELL D., and BROWN, FRANCIS (Drs. and Professors in Union Theol. Seminary, New York). *Διδ. τ. δωδ. Απ. Teaching of the Twelve Apostles. Recently discovered and published by Philotheos Bryennios, Metropolitan of Nicomedia. Edited with a Translation, Introduction, and*

Notes. New York: Charles Scribner's Sons, 1884. Pages vi. 37. *A new edition revised and greatly enlarged.* N. Y. 1885. cxv. and 85 pages.

The first edition was issued a few days after the arrival of the first copy of the edition of Bryennios from Constantinople, *via* Leipzig, and had the unprecedented sale of nearly eight thousand copies in a few months. It was, however, prepared, as the writers say, "in great haste (March 17-25), in order to give speedy circulation to Bryennios' great discovery." The new edition was published March 25, 1885, with learned Prolegomena by Prof. Brown, (cxv. pages), a revision of the translation, pp. 2-29, by both editors, and valuable explanatory notes by Prof. Hitchcock, pp. 31-64, to which is added an Appendix by Prof. Schaff, pp. 65-77. Among the special features the editors (Preface, p. iv) point out the discussions on the integrity of the text, the relations between the *Did.* and kindred documents, with translations of these and of Krawutzcky's reproduction of "the Two Ways," on the peculiarities of the Greek Codex, the printed texts, and the recent literature. Dr. Hitchcock has also paid special attention to the vocabulary of the *Did.* as compared with that of the New Testament and the Septuagint.

LINCOLN, HEMAN (Prof. in Newton Theolog. Institution, Mass.): a notice in the "Bibliotheca Sacra" (now published at Oberlin, Ohio, formerly at Andover) for July, 1884, pp. 590-594; and a notice of Schaff, in the "Baptist Quarterly Review" for July, 1885. See p. 312.

LONG, PROF. J. C.: *Sources of the Teaching,* in the "Baptist Quarterly," July–Sept., 1884.

Puts the *Did.* as late as or later than the Apost. Const., *i. e.* in the fourth century. Impossible.

POTWIN, LEMUEL S. (Prof. in Adelbert College, Cleveland, Ohio): *The Vocabulary of the " Teaching of the Apostles."* In the "Bibliotheca Sacra," for Oct., 1884, pp. 800-817.

P. gives an alphabetical list of the words of the *Did.* that are not found in the N. T., with explanatory notes and references, compares the vocabulary of the *Did.* with that of Barnabas, and concludes that the last chapters of B. are a confused amplification of the first five chapters of the *Did.*

SCHAFF, Philip: *The Oldest Church Manual,* etc. New York, May, 1885; second ed., 1886; third ed., 1888. See note at the end of this chapter.

STARBUCK, REV. C. C., and SMYTH, Prof. EGBERT C., D.D. (Prof. of Church History in Andover Theol. Seminary): *Teaching of the Twelve Apostles.* Translation and Synopsis of the Introduction of Bryennios. In the "Andover Review" for April, 1884.

This article appeared almost simultaneously with the edition of Profs. Hitchcock and Brown, and likewise had a very large circulation.

SMYTH, EGBERT C.: *Baptism in the " Teaching" and in early Christian Art.* In the "Andover Review" for May, 1884, pp. 533-547.

TEACHING OF THE TWELVE APOSTLES. *Text and Translation together with Critical and Illustrative Papers by Eminent Scholars.* Reproduced from "The Journal of Christian Philosophy." New York (ed. and publ. by J. A. Paine, 30 Bible House), April, 1884. 84 pages.

Contents: Gr. text and trsl. by S. STANHOPE ORRIS; Genuineness, Priority,

Source and Value of the Teaching, by J. RENDEL HARRIS; Phraseology by ISAAC H. HALL; Comments by ELIJAH R. CRAVEN.

V.—FRENCH EDITIONS AND DISCUSSIONS.

BONET-MAURY, GASTON (Prof. in the Faculté de Théologie Protestante in Paris): *La doctrine des douze apôtres*, Paris (Fischbacher, 33 rue de Seine) 1884, 36 pages.

A good French translation with critical and historical notes, first published in the "Critique philosophique" and "Critique religieuse." Assigns the book to Egypt between 160 and 190, and agrees with Hilgenfeld that it has a Montanistic coloring. He sums up the result on page 36 as follows: "*C'est ainsi que nous nous représentons les destinées de ce petit livre qui, dès son apparition, a été salué par les acclamations des exégètes et des historiens, comme un témoin vénérable de l'Église du second siècle. . . . Pour nous, d'accord avec Mgr. Bryennios, et MM. Harnack et Hilgenfeld, nous conservons à la Didachè une place d'honneur entre le pasteur d'Hermas et les Homélies Clémentines. Elle nous offre, en son ensemble, un monument authentique de ce christianisme essentiellement moral, qui éclate dans des Évangiles synoptiques et s'était conservé au sein des judéo—chrétiens d'Égypte et de Palestine.*"

DUCHESNE, Abbé LOUIS, notice in "Bulletin Critique," Paris, 1884, Nos. 5, 17, 19. Massebieau says: "un court et bon article."

MASSEBIEAU, L. (Prof. in the Faculty of Protest. Theol. in Paris): *L'enseignement des douze apôtres*, Paris (Ernest Leroux), 1884, 36 pages [from "Revue de l'Hist. des Religions," Sept.-Oct. 1884]. Also: *Communications sur la Didachè*, in "Témoignage" of 7 février, 1885.

He briefly but ably discusses the contents of the *Did.*. and assigns it to Rome at the end of the first century (p. 35). He well states the relation between the *Did.* and Barnabas (p. 16): "*L'épître de Barnabas qu'on situe en général à la fin du premier siècle contient dans ses chapitres XVII.-XXI. une description des deux voies, relativement courte, et qui coïncide presque entièrement avec des passages de notre première partie. On a contesté, il est vrai l'authenticité de ces derniers chapitres de l'épître, mais les témoignages de Clément d'Alexandrie et d'Origène sont suffisamment rassurants à cet égard. Ici, dans la description de la première voie l'ordre que nous connaissons est bouleversé. On dirait que les phrases se succèdent au hasard. Ainsi les passages relatifs à la deuxième table de la loi sont jetés loin les uns des autres sans qu'un puisse savoir pourquoi. Il est impossible d'admettre que l'auteur de la Didachè, pour réaliser quelques parties de son plan si régulier, ait glané çà et là dans ces chapitres de Barnabas quelques phrases ou parties de phrases si étrangement disposées. On comprend, au contraire, que l'auteur de l'épître de Barnabas désirant après tant d'allégories donner quelques leçons de morale pratique, et passant ainsi comme il le dit à une autre sorte d'enseignement, pressé d'ailleurs d'en finir, se soit servé de lambeaux d'un autre écrit qui lui restaient dans la mémoire et les ait mêlés à sa prose comme ils lui venaient à l'esprit.*"

MATHIEAU, S.: *Les origines de l'épiscopat*, in the "Revue de théologie," Montauban, July–Sept., 1884.

MÉNÉGOZ, E.: Several articles in the Lutheran journal, "Le Témoignage," Paris, 1884, 23 février (*une découverte importante*); 1 mars (*les origines de l'épiscopat*); 8 mars (*les parasites dans l'église primitive*); 15 mars (*le chemin de la vie*); 29 mars (*les choses finales*); 5 jouillet (*l'agape*); 1885, 3 janvier (*une nouvelle étude sur la Didachè*), 28 mars (*Le caractère de la Did.*); 4 avril (*La doctrine relig. de la Did.*); 11 avril (*La Did. et l'interprétation du N. T.*); 18 avril (*La date de la Did.*); 25 avril (*Les indices de la haute antiquité de la Did.*). M. assigns the *Did.* to 80–100. The first six chapters are not a manual of religious instruction, but a liturgical exhortation to lead a Christian life addressed to proselytes at the moment of their Baptism. "*Ce qu'on a pris pour un résumé de la religion chrétienne, n'est autre chose qu' une exhortation à mener une vie digne du chrétien, adressée au prosélyte au moment du baptême.*" Mars 28, 1885, p. 100. In this way Ménégoz explains the absence of dogmatic instruction.

MURALT, E. DE.: *L'enseignement des douzes apôtres*, in "Revue de théologie et de philosophie" for May, 1884, pp. 278–291.

RÉVILLE, JEAN: *Une importante découverte*, in "La Rennaissance," for Febr. 29, 1884.

SABATIER, PAUL (*ancien élève de la Faculté de théologie protestante de Paris, pasteur à l'église Saint Nicolas à Strasbourg, Alsace*): *La Didachè*, in the "Église libre," 1884, Nos. 11–18. The same: $\Delta\iota\delta\alpha\chi\dot{\eta}\ \tau\tilde{\omega}\nu\ \iota\beta'\ \dot{\alpha}\pi o\sigma\tau\acute{o}\lambda\omega\nu$. *La Didachè ou l'enseignement des douze apôtres. Texte grec retrouvé par Mgr. Philotheos Bryennios, métropolitain de Nicomédie publié pour la première fois en France avec un commentaire et des notes*. Paris (libr. Fischbacher), 1885. 165 pages.

Unfortunately I did not receive this book till to-day (May 9), after this Ch. was already set in type. But I can add the table of contents and state the result of a cursory inspection. I. Introduction, bibliography, and the Greek text of the *Did.* for the first time reprinted in France. II. French translation of the *Did.* III. Eight historical and critical studies on the Catechetical section, on Baptism, on Fasting and Prayer, on the Eucharist, on the Spiritual Gifts and ecclesiastical Offices, on Deacons and Bishops, on the last things, on the Date and Origin of the *Did.* Sab. assigns it to Syria and to the middle of the first century: "*Nous n'hesitons pas à fair remonter la Did. au milieu du premier siècle, avant les grandes courses missionaires de Paul.*" The author is well acquainted with the literature on the subject, but was misinformed that the *Didachè* was *telegraphed* to America (p. 5). The book is the most important contribution in the French language. He informs me by letter, April 27, 1885, that a new edition is already called for. It is remarkable that the Protestants of France are far ahead of their Roman Catholic countrymen in the interest they have taken in this discovery, and that the principal works on the *Did.* have proceeded from the new Protestant Theological School of Paris.

VI.—Editions and Discussions in Dutch, Norwegian, Danish, and Swedish.

BERGGREN, J. E.: *Om den nyligen återfunna skriften, "De tolf apostlarnes lära."* In "Teologisk Tidsskrift grundad af A. F. Beckman, etc. Upsala, 1884, Tredje Häftet, pp. 200-206.

A Swedish translation of the *Did.* with a brief introduction.

CASPARI, C. P. (Dr. and Prof. of Theology in Christiania): *Den aeldste Kircheordning.* In "Luthersk Ugeskrift," Lördag, June 14 and 21, 1884, Nos. 24 and 25. A Norwegian journal of the Lutheran Church.

Translation and Notes. Dr. C., well known by his antiquarian researches on the baptismal creeds, etc., asserts the priority of the *Did.* over the Ep. of Barnabas, and regards it as a Judæo-Christian (but not Ebionite) production of Palestine, written before A.D. 120, probably before 100. He notes the silence respecting doctrines, in which respect the *Did.* resembles the Epistle of James. The *Did.* is literally built upon the Gospel of Matthew.

HELVEG, FR.: *Fra Kirkens Oldtid.* In "Dansk Kirketidende," 1884, Nos. 24 and 25.

Danish translation and Notes. H. dates the *Did.* from about time of Justin Martyr.

PAULSSEN, A. S.: *Et igenfundet Skrift fra Kirkens ældste Tider.* In "Theologisk Tidsskrift for den danske Folkekirke." B. I. H. 4 pp. 576-589. Kjöbenhavn, 1884.

A translation with notes. Paulssen holds that the *Did.* is older than Barnabas, and was written shortly after the Apostolic period, at all events in the first half of the 2d century. Paulssen uses the silence of Chap. VII. respecting the Apostles' Creed as an argument against the Grundtvigian theory that the Apostles' Creed as well as the Lord's Prayer was taught by the Lord himself, and that their reception, along with Baptism, constitute the condition of salvation.

PRINS, J. J.: *Bryennios Διδ. τ. δ. ἀπ. E codice Hierosolymitano, nunc Constantinopolitano, nupperrime primum edita. In usum studiosæ juventutis repetit.* Ludg. Bat. (E. J. Brill), 1884, 16 pages.

RÖRDAM, Thomas: *Den apostoliske Troesbekjen.* In "Theol. Tids. f. d. danske Folkekirke." Kjöbenhavn. B. II. H. 1, pp. 127-130.

VARMING, C.: *De tolv apostles lærdom. Et skrift fra det andet Kristelige århundrede, oversat.* Kjöbenhavn, 1884, 35 pages.

"Theologisk Tidsskrift for den ev. luth. Kirke i Norge" (Christiania), New Series, X., 1884, I. Greek text, reprinted from Bryennios.

Note on the Fac-similes in this Work.

The fac-similes of the Jerusalem MS. on pp. 6 and 7, and the picture of the Jerusalem Monastery facing the first chapter, were obtained for the author by influential friends in Constantinople last summer, but not without difficulty. A few extracts from a letter dated Constantinople, July 1, 1884, will interest the reader.

"When Dr. W. informed me of your desire to have a photograph of the first and last pages of the Διδαχή, and consulted me as to the means of accomplishing it, I was very doubtful of success. It was concluded, however, that Dr. W., accompanied by an English clerical friend well known for his interest in the Greeks, should visit the Monastery of the Jerusalem Patriarchate in Stamboul, and, if possible, obtain the permission for me to come privately, at some convenient time, and take the photograph.

"They went and were courteously received, and it was agreed that I should go at 10 o'clock on Thursday. I went accompanied only by one of our Senior Class, a Greek. We were politely received, and, after some delay, escorted to the Library. The representative of the Jerusalem Patriarch (the Archimandrite Polycarp) asked the Librarian for the MS., and, taking it in his hands, turned to the first page of the *last leaf*, put a piece of white paper under it, and, with another piece of white paper, covered the preceding page, and then said to me, 'Now it is ready for you to copy.' I asked, 'Why have you chosen this page rather than some other?' He replied, 'Because this is the most important page of the book. It contains the subscription of the copyist *and the date* at which it was finished.' I looked at it and read: 'Finished in the month of June—year 6364, by the hand of Leon, the notary and sinner.' I asked what the upper portion (five and a half lines) was. I was told they were the concluding lines of the *Teaching*. I saw and deciphered the last words, ἔρρωσθε εἰς τέλος ἐν ὑπομονῇ Ἰησοῦ Χριστοῦ. I was not familiar with the *Teaching*. I had no copy of it, and had never had the book in my hands more than an hour, and that more for a cursory examination of the Introductory and Historical Notes of Bryennios than anything else. So I was quite ready to believe the statement; besides, I had no reason whatever for disbelieving or being suspicious after once the permission had been given for me to take a copy. I asked, 'What is this below the subscription and date (the lower two-thirds of the page)?' I was told it was some addition in the form of a note or comment from the same hand. There was an evident disinclination to allow me to handle or examine the MS., which I understood simply as the usual jealousy in guarding such treasures. I had a definite object before me: the securing of a photograph. The room was dark. Objection was made to taking the MS. out of the room. I finally succeeded in getting it into the vestibule just outside the door, where the light from a window would fall upon it. A young Deacon was told to hold it before my instrument, which I had unpacked and set up, but I induced them to allow him to place it on the sill of a window opening into an inner room, and fasten it with a piece of string, which I furnished from my pocket, to the iron gratings. This was all done without my having touched the precious volume with my hands.

"I exposed my plates in duplicate (in case of accident), enveloped my dark slide in its covering, and then for the first time, my work being finished, I took hold of the book, untied its fastenings, and carefully carried it into the inner room and with thanks placed it in the hands of the Librarian. I had been intending all the time to ask the favor of a half-hour's perusal of the MS. after my work was finished; but overhearing a remark of one of the aged monks present, I had a benevolent impulse. I said to them, I have one plate more with me which I would like to place at your service in case there is anything which you would like to have photographed. They were greatly pleased, and said they had for a long time wished for a view of their premises. So I found a window in a neighboring house from which I got a nice view. Then I hurried off to take the steamer for home. Friday I developed my plates, printed off a proof or two, and left them to soak in the water over night. Saturday Dr. W. was anxious to get his letter off to you, so I took the two proofs out of the water, hastily dried them and gave them to him to send to you with my compliments, and simply telling him what I was told as to the contents of the page copied. . . . During the week I printed off two or three more copies, and sent one of them to the English friend who accompanied Dr. W. in his visit to the Monastery. After a week had elapsed he wrote me a note that he was sorry to be unable to find upon the page *any portion of the 'Teaching.'* This startled me and set me to work investigating the matter. I found upon examining the Greek edition of the $διδαχη$ published here last year that the subscription and the genealogical addition on the lower part of the page were there given on the last page of the Introduction, but no mention was made anywhere of the five and a half lines at the top, and that strictly speaking there was no part of the $διδαχη$ in the photographic copy. I informed Dr. W. of my disappointment in this and of my intention at my earliest convenience to try again. This was on Friday. I had examinations to attend to until this morning, Tuesday; so this morning I took an early start accompanied by an associate, Prof. Grosvenor, and went again to the Library with some little misgiving, but full of hope that by means of a conciliatory present of several copies of nice photographs of the Library and School such a friendly footing would be gained that I could get just what I wanted, and what that was I knew pretty well, because I had in the last four days read and pretty well digested the 'Teaching.'

"We were, I may say, cordially received by the Librarian, but when the Superior came in I saw by his countenance that trouble was in store for us. To make a long story short, nearly an hour's argument, remonstrance and entreaty failed to make any impression upon him. He would not allow a page of the 'Teaching' to be copied. His argument, so far as he argued, was that what I had already *was a part* of the 'Teaching,' that it was the essential part, the proof of its genuineness, etc. etc. After long discussion I came away not at all settled in my mind as to the exact reasons for the refusal. The election of a Patriarch of Constantinople is to take place next week. The Archbishop Philotheos (Bryennios) is a prominent candidate. I have an impression that these Jerusalem people are not of his party. Many other theories have presented themselves to my mind. One thing I am quite convinced of, that in promising the permission to photograph there was no intention to give any other than the page selected, and had I insisted on examining for myself and copying some other page than the one offered, the volume would have quickly been put back into its drawer and we should have got nothing. As it is, we have the last page but one of the *volume* in which the $\delta\iota\delta\alpha\chi\acute{\eta}$ is found and a fair specimen of the chirography and style of the whole work, called in Europe '*The Jerusalem Manuscript,*' but which these monks now for the sake of justifying their position call the $\delta\iota\delta\alpha\chi\acute{\eta}$, although it contains 7 treatises and on 120 pages of vellum, of which the 'Teaching' only fills four. . . .

"I shall, after some time, try and bring some other influences to bear upon our monastic friends, and if possible will yet try to get what you want. In the meantime please accept my personal salutations, and the assurance of my readiness to oblige you in any way in my power.

"P. S.—You will be perhaps interested in the View of the Library. The monks are standing in front of the Library, and in the doorway (rather deeply shaded by the trunk of the tree) may be seen the Librarian holding the MS. in his hand. The large building in the background is a magnificent building just erected for the Greek National School through the munificence of some rich patriotic Greeks of this city. In the picture the monks are looking towards the Golden Horn and Pera, *i. e.*, to the N. E."

* * *

I afterwards (August, 1884) secured a photograph of the page which contains the first four lines of the *Didache*. The same photographs were subsequently (Jan. 31, 1885) obtained by Rev. Dr. Hale. See above, p. 151.

THE DOCUMENTS.

I. THE DIDACHE. Greek and English, with Comments.
II. A LATIN FRAGMENT OF THE DIDACHE. With a Critical Essay.
III. THE EPISTLE OF BARNABAS. Greek and English. ןבר
IV. THE SHEPHERD OF HERMAS. Greek and English.
V. THE APOSTOLICAL CHURCH ORDER. Greek and English.
VI. THE APOSTOLICAL CHURCH ORDER from the COPTIC. English Version.
VII. THE SEVENTH BOOK OF THE APOSTOLICAL CONSTITUTIONS. Greek and English.
A Letter and Communication from Metropolitan BRYENNIOS.
Addenda to second edition.

DOCUMENT I.

THE DIDACHE IN GREEK AND ENGLISH.

With Explanatory Notes.

THE Greek text is an exact reprint of the Jerusalem Manuscript. The textual emendations and conjectures are given in the notes. The Jerusalem MS. has no divisions into chapters and verses. Bryennios has divided the book judiciously into sixteen chapters. The divisions into verses or lines differ in various editions. Instead of adding to the confusion, I have adopted the convenient versicular arrangement of Prof. Harnack, which is followed also by Krawutzcky and De Romestin, and is likely to prevail. I have added the chapter headings, textual emendations, and Scripture references.

The explanatory foot-notes should be used in connection with the preceding discussions. It is but just to say in advance, that most of the Biblical and Patristic parallels which have since been quoted from book to book (often without the least acknowledgment) were already pointed out by the learned discoverer and first editor, who was thoroughly equipped for his task.

The different writers are quoted with the following abbreviations:

Br. = Bryennios.   (Greek.)
Ha. = Harnack.   (German.)
Hi. = Hilgenfeld.   Do.
W. = Wünsche.   Do.
Z. = Zahn.   Do.
Fa. = Farrar.   (English).
R. = De Romestin.   Do.
Sp. = Spence.   Do.
J. W. = John Wordsworth.   Do.
Fi. = Fitzgerald.   (American.)
G. = Gardiner.   Do.
H. & B. = Hitchcock & Brown.   Do.
H. & N. = Hall & Napier.   Do.

O. = Orris.   (American.)
St. = Starbuck.   Do.
B.-M. = Bonet-Maury.   (French.)
Ma. = Massebieau.   Do.
Sa. = Sabatier.   Do.
Ca. = Caspari.   (Norwegian.)
For the titles see Lit. in Ch. XXXIII.

ΔΙΔΑΧΗ	TEACHING
ΤΩΝ	OF THE
ΔΩΔΕΚΑ ΑΠΟΣΤΟΛΩΝ.	TWELVE APOSTLES.

Διδαχὴ Κυρίου διὰ τῶν δώδεκα ἀποστόλων τοῖς ἔθνεσιν.	The Teaching of the Lord by the Twelve Apostles to the Gentiles.
Κεφ. α'.	CHAP. I.
	THE TWO WAYS. THE WAY OF LIFE.
1. Ὁδοὶ δύο εἰσί, μία τῆς	1. There are two Ways, one

NOTES TO CHAPTER I.

THE TITLE.—The larger title is probably the original one, the shorter an abridgment. The clause *to the Gentiles*, indicates the Jewish Christian origin. The writer means to give the teaching of the Lord himself in his Gospel, at least in the first six chapters, which repeat substantially the Sermon on the Mount. In subsequent quotations the title is still more abridged by the omission of *Twelve*, for the sake of convenience, or in justice to Paul (who, however, is not by that designation excluded from the Apostolate any more than in Acts vi. 2 ; 1 Cor. xv. 5 ; Rev. xxi. 14). The title is derived from Acts ii. 42 (ἦσαν δὲ προσκαρτεροῦντες τῇ διδαχῇ τῶν ἀποστόλων καὶ τῇ κοινωνίᾳ, τῇ κλάσει τοῦ ἄρτου καὶ ταῖς προσευχαῖς), and Matt. xxviii. 19 (μαθητεύσατε πάντα τὰ ἔθνη). The book is called by Athanasius (*Ep. Fest.* 39) : διδαχὴ καλουμένη τῶν ἀποσόλων (the so-called *D. of the Apostles;* implying that it is not strictly apostolical or canonical, but ecclesiastical only and apocryphal) ; by Nicephorus (*Stichometria*) : διδαχὴ τῶν ἀποστόλων ; but by Eusebius with a slight difference (*H. E.* iii. 25) : τῶν ἀποστόλων αἱ λεγόμεναι διδαχαί (the so-called *Doctrines of the Ap.*) and by Pseudo-Cyprian (*De Aleatoribus*) : *Doctrinæ Apostolorum.* Rufinus mentions likewise a *Doctrina Apostolorum* among the ecclesiastical books, and one called *Duæ Viæ* or *Judicium Petri*, which is probably identical with the first six chapters, or may be a still earlier lost document of similar character. See Ch. X. p. 18 sq. and Ch. XXX.

Ver. 1 and 2. Scripture parallels on the *Two Ways:* Matt. vii. 13, 14 ;

ζωῆς καὶ μία τοῦ θανάτου· | of Life and one of Death;[a]
διαφορὰ δὲ πολλὴ μεταξὺ τῶν | but there is a great difference
δύο ὁδῶν. | between the two Ways.

2. Ἡ μὲν οὖν ὁδὸς τῆς ζωῆς | 2. Now the Way of Life is
ἐστιν αὕτη· πρῶτον, ἀγα- | this: First, Thou shalt love
πήσεις τὸν Θεὸν τὸν ποιήσαν- | God who made thee; sec-

---

[a] Jer. xxi. 8. Comp. Deut. xxx. 15, 16, 19; Matt. vii. 13, 14.

Deut. xxx. 19; Jer. xxi. 8., 2 Pet. ii. 2. Post-Apostolic parallels: Ep. Barnabæ, ch. xvii: "*There are two Ways* of teaching and authority, the Way of Light and the Way of Darkness; *but there is a great difference between the two Ways.*" Ch. xix.: "*Now the Way* of Light *is this* . . . *thou shalt love Him who made thee* . . . thou shalt love *thy neighbor* above thy soul." Pastor Hermæ, *Mand.* vi. 1, 2: "The way of righteousness is straight, but that of unrighteousness is crooked . . . There are two angels with a man, one of righteousness, and the other of iniquity." The Testaments of the Twelve Patriarchs, a Jewish Christian book (ed. Migne, in "Patrol. Gr." ii. col. 1120): "God gave to the children of men *two Ways* . . . of good and evil" (δύο ὁδοὺς ἔδωκεν ὁ θεὸς τοῖς υἱοῖς ἀνθρώπων, δύο διαβούλια καὶ δύο πράξεις, καὶ δύο τόπους καὶ δύο τέλη . . ὁδοὶ δύο, καλοῦ καὶ κακοῦ). Apost. Church Order, cap. iv.: "John said, '*There are two Ways, one of life and one of death,*'" etc. Apost. Constitutions, vii. 1 (ed. Ueltzen, p. 160; Lagarde, p. 197): "We say, *There are two Ways, one of Life and one of Death;* but there is no comparison between the two, *for the difference is great*, or rather they are entirely separate; and the Way of Life is that of nature, but the Way of Death was afterwards introduced, as it is not according to the mind of God but from the scheme of the adversary." The pseudo-Clementine Homilies, v. 7 (Dressel's ed. p. 177), likewise speak of two Ways, the broad Way of the lost and the narrow Way of the saved (ἡ τῶν ἀπολλυμένων ὁδὸς πλατεῖα καὶ ὁμαλωτάτη . . . ἡ δὲ τῶν σωζομένων στενὴ μὲν καὶ τραχεῖα), with evident reference to Matt. vii. 13, 14. Clement of Alexandria (*Strom.* v. 5) says: "The Gospel [Matt. vii. 13, 14] proposes two Ways, as do likewise the *Apostles* [probably the *Didache*], and all the Prophets (Jer. xxi. 8). They call the one narrow and circumscribed (στενὴν καὶ τεθλιμμένην), which is hemmed in according to the commandments and prohibitions, and the opposite one, which leads to destruction, broad and roomy (πλατεῖαν καὶ εὐρίχωρον), open to pleasures and wrath." (*Strom.* v. 5, in Migne's ed. ii. col. 54).

2. *Thou shalt love God who made thee.*] Barnabas and the Apost. Ch. Order add the important clause: "Thou shalt glorify Him who redeemed thee from death." The omission is no trace of Ebionitic hostility to the doctrine of the atonement (Krawutzcky), but due to the priority and greater simplicity of the *Did.* So is also the omission of "from thy whole heart." (Ap. Ch. Ord.)

2. *And all things.*] The negative form of the golden rule. So also in

τά σε· δεύτερον, τὸν πλησίον σου ὡς σεαυτόν· πάντα δὲ ὅσα ἐὰν θελήσῃς μὴ γίνεσθαί σοι, καὶ σὺ ἄλλῳ μὴ ποίει.

3. Τούτων δὲ τῶν λόγων ἡ διδαχή ἐστιν αὕτη· Εὐλογεῖτε τοὺς καταρωμένους ὑμῖν καὶ προσεύχεσθε ὑπὲρ τῶν ἐχθρῶν ὑμῶν, νηστεύετε δὲ ὑπὲρ τῶν διωκόντων ὑμᾶς· ποία γὰρ χάρις, ἐὰν ἀγαπᾶτε τοὺς ἀγαπῶντας ὑμᾶς; οὐχὶ καὶ τὰ ἔθνη τὸ αὐτὸ ποιοῦσιν; ὑμεῖς δὲ ἀγαπᾶτε τοὺς μισοῦντας ὑμᾶς καὶ οὐχ ἕξετε ἐχθρόν.

4. Ἀπέχου τῶν σαρκικῶν καὶ σωματικῶν* ἐπιθυμιῶν.

ondly, thy neighbor as thyself;[a] and all things whatsoever thou wouldst not have done to thee, neither do thou to another.[b]

3. Now the teaching of these [two] words [of the Lord] is this: Bless those who curse you, and pray for your enemies,[c] and fast for those who persecute you; for what thank is there if ye love those who love you? Do not even the Gentiles the same?[d] But love ye those who hate you, and ye shall not have an enemy.

4. Abstain from fleshly and bodily [worldly][e] lusts. If

---

[a] Matt. xxii. 37, 39.
[b] Comp. Matt. vii. 12; Luke vi. 31.
[c] Comp. Matt. v. 48; Luke vi. 27, 28.
[d] Comp. Matt. v. 46; Luke vi. 32.
[e] 1 Pet. ii. 11.

* κοσμικῶν, Br. W. F. H. & B. Sp. Sa.; but σωματικῶν is retained by Hi. Ha. R.

Const. Ap. vii. 1; in Tobit iv. 15; in the Talmud (as coming from the renowned Hillel: "Do not to thy neighbor what is disagreeable to thee"); in Buddhist and Chinese ethics, and among the Stoics ("*quod tibi fieri non vis, alteri ne feceris*"). Matthew (vii. 12) and Luke (vi. 31) give the positive form, which is much stronger. There is a great difference between doing no harm and doing good. The former is consistent with extreme selfishness. Some MSS. add the negative form in Acts xv. 29. See Tischend.

3. *Fast for them.*] A post-scriptural addition, which may be as innocent as prayer for our enemies, or may contain the germ of a doctrinal error. Spence: "Probably an oral tradition of the Master's words." Ha. quotes a parallel passage of unknown authorship from Origen, *Hom. in Lev.* x.: "*Invenimus in quodam libello ab apostolis dictum: 'Beatus est qui etiam jejunat pro eo ut alat pauperem.'*" Epiphanius (*Hær.* lxx. 11) quotes from the Apost. Constitutions: "When they (the Jews) feast, ye shall fast and mourn for them."

3. *Ye shall not have an enemy.*] Love conquers enmity and turns even foes into friends. A beautiful sentiment. A similar idea in 1 Pet. iii. 13. Sp. again conjectures here an oral tradition of Christ's sayings.

Ἐάν τις σοι δῷ ῥάπισμα εἰς τὴν δεξιὰν σιαγόνα, στρέψον αὐτῷ καὶ τὴν ἄλλην, καὶ ἔσῃ τέλειος· ἐὰν ἀγγαρεύσῃ σέ τις μίλιον ἕν, ὕπαγε μετ' αὐτοῦ δύο· ἐὰν ἄρῃ τις τὸ ἱμάτιόν σου, δὸς αὐτῷ καὶ τὸν χιτῶνα· ἐὰν λάβῃ τις ἀπὸ σοῦ τὸ σόν, μὴ ἀπαίτει· οὐδὲ γὰρ δύνασαι.

5. Παντὶ τῷ αἰτοῦντί σε δίδου, καὶ μὴ ἀπαίτει· πᾶσι γὰρ θέλει δίδοσθαι ὁ πατὴρ ἐκ τῶν ἰδίων χαρισμάτων. Μακάριος ὁ διδοὺς κατὰ τὴν ἐν-

any one give thee a blow on the right cheek turn to him the other also,[a] and thou shalt be perfect.[b] If any one press thee to go with him one mile, go with him two;[c] if any one take away thy cloak, give him also thy tunic;[d] if any one take from thee what is thine, ask it not back,[e] as indeed thou canst not.

5. Give to every one that asketh thee, and ask not back,[f] for the Father wills that from his own blessings we should give to all. Blessed

---

[a] Matt. v. 39; Luke vi. 29.
[c] Matt. v. 41.
[e] Luke v. 30; Comp. Matt. v. 42.
[b] Comp. Matt. v. 48; xix. 21.
[d] Matt. v. 40; Luke vi. 29.
[f] Luke vi. 30.

---

4. σωματικῶν.] So the MS. Br.: τὸ χειρόγραφον ἔχει σωματικῶν, ὃ οὐδὲν διαφέρει τοῦ σαρκικῶν. He adopts κοσμικῶν, *worldly*, and quotes 1 Pet. ii. 11 (ἀπέχεσθαι τῶν σαρκικῶν ἐπιθυμιῶν); Tit. ii. 12 (τὰς κοσμικὰς ἐπιθυμίας); 2 Clem. ad Cor. xvii. (ἀπὸ τῶν κοσμικῶν ἐπιθυμιῶν); Const. Ap. Const. vii. 2.

τέλειος.] Comp. Ch. vi. 2; x. 5; xvi. 2. Probably with reference to Matt. v. 48; xix. 21. The germ of the doctrine of perfection, as distinct from ordinary virtue.

ἀγγαρεύω.] A word of Persian origin, which occurs Matt. v. 41; xxvii. 32; Mark, xv. 21. It is the technical term for pressing men and beasts into public service for transmission of royal messages and for military purposes—a matter very obnoxious to the Jews. The E. V. translates it *compel*.

ἱμάτιον ... χιτῶνα.] The *Did.* follows here the more natural order of Luke vi. 29: "From Him that taketh away thy cloke [the outer garment, mantle], withhold not thy coat [the inner garment, tunic] also;" while Matt. v. 40, reads: "If any one ... take away thy coat, let him have thy cloke also."

οὐδὲ γὰρ δύνασαι.] "Thou canst not even do so," if thou wouldest, because a Christian ought not to use force, or go to law before Gentile courts. 1 Cor. vi. 1. As a statement of the mere fact that forcible resistance to a stronger one is useless, it would be trivial. Ha. suggests unnecessarily a different reading: καίπερ δυνάμενος. The clause is omitted in Const. Ap. vii. 2.

τολήν· ἀθῷος γάρ ἐστιν· οὐαὶ τῷ λαμβάνοντι· εἰ μὲν γὰρ χρείαν ἔχων λαμβάνει τις, ἀθῷος ἔσται· ὁ δὲ μὴ χρείαν ἔχων δώσει δίκην, ἱνατί* ἔλαβε καὶ εἰς τί, ἐν συνοχῇ δὲ γενόμενος ἐξετασθήσεται περὶ ὧν ἔπραξε, καὶ οὐκ ἐξελεύσεται ἐκεῖθεν μέχρις οὗ ἀποδῷ τὸν ἔσχατον κοδράντην.

is he that gives according to the commandment, for he is guiltless. Woe to him that receives; for if any one receives, having need, he shall be guiltless, but he that has not need shall give account, why he received and for what purpose, and coming into distress he shall be strictly examined concerning his deeds, and he shall not come out thence till he have paid the last farthing.[a]

---

* ἵνα τι, Hi. Ha.   [a] Matt. v. 26.

---

5. *Blessed is he,* etc.] Comp. Acts xx. 85: "It is more blessed to give than to receive." Hermas (*Mand.* ii.): "Give to all, for God wishes his gifts to be shared by all" (πᾶσιν δίδου· πᾶσιν γὰρ ὁ θεὸς δίδοσθαι θέλει ἐκ τῶν ἰδίων δωρημάτων). Quoted by Br.; see Funk's *Patr. Ap.* i. 390.

According to the commandment.] of the Lord. Comp. Matt. v. 7, 42; Rom. xii. 8.

ἀθῷος], *unpunished, innocent* (from a priv. and θωή, penalty); only twice in the N. T. Matt. xxvii. 4 (αἷμα ἀθῷον, where, however, Westcott and Hort read αἷμα δίκαιον) and ver. 24, where Pilate says, "I am innocent of the blood of this righteous man." Also in the Sept., Deut. xxvii. 25; Jer. xxvi. 15; Hermas, *Mand.* i.: ὁ οὖν διδοὺς ἀθῷός ἐστιν. The Ap. Ch. O. omits it.

Woe to him that receives.] Alms without needing them. 2 Thess. iii. 10: "If any one will not work, neither let him eat." Ap. Const. iv. 3: "Woe to those who have, and who receive in hypocrisy, or are able to support themselves, and wish to receive from others; for both of them shall give account to the Lord God in the day of judgment."

Till he have paid the last farthing.] *Farthing* (κοδράντης=*quadrans*, *i. e.* a quarter of an *as*) is the smallest denomination of coin and indicates that the debt will be exacted to the last balance. This passage, like Matt. v. 26, on which it is based, has been interpreted by Roman Catholics as referring to the future state and containing the germ of the doctrine of purgatory (as afterwards developed by Augustin and Pope Gregory I.). Matthew has *prison* (φυλακή) for *distress,* συνοχή, which occurs Luke, xxi. 25; 2 Cor. i. 1, and may here mean *imprisonment*. H. and Br.: "under confinement;" H. and N.: "Into straits (confinement);" Sp.: "in sore straits."

6. Ἀλλὰ καὶ περὶ τούτου δὲ* εἴρηται· ἱδρωτάτω† ἡ ἐλεημοσύνη σου εἰς τὰς χεῖράς σου, μέχρις‡ ἂν γνῷς τίνι δῷς.

6. But concerning this also it hath been said, "Let thine alms sweat (drop like sweat) into thy hands till thou know to whom thou shouldst give."

Κεφ. β′.

CHAP. II.

THE SECOND GREAT COMMANDMENT.
WARNING AGAINST GROSS SINS.

1. Δευτέρα δὲ ἐντολὴ τῆς διδαχῆς·

1. And the second commandment of the Teaching is:

---

* δή, (truly), Br., &c. † ἱδρωσάτω, Br. Ha. H. & B. Sp.; ἱδρυσάτω, Hi.
‡ μέχρις, B., &c., or μέχρι, so long as, until

6. *ἱδρωτάτω.*] An error of the scribe. Br. corrects ἱδρωσάτω (from ἱδρόω, to sweat, to perspire). Hi. conjectures ἱδρυσάτω (from ἱδρύω, to settle, to fix), and explains (p. 104): "*Collocet misericordia tua stipem in manibus tuis.*" Contrary to εἰς. Zahn proposes μὴ δραχ9ήτω, "nicht soll (mit der Faust) gepackt (und festgehalten) werden dein Almosen in deinen Händen bis du weisst, wem du geben sollst." This would give the opposite sense and encourage promiscuous almsgiving, but the emendation is forced and inconsistent with εἰς. The verb ἱδρόω is classical, and the noun ἱδρώς, sweat, occurs Luke xxii. 44. Potwin suggests ἱερωτάτη, sacrosancta, to get out of "the sweat" and toil of the sentence.

Let thine alms drop like sweat into thy hand.] The meaning is, keep your money in your hands, until it makes them sweat. A curious passage quoted as Scripture (εἴρηται), from oral tradition, or an unknown apocryphal book, or some living Prophet. A similar sentence, however, occurs in Ecclesiasticus, xii. 1–6 (ἐὰν εὖ ποιῇς, γνῶθι τίνι ποιεῖς, κ. τ. λ.). Assuming the reading of the MS. as amended by Br., the sentence is a warning against indiscriminate and injudicious almsgiving, and shows that the author of the *Did.* did not understand the commands of the Sermon on the Mount in a strictly literal sense; otherwise he would contradict what he said in the preceding lines. The Ap. Const. (vii. 2) omit the passage. The abuse of promiscuous charity by idlers and impostors led to the practice of giving alms through the bishop, who would inquire into the merits of each case. Br. quotes Justin M. to this effect. Dr. Hort suggests the negative μή before the verb, to maintain the continuity of the passage.

NOTES ON CHAPTER II.

This chapter is an expansion of the commandments of the second table of the Decalogue with reference to prevailing heathen vices. It contains twenty-five points of warning. The first ten refer to the commandments of the second table, the rest mostly to sins of the tongue, especially to those against charity. (Ha. and R.) In the specification of the commandments the author seems to have had Rom. xiii. 9 before him: "For this, Thou

2. Οὐ φονεύσεις, οὐ μοιχεύσεις, οὐ παιδοφθορήσεις, οὐ πορνεύσεις, οὐ κλέψεις, οὐ μαγεύσεις, οὐ φαρμακεύσεις οὐ φονεύσεις τέκνον ἐν φθο-

2. Thou shalt not kill.[a] Thou shalt not commit adultery;[b] thou shalt not corrupt boys; thou shalt not commit fornication. Thou shalt not

---

[a] Ex. xx. 13.   [b] Ex. xx. 14.

---

shalt not commit adultery, Thou shalt not kill, Thou shalt not steal, Thou shalt not covet, and if there be any other commandment, it is summed up in this word, namely, Thou shalt love thy neighbor as thyself."

2. οὐ παιδοφθορήσεις.] παιδοφθορέω, *to seduce boys, to commit pæderasty*, is not used in the N. T., nor in the Sept., but by Barnabas, Justin M., Ap. Const., Clement of Alex. (quoted by Bryennios), and in classical writers. An unnatural and revolting vice very prevalent among the heathen, even among the best classes in Greece, but severely condemned by the Mosaic law, as an abomination punishable with death, Lev. xviii. 22 ; xx. 13, and by Paul, Rom. i. 27 ; 1 Cor. vi. 9 ; 1 Tim. i. 10 ("abusers of themselves with men").

οὐ πορνεύσεις.] Fornication and concubinage were not considered sinful among the heathen. Adultery was condemned, but only as an interference with the rights of a freeman.

οὐ μαγεύσεις, κ. τ. λ.] The practice of magic and enchantments is condemned, Ex. xxii. 18 ; Lev. xix. 26 ; xx. 6 ; Deut. xviii. 11, 12 ; Gal. v. 20 ; comp. Rev. ix. 21 ; xviii. 23 ; xxi. 8 ; xxii. 15. The verb μαγεύω is used Acts viii. 9 ; μαγεία or μαγία, Acts viii. 11 ; μάγος in the sense of sorcerer, Acts xiii. 6, 8. φαρμακεύω is classical and used in the Sept. The N. T. has the nouns φαρμακεία and φαρμακός.

Thou shalt not procure abortion, nor shalt thou kill the new-born child.] Against the fearful crime of infanticide in all its forms Christianity raised its indignant protest through Justin Martyr, Tertullian, Lactantius, and synodical legislation. A council of Ancyra, 314 (can. xxi.; see Fulton's *Index Can.* p. 209) imposes ten years' penance upon women who "commit fornication and destroy that which they have conceived, or who are employed in making drugs for abortion." The exposure of poor or sickly children by parents was very general and was approved, for the public interest, even by Plato, Aristotle, and Seneca. Gibbon says (*Decline and Fall*, ch. xliv.): "The Roman Empire was stained with the blood of infants, till such murders were included, by Valentinian and his colleagues, in the letter and spirit of the Cornelian law. The lessons of jurisprudence and Christianity had been inefficient to eradicate this inhuman practice, till their gentle influence was fortified by the terrors of capital punishment." See my *Church Hist.* ii. 360 ; iii. 114. For γεννηθέντα in the MS. Br. substitutes γεννηθέν (*conceived, begotten,* comp Matt. i. 20). He quotes a parallel passage from the apocryphal book of Wisdom xii. 5 "the unmerciful murderers of their children" (τέκνων φονέας ἀνελεήμονας). φθορά in the sense of *abortion* occurs in Barnabas, Clement of Alex., and Ap. Const.

ρᾷ, οὐδὲ γεννηθέντα* ἀποκτενεῖς. Οὐκ ἐπιθυμήσεις τὰ τοῦ πλησίον.

3. Οὐκ ἐπιορκήσεις, οὐ ψευδομαρτυρήσεις, οὐ κακολογήσεις, οὐ μνησικακήσεις.

4. Οὐκ ἔσῃ διγνώμων οὐδὲ δίγλωσσος· παγὶς γὰρ θανάτου ἡ διγλωσσία.

5. Οὐκ ἔσται ὁ λόγος σου

steal.[a] Thou shalt not use witchcraft; thou shalt not practice sorcery. Thou shalt not procure abortion, nor shalt thou kill the new-born child. Thou shalt not covet thy neighbor's goods.[b]

3. Thou shalt not forswear thyself.[c] Thou shalt not bear false witness.[d] Thou shalt not speak evil; thou shalt not bear malice.

4. Thou shalt not be double-minded nor double-tongued; for duplicity of tongue is a snare of death.

5. Thy speech shall not be

---

[a] Ex. xx. 15. [b] Ex. xx. 17.
[c] Matt. v. 33. [d] Ex. xx. 16.

* γεννηθὲν, B. Hi. Ha. W. H. & B. Sp.

---

3. οὐ κακολογήσεις, κ. τ. λ.] Fa.: *thou shalt not speak evil, nor cherish a grudge.* H. and B.: "*Thou shalt not revile, thou shalt not be revengeful.*" κακολογέω occurs repeatedly in the Sept. and the N. T.; μνησικακέω, *to remember past injuries*, is classic and used in the Sept. for different Hebrew words (see Trommius), but not in the N. T. Br. and Sp. quote a parallel from the Testaments of the Twelve Patriarchs (Zabulon, 8): "My children, be ye devoid of malice (ἀμνησίκακοι) and love one another, and do not each of you be careful to mark your brother's badness (κακίαν), for this breaks up unity and scatters to the winds all idea of kinship, and harasses the soul, for the malicious man (μνησίκακος) has no bowels of compassion." Sp. remarks: "The special features which distinguished the sect of the Nazarenes, gentleness, benevolence, kindness, characterize both these early Christian writings" (the *Did.* and the Testaments of the 12 Patr).

4. οὐκ ἔσῃ διγν.] διγνώμων (δίγνωμος) and δίγλωσσος (δίγλωττος) are classic, the latter in the primary linguistic sense (*bilingual;* hence δίγλωσσος as a noun, an *interpreter*). The former is not biblical, but δίγλωσσος in the moral sense (*deceitful*, speaking one thing and meaning another) occurs in the Sept., Prov. xi. 13; Sirach v. 9, 14; xxviii. 13, and δίλογος (*double-tongued*) in 1 Tim. iii. 8.

διγλωσσία.] Not found in the dictionaries, classical or biblical, but easily coined from the adjective. Barn. uses it ch. xix. 7.

5. μεμεστωμένος πράξει.] Fa.: *filled with fact.* St.: *filled with deed.*

ψευδής, οὐ κενός, ἀλλὰ μεμεστωμένος πράξει.

6. Οὐκ ἔσῃ πλεονέκτης οὐδὲ ἅρπαξ οὐδὲ ὑποκριτὴς οὐδὲ κακοήθης οὐδὲ ὑπερήφανος. Οὐ λήψῃ βουλὴν πονηρὰν κατὰ τοῦ πλησίον σου.

7. Οὐ μισήσεις πάντα ἄνθρωπον, ἀλλὰ οὓς μὲν ἐλέγξεις, περὶ δὲ ὧν προσεύξῃ, οὓς δὲ ἀγαπήσεις ὑπὲρ τὴν ψυχήν σου.

false, nor vain, but fulfilled by deed.

6. Thou shalt not be covetous, nor rapacious, nor a hypocrite, nor malignant, nor haughty. Thou shalt not take evil counsel against thy neighbor.

7. Thou shalt not hate any one, but some thou shalt rebuke* and for some thou shalt pray, and some thou shalt love above thine own soul (or, life).

Κεφ. γ'.

1. Τέκνον μου, φεῦγε ἀπὸ

CHAP. III.

WARNING AGAINST LIGHTER SINS.

1. My child, flee from every

* Lev. xix. 17.

R.: *filled by deed.* Ha.: *erfüllt mit That.* Comp. Acts. ii. 13 (γλεύκους μεμεστωμένοι); Rom. xv. 14 (μεσθοὶ ἀγαθωσύνης); Jas. iii. 17 (σοφία μεστὴ ἐλέους). For the sentiment comp. Matt. xxiii. 3; 1 John, iii. 18; Jas. i. 22.

6. ἅρπαξ.] R.: *an extortioner.* In Matt. vii. 15 the false Prophets are called λύκοι ἅρπαγες. In 1 Cor. v. 10, 11 πλεονέκτης—ἅρπαξ. Br. compares also Clemens Rom. 1 Cor. xxxv.

ὑπερήφανος] Fa.: *overweening.* Sp.: *proud.* It occurs Luke i. 51; Rom. i. 30; 2 Tim. iii. 2; Jas. iv. 6; 1 Pet. v. 5; and the noun, ὑπερηφανία in Mark vii. 22.

οὐ λήψῃ, κ. τ. λ.] The same warning in Barn. xix. 3.

7. οὐ μισήσεις πάντα.] A common Hebraism for οὐδείς. *no one.* An indication of the Hebrew origin of the writer. Barn. xix. 11 changed this sentence into εἰς τέλος μισήσεις τὸν πονηρόν (Satan, *the evil one,* is meant; otherwise it would be unchristian). Comp. Jude 22: "On some have mercy who are in doubt (or, while they dispute with you); and some save, snatching them out of the fire; and on some have mercy with fear."

ὑπὲρ τὴν ψυχήν σου]. H. and B., O.: *above thy life.* H. and N.: *more than thy own life.* Not: *for thy soul's good.* Barn. xix. 5: ἀγαπήσεις τὸν πλησίον σου ὑπὲρ τὴν ψυχήν σου. For the idea comp. Phil. ii. 30 ("hazarding his life" for others); Rev. xii. 11 ("they loved not their life even unto death").

NOTES ON CHAPTER III.

Ch. III. contains as it were a second Decalogue against more refined sins

παντὸς πονηροῦ καὶ ἀπὸ παν- | evil, and from every thing
τὸς ὁμοίου αὐτοῦ. | that is like unto it.*

2. Μὴ γίνου ὀργίλος·* ὁδη- | 2. Be not prone to anger,
γεῖ γὰρ ἡ ὀργὴ πρὸς τὸν φό- | for anger leadeth to murder;
νον· μηδὲ ζηλωτὴς μηδὲ ἐρισ- | nor given to party spirit, nor
τικὸς μηδὲ θυμικός· ἐκ γὰρ | contentious, nor quick-tem-
τούτων ἁπάντων φόνοι γεν- | pered (or, passionate); for
νῶνται. | from all these things mur-
 | ders are generated.

3. Τέκνον μου, μὴ γίνου | 3. My child, be not lust-

---

* ὀργίλος, Br.   *Comp. 1 Thess. v. 22.

---

and passions of the heart which lead to the grosser sins of deed, as anger to murder, lust to adultery, superstition to idolatry, lying to theft. Herein is seen the superiority of the gospel ethics over the law. For the idea compare Matt. v. 28; 2 Pet. ii. 14; Jas. i.14, 15.

. 1. The affectionate address, "my child," occurs five times in this ch.. and again once in ch. iv., and "children" in ch. v. Used in the same spiritual sense in the Proverbs (i. 8, 15; ii. 1, etc.), in Sirach (ii. 1; iii. 1, 14; iv. 1, 23, etc.), and in the N. T. (Gal. iv. 19; 1 John, ii. 1, 12; iii. 7, etc.). See the note of Br.

ἀπὸ παντὸς ὁμοίου αὐτοῦ.] Br. and others naturally refer to 1 Thess. v. 22, ἀπὸ παντὸς εἴδους πονηροῦ ἀπέχεσθε, "*abstain from every form* (or, *appearance*) *of evil.*" It is probably a reminiscence.

2. *given to party spirit.*] Fa.: *a hot partisan.* H. and Br., H. and N., St., O.: *jealous.* Sp : a *fanatic.* ζηλωτής, *zealous*, in the good sense, 1 Cor. xiv. 12. ζηλωταὶ τοῦ νόμου, zealots in behalf of the Jewish law and institutions, Acts, xxi. 20 ; xxii. 3 The party of the Zealots, called Ζηλωταί, arose during the bloody Jewish war, and under the pretext of zeal for the law committed the greatest crimes. Josephus often mentions them in *Bell. Jud.* Spence thinks that the *Did.* warns against sympathizing with these brave but mistaken patriots ; but this would put the composition before A.D. 70.
ἐριστικός and θυμικός are classical, but not biblical.

3. αἰσχρολόγος.] H. and B., and F.: *foul-mouthed;* Sp.: *a coarse talker ;* O.: *of foul speech ;* G.: *filthy speaker.* Br. quotes Col. iii. 8 (αἰσχρολογία, *shameful speaking*), and Eph. v. 4 (αἰσχρότης, *filthiness*). The adjective occurs neither in the N. T. nor in the Sept., but in ecclesiastical Greek.

ὑψηλόφθαλμος] literally *lofty-eyed ;* Fa.: *a man of high looks ;* G.: *one who casts lewd eyes ;* F.: *supercilious ;* H. and N.: *of lofty eye ;* O.: *of leering eyes ;* St.· *a greedy gazer ;* R.: *a lifter up of the eyes (to sin)*; Sp.: *one who makes signs with the eyes.* The word is not hapaxlegomenon, as Ha. says, but occurs once more in the Eccles Canons (9), where Simon says : μὴ γίνου αἰσχρολόγος, μηδὲ ὑψηλόφθαλμος. The Ap. Const. vii. 6 substitute for it ῥιψόφθαλμος, *casting the eyes about, casting lewd glances,* ἐπιθυμητής· ὁδηγεῖ γὰρ ἡ ἐπιθυμία πρὸς τὴν πορνείαν· μηδὲ αἰσχρολόγος μηδὲ ὑψηλόφθαλμος· ἐκ γὰρ τούτων ἁπάντων μοιχεῖαι γεννῶνται.

ful, for lust leadeth to fornication; neither be a filthy talker, nor an eager gazer; for from all these are generated adulteries.

4. Τέκνον μου, μὴ γίνου οἰωνοσκόπος· ἐπειδὴ ὁδηγεῖ εἰς τὴν εἰδωλολατρίαν·* μηδὲ ἐπαοιδὸς μηδὲ μαθηματικὸς μηδὲ περικαθαίρων, μηδὲ θέλε αὐτὰ βλέπειν· ἐκ γὰρ τούτων ἁπάντων εἰδωλολατρία † γεννᾶται.

4. My child, be not an observer of birds [for divination] for it leads to idolatry; nor a charmer (enchanter), nor an astrologer, nor a purifier (a user of purifications or expiations), nor be thou willing to look on those things; for from all these is generated idolatry.

5. Τέκνον μου, μὴ γίνου ψεύστης· ἐπειδὴ ὁδηγεῖ τὸ ψεῦσμα εἰς τὴν κλοπήν· μηδὲ

5. My child, be not a liar, for lying leads to theft; nor avaricious, nor vainglorious,

---

* εἰδωλολατρείαν, Br. Hi. W. Sp.   † εἰδωλολατρεία, B. Hi. W. Sp.

---

leering. Comp. 2 Pet. ii. 14: "having eyes full of adultery." Br. quotes also two parallel passages from the Testaments of the Twelve Patriarchs. Potwin: "Perhaps the exhortation has women chiefly in mind, and condemns the opposite of modest, downcast looks." Sirach xxvi. 9 (12). πορνεία γυναικὸς ἐν μετεωρισμοῖς ὀφθαλμῶν καὶ ἐν τοῖς βλεφάροις αὐτῆς γνωσθήσεται.

4. οἰωνοσκόπος.] = οἰωνιστής (from οἰωνός, a large bird), an augur who foretells from the flight and cries of birds (Vogelschauer). H. and B., and Sp.: an omen-watcher; H. and N.: an observer of omens; Fa.: a forecaster; St.: a drawer of auguries; O.: an augur. Classical, but not in N. T. The verb appears in the Sept. Lev. xix. 26 (μὴ οἰωνιεῖσθε), comp. Deut. xviii. 10 (οἰωνιζόμενος). Sorcery and enchantments were very common among Jews and Gentiles.

μαθηματικός.] Used as adjective and noun, a mathematician, an astronomer; in later writers of the second century, an astrologer. So also the Latin mathematicus. See quotations in Liddell and Scott, from Sextus Empiricus, Juvenal, Tacitus.

περικαθαίρων.] Used Deut. xviii. 10, embraces here all kinds of heathen sacrifices and lustrations for averting disease. The Apost. Const. vii. 32, add to this list other strange terms. See the note of Br.

5. μὴ γίνου ψεύστης, κ. τ. λ.] This is the passage quoted by Clement of Alex. as "Scripture." See ch. XXVI. p. 115.

φιλάργ. κ. τ. λ.] Fa. and Sp.: a lover of money, nor vainglorious.

φιλάργυρος μηδὲ κενόδοξος·
ἐκ γὰρ τούτων ἁπάντων κλοπαὶ γεννῶνται.

6. Τέκνον μου, μὴ γίνου
γόγγυσος· ἐπειδὴ ὁδηγεῖ εἰς
τὴν βλασφημίαν· μηδὲ αὐ-
θάδης μηδὲ πονηρόφρων· ἐκ
γὰρ τούτων ἁπάντων βλασ-
φημίαι γεννῶνται.

7. Ἴσθι δὲ πραΰς, ἐπεὶ οἱ
πραεῖς κληρονομήσουσι τὴν
γῆν.

8. Γίνου μακρόθυμος καὶ
ἐλεήμων καὶ ἄκακος καὶ ἡσύχιος καὶ ἀγαθὸς καὶ τρέμων
τοὺς λόγους διὰ παντός, οὓς
ἤκουσας.

9. Οὐχ ὑψώσεις σεαυτὸν
οὐδὲ δώσεις τῇ ψυχῇ σου θράσος. Οὐ κολληθήσεται ἡ ψυ-
χή σου μετὰ ὑψηλῶν, ἀλλὰ
μετὰ δικαίων καὶ ταπεινῶν
ἀναστραφήσῃ.

10. Τὰ συμβαίνοντά σοι

for from all these things are generated thefts.

6. My child, be not a murmurer, for it leads to blasphemy; neither self-willed (presumptuous), nor evil-minded, for from all these things are generated blasphemies.

7. But be thou meek, for the meek shall inherit the earth.^a

8. Be thou long-suffering, and merciful, and harmless, and quiet, and good, and trembling continually at the words which thou hast heard.^b

9. Thou shalt not exalt thyself, nor shalt thou give audacity (presumption) to thy soul. Thy soul shall not be joined with the lofty, but with the just and lowly shalt thou converse.^c

10. The events that befall

---

^a Matt. v. 5.   ^b Comp. Isa. lxvi. 2, 5.   ^c Comp. Rom. xii. 16.

6. γόγγυσος.] Post-classical, but in Apost. Const. vii. 7. Br. quotes Jude ver. 16, "these are murmurers" (γογγυσταί); Phil. ii. 14, "do all things without murmurings" (χωρὶς γογγυσμῶν).

αὐθάδης.] Occurs in Titus i. 7; and 2 Pet ii. 10: τολμηταί, αὐθάδεις, δόξας οὐ τρέμουσιν, βλασφημοῦντες.

7. πραΰς, κ. τ. λ.] Almost literally from Matt. v. 5. Br. quotes also Col. ii. 12 (ἐνδύσασθε—πραότητα); Eph. iv. 32; 1 Thess. v. 14, 15; Hermas, Mand. v.

8. τρέμων.] Isa. lxvi. 2 (Sept.), τρέμοντα τοὺς λόγους μου.

9. θράσος] presumption, overboldness. Classical and in the Sept. The N. T. has θάρσος, courage, once, in Acts xxviii. 15. Aristotle (Nicomach. Ethics, Bk. iii. ch. 7) distinguishes between the coward (δειλός), the rash man (θρασύς), and the brave man (ἀνδρεῖος); the last holds the mean between the two extremes and is neither desponding nor precipitate, but tranquil before action, and full of spirit in action.

10. τὰ συμβαίν., κ. τ. λ.] Comp. Matt. x. 29, 30; Heb. xii. 7–11. Si-

ἐνεργήματα ὡς ἀγαθὰ προσ-
δέξῃ, εἰδὼς ὅτι ἄτερ Θεοῦ
οὐδὲν γίνεται.

thee thou shalt accept as good,
knowing that nothing happens without God.

Κεφ. δ′.

CHAP. IV.

SUNDRY WARNINGS AND EXHORTATIONS.

1. Τέκνον μου, τοῦ λαλοῦντός σοι τὸν λόγον τοῦ Θεοῦ μνησθήσῃ νυκτὸς καὶ ἡμέρας, τιμήσεις δὲ αὐτὸν ὡς Κύριον· ὅθεν γὰρ ἡ κυριότης λαλεῖται, ἐκεῖ Κύριός ἐστιν.

1. My child, thou shalt remember night and day him that speaks to thee the word of God, and thou shalt honor him as the Lord, for where the Lordship is spoken of, there is the Lord.

2. Ἐκζητήσεις δὲ καθ' ἡμέ-

2. And thou shalt seek out

rach ii. 4: "Whatever is brought upon thee take cheerfully." Barn. xix. 6. Quoted by Origen as "divine Scripture" (*De Princ.* III. 2, 17): *omnia quæ accidunt . . . a Deo illata suscipere, scientes quod sine Deo nihil fit.*" Clement of Alex. describes the Christian Gnostic (philosopher) as a man "who takes everything for good, though it may seem evil, and who is not disturbed by anything that happens" (*Strom.* vii. 12, 13).

ἄτερ] *without, apart from.* A poetic word used by Homer and Pindar (ἄτερ Ζηνός, *without Zeus, i. e., without his will*); also occurring twice in the N. T. (Luke xxii. 6, 35), and in 2 Macc. xii. 15. Barnabas has ἄνευ instead.

NOTES TO CHAPTER IV.

This chapter enjoins duties on Christians as members of the Church.

1. *Thou shalt remember.*] Comp. Heb. xiii. 7: "Remember them that had the rule over you, who spake unto you the word of God." The rulers are all the church officers, Apostles, Prophets, Teachers, Bishops and Deacons (comp. XI. 2, 4; XV. 2).

Honor him as the Lord.] Comp. XI. 2; Matt. x. 40–42; Gal. iv. 14: "Ye received me as an angel of God, even as Christ Jesus."

κυριότης] variously rendered, *Lordship* (R., St., Ha.: *Herrschaft*); *the glory of the Lord* (G., Sp., W.); *that which pertaineth to the Lord* (H. and B.); *lordly rule* (H. and N.); *sovereignty of the Lord* (O.). The word is not classical, but occurs, without the article, four times in the N. T. (Eph. i. 21; Col. i. 16; Jude 8; 2 Pet. ii. 10), and is always rendered *dominion* in the R. V. The Ap. Const. vii. 9 gives an explanatory substitute: "Where is the *teaching concerning God* (ἡ περὶ Θεοῦ διδασκαλία), there God is present." It refers to Christ, his person, word and work, as "the Lord of glory," Jas. ii. 1, and gives a hint of the Christology which underlies the *Did.*

2. *Thou shalt seek out*, etc.] A strong sense of the communion of saints pervades this treatise. "Saints" is used in the N. T. sense for all believers. So also X. 6, "if any one be holy."

Rest upon their words.] H. and B.: *refreshed by.* So also Ha.: *dass du*

ραν τὰ πρόσωπα τῶν ἁγίων, ἵνα ἐπαναπαῇς* τοῖς λόγοις αὐτῶν.

3. Οὐ ποθήσεις† σχίσμα, εἰρηνεύσεις δὲ μαχομένους· κρινεῖς δικαίως, οὐ λήψη πρόσωπον ἐλέγξαι ἐπὶ παραπτώμασιν.

4. Οὐ διψυχήσεις, πότερον ἔσται ἢ οὔ.

day by day the faces of the saints, that thou mayest rest upon their words.

3. Thou shalt not desire (make) division, but shalt make peace between those at strife. Thou shalt judge justly ; thou shalt not respect a person (or, show partiality) in rebuking for transgressions.

4. Thou shalt not be doubleminded (doubtful in thy mind) whether it shall be or not.ᵃ

ᵃComp. Sir. i. 28 ; James i. 8 ; iv. 8.

* ἐπαναπαύῃ, Br. Sp. Sa.; ἐπαναπαῇς, Ha. Hi.

† ποιήσεις, Ha. Hi. The reading of the Jerus. MS. is retained by W. R. Sp. Sa.

durch ihre Gespräche (?) *erquickt werdest.* Br. reads ἐπαναπαύῃ, Hi. and Ha. ἐπαναπαῇς, to conform to the corresponding passage in Ap. Const. vii. 9. ἀναπαύω, *to give rest, to refresh,* occurs 12 times in the N. T.; ἐπανπαύομαι, *to rest upon,* only twice, Luke x. 6; Rom. ii. 17.

3. οὐ ποθήσεις σχίσμα.] So the MS. Hi., Ha., and Z. adopt ποιήσεις, which is easier and sustained by the parallel passages in Barnabas (xix.) and Ap. Const. vii. 10. ποθέω is classical and Hellenistic, but does not occur in the N. T., which has ἐπιποθέω 9 times, and ἐπιπόθησις twice, ἐπιπόθητος once, and ἐπιποθία once. σχίσμα is used here in the same sense as 1 Cor. i. 10 and xi. 18, of parties or factions within the church.

εἰρηνεύω.] Here transitive, *to make peace,* as also in Clemens Rom., and in 1 Macc. vi. 60. In the N. T. it is intransitive, *to have peace,* or *to be at peace* (in 4 places).

4. διψυχήσεις] *be of two minds* (F., Fa., R.); *waver in soul* (St.); *hesitate* (H. and B., Sp.); *be undecided* (H. and N.); *doubt in thy heart* (G.). The verb occurs in Clement of Rome, Barnabas, Hermas, and Cyril of Alex.; the adj. δίψυχος in Philo and James. The warning refers not to the Divine judgment (Ha.: *Zweifle nicht, ob Gottes Gericht kommen wird oder nicht*), but to doubtfulness in prayer. Br. compares Sirach i. 28: μὴ προσέλθῃς αὐτῷ (τῷ Θεῷ) ἐν καρδίᾳ δισσῇ, and James i. 8: ἀνὴρ δίψυχος ἀκατάστατος ἐν πάσαις ταῖς ὁδοῖς αὐτοῦ. Comp. also Jas. iv. 8; Matt. xxi. 22; 1 John v. 14, 15. Ap. Const. vii. 11 correctly understand it: οὐ διψυχήσεις ἐν προσευχῇ σου. Br. quotes also Hermas, who says (*Mand.* ix. on Prayer): "Remove doubt from thyself, and doubt not to ask anything from God. Neither say within thyself, How can I ask and re-

5. Μὴ γίνου πρὸς μὲν τὸ λαβεῖν ἐκτείνων τὰς χεῖρας, πρὸς δὲ τὸ δοῦναι συσπῶν.

6. Ἐὰν ἔχῃς, διὰ τῶν χειρῶν σου δώσεις λύτρωσιν ἁμαρτιῶν σου.

7. Οὐ διστάσεις δοῦναι οὐ-

5. Be not one that stretches out his hands for receiving, but draws them in for giving.[a]

6. If thou hast [anything], thou shalt give with thy hands a ransom for thy sins.[b]

7. Thou shalt not hesitate

---

[a] Ecclus. iv. 31.   [b] Comp. Dan. iv. 27; Tobit iv. 10, 11.

ceive from the Lord, seeing that I have committed so many sins against Him? Reason not thus with thyself, but turn unto the Lord with thy whole heart and ask from Him, nothing doubting, and thou shalt know his great compassion, that He will not abandon thee, but will fulfil the request of thy soul. For He is not as men who bear malice, but He himself is without malice, and has compassion on his work."

5. A graphic description of generous liberality, a quotation from Sirach iv. 31: μὴ ἔστω ἡ χείρ σου ἐκτεταμένη εἰς τὸ λαβεῖν καὶ ἐν τῷ ἀποδιδόναι συνεσταλμένη. For συσπῶν (συσπάω, to draw together, to contract, in Plato, Aristotle, Lucian, etc., but not in Sept. nor in N. T.) the Ap. Const. vii. 11 substitute συστέλλων, in partial conformity to Sirach. Active charity and self-denying generosity is made a very prominent virtue in the *Did.*, as it was among the primitive Christians notwithstanding their general poverty. Different renderings: Fa. and Sp.: *one who stretches out his hands to receive and clenches them tight for giving.* H. and N.: *a stretcher forth . . . to receive, and a drawer back to give.* R.: *one that stretcheth out, but shutteth them close.* F.: *one who holds open the hands to receive but clinched toward giving.* St.: *extending . . . contracting.* G.: *stretch out, draw back.*

6. *If thou hast, etc.*] May be understood of the meritoriousness and atoning efficacy of almsgiving as an equivalent (λύτρον, *ransom*). This error crept very early into the church, but has, like most errors, an element of truth which gives it power and tenacity. Br. quotes several parallel passages. Comp. Prov. xvi. 6: "By mercy and truth iniquity is purged;" Dan. iv. 27 (in Sept. iv. 24) where Daniel counsels King Nebuchadnezzar: "Break off thy sins by righteousness and thine iniquities by showing mercy to the poor." Tobit iv. 10: ἐλεημοσύνη ἐκ θανάτου ῥύεται καὶ οὐκ ἐᾷ εἰσελθεῖν εἰς τὸ σκότος. 11: δῶρον γὰρ ἀγαθόν ἐστιν ἐλεημοσύνη πᾶσι τοῖς ποιοῦσιν αὐτὴν ἐνώπιον τοῦ ὑψίστου. Testaments of the Twelve Patriarchs (Zabulon, 8): "In proportion as a man is pitiful towards his neighbor will the Lord be pitiful towards him" (ὅσον γὰρ ἂν ἄνθρωπος σπλαγχνίζεται εἰς τὸν πλησίον, τοσοῦτον Κύριος εἰς αὐτόν).

7. *Nor in giving shalt thou murmur.*] Comp. 2 Cor. ix. 7: "God loveth a cheerful giver." 1 Pet. iv. 9: "Use hospitality one to another without

δὲ διδοὺς γογγύσεις· γνώσῃ γὰρ τίς ἐστιν ἡ* τοῦ μισθοῦ καλὸς ἀνταποδότης.

8. Οὐκ ἀποστραφήσῃ τὸν ἐνδεόμενον, συγκοινωνήσεις δὲ πάντα τῷ ἀδελφῷ σου καὶ οὐκ ἐρεῖς ἴδια εἶναι· εἰ γὰρ ἐν τῷ ἀθανάτῳ κοινωνοί ἐστε, ποσῷ μᾶλλον ἐν τοῖς θνητοῖς;

9. Οὐκ ἀρεῖς τὴν χεῖρά σου

to give, nor in giving shalt thou murmur, for thou shalt know who is the good recompenser of the reward.

8. Thou shalt not turn away him that needeth, but shalt share all things with thy brother, and shalt not say that they are thine own;[a] for if you are fellow-sharers in that which is imperishable (immortal), how much more in perishable (mortal) things?[b]

9. Thou shalt not take

---

[a] Acts, iv. 32.   [b] Comp. Rom. xv. 27.

* ὁ, Br. et al.

murmuring." Fa. deems it probable that the Didachographer had read the first Ep. of Peter.

8. *Thou shalt not turn away*, etc.] This points to the community of goods, which was introduced at Jerusalem in the pentecostal fervor of brotherly love, but passed away with the growth and changed circumstances of the church; at least we find it in no other congregation. The Agape remained for a while as a reminder of that state. The Acts in describing it uses in part the same words (iv. 32): "And the multitude of them that believed were of one heart and soul: and not one of them said that aught of the things which he possessed was his own (ἴδιον εἶναι), but they had all things common."

If you are fellow-sharers] Or, *partakers, partners, joint participants*. In Rom. xv. 27 the Gentiles are represented as debtors to the Jews for the spiritual gifts received from them. The idea is the same, but πνευματικά and σαρκικά are used for ἀθάνατον and θνητά. For ἀθάνατος, which is classical and Hellenistic, the N. T. uses ἄφθαρτος (in 7 places, *e. g.*, 1 Pet. iii. 4; 1 Tim. i. 17). It has also the substantives ἀφθαρσία (8 times), and ἀθανασία (3 times).

9. *From their youth up*, etc.] Christian family nurture enjoined, Eph. vi. 4: "Nurture your children in the chastening and admonition of the Lord." It is said of Timothy that from childhood (ἀπὸ βρέφους, *from a babe*) he knew the sacred writings, 1 Tim. iii. 15. Clement of Rome (Ep. to the Cor. xxi.): "Let your children be sharers in true Christian training." Hermas (*Vis.* I. 3): "Fail not to rebuke thy children, for I know that if they shall repent with all their heart, they shall be written in the book of life, together

ἀπὸ τοῦ υἱοῦ σου ἢ ἀπὸ τῆς θυγατρός σου, ἀλλὰ ἀπὸ νεότητος διδάξεις τὸν φόβον τοῦ Θεοῦ.

10. Οὐκ ἐπιτάξεις δούλῳ σου ἢ παιδίσκῃ, τοῖς ἐπὶ τὸν αὐτὸν Θεὸν ἐλπίζουσιν, ἐν πικρίᾳ σου, μήποτε οὐ μὴ φοβηθήσονται τὸν ἐπ᾽ ἀμφοτέροις Θεόν· οὐ γὰρ ἔρχεται κατὰ πρόσωπον καλέσαι, ἀλλ᾽ ἐφ᾽ οὓς τὸ πνεῦμα ἡτοίμασεν.

11. Ὑμεῖς δὲ δοῦλοι * ὑποταγήσεσθε τοῖς κυρίοις ἡμῶν†

away thy hand from thy son or from thy daughter, but from [their] youth up thou shalt teach [them] the fear of God.

10. Thou shalt not in thy bitterness lay commands on thy man-servant (bondman), or thy maid-servant (bondwoman), who hope in the same God, lest they should not fear Him who is God over [you] both;* for He comes not to call [men] according to the outward appearance (condition), but [he comes] on those whom the Spirit has prepared.

11. But ye, bondmen, shall be subject to our (your) mas-

* Comp. Eph. vi. 9 (Col. iv. 1).

* οἱ δοῦλοι, Br. Ha. Hi. Sa.   † ὑμῶν, Br. &c.

with the saints." (Quoted by Br.) The Jews and Christians were far ahead of the cultivated heathen in religious knowledge and intelligence.

10, 11. The same view of slavery as that taken Eph. vi. 5–9; Tit. ii. 9; the Ep. to Philemon, and 1 Pet. ii. 18. It is not forbidden by the Apostles, but regulated, moderated, and put in the way of ultimate abolition by the working of the Christian spirit of love and brotherhood infused into the master and slave. Br. quotes Ignatius *Ad Polyc.* iv. (in Funk's ed. i. 248): "Do not despise either male or female slaves, yet neither let them be puffed up, but rather let them submit themselves the more for the glory of God that they may win a better liberty from God. Let them not desire to be set free at public cost [at the expense of the church], lest they be found slaves to their own lusts." This is, however, not to be understood as prohibiting emancipation at private expense, which was at all times encouraged by the church and regarded as a meritorious deed. See *Church History*, I. 444 sqq.; II. 347 sqq.

10. *Whom the Spirit has prepared.*] A clear allusion to the work of the Spirit in the human heart. Comp. Rom. viii. 29, 30. The only other place where the Holy Spirit is mentioned is in the baptismal formula, ch. VII.

11. Br. corrects ἡμῶν of the MS. to ὑμῶν, which is accepted by most editors.

ὡς τύπῳ Θεοῦ ἐν αἰσχύνῃ καὶ φόβῳ.

12. Μισήσεις πᾶσαν ὑπόκρισιν καὶ πᾶν ὃ μὴ ἀρεστὸν τῷ Κυρίῳ.

13. Οὐ μὴ ἐγκαταλίπῃς ἐντολὰς Κυρίου, φυλάξεις δὲ ἃ παρέλαβες, μήτε προστιθεὶς μήτε ἀφαιρῶν.

14. Ἐν ἐκκλησίᾳ ἐξομολογήσῃ τὰ παραπτώματά σου, καὶ οὐ προσελεύσῃ ἐπὶ προσευχήν σου ἐν συνειδήσει πονηρᾷ.

Αὕτη ἐστὶν ἡ ὁδὸς τῆς ζωῆς.

Κεφ. ε'.

1. Ἡ δὲ τοῦ θανάτου ὁδός ἐστιν αὕτη· πρῶτον πάντων

ters as to the image of God in reverence (modesty) and fear.ᵃ

12. Thou shalt hate all hypocrisy, and everything that is not pleasing to the Lord.

13. Thou shalt not forsake the commandments of the Lord, but thou shalt keep what thou hast received, neither adding [thereto] nor taking away [therefrom].ᵇ

14. In the congregation (in church) thou shalt confess thy transgressions,ᶜ and thou shalt not come to thy prayer (or, place of prayer) with an evil conscience.

This is the way of life.

CHAP. V.

THE WAY OF DEATH.

1. But the way of death is this.

ᵃ Comp. Eph. vi. 5 (Col. iii. 22).   ᵇ Deut. xii. 32.   ᶜ Comp. James v. 16.

13. *Neither adding nor taking away.*] Deut. iv. 2: "Ye shall not add unto the word which I command you, neither shall ye diminish aught from it." Comp. Deut. xii. 32; Prov. xxx. 6; Rev. xxii. 18, 19.

14. *In the congregation thou shalt confess.*] The earliest mention of public confession of sins, after that in Jas. v. 16: "Confess your sins one to another." In ch. XIV. 1, confession is required before partaking of the Eucharist.

ἐπὶ προσευχήν.] May be *prayer*, or the *house of prayer* (Acts xvi. 13). συνείδησις πονηρᾷ is probably a reminiscence of Heb. x. 22.

NOTES TO CHAPTER V.

Chapter V. describes the Way of Death by a catalogue of sins, which faithfully reflects the horrible immorality of heathenism in the Roman empire, and is confirmed by Seneca, Tacitus, and other serious classics. Comp. the summaries in Rom. i. 18–32, and Apoc. xxii. 15. The chapter agrees almost verbatim with the 20th chapter of Barnabas, and has a parallel in Hermas, *Mand*. viii. Eight words in it are not found in the N. T.

1. ἀλαζονεία or ἀλαζονία occurs in Jas. iv. 16, *vauntings* (R. V.), and

πονηρά ἐστι καὶ κατάρας μεστή· φόνοι, μοιχεῖαι, ἐπιθυμίαι, πορνεῖαι, κλοπαί, εἰδωλολατρίαι*, μαγεῖαι, φαρμακίαι† ἁρπαγαί, ψευδομαρτυρίαι, ὑποκρίσεις, διπλοκαρδία, δόλος, ὑπερηφανία, κακία, αὐθάδεια, πλεονεξία, αἰσχρολογία, ζηλοτυπία, θρασύτης, ὕψος, ἀλαζονεία.

2. Διῶκται ἀγαθῶν, μισοῦντες ἀλίθειαν, ἀγαπῶντες ψεῦδος, οὐ γινώσκοντες μισθὸν δικαιοσύνης, οὐ κολλώμενοι ἀγαθῷ οὐδὲ κρίσει δικαίᾳ, ἀγρυπνοῦντες οὐκ εἰς τὸ ἀγαθόν, ἀλλ' εἰς τὸ πονηρόν· ὧν μακρὰν πραΰτης καὶ ὑπομονή, μάταια ἀγαπῶντες, διώκοντες ἀνταπόδομα, οὐκ ἐλεοῦντες πτωχόν, οὐ πονοῦντες ἐπὶ καταπονουμένῳ, οὐ γινώσκοντες τὸν ποιήσαντα αὐτούς, φονεῖς τέκνων, φθορεῖς πλάσματος Θεοῦ, ἀπο-

First of all it is evil and full of curse; murders, adulteries, lusts, fornications, thefts, idolatries, witchcrafts, sorceries, robberies, false-witnessings, hypocrisies, double-heartedness, deceit, pride, wickedness, self-will, covetousness, filthy-talking, jealousy, presumption, haughtiness, boastfulness.

2. Persecutors of the good, hating truth, loving a lie,ᵃ not knowing the reward of righteousness, not cleaving to that which is good nor to righteous judgment, watchful not for that which is good but for that which is evil; far from whom is meekness and endurance, loving vanity, seeking revenge, not pitying the poor, not toiling with him who is vexed with toil, not knowing Him that made them, murderers of children,

---

* εἰδωλολατρεῖαι, Br. Hi. W. H. & B.
† φαρμακεῖαι, Br. Hi. W. H. & B.

ᵃ Comp. Rev. xxii. 15.

ἀλαζονία τοῦ βίου, *vainglory of life* (R. V.), in 1 John ii. 16; ἀλαζών, *boastful*, in Rom. i. 30; 2 Tim. iii. 2.

2. ἀγαπῶντες ψεῦδος.] Perhaps from Rev. xxii. 15: φιλῶν καὶ ποιῶν ψεῦδος, *loving and making a lie*.

κολλώμενοι ἀγαθῷ] Probably from Rom. xii. 9: κολλώμενοι τῷ ἀγαθῷ, *cleaving to that which is good*.

πανθαμάρτητοι] Fa.: *sinners in all respects;* H. and N.: *utter sinners;* Sp.: *sinners in everything;* H. and B.: *universal sinners*. The word is found only in Barnabas (xx.), and in Ap. Const. vii. 18; and πανθαμάρτωλος in Clemens. 2 Cor. xviii.: "For I myself too, being an utter sinner and not yet escaped from temptation, but being still amidst the engines of the devil, do my diligence to follow after righteousness" (see Lightfoot, *Appendix to S. Clement of Rome*, pp. 337 and 389).

στρεφόμενοι τὸν ἐνδεόμενον, καταπονοῦντες τὸν θλιβόμενον, πλουσίων παράκλητοι, πενήτων ἄνομοι κριταί, πανθαμάρτητοι· ῥυσθείητε, τέκνα, ἀπὸ τούτων ἁπάντων.

destroyers of the handiwork of God, turning away from the needy, vexing the afflicted, advocates of the rich, lawless judges of the poor, wholly sinful.

May ye, children, be delivered from all these.

Κεφ. ς'.

CHAP. VI.

WARNING AGAINST FALSE TEACHERS AND THE WORSHIP OF IDOLS.

1. Ὅρα μή τις σε πλανήσῃ ἀπὸ ταύτης τῆς ὁδοῦ τῆς διδαχῆς, ἐπεὶ* παρεκτὸς Θεοῦ σε διδάσκει.

2. Εἰ μὲν γὰρ δύνασαι βασ-

1. Take heed that no one lead thee astray from this way of teaching, since he teacheth thee apart from God.

2. For if indeed thou art

---

* ἐπειδή, Hi.

NOTES TO CHAPTER VI.

1. *From this way of teaching.*] Barnabas xviii. 1; ὁδοὶ δύο εἰσὶ διδαχῆς.

παρεκτὸς θεοῦ] R.: *not according to God.* παρεκτός is not classical, but occurs three times in the N. T.

2. *The whole yoke of the Lord.*] Matt. xi. 29: "Take my yoke (τὸν ζυγόν μου) upon you ... my yoke is easy and my burden is light." In the Council of Jerusalem, A.D. 50, Peter said, Acts xv. 10, 11, in opposition to the strict Jewish party: "Why tempt ye God, that ye should put a yoke (ζυγόν) upon the neck of the disciples, which neither our fathers nor we were able to bear (βαστάσαι)? But we believe that we shall be saved through the grace of the Lord Jesus, in like manner as they [the Gentiles]." This was the principle of Paul. But a Jewish-Christian reaction took place a year or two afterwards at Antioch under the authority of James of Jerusalem, and even Peter and Barnabas were carried away by the over-conservative current (Gal. ii. 12). Hence the temporary breach between Paul and Peter, and the bold remonstrance of the former in the presence of the congregation, which consisted of Jewish and Gentile converts. It must have been a most serious crisis when the two greatest Apostles in the midst of their career of usefulness stood face to face against each other, and Paul charged Peter with hypocrisy for denying, by his timid conduct in Antioch, the doctrine he had proclaimed a year before at Jerusalem. It foreshadowed the antagonism between the conservative and progressive, the legalistic and evangelical tendencies which run through church history; it was typical

τάσαι ὅλον τὸν ζυγὸν τοῦ Κυρίου, τέλειος ἔσῃ· εἰ δ' οὐ δύνασαι, ὃ δύνῃ τοῦτο ποίει.   able to bear the whole yoke of the Lord, thou wilt be perfect; but if thou art not able, do what thou canst.

of the conflict between Catholicism and Protestantism. The writer of the *Didache* evidently belonged to the Jewish-Christian party, and in this again to James rather than Peter. James stood at the head of the right wing on the very border of what was afterwards called the Ebionitic heresy, yet differing from it in spirit and aim. Peter occupied a position in the centre between James and Paul. By "the whole yoke of the Lord," the *Did.* means, no doubt, the ceremonial law which Peter had pronounced unbearable, but which James and his sympathizers seem to have borne to the end of their lives from habit and reverence for their ancestral traditions. But the *Did.* shows here a mild and tolerant spirit. The whole yoke is not required, but only as much as one is able to bear. No reflection is cast upon those who cannot bear it.

Ha. has here a long note trying to show that the *Didache* means by "the whole yoke" the counsels of perfection or the requirements of monastic asceticism, especially celibacy. But celibacy is nowhere mentioned in the *Did.* and its over-estimate had no root in the Old Testament where the family occupies a much higher place. All the leaders of the theocracy, the patriarchs, Moses, Aaron, Samuel, David, and several of the Prophets were married men. So was St. Peter. The contempt of marriage was of heathen origin and connected with the dualistic theory held by all the Gnostic sects. Paul denounces it as a doctrine of demons, 1 Tim. iv. 1, 2.

Thou wilt be perfect.] Matt. xix. 21 (εἰ θέλεις τέλειος εἶναι). This passage was very early made the basis of the doctrine of perfection and of a distinction between a lower morality for the masses and a higher morality for the elect few who renounce property and marriage for the sake of Christ, and thus literally follow him. This higher morality acquired a correspondingly higher merit. It is the foundation of the practice of the orthodox Ascetics who abstained from flesh, wine, and marriage for their own good without denouncing them, and of the heretical Enkratites (Ἐγκρατεῖς, Ἐγκρατῖται) who based their abstinence on the essential impurity of the things renounced. In the Nicene age the ascetic tendency assumed an organized form in the system of monasticism, which swept with irresistible moral force over the whole Catholic church, East and West, and found enthusiastic advocates among the greatest of the fathers; as Athanasius and Chrysostom, Jerome and Augustin. How far the Didachographer favored this higher morality does not appear from his book; but from a reference to the community of goods, IV. 8, we may infer that he included voluntary poverty in his ideal of perfection. James of Jerusalem is described by Hegesippus, an orthodox Jewish Christian from the middle of the second century, as a saint of the Nazarite and Essenic type. See *Church History*, i. 276 sq.; ii. 742 sqq.

If thou art not able, etc.] Comp Matt. xix. 11: "All men cannot receive

3. Περὶ δὲ τῆς βρώσεως, ὃ δύνασαι βάστασον· ἀπὸ δὲ τοῦ εἰδωλοθύτου λίαν πρόσ-

3. And as regards food, bear what thou canst, but against idol-offerings be ex-

this saying, but they to whom it is given;" 1 Cor. vii. 7: "Each man hath his own gift from God, one after this manner, and another after that."

3. *As regards food.*] The Levitical law concerning clean and unclean meats. Peter clung to that distinction till he was taught a more liberal view by the revelation at Joppa (Acts x.). The Council of Jerusalem adopted a compromise between the Jewish and Hellenic Christians and prohibited meat which had been offered to the gods (ἀπέχεσθαι εἰδωλοθύτων) and was contaminated with idolatry (Acts xv. 20, 29). The synodical letter was written by James and begins with χαίρειν (ver. 23), like his Epistle (1. 1). To this decree the *Did.* refers and puts upon it a strict construction, like John, Apoc. ii. 14, 20 (where the eating of idol offerings is associated with fornication); while Paul takes a more liberal view and puts the abstinence from such meat on the law of expediency and regard for the conscience of weaker brethren, 1 Cor. viii. 4-13; x. 18, 19, 28, 29; comp. Rom. xiv. 20 sq. The same prohibition was, however, repeated by writers of the second century, *e. g.* Justin Martyr (*Dial. c. Tryph. Jud. c.* xxxiv. and xxxv.), and by the Council of Gangra (in the second canon), and in the sixty-third of the Apost. Canons (see Fulton's *Index Can.* pp 101 and 223). The Greek church regards the decree of Jerusalem as binding for all time. The Latin church followed Paul.

Dead gods.] Comp. 1 Cor. viii. 4. Br. quotes from the so-called second Ep. of Clement to the Cor. c. iii.: ἡμεῖς οἱ ζῶντες τοῖς νεκροῖς θεοῖς οὐ θύομεν καὶ οὐ προσκυνοῦμεν αὐτοῖς, and from the Ep. to Diognetus, c. ii., where the idol gods are called κωφά, τυφλά, ἄψυχα, ἀναίσθητα, ἀκίνητα (deaf, blind, lifeless, destitute of feeling, incapable of motion.)

Here closes the catechetical section. It is purely ethical and practical. But religious instruction necessarily is also historical and dogmatical. It cannot be supposed that this was altogether omitted. How could catechumens be expected to believe in Christ as their Lord and Saviour without some knowledge of his person and work, his life, death and resurrection? The *Didache* implies such additional teaching by its frequent references to the Gospel and the commandments of the Lord from which nothing should be taken away (IV. 13), and by its allusion to the preparatory work of the Holy Spirit in the heart (IV. 10). Much was added by the regular teachers who preached to the catechumens "the word of God" and the "Lordship" of Christ (IV. 1), and by the saints whose faces they should seek day by day (IV. 2). But the moral instruction in the fundamental duties of the Christian was of immediate and primary importance. Very often the preparation for Baptism was even much shorter than here, as in the case of the pentecostal converts (Acts ii.), of the Eunuch (ch. viii.), of Cornelius (ch. x.), and of the jailer at Philippi (xvi. 31). Instruction is supposed to continue after Baptism in the bosom of the Church, which is a training-school for heaven.

ἔχε· λατρεία γάρ ἐστι θεῶν νεκρῶν.   ceedingly on thy guard, for it is a service of dead gods.

Κεφ. ζ́.   CHAP. VII.

BAPTISM.

1. Περὶ δὲ τοῦ βαπτίσματος, οὕτω βαπτίσατε· ταῦτα πάντα προειπόντες, βαπτίσατε εἰς τὸ ὄνομα τοῦ Πατρός

1. Now concerning baptism, baptize thus: Having first taught all these things, baptize ye into the name of

---

NOTES TO CHAPTER VII.

In the first six chapters the Catechumen was addressed as "my child." Chs. VII.-XVI. are addressed to the church members and congregations. Hence the plural, ye (βαπτίσατε VII. 1; comp. ὑμῶν, VIII 1; προσεύχεσθε, VIII. 3; εὐχαριστῆτε, IX. 1; X. 1; ὑμᾶς, XI. 1, 4; κλάσατε, XIV. 1; χειροτονήσατε, XV. 1, γρηγορεῖτε, XVI. 1, etc.). Baptism is first treated of because it is the solemn introduction of the convert into the privileges and duties of church membership. Comp. on this chapter the previous discussions, pp. 29 sqq.

περὶ δέ] δέ and ταῦτα πάντα προειπόντες show the connection with the preceding catechetical instruction which terminates in Baptism. In the case of infant-Baptism, which is not contemplated in the *Did.*, instruction *follows* and looks to confirmation as its aim.

ταῦτα πάντα προειπόντες] Fa.: *having taught all that goes before.* St. and R.: *having said (taught) beforehand all these things.* H. and N.: *having first said all these things.* Sp.: *having first rehearsed all these things.* H. and B.: *having first uttered.* A free rendering would be: *after the preceding instruction in all these things.* It is referred to the first six chapters, except by Bielenstein, who understands by it a baptismal address.

βαπτίσατε] No special officer is mentioned; any Christian, it seems, could baptize at that time. Jesus himself never baptized (John iv. 2), Paul only in exceptional cases (1 Cor. i, 14-17). Justin Mart. mentions no particular baptizer, but Ignatius (*Ad Smyrn.* viii. 2) represents Baptism as a prerogative of the Bishop, or at least as requiring his presence: "It is not lawful without the Bishop either to baptize or to celebrate the Agape; but whatsoever he shall approve of, that is also pleasing to God, so that everything that is done may be secure and valid."

εἰς τὸ ὄνομα, κ. τ. λ.] *into* (not *in*, as in the A. V.) *the name, i. e.* into communion and covenant relationship with the revealed persons of the Holy Trinity. The *Did.* gives the precise baptismal formula, Matt. xxviii. 19. One of the exact quotations. The first proof of the use of this formula. It includes belief in the divinity of Christ and the Holy Spirit, as co-ordinated with the Father. In ver. 3 the article before the divine names is omitted by carelessness. Baptism in the name of Jesus only, is not mentioned; nor is

καὶ τοῦ Υἱοῦ καὶ τοῦ ἁγίου Πνεύματος ἐν ὕδατι ζῶντι.

2. Ἐὰν δὲ μὴ ἔχῃς ὕδωρ ζῶν, εἰς ἄλλο ὕδωρ βάπτισον· εἰ δ' οὐ δύνασαι ἐν ψυχρῷ, ἐν θερμῷ.

3. Ἐὰν δὲ ἀμφότερα μὴ

the Father, and of the Son, and of the Holy Ghost, in living water.

2. And if thou hast not living water, baptize into other water; and if thou canst not in cold, then in warm (water).

3. But if thou hast neither,

---

the threefold repetition, but this must be inferred from τρίς in ver. 3. Tertullian, *Adv. Prax.* xxvi.: "*Nec semel, sed ter, ad singula nomina in personas singulas tinguimur.*"

ἐν ὕδατι ζῶντι] Comp. John iv. 10, 11; vii. 38. Living water is fresh, clean water in motion, *i. e.*, river-water or spring-water, as distinct from stagnant water. Br.: ὕδωρ ζῶν λέγει τὸ ἄρτι ἀπὸ τοῦ φρέατος ἠντλημένον, τὸ ὑπόγυιον, τὸ πρόσφατον καὶ νεαρόν. Ha. would confine *living* water to river-water, and translates *fliessendes Wasser*. The preference of the ante-Nicene Church was for Baptism in a running stream, as the Jordan, the Nile, the Tiber; the baptized standing, undressed, knee-deep or waist-deep in the water, while the baptizer on the shore, slightly clothed, dipped the candidate's head under the water and helped him out of the river. See the illustrations from the Catacombs, p. 88 sqq. The preference for river-Baptism was based on the typical baptism of Christ in the Jordan, and continued till the age of Constantine, when special Baptisteries were built with different apartments and other conveniences, for both sexes and all seasons of the year. Harris (*Teach. of the Ap. and the Sibyll. Books*, p. 13) quotes a parallel from the Sibylline Oracles, IV. 164 [not 165, as he has it].

Ἐν ποταμοῖς λούσασθε ὅλον δέμας ἀεναοισι.

"In perennial streams wash the whole form (body)."

2. εἰς ἄλλο ὕδωρ] Br.: μὴ πρόσφατον μὲν καὶ νεαρόν, ψυχρὸν δέ. Cold water in pools, reservoirs, cisterns, baths. In Galilee the lake was most convenient. In and around Jerusalem the Kidron is dry during the summer, but there are large pools (Bethesda, Hezekiah, the upper and lower Gihon); and almost every house has a cistern filled with rain-water. The same choice is given by Tertullian, *De Bapt.* iv.: "*Nulla distinctio est, mari quis an stagno, flumine an fonte, lacu an alveo diluatur.*"

ἐν θερμῷ] Warm water does not so well symbolize the refreshing, regenerating agency of the Holy Spirit as cold water, but it was permitted in cases of sickness, in cold climates, and inclement seasons. The sacrament was then probably administered at home or in public baths. Br.: εἴτε δι' ἀσθένειαν καὶ ἀρρωστίαν τοῦ σώματος, εἴτε καὶ διὰ τὴν ὥραν τοῦ ἔτους, βάπτισον ἐν θερμῷ ἤτοι χλιαρῷ. Then he quotes from Gregory of Nyssa, who says that all kinds of water are good for Baptism, provided there is faith on the part of the baptized and the blessing of the baptizer. Farrar infers that the writer lived in a cold region.

3. *But if thou hast neither*] *i. e.* neither living water nor other water (cold

ἔχῃς, ἔκχεον εἰς τὴν κεφαλὴν τρὶς ὕδωρ εἰς ὄνομα Πατρὸς καὶ Υἱοῦ καὶ ἁγίου Πνεύματος.

pour [water] thrice upon the head into the name of the Father, and of the Son, and of the Holy Ghost.

---

or warm) in sufficient quantity for immersion. So J. W., Fa., R., Ma. (*en quantité suffisante*), and others. Immersion must be meant in all previous modes, else there would be no difference between them and the last. So also Br.: ἐὰν μήτε ψυχρὸν μήτε θερμὸν ὕδωρ ἔχῃς ἱκανόν ἐ`ς τὸ βάπτισμα, but he adds as an additional condition the necessity of Baptism (καὶ ἀνάγκη ἐπιστῇ τοῦ βαπτίσματος), and confines the permission of pouring to cases of severe sickness (*in periculo mortis*), or what is called clinical Baptism, referring to Tertullian and Cyprian. Fa. assents. But the *Did.* mentions only the scarcity of water, not the state of the candidate. The restriction to cases of sickness, and the disqualification for the priesthood of persons baptized by aspersion on the death-bed, seem to date from the third century. Cyprian (250) had to refute existing doubts on the validity of clinical Baptism. The doubts, however, were not based so much on the defective mode, but on the suspicion of the sincerity of motive.

ἔκχεον, κ. τ. λ.] The first instance of Baptism by pouring or aspersion, and that without the least doubt of its validity. A remarkable passage, which has elicited much discussion and controversy. B. Maury (p. 29): "*Voilà le plus ancien exemple du baptême par aspersion, sans que le moindre doute soit élevé sur sa validité.*" Harn.: "*Wir haben hier das älteste Zeugniss für die Zulassung der Aspersionstaufe; besonders wichtig ist, dass der Verf. auch nicht das geringste Schwanken über ihre Gültigkeit verräth. Die Zeugnisse für ein frühes Vorkommen der Aspersion waren bislang entweder, was ihre Zeit (so die bildlichen Darstellungen der Aspersion; s. Kraus, Roma Sotter. 2. Aufl. S. 311 f.), oder was ihre Beweiskraft (Tert. de pœnit. 6; de bapt. 12) betrifft, nicht genügend sichere; jetzt ist ein Zweifel nicht mehr möglich. Aber die Bedenken über ihre volle Gültigkeit mögen in manchen Landeskirchen uralt gewesen sein; doch kann man sich auf Euseb. H. E. vi. 43, 14, 15, für dieselben nur mit Zurückhaltung berufen; dagegen auf Cypr. ep. 69, 12–14, und auf die Praxis des Orients. Unserem Verf. ist die Aussprechung der drei heiligen Namen die Hauptsache und desshalb auch die dreimalige Aspersion.*" Farrar: "In this permission of (trine) affusion our [Church of England] rubric is anticipated by eighteen centuries. The allusion, however, seems to be to private baptisms *in periculo mortis*. Infant-Baptism is not here contemplated."

εἰς τὴν κεφαλήν] The application of water to the head, as the seat of intelligence, is absolutely essential and the chief part of Baptism; but the wetting of other parts of the body is not indispensable.

τρίς] Trine immersion in the name of the three persons of the Trinity is the universal rule in the Eastern churches. In the West single immersion was practiced for a while in Spain, and sanctioned by Pope Gregory I.; but the Roman Rituals prescribe trine immersion and trine affusion. See Ch. XVII.

4. Πρὸ δὲ τοῦ βαπτίσματος προνηστευσάτω ὁ βαπτίζων καὶ ὁ βαπτιζόμενος* καὶ εἴ τινες ἄλλοι δύνανται· κελεύεις† δὲ νηστεῦσαι τὸν βαπτιζόμενον πρὸ μιᾶς ἢ δύο.

4. But before Baptism let the baptizer and the baptized fast, and any others who can; but thou shalt command the baptized to fast for one or two days before.

Κεφ. η´.

CHAP. VIII.

FASTING AND PRAYER.

1. Αἱ δὲ νηστεῖαι ὑμῶν μὴ ἔστωσαν μετὰ τῶν ὑποκριτῶν· νηστεύουσι γὰρ δευτέ-

1. Let not your fasts be with the hypocrites,* for they fast on the second and fifth

---

* Comp. Matt. vi. 16.

* οἱ βαπτιζόμενοι, Hi.   † κελεύσεις, Br. Hi. Sa. &c.

4. Fasting before Baptism was the general practice in the ante-Nicene age, as we learn from Justin M. and Tertullian. In the Ap. Const. vii. 22, it is enforced by the fasting of Christ *after* Baptism, which He did not need himself, but by which He set us an example. The fasting of the baptizers probably soon went out of use, and is not mentioned in the Ap. Const. It indicates the early age of the *Did.* and the family feeling of the community from which it proceeded.

κελεύεις] Br. reads κελεύσεις. Ha. retains the reading of the MS. in the text, but translates *gebiete*. The command goes beyond the N. T., and is one of the "commandments of men." It was probably based on Matt. xvii. 21 (text rec.); Mark ix. 29: "This kind goeth not out save by prayer and fasting." There is no trace of exorcism in the *Did.*, but it was connected with Baptism in the second century. The rule of fasting is still observed in the East in cases of adult Baptism, which are very rare. In England, down to the time of the Reformation, the candidates for Confirmation and the Bishop were required to fast before the ceremony.

NOTES TO CHAPTER VIII.

1. μετὰ τῶν ὑποκριτῶν] in common, or together with those of the hypocrites, *i. e.*, the Pharisees, as in ver. 2 (not the Jews generally, as Ha. deems probable). Comp. Matt. vi. 16 : "When ye fast, be not as the hypocrites, of a sad countenance." In Luke xviii. 12, the Pharisee in the Temple boasts: "I fast twice in the week." This is the only allusion to Jews in the *Did.*, which differs on the one hand from the anti-Jewish violence of Barnabas, and on the other from the Judaizing sympathy of the Ebionites. Christ opposes the *spirit* of hypocritical and ostentatious fasting, but gives no direction as to days. The *Did.* opposes the Jewish fast *days*, and replaces them by two other fast days. Christian Judaism *versus* Mosaic Judaism. Another indication of the early date and Jewish origin of the

ρᾳ σαββάτων καὶ πέμπτῃ·
ὑμεῖς δὲ νηστεύσατε τετράδα
καὶ παρασκευήν.

2. Μηδὲ προσεύχεσθε ὡς οἱ
ὑποκριταί, ἀλλ' ὡς ἐκέλευσεν
ὁ Κύριος ἐν τῷ εὐαγγελίῳ
αὐτοῦ οὕτως προσεύχεσθε·

day of the week; but ye
shall fast on the fourth day,
and the preparation day
(Friday).

2. Neither pray ye as the
hypocrites,* but as the Lord
commanded in His Gospel, so
pray ye: "Our Father, who

---

* Comp. Matt. vi. 5.

Did. Stated fasting soon became a general custom of the Catholic church. See the passages of Barnabas, of Hermas, Tertullian, Clement of Alex., Origen, Epiphanius, quoted by Br. and Ha. Origen says (*Homil. x. in Levit.*): "*Habemus quartam et sextam septimanæ dies, quibus solemniter jejunamus.*" A change of the day is no guarantee against hypocrisy and self-righteousness.

The Jewish fasts were fixed on Monday and Thursday of the week in commemoration of Moses' ascent to, and descent from, Mt. Sinai; the Christian fasts on Wednesday (τετράς, *feria quarta*) and Friday (παρασκευή, *parasceve, feria sexta*) as the days of the Betrayal and Crucifixion of the Lord, with reference to Matt. ix. 15: "When the bridegroom shall be taken away from them, then they will fast." They were called στάσεις, *dies stationum, semijejunia*. Wednesday dropped gradually out of use as a fast day. After the Council of Elvira, 305, Saturday came to be observed in the West.

These days of fasting, together with the joyous Lord's Day, mentioned in Ch. XIV., determine the Christian week. The death and resurrection of our Lord were the controlling idea of Christian life and Christian worship. But no allusion is made in the *Did.* to the annual festivals and the ecclesiastical year, which was developed gradually from the same central facts.

παρασκευή] the Jewish designation of Friday, on which preparations were made for the proper observance of the Sabbath. Matt. xxvii. 62; Mark xv. 42; Luke xxiii. 54; John xix. 14, 31, 42. It was also called προσάββατον (Sabbath eve), Judith viii. 6; Mark xv. 42. The name is retained in the Greek liturgies and in the Latin office for Good Friday, *Feria sexta in Parasceve*.

2. *As the Lord commanded in His Gospel.*] A distinct reference to St. Matthew. The oldest testimony to its existence and use.

Our Father, etc.] The first quotation of the Lord's Prayer, and the first testimony to its use as a form in daily devotion. The text is taken from Matthew vi. 5-13 (not from the shorter form of Luke), with three unimportant differences unsupported by MS. authority, viz.: 1) ἐν τῷ οὐρανῷ for the favorite plural of Matthew; 2) the omission of the article before γῆς, and 3) τὴν ὀφειλήν for the plural τὰ ὀφειλήματα. The other differences are textual. The *Did.* sustains the textus receptus: 1) in ἐλθέτω for ἐλθάτω, 2) in ἀφίεμεν (*we forgive*) instead of ἀφήκαμεν (*we have forgiven*), which is supported by ℵ, *, B, Z, Origen, and preferred by Tischend.,

Πάτερ ἡμῶν ὁ ἐν τῷ οὐρανῷ, ἁγιασθήτω τὸ ὄνομά σου, ἐλθέτω ἡ βασιλεία σου, γεννηθήτω* τὸ θέλημά σου ὡς ἐν οὐρανῷ καὶ ἐπὶ γῆς. τὸν ἄρτον ἡμῶν τὸν ἐπιούσιον δὸς ἡμῖν σήμερον, καὶ ἄφες ἡμῖν τὴν ὀφειλὴν ἡμῶν ὡς καὶ ἡμεῖς ἀφίεμεν τοῖς ὀφειλέταις ἡμῶν, καὶ μὴ εἰσενέγκῃς ἡμᾶς εἰς πειρασμόν, ἀλλὰ ῥῦσαι ἡμᾶς ἀπὸ τοῦ πονηροῦ· ὅτι σοῦ ἐστιν ἡ δύναμις καὶ ἡ δόξα εἰς τοὺς αἰῶνας.	art in heaven, hallowed be Thy Name. Thy Kingdom come. Thy will be done, as in heaven, so on earth. Give us this day our daily (needful) bread. And forgive us our debt as we also forgive our debtors. And bring us not into temptation, but deliver us from the evil one (or, from evil). For Thine is the power and the glory for ever."ᵃ
3. Τρὶς τῆς ἡμέρας οὕτω προσεύχεσθε.	3. Pray thus thrice a day.

ᵃ Matt. vi. 9-13.   * γενηθήτω, Br. Hi. W. &c.

Westc. and Hort, and the E. R.); and 3) in the insertion of the doxology, though only in part, the βασιλεία and the ἀμήν being omitted. Gregory of Nyssa (as quoted by Tischend. and Hort) has the same form, ὅτι αὐτῷ ἡ δύναμις καὶ ἡ δόξα.

The doxology is absent from the oldest MS. and other authorities, and came into the text from liturgical and devotional use, as we can clearly see here. Dr. Hort says: "There can be little doubt that the doxology originated in liturgical use in Syria, and was then adopted into the Greek and Syriac-Syrian texts of the N. T. It was probably derived ultimately from 1 Chron. xxix. 11 (Heb.), but, it may be, through the medium of some contemporary Jewish usage : the people's response to prayers in the temple is said to have been, 'Blessed be the name of the glory of his kingdom for ever and ever.'" (*Notes on Select Readings*, p. 9.) The doxology varies as to length and wording in different texts and liturgies, until from the time of Chrysostom it assumed its traditional form, but in the Latin and Anglican services the shorter form without the doxology is still alternately used with the other.

3. *Thrice a day.*] Indicates the beginning of Christian regularity and formalism in devotion, in imitation of the Jewish hours of prayer, Dan. vi. 10 (comp. Ps. lv. 17) ; Acts ii. 1, 15; iii. 1; x. 9. Tertullian (*De Orat.* xxv. and *De Jejun.* x.) derives from these passages the duty to pray at the third, sixth and ninth hour (*i. e.* morning, noon, and afternoon or evening), in addition to the ordinary prayers at sunrise and bed-time which need no admonition. He supposes (*De Orat.* x.) that these devotions include the Lord's Prayer (*præmissa legitima et ordinaria oratione quasi fundamento*). See the note of Ha., p. 27, and the ample quotations of Br. p. 31-33.

Κεφ. Θ'.   CHAP. IX.

THE AGAPE AND THE EUCHARIST.

1. Περὶ δὲ τῆς εὐχαριστίας, οὕτω* εὐχαριστήσατε.
    1. Now as regards the Eucharist (the Thank-offering),

---

* οὕτως, B. &c.

NOTES TO CHAPTER IX.

Chs. IX. and X. contain three eucharistic prayers, the oldest known Christian prayers after those in the N. T., with the exception, perhaps, of the intercessory prayer of the Roman church, which is found at the close of the Clementine Epistle to the Corinthians in the complete copy of the Jerusalem MS. (edited by Bryennios, 1875; see *Church History*, ii. 228). They furnish, together with the Lord's Prayer, the elements of a primitive liturgy, and deserve the careful attention of liturgical scholars. They correspond to the Jewish Passover eulogiæ. They are very remarkable for their brevity, simplicity, and high-toned spirituality, but also for the absence of any allusion to the atoning sacrifice of Christ, except perhaps in the mystic meaning of " the *vine* of David " and the *broken* bread. Not even the words of institution, " This is My body," " This is My blood," are mentioned, much less is any theory of the real presence intimated or implied. The prayers are too low for the sacrament, and yet too high for an ordinary meal. But we must remember: 1) The brief and fragmentary character of this section, and the express reference to the extemporaneous effusions of the Prophets which were to follow and to supplement the liturgical forms (X. 7); 2) the designation of the Eucharist as a *sacrifice* foretold by the Prophets, to be celebrated every Lord's Day (XIV. 3), after a public confession of sin and a reconciliation of brethren at strife (XIV. 1, 2); and, 3) the Johannean phraseology and tone of these prayers, which we have previously pointed out (p. 80 sq.). If we read such expressions as " spiritual food and drink " (X. 3), " eternal life " (IX. 3; X. 3), " perfect her in Thy love " (X. 5), in the light of Christ's mysterious discourse after the feeding of the five thousand, and of his Sacerdotal Prayer, and take them in their full Johannean meaning, there can be no doubt that the author believed in the atonement for sin by the sacrifice of our Lord, of which the Eucharist is the perpetual memorial. B. M.: "*Ces prières respire un vif sentiment de gratitude pour Dieu et de solidarité avec tous les membres de l'Église, dispersés aux quatre vents du ciel.*" He likewise points to the striking resemblance of these prayers to the Sacerdotal Prayer, but derives them from oral tradition rather than from the fourth Gospel.

1. εὐχαριστία] In the N. T.: *thankfulness*, or *thanksgiving*, especially also before a meal. The verbs εὐχαριστέω and εὐλογέω are used by our Saviour in blessing the bread and the cup at the Last Supper, Matt. xxvi. 27; Luke, xxii. 17, 19; 1 Cor. xi. 24. Hence in post-Apostolic and Patristic writers *Eucharist* was the technical term for the Lord's Supper as a sacrifice of thanksgiving for all the gifts of God, especially for the redemption of Christ. It was usually applied to the whole act of celebration, with or without the Agape, but sometimes also to the consecrated elements, by

2. Πρῶτον περὶ τοῦ ποτη- 2. First for the cup:
ρίου. Εὐχαριστοῦμέν σοι, "We give thanks to Thee,
Πάτερ ἡμῶν, ὑπὲρ τῆς ἁγίας our Father, for the holy vine
ἀμπέλου Δαβὶδ τοῦ παιδός of David Thy servant, which
σου, ἧς ἐγνώρισας ἡμῖν διὰ thou hast made known to us

give thanks after this manner:

Ignatius, Justin M., Irenæus, and others. Here it includes the Agape. See the notes of Br., and Suicer, *Thesaur.* sub εὐλογία. B. Maury (p. 81): "*L'eucharistie est pour notre auteur, à la fois un repas fraternel (car elle est jointe à l'agape), une action de grâces pour le bienfait de la revelation de Jesus pour les fruits de la terre et une oblation des cœurs purifié et réconciliés, comme étant le sacrifice le plus agréable à Dieu.*"

2. *First for the cup.*] For the order see Luke xxii. 17-19; 1 Cor. x. 16. In ver 5 ("let no one eat or drink") the usual order is implied.

ὑπὲρ τῆς ἁγίας ἀμπέλου Δαβίδ] A peculiar expression. It may mean the Christian church, as the true theocracy, the Lord's vineyard; comp. Ps. lxxx. 15: "the vineyard which thy right hand hath planted;" Isa. v. 1 sqq.; Jer. ii. 21; xii. 10. But it is probably a mystic name of Christ, suggested by the parable of the Vine, John xv. 1: "I am the true vine;" comp. Ps. lxxx. 8: "Thou hast brought a vine out of Egypt;" and Matt. xxvi. 29: "this fruit of the vine." This interpretation would imply a reference to the atoning blood. Clement of Alexandria (*Quis dives salvus*, 29), uses the same expression, probably in view of this passage and with reference to the sacrament of the Lord's Supper. "This (Jesus)," he says, "who poured out for us the wine of the vine of David, that is to say, His blood" (οὗτος ὁ τὸν οἶνον, τὸ αἷμα τῆς ἀμπέλου τῆς Δαβίδ, ἐκχέας ἡμῖν). Br. quotes also another passage from the same author (*Pædagogue* i. 5): "For the vine produces wine as the Word produces blood, and both drink for the health of men; the wine, for the body, the blood for the spirit" (φέρει γὰρ οἶνον ἡ ἄμπελος ὡς αἷμα ὁ λόγος, ἄμφω δ᾽ ἀνθρώποις ποτὸν εἰς σωτηρίαν, ὁ μὲν οἶνος τῷ σώματι, τὸ δὲ αἷμα τῷ πνεύματι). Origen (*Hom.* vi. in *Jud.*) calls Christ "the true vine from the root of David." (See Append.). The vine was a favorite symbol of Christ in the pictures of the Catacombs. See *Ch. Hist.* ii. 273 sq.

Thy servant] παῖς means both *son* and *servant*, and is used of Christ by St. Peter four times in Acts iii. 13, 26; iv. 27, 30; with reference to the servant of Jehovah (עֶבֶד יְהוָה) in Isaiah xlii. 1 (quoted by Matt. xii. 18).

An indication of the antiquity of the *Did.* and probably also of a knowledge of Acts (but not of Ebionitism; for Christ is called the Son of God in the baptismal formula, VII. 1, and indirectly in XVI. 4, see note there). The designation was a liturgical form. In the prayer of the Roman church in the first Ep. of Clemens, ch. lix. (recovered by Br. in 1875), Christ is three times called παῖς and παῖς ἠγαπημένος. Polycarp used it twice in his last prayer, according to the *Martyr. Polyc.* c. xiv. (Funk, *P. Aps.* i. 298), namely, ὁ τοῦ ἀγαπητοῦ καὶ εὐλογητοῦ παιδός σου Ἰησοῦ Χριστ-

Ἰησοῦ τοῦ παιδός σου· σοὶ ἡ δόξα εἰς τοὺς αἰῶνας.

3. Περὶ δὲ τοῦ κλάσματος·

Εὐχαριστοῦμέν σοι, Πάτερ ἡμῶν, ὑπὲρ τῆς ζωῆς καὶ γνώσεως, ἧς ἐγνώρισας ἡμῖν διὰ Ιησοῦ τοῦ παιδός σου· σοὶ ἡ δόξα εἰς τοὺς αἰῶνας.

4. Ὥσπερ ἦν τοῦτο * κλάσμα διεσκορπισμένον ἐπάνω τῶν ὀρέων καὶ συναχθὲν ἐγένετο ἕν, οὕτω συναχθήτω σου ἡ ἐκκλησία ἀπὸ τῶν πε-

through Jesus, Thy servant: to Thee be the glory for ever."

3. And for the broken bread:

"We give thanks to Thee, our Father, for the life and knowledge which Thou hast made known to us through Jesus, Thy servant: to Thee be the glory for ever.

4. "As this broken bread was scattered upon the mountains and gathered together became one, so let Thy church be gathered together

---

* τό inserted after τοῦτο by v. Gebh. IIa. Z.

τοῦ, and διὰ ἀγαπητοῦ σου παιδός. It is retained several times in the prayers of the Apost. Const. viii. 5, 14, 39, 40, 41.

3. κλάσμα] A fragment (from κλάω, to break), the broken bread of the Agape and the Eucharist. The noun (in the plural) is so used in the accounts of the miraculous feeding (Matt. xiv. 20 ; Mark vi. 43; viii. 19, 20 ; John vi. 12, 13), and the verb κλάσαι τὸν ἄρτον, of the Agape and the Lord's Supper (Matt. xxvi. 26 ; Mark xiv. 22 ; Luke xxii. 19 ; Acts ii. 46; xx. 7, 11 ; 1 Cor. x. 16). Metaphorically, it designates the body of Christ, as broken really on the cross and typically in the Eucharist, 1 Cor. xi. 24: τὸ σῶμα τὸ ὑπὲρ ὑμῶν κλώμενον (tex. rec. and in margin of R. V.). "The breaking of bread" (ἡ κλάσις τοῦ ἄρτου) was an apostolic term for the Agape and the Lord's Supper combined, Acts ii. 42.

4. *Scattered* (in grains) *upon the mountains*, or, *hills*.] Entirely inapplicable to Egypt, and hence omitted in the Egyptian prayer quoted below, but quite appropriate in a hilly country like Syria and Palestine, where the *Did.* originated.

Gathered together, became one.] The idea was probably suggested by 1 Cor. x. 17, where Paul, with reference to the communion, says: "We, who are many, are one bread, one body: for we all partake of the one bread." Irenæus (*Adv. Hær.* iv. 18, 5) speaks of "the bread which is produced from the *earth* (ἀπὸ τῆς γῆς ἄρτος), when it receives the invocation of God, is no longer common bread, but the Eucharist, consisting of two realities, earthly and heavenly."

Let Thy church be gathered together into Thy kingdom.] An important distinction between the ἐκκλησία and the βασιλεία, which occurs again in the third prayer X. 5. The Church is a training-school for the kingdom

ράτων τῆς γῆς εἰς τὴν σὴν βα-
σιλείαν· ὅτι σοῦ ἐστιν ἡ δόξα
καὶ ἡ δύναμις διὰ Ἰησοῦ Χριστοῦ εἰς τοὺς αἰῶνας.

5. Μηδεὶς δὲ φαγέτω μηδὲ
πιέτω ἀπὸ τῆς εὐχαριστίας
ὑμῶν, ἀλλ' οἱ βαπτισθέντες
εἰς ὄνομα Κυρίου· καὶ γὰρ
περὶ τούτου εἴρηκεν ὁ Κύ-

from the ends of the earth
into Thy kingdom, for Thine
is the glory and the power
through Jesus Christ for
ever."

5. But let no one eat or
drink of your Eucharist, except those baptized into the
name of the Lord ; for as regards this also the Lord has

of God. The Church is manifold and will pass away with its various organizations; the kingdom is one and will last forever, now as a kingdom of grace, then as a kingdom of glory. This distinction was obscured in the Roman church, which identifies herself with *the* church catholic, and the church with the kingdom. It was measurably restored by the Protestant distinction between the visible and invisible church. The difference is very apparent in the parables which illustrate the kingdom, and in such passages as "to them (to the poor in spirit, to the children) belongs the kingdom of heaven;" "to enter the kingdom" (Matt. v. 3; xviii. 3, 4; Mark, x. 14; John, iii. 5), or "the kingdom of God is not meat and drink, but righteousness and peace and joy in the Holy Ghost" (Rom. xiv. 17). In such cases it would be improper to substitute "the church." It is significant that Christ uses ἐκκλησία only twice (in Matthew and nowhere else), but βασιλεία (with τῶν οὐρανῶν or τοῦ Θεοῦ) twenty-three times in Matthew alone. The eschatological aim of this prayer is remarkable and was suggested by Matt. xxvi. 29, and 1 Cor. xi. 26 ("till He come"). "*Es ist*," says Ha., "*der höchsten Beachtung werth, dass der Verfasser im Abendmahl eine eschatologische Allegorie gefunden hat, die [uns] sonst nirgends begegnet.*"

From the ends of the earth.] Comp. X. 5, "from the four winds." Matt. xxiv. 31: "they [the angels] shall gather together His elect from the four winds, from one end of heaven to the other."

5. *Except those baptized.*] The communion is for baptized believers, and for them only. Baptism is the sacramental sign and seal of regeneration and conversion; the Lord's Supper is the sacrament of sanctification and growth in spiritual life. Justin Martyr (*Apol.* I. c. lxvi.) says: "This food is called among us the Eucharist (εὐχαριστία), of which no one is allowed to partake but he who believes that the things which are taught by us are true, and who has been washed with the washing that is for the remission of sins and unto regeneration, and who is so living as Christ has delivered. For not as common bread and common drink (ὡς κοινὸν ἄρτον οὐδὲ κοινὸν πόμα) do we receive these [elements]." In the second century the divine service was sharply divided into two parts, the service of the catechumens (*missa catechumenorum*) and the service of the faithful (*missa fidelium*). Hence the Ap. Const.. vii. 25, lay great stress on the exclusion of unbelievers from the Eucharist.

ριος· Μὴ δῶτε τὸ ἅγιον τοῖς κυσί.

said: "Give not that which is holy to the dogs."[a]

Κεφ. ί.

1. Μετὰ δὲ τὸ ἐμπλησθῆναι οὕτως εὐχαριστήσατε·

CHAP. X.
POST-COMMUNION PRAYER.

1. Now after being filled, give thanks after this manner:

[a] Matt. vii. 6.

Give not, etc.] A justifiable application of the warning of Christ, Matt. vii. 6. Ha. aptly quotes Tertullian, *De Præscr.*, xli., who says of the services of the heretics that they throw "*sanctum canibus et porcis margaritas*."

A remarkable parallel prayer to the thanksgiving for the bread, to which Dr. Swainson first called attention, and which is quoted also by De Romestin (p. 100), is found in Pseudo-Athanasius *De Virginitate*, *s. De Ascesi*, § 13 (Athan. *Opera* ed. Migne. iv. 266, in Tom. xxviii. of his "Patrol. Gr."). Here the virgin is directed "ὅταν κατεσθῆς ἐπὶ τῆς τραπέζης καὶ ἔρχῃ κλάσαι τὸν ἄρτον .. εὐχαριστοῦσα λέγε, εὐχαριστοῦμέν σοι, Πάτερ ἡμῶν, ὑπὲρ τῆς ἁγίας ἀναστάσεως σου, διὰ γὰρ Ἰησοῦ τοῦ παιδός σου ἐγνώρισας ἡμῖν αὐτήν, καὶ καθὼς ὁ ἄρτος οὗτος διεσκορπισμένος ὑπῆρχεν ὁ ἐπάνω ταύτης τῆς τραπέζης καὶ συναχθεὶς ἐγένετο ἕν, οὕτως ἐπισυναχθήτω σου ἡ ἐκκλησία ἀπὸ τῶν περάτων τῆς γῆς εἰς τὴν βασιλείαν σου, ὅτι σου ἐστὶν ἡ δύναμις καὶ ἡ δόξα εἰς τοὺς αἰῶνας. ἀμήν." The words ἐπάνω τῶν ὀρέων, "upon the hills," so inapplicable to Egypt, are omitted after διεσκορπισμένος.

NOTES TO CHAPTER X.

Ch. X. contains the post-communion prayer. Like all similar prayers of later times, it consists of two parts, thanksgiving and intercession. It follows in this respect Jewish precedent. The prayer after drinking the Hallel cup at the Passover reads thus : " Blessed be Thou, O Lord our God, King of the world, for the vine and the fruit of the vine, and for the harvest of the field, and for the glorious, good and roomy land which Thou didst give to our fathers in Thy good pleasure, that they might eat of its fruit and be satisfied by its bounty. Have mercy, O Lord our God, upon us and upon Israel, Thy people, and upon Jerusalem, Thy city [and upon Thine altar and Thy temple ; and build Jerusalem, the holy city, speedily in our days, and bring us thither and make us rejoice in her, that we may eat of her fruit and be satisfied with her bounty, and praise Thee in holiness and purity ; and refresh us on this festive day of unleavened bread]; for Thou, O Lord, art good and doest good to all [so shall we thank Thee for the land and for the fruit of the vine]. Blessed be Thou, O Lord, for the land and its fruits, for ever. Amen." The bracketed sentences seem to presuppose the second destruction of Jerusalem, and are omitted in an Oxford MS. of the twelfth century. See G. Bickell, *Messe und Pascha*, Mainz, 1872, and the Innsbruck "Zeitschrift für kath. Theol." 1880, 90–112.

1. μετὰ δὲ τὸ ἐμπλησθῆναι] Changed by the Ap. Const. into μετὰ

2. Εὐχαριστοῦμέν σοι, Πάτερ ἅγιε, ὑπὲρ τοῦ ἁγίου ὀνόματός σου, οὗ κατεσκήνωσας ἐν ταῖς καρδίαις ὑμῶν* καὶ ὑπὲρ τῆς γνώσεως καὶ πίστεως καὶ ἀθανασίας, ἧς ἐγνώρισας ἡμῖν διὰ Ἰησοῦ τοῦ παιδός σου· σοὶ ἡ δόξα εἰς τοὺς αἰῶνας.

3. Σύ, δέσποτα παντοκράτορ, ἔκτισας τὰ πάντα ἕνεκεν τοῦ ὀνόματός σου, τροφήν τε καὶ ποτὸν ἔδωκας τοῖς ἀνθρώποις εἰς ἀπόλαυσιν ἵνα σοι εὐχαριστήσωσιν, ἡμῖν δὲ ἐχαρίσω πνευματικὴν τροφὴν καὶ

2. "We thank Thee, Holy Father, for Thy holy Name, which Thou hast caused to dwell (tabernacle) in our hearts, and for the knowledge and faith and immortality which Thou hast made known to us through Jesus Thy Servant, to Thee be the glory for ever.

3. "Thou, O, Almighty Sovereign, didst make all things for Thy Name's sake; Thou gavest food and drink to men for enjoyment that they might give thanks to Thee; but to us Thou didst

---

* ἡμῶν, Br. &c.

μετάληψιν, *after partaking* of the communion. But the *Did.* must mean a regular meal, the Agape then still being connected with the sacramental celebration, as in the church at Corinth (1 Cor. xi. 20–22); it was separated in the time of the younger Pliny and Justin Martyr. John (vi. 12) uses the phrase ὡς δὲ ἐνεπλήσθησαν, "when they were filled," of the feeding of the five thousand.

2. *Holy Father*] The same address in the Sacerdotal Prayer, John xvii. 11, but nowhere else. God is next addressed as "Almighty Sovereign" (ver. 3) and last as "Lord," (ver. 8.) These terms correspond, as Ha. points out, to the three divisions of the prayer: 1) thanks for the revelation and redemption through Christ, 2) thanks for the creation and spiritual food and drink and eternal life through Christ, 3) intercession for the church of God. A similar division in Justin M. *Apol.*, i. LXV.

Caused to dwell] κατασκηνόω, *to pitch tent, to encamp*, has here the transitive sense as in the Sept. Ps. xxii. 2 ; 2 Chr. vi. 2. The simple verb is a favorite term of St. John, who uses it intransitively with reference to the Shekina, the indwelling of Jehovah in the Holy of Holies ; comp. John i, 14 ἐσκήνωσεν ἐν ἡμῖν); Apoc. xxi. 3 (σκηνώσαι μετ' αὐτῶν).

3. *Almighty Sovereign*] or *Ruler*. παντοκράτωρ, in the Sept., often in the Apoc., and in 2 Cor. vi. 18 (in a quotation from the Sept.). Introduced into the Apostles' Creed: πιστεύω εἰς θεὸν παντοκρατορα, *Credo in Deum Patrem omnipotentem*. On δεσπότης see the note of Hitchcock, p. 51.

ποτὸν καὶ ζωὴν αἰώνιον διὰ τοῦ παιδός σου.

4. Πρὸ πάντων εὐχαριστοῦμέν σοι ὅτι δυνατὸς εἶ σύ†· ἡ δόξα εἰς τοὺς αἰῶνας.

5. Μνήσθητι, Κύριε, τῆς ἐκκλησίας σου τοῦ ῥύσασθαι αὐτὴν ἀπὸ παντὸς πονηροῦ καὶ τελειῶσαι αὐτὴν ἐν τῇ ἀγάπῃ σου, καὶ σύναξον αὐτὴν ἀπὸ τῶν τεσσάρων ἀνέμων τὴν ἁγιασθεῖσαν εἰς τὴν σὴν βασιλείαν, ἣν ἡτοίμασας

freely give spiritual food and drink and eternal life through Thy servant.

4. "Before all things we give thanks to Thee that Thou art mighty; to Thee be the glory for ever.

5. "Remember, O Lord, Thy Church to deliver her from all evil and to perfect her in Thy love; and gather her together from the four winds,ᵃ sanctified for Thy kingdom which Thou didst prepare for her; for Thine

---

ᵃ Matt. xxiv. 31.

†σοί, substituted for σύ by Br. Hi. Z. σοί inserted after σύ by Ha.

Spiritual food and drink, etc.] A spiritual conception of the Eucharist based on the Lord's discourse on the bread of life, John vi. 35 sqq. Ignatius and Justin Martyr first suggested a strongly realistic conception, which terminated at last in the dogma of transubstantiation. Ignatius (*Ad Ephes.* xx.) calls the Eucharist a medicine of immortality (φάρμακον ἀθανασίας) and an antidote against death. Justin M. speaks of a change (μεταβολή) of the elements. But the African and Alexandrian fathers favored a spiritual conception till the time of Augustin, who was the chief authority for that view (afterwards advocated by Ratramnus and Berengar, but forced to give way to transubstantiation).

Deliver her from every evil] Comp. John xvii. 15, and Matt. vi. 13 (ῥῦσαι ἡμᾶς ἀπὸ τοῦ πονηροῦ).

5. τελειῶσαι αὐτὴν ἐν τῇ ἀγάπῃ σου.] A peculiarly Johannean expression. Comp. John xvii. 23 (ἵνα ὦσιν τετελειωμένοι εἰς ἕν); 1 John ii. 5; ἡ ἀγάπη τοῦ θεοῦ τετελείωται); iv. 12–18 (ἡ τελεία ἀγάπη).

τὴν ἁγιασθεῖσαν] sanctified by the sacrifice of Christ; comp. John xvii. 19: ὑπὲρ αὐτῶν ἐγὼ ἁγιάζω ἐμαυτόν, ἵνα ὦσι καὶ αὐτοὶ ἡγιασμένοι ἐν ἀληθείᾳ, and Heb. x. 10: ἡγιασμένοι ἐσμὲν διὰ τῆς προσφορᾶς τοῦ σώματος Ἰησοῦ Χριστοῦ ἐφάπαξ. Ha. inserts a comma after ἁγιασθεῖσαν, and connects εἰς τὴν σὴν βασ. with the verb σύναξον. Br. omits the comma and explains: "sanctified in order to inherit the kingdom." So also B. M.: "*elle qui a été sanctifiée en vue de ton royaume que tu lui a préparé.*" Sa.: "*après l'avoir sanctifiée pour ton royaume,*" etc.

Which Thou didst prepare for her.] This includes the doctrine of foreordination. Comp. Matt. xxv. 34, κληρονομήσατε τὴν ἡτοιμασμένην

αὐτῇ· ὅτι σοῦ ἐστιν ἡ δύνα- | is the power and the glory
μις καὶ ἡ δόξα εἰς τοὺς αἰῶ- | for ever.
νας.

6. Ἐλθέτω χάρις καὶ παρελ-
θέτω ὁ κόσμος οὗτος. Ὡς
ἀννὰ† τῷ θεῷ * Δαβίδ. Εἴ
τις ἅγιός ἐστιν, ἐρχέσθω· εἴ
τις οὐκ ἔστι, μετανοείτω· μα-
ραναθά. Ἀμήν.

6. "Let grace come, and let this world pass away.[a] Hosanna to the God (Son) of David. If any one is holy let him come, if any one is not holy let him repent. Maranatha.[b] Amen."

---

[a] Comp. 1 Cor. vii. 31.   [b] 1 Cor. xvi. 22.

*Ὡσαννά, Br. Hi. Ha. W.
†υἱῷ, Br. Hi. W. H. & B. Sp., but Ha. R. retain θεῷ.

ὑμῖν βασιλείαν ἀπὸ καταβολῆς κόσμου. On the distinction between the church and the kingdom see note on IX. 4.

6. *Let grace come, etc.*] Or, to retain the paronomasia : "Let grace appear, and let the world disappear." Comp. 1 Cor. vii. 31: "the fashion of this world passeth away." ἐλθέτω χάρις must be explained in the eschatological sense of the grace of the second coming ; comp. 1 Pet. i. 13 (τὴν χάριν ἐν ἀποκαλύψει Ἰησοῦ Χρ.); and Apoc. xxii. 17, 20. Hence the conjecture of Potwin, Χριστός for χάρις, is unnecessary. The opposite anti-millennarian tendency and the mighty missionary impulse of the Church led afterwards to pray for the *delay* of the end of the world, as Tertullian, contrary to his own millennarian views, records in *Apol.* c. xxxix.: "*oramus pro mora finis.*" See Ha., p. 35.

To the God of David.] A strong testimony for the author's belief in the divinity of Christ, to whom it must refer in connection with his coming here spoken of. It may be traced back to our Lord's interpretation of the Messianic Ps. cx. 1 ("The Lord said unto my Lord") in Matt. xxii. 42-46. Br. and Hi. conjecture τῷ υἱῷ, for τῷ θεῷ, to conform the passage to Matt. xxi. 9, 15 : "Hosanna to the *Son* of David." But Ha. defends the reading of the MS. with six arguments. There arose an early prejudice against the designation of Christ as David's *Son ;* Barnabas calls it an "error of the sinners," and substitutes for it "the Lord of David." It is much easier to account for the change of θεῷ into υἱῷ than *vice versa*.

Let him repent.] Here, according to liturgical usage, would be the place for the communion ; but as this was indicated at the close of the preceding prayers (IX. 5), we must understand this as an invitation to catechumens and unbelievers to join the Church. There was at the time not yet a strict separation of the two parts of the service, the *missa catechumenorum* and the *missa fidelium*, as in the third century. In some American churches it is customary to exhort the non-communicants after the communion to repent and to unite with God's people. Br. explains: "Let the saints come to meet the Lord. As many as are unbelievers, and not yet washed in the laver of

7. Τοῖς δὲ προφήταις ἐπιτρέπετε εὐχαριστεῖν ὅσα θέλουσιν.

Κεφ. ιαʹ.

1. Ὅς ἂν οὖν ἐλθὼν διδάξῃ

7. But permit the Prophets to give thanks as much as [in what words] they wish.

CHAP. XI.

APOSTLES AND PROPHETS.

1. Whosoever then comes

grace, or who have fallen away, let them repent. May the Lord come and his kingdom." Ha.: *"Das ἔρχέσθω bezieht sich auf den Zutritt zu der versammelten, auf ihren Herrn wartenden Gemeinde; an die spätere, ähnlich lautende Formel in Bezug auf den Zutritt zum Genuss der heil. Speise, ist nicht zudenken."*

Maran-atha] Aramæan (מָרָן אֲתָה), *i. e., the Lord cometh* (κύριος ἔρχεται); comp. 1 Cor. xvi. 22, where the same word occurs, and Apoc. xxii. 20: "Amen: come, Lord Jesus" (ἔρχου, κύριε Ἰησοῦ). The word was a reminder of the second coming, perhaps "a mysterious pass-word of the early Christians" (Bisping). Harnack: *"Man beachte, wie dieses uralte, dramatisch aufgebaute Stossgebet (vota suspirantia, sagt Tertullian) die Gemeinde schliesslich in den Moment der Wiederkunft Christi versetzt; so lebendig war die Hoffnung auf die Nähe derselben."* Sabatier: *"Le cri de Maranatha annonce la venue du Seigneur, non dans les espèces consacrées, mais son retour glorieux sur les nuées du ciel."* Field (in his *Otium Norvicense, Pars tertia*, a criticism of the Revised N. T., 1881. p. 110), renders the Syriac *Moran etho*: *"Our Lord came,"* or rather *"Our Lord is come"* (not "cometh"), since the Syriac verb represents either ἦλθε (Jude, ver. 14), or ἥκει (Luke xv. 27; 1 John v. 20). "Accordingly Theodoret and Schol. Cod. 7, explain the word to mean ὁ κύριος ἦλθεν; Schol. Cod. 19, ὁ κύριος παραγέγονεν; and Schol. Cod. 46, ὁ κύριος ἡμῶν ἥκει."

7. *Permit the Prophets.*] The whole congregation is addressed as having control over this matter. The liberty of extemporaneous prayer combined with liturgical forms. First, full liberty for all to pray in public meeting, 1 Cor. xiv. 29, 31; then restriction of liberty to the prophets, as here; at last prohibition of free prayer. Justin Martyr, whom Br. aptly quotes, accords the same freedom to the presiding minister, or bishop (*Apol.* i. lxvii): "When our prayer is ended, bread and wine and water are brought, and the President (ὁ προεστώς) in like manner offers prayers and thanksgivings according to his ability (ὅση δύναμις αὐτῷ)." The people were to respond, "Amen." Clement of Rome, like Paul, warns the Corinthians against disorder and confusion, *Ad. Cor.* cap. xli.: "Let each of you, brethren, in his own order give thanks unto God (ἐν τῷ ἰδίῳ τάγματι εὐχαριστείτω τῷ θεῷ), maintaining a good conscience and not transgressing the appointed rule of his service (τὸν ὡρισμένον τῆς λειτουργίας αὐτοῦ κανόνα), but acting with all seemliness." Ha.: *"In der Did. gelten die Propheten als die Virtuosen des Gebets."*

NOTES TO CHAPTER XI.

Here begins the directory of discipline and the officers of the Church, Chs. XI.-XIII., and Ch. XV. See the general discussion, pp. 62 sqq.

ὑμᾶς ταῦτα πάντα τὰ προειρημένα, δέξασθε αὐτόν·

2. Ἐὰν δὲ αὐτὸς ὁ διδάσκων στραφεὶς διδάσκῃ ἄλλην διδαχὴν εἰς τὸ καταλῦσαι, μὴ αὐτοῦ ἀκούσητε· εἰς δὲ τὸ προσθεῖναι δικαιοσύνην καὶ γνῶσιν Κυρίου, δέξασθε αὐτὸν ὡς Κύριον.

3. Περὶ δὲ τῶν ἀποστόλων καὶ προφητῶν κατὰ τὸ δόγμα τοῦ εὐαγγελίου οὕτως ποιήσατε.

4. Πᾶς δὲ ἀπόστολος ἐρχόμενος πρὸς ὑμᾶς δεχθήτω ὡς Κύριος.

and teaches you all the things aforesaid, receive him.

2. But if the teacher himself being perverted teaches another teaching to the destruction [of this], hear him not, but if [he teach] to the increase of righteousness and the knowledge of the Lord, receive him as the Lord.

3. Now with regard to the Apostles and Prophets, according to the decree (command) of the gospel, so do ye.

4. Let every Apostle that cometh to you be received as the Lord.[a]

---

[a] Matt. x. 40.

2. *Hear him not.*] 2 John 10: "If any one cometh unto you, and bringeth not this teaching, receive him not into your house."

Receive him as the Lord.] Matt. x. 40: "He that receiveth you receiveth me, and he that receiveth me receiveth Him that sent me." John xiii. 20. Br. quotes also Ignatius, *Ad. Eph.* vi.

3. *Apostles and Prophets.*] The first order of ministers whose field is the world. They have their commission directly from the Lord: while Bishops and Deacons are elected by the congregation, XV. 1.

The decree of the Gospel.] The directions of Christ in sending out the Twelve and the Seventy, Matt. x. 5-12; Luke ix. 1-6; x. 4-21. δογμα in the sense of *decree, ordinance*, as in Luke ii. 1; Acts xvi. 4; xvii. 7; Eph. ii. 15.

4. *Apostle.*] In a wider and secondary sense; as in Acts xiv. 4, 14; Rom. xvi. 7; 1 Cor. xv. 5, 7; 1 Thess. ii. 6. A wandering evangelist or itinerant preacher who carries the Gospel to the unconverted, and is therefore not allowed to remain in one place. See the description of this class of ministers in Euseb. H. E. iii. 37, quoted on p. 68. Hermas uses the term likewise in the wider sense and speaks of forty Apostles and Teachers, *Simil.* ix. 15, 16. 17, 25; *Vis.* iii. 5. The *Did.* cannot mean the original Twelve and Paul, for to them the restriction of ver. 5 would not apply (Paul sojourned three years in Ephesus, and eighteen months, and again three months in Corinth). It is a second and weaker generation. An indication that the book was written after A.D. 70. According to Mommsen, in *Corpus Inscript. Lat.*, Tom. ix. num. 648 (Berol. 1883), the Jews used the term "Apostle" till the sixth century for a special class of officials. This is con-

5. Οὐ* μενεῖ δὲ ἡμέραν μίαν, ἐὰν δὲ ᾖ χρεία, καὶ τὴν ἄλλην, τρεῖς δὲ ἐὰν μείνῃ, ψευδοπροφήτης ἐστίν.

6. Ἐξερχόμενος δὲ ὁ ἀπόστολος μηδὲν λαμβανέτω εἰ μὴ ἄρτον ἕως οὗ αὐλισθῇ· ἐὰν δὲ ἀργύριον αἰτῇ, ψευδοπροφήτης ἐστί.

7. Καὶ πάντα προφήτην λαλοῦντα ἐν πνεύματι οὐ πειρά-

5. But he shall not remain [longer than] one day; and, if need be, another [day] also; but if he remain three [days] he is a false prophet.

6. And when the Apostle departeth, let him take nothing except bread [enough] till he reach his lodging (night-quarters). But if he ask for money, he is a false prophet.

7. And every prophet who speaks in the spirit ye shall

---

* οὐ, om. Hi.; οὐ μενεῖ δὲ εἰ μή, Ha.; οὐ, with μενέτω: "when he makes a stay, *let him do it* for one day (only)," Zahn.

---

firmed by the Theodosian Code (Lib. xvi. Tit. viii., Lex 14), which speaks of Jewish Presbyters and those "*quos ipsi Apostolos vocant.*"

5. *Not longer than one day.*] The Jerus. MS. is here evidently defective. Hi. omits οὐ, Ha. inserts εἰ μή (comp. XII. 2), Z. changes οὐ into οὖ and supplies μενέτω (*where* he makes a stay, *let him stay* only for a day).

Three days.] Two or three days of hospitality are granted to every wayfaring Christian brother, XII. 2, but to an Apostle only one or two days. This restriction indicates a frequent abuse of the Apostolic or Evangelistic office for purposes of gain. Lucian's historical novel *Peregrinus Proteus*, in which he ridicules both the Cynic philosophy and the Christian religion, furnishes a commentary.

A false Prophet.] Here equivalent for false Apostle. False Apostles are mentioned 2 Cor. xi. 13; Rev. ii. 2, 20; false Prophets, Matt. vii. 15; xxiv. 11; Mark xiii. 22; Luke vi. 26; 2 Pet. ii. 1; 1 John iv. 1. Ha. quotes Tertullian *De Præser.* iv.: "*Qui pseudo-prophetæ sunt, nisi falsi prædicatores? Qui pseudo-apostoli nisi adulteri evangelisatores?*"

Hermas, in the *Eleventh Commandment*, draws from experience an interesting comparison between true and false Prophets. The true Prophet, he says, is "gentle, quiet, humble, and abstains from all wickedness and from the vain desire of this world, and makes himself the poorest of all men;" while the false Prophet "exalts himself, is hasty, shameless, talkative, and takes hire for his prophecy." Comp. the notes of Ha. and the art. of Bonwetsch, *Die Prophetie im apost. und nach-apost. Zeitalter*, quoted p. 143.

6. Comp. Matt. x. 9, 10; Mark vi. 8; Luke ix. 3.

7. *Speaks in (the) spirit.*] ἐν πνεύματι, without the article, in distinction from ἐν νοΐ, that is in ecstasy, or in a highly exalted state of mind when it is the organ of the Holy Spirit. 1 Cor. xii. 8; xiv. 2; Rev. i. 10; iv. 2.

σετε ουδέ διακρινεῖτε· πᾶσα γὰρ ἁμαρτία ἀφεθήσεται, αὕτη δὲ ἡ ἁμαρτία οὐκ ἀφεθήσεται.

8. Οὐ πᾶς δὲ ὁ λαλῶν ἐν πνεύματι προφήτης ἐστίν, ἀλλ ἐὰν ἔχῃ τοὺς τρόπους Κυρίου. Ἀπὸ οὖν τῶν τρόπων γνωσθήσεται ὁ ψευδοπροφήτης καὶ ὁ προφήτης.

9. Καὶ πᾶς προφήτης ὁ ρίζων* τράπεζαν ἐν πνεύματι οὐ φάγεται ἀπ᾽ αὐτῆς, εἰδὲ μήγε ψευδοπροφήτης ἐστί.

10. Πᾶς δὲ προφήτης διδάσκων τὴν ἀλήθειαν, εἰ ἃ διδάσκει οὐ ποιεῖ, ψευδοπροφήτης ἐστί.

11. Πᾶς δὲ προφήτης δεδοκιμασμένος ἀληθινὸς ποιῶν† εἰς μυστήριον κοσμικὸν‡ ἐκ-

not try nor prove; for every sin shall be forgiven, but this sin shall not be forgiven.

8. Not every one that speaks in the spirit is a Prophet, but only if he has the behavior (the ways) of the Lord. By their behavior then shall the false prophet and the [true] Prophet be known.

9. And no Prophet that orders a table in the spirit eats of it [himself], unless he is a false prophet.

10. And every Prophet who teaches the truth if he does not practice what he teaches, is a false prophet.

11. And every approved, genuine Prophet, who makes assemblies for a worldly mys-

---

* ὁρίζων, Br. et al.   † ῥυῶν, Hi.
‡ κοσμικῶν, Hi., κόσμιον, Petersen; ποιῶν μυστ. κοσμ. εἰς ἐκκλ. Z.

This sin shall not be forgiven.] Matt. xii. 31: "Every sin and blasphemy shall be forgiven unto men; but the blasphemy against the Spirit shall not be forgiven."

8. Conformity to the Lord's example is the criterion of a true Prophet. "By their fruits ye shall know them." Comp. Matt. vii. 15-23.

9. *Order a table.*] A love-feast ordered in ecstasy. A strange fact not mentioned elsewhere. The true Prophet will not profane a sacred ordinance to personal uses by making a meal of the Eucharist. Gordon proposes a different reading, ὁ ῥέζων, "*who is offering.*" ῥέζω is a rare poetic word occurring in Homer and Hesiod, in the sense *to perform a sacrifice.*

11. κοσμικόν.] *Belonging to this world* (in a local, not in a moral sense), *mundane, worldly* or *earthly*, as opposed to ἐπουράνιον, *heavenly;* comp. Heb. ix. 1, where the tabernacle is called τὸ ἅγιον κοσμικόν, the sanctuary of this world, as distinct from the sanctuary in heaven. In Rabbinical Hebrew it was used as a substantive.

ποιῶν εἰς μυστήριον κοσμικὸν ἐκκλησίας.] Another translation: "who acts with reference to an earthly mystery of the church." The most difficult passage in the *Did.* and not yet satisfactorily explained. Br. admits that it is

κλησίας, μὴ διδάσκων δὲ ποι-   tery [?], but does not teach
εῖν ὅσα αὐτὸς ποιεῖ, οὐ κρι-   [others] to do what he him-
θήσεται ἐφ᾿ ὑμῶν· μετὰ Θεοῦ   self does, shall not be judged

---

obscure and indistinct (σκοτεινὸν καὶ ἀσαφές), and proposes his explanation with diffidence (p. 44). ποιῶν seems to require an object; ἐκκλησίας may be the plural accusative depending on ποιῶν, or the singular genitive depending on μυστήριον. The earthly mystery may be a mystery in the Church, or the Church itself, as the Gospel is called a mystery (Rom. xvi. 25, 26). For the absence of the article in the latter case, comp. Heb. ii. 12 (ἐν μέσῳ ἐκκλ.) and 3 John 6.—Different renderings : Fa.: *who makes assemblies for a mystery of this world.* H. and B.: *acting with a view to the mystery of the church on earth.* St.: *dealing with reference to the mystery of the church here below.* H. and N.: *working unto the mystery of the church in the world.* O.: *with a view to the world-mystery of the church.* Sp.: *who summons assemblies for the purpose of showing an earthly mystery.* W.: *der Versammlungen zu einem Geheimniss vor der Welt macht.* Ha.: *der im Hinblick auf das irdische Geheimniss der Kirche handelt.* Z.: *wenn er eine symbolische Handlung weltlicher Art vollzieht.* Kr.: *wenn er in Bezug auf die Ehe die etwas Weltliches und doch in der Kirche (nach Eph. V. 32) etwas Geheimnissvolles ist, für seine Person starke Dinge leistet (durch Verheirathung und Wiederverheirathung).* B.-M.: *exerçant son corps (?) en vue du mystère terrestre de l'église (sans imposer aux autres ses pratiques ascétiques).* Sa.: *travaillant au mystère terrestre de l'église.* Hi. changes the reading ποιῶν into μυῶν, and κοσμικόν into κοσμικῶν, "*initians in mysterium secularium ecclesias*" (with reference to the Gnostic and Montanistic distinction between psychical or secular, and pneumatic or spiritual churches), but has found no response. Petersen (p. 8) proposes κόσμιον, *chaste*, in opposition to the unchaste mysteries of the heathen; likewise without response.

Interpretations: (1) Br., Z., Fa., R., Sp.: symbolical actions like those of Isaiah (xx. 2, 4), Jeremiah (xix. 1; xxvii. 2; xxviii. 10), Ezekiel (iv. 12–v. 3), Hosea (i. 2 sqq.), Agabus (Acts xi. 28; xxi. 11). Br.: ἐκκλησιάζων τὸν λαὸν εἰς τὸ ἐπιδεῖξαι αὐτῷ ἔργον συμβολικόν ὁ αὐτὸς ἐργάζεται ἐπὶ παρακλήσει καὶ νουθεσίᾳ τῶν πιστῶν. The Prophet would at times perform a striking and exciting symbolic action, like the old Prophets; but in all these dramatic shows there was grave danger of vanity and imposition for the sake of gain. Hence the author, while permitting such exceptional exhibitions, guards against abuse by insisting that the Prophet should receive no pay, and not teach others to perform like acts. (2) Ha.: abstinence from marriage. He refers to Eph. v. 32, Ignatius, *Ad Polyc.* v., and Tertullian, *De Monog.*, xi., which recommend celibacy as being more consistent with a perfect Christian than marriage. But this is far-fetched, and by the great mystery Paul does not mean celibacy, but marriage or rather the union of Christ with his church. Besides celibacy needed no apology in view of the ascetic tendency which set in very early in opposition to the bottomless sexual depravity of the heathen world. (3) Krawutzcky (in his second article, *l. c.*, p. 581, note) takes the very opposite view, that the *Did.* allows

γὰρ ἔχει τὴν κρίσιν· ὡσαύ- | by you; for he has his judg-
τως γὰρ ἐποίησαν καὶ οἱ ἀρ- | ment with God (or, his judg-
χαῖοι προφῆται. | ment is in the hands of God);
for so did also the ancient
Prophets.

12. Ὅς δ' ἂν εἴπῃ ἐν πνεύ- | 12. But whosoever says in
ματι· Δός μοι ἀργύρια ἢ ἕτε- | the spirit: Give me money
ρά τινα, οὐκ ἀκούσεσθε αὐ- | or any other thing, ye shall
τοῦ· ἐὰν δὲ περὶ ἄλλων ὑσ- | not listen to him; but if he

the Prophets to marry and even to remarry, after the example of some of the Hebrew Prophets, provided only they do not teach others to imitate their example. He refers to the case of Hos. i. 2; iii. 1; but this marriage to an adulteress is probably to be understood figuratively. (4) E. B. Birks (in "The Guardian" for June 11, 1884): "making garniture of a church for a sacramental celebration." Prophets may make shrines or altars for the celebration of the Eucharist so long as they do not encourage others in setting up separate conventicles. (5) Hicks in "The Guardian," approved by E. Venables in "The British Quart. Rev." for May, 1885 (p. 353): calling assemblies of the church for the purpose of revealing future events in the world's history, as were foretold by Agabus (Acts xi. 28), or impending judgments on the enemies of the church. Such predictions might provoke disloyalty to the civil government. This gives very good sense. (6) Gordon: "doing with an eye to the church's mystery in the world," *i.e.*, the hidden potency of the Kingdom of God on earth. (7) Sabatier identifies the mystery of the Church with the mystery of the Gospel, Eph. vi. 19, and contrasts it with the mystery of iniquity, 2 Thess. ii. 7. "*Annoncer l'Evangile, c'est hâter la venue des temps, c'est aider le mystère terrestre de l'Église*" (comp. Apoc. x. 7: "then is finished the mystery of God, according to the good tidings which he declared to his servants the prophets").—I venture, modestly, to suggest two more interpretations. (8) "The earthly mystery of the church" is the sacrament or the sacrifice of the Eucharist, which in the Greek church is emphatically called μυστήριον (comp. Eph. v. 32). This might be supported by the connection with "the ordering a table" just spoken of (XI 9), and with Chs. IX. and X. and XIV., all of which treat of the Eucharistic sacrifice; but it does not suit the last clause of the verse. (9) The observance of the ceremonial law, or the bearing of the whole yoke; comp. VI. 2 and the note there. Upon the whole, however, the interpretation of Br. is, perhaps, the least objectionable, and next to it that of Hicks.

The ancient Prophets] of the Old Testament. Symbolic actions are reported of several of them, Isaiah, Jeremiah, Ezekiel, Hosea. The reference to the Hebrew Prophets is natural, and it is necessary if we assign the *Did.* to the first century. Ha. and Hi., who date it from the middle of the second century, understand the early *Christian* Prophets, as Agabus, the daughters of Philip, Judas, Silas, Quadratus. But they could hardly be called ἀρχαῖοι even then without distinguishing them from the still older Hebrew Prophets.

τερούντων εἴπῃ δοῦναι, μηδεὶς αὐτὸν κρινέτω.

Κεφ. ιβ´.

1. Πᾶς δὲ ὁ ἐρχόμενος ἐν ὀνόματι Κυρίου δεχθήτω, ἔπειτα δὲ δοκιμάσαντες αὐτὸν γνώσεσθε, σύνεσιν γὰρ ἕξεται*, δεξιὰν καὶ ἀριστεράν.

2. Εἰ μὲν παρόδιός ἐστιν ὁ ἐρχόμενος, βοηθεῖτε αὐτῷ ὅσον δύνασθε· οὐ μενεῖ δὲ πρὸς ὑμᾶς εἰ μὴ δύο ἢ τρεῖς ἡμέρας, ἐὰν ᾖ ἀνάγκη.

3. Εἰ δὲ θέλει πρὸς ὑμᾶς καθῆσθαι†, τεχνίτης ὤν, ἐργαζέσθω καὶ φαγέτω.

bid you to give for others that lack, let no one judge him.

Chap. XII.
Receiving Disciples.

1. Let every one that comes in the name of the Lord be received, and then proving him ye shall know him; for ye shall have understanding right and left.

2. If indeed he who comes is a wayfarer, help him as much as ye can; but he shall not remain with you longer than two or three days, unless there be necessity.

3. If he wishes to settle among you, being a craftsman (artisan), let him work and eat (earn his living by work).

---

* ἕξετε, Br. &c.   † καθῆσαι, Br.; καθίσαι, Ha. Hi. Z.

Notes to Chapter XII.

1. *Every one*] who professes Christ. Hospitality is to be exercised to all without distinction, but not to the extent of encouraging idleness. Every one who can must work. Comp. 2 Thess iii. 10–12.

Ye shall know, etc.] Ye shall know the difference between right and wrong, between true and false Christianity. The Ap. Const. vii. 28 paraphrase the passage: "Ye are able to know the right hand from the left and to distinguish false teachers from true teachers." Br. refers to 2 Cor. vi. 7 (" by the armor of righteousness on the righth and and the left"); 2 Tim. ii. 7(" the Lord shall give thee understanding in all things "). Ha. takes σύνεσιν ἕξετε as a parenthesis.

2. παρόδιος.] Post-classical for παροδίτης, *traveller.* The Sept. has πάροδος, 2 Kings xii. 4 (which in classical Greek means *entrance, side-entrance*). Paul uses ἐν παρόδῳ, *by the way,* 1 Cor. xvi. 7. The Jews, having no country of their own, and being engaged in merchandise were great travellers, and so were the Jewish Christians (as Aquila and Priscilla, whom we find in Rome, Corinth, and Ephesus, Acts xvi. 3–5; xviii. 2). This habit tended to strengthen the ties of brotherhood and to promote catholicity.

3. *Let him work, etc.*] 2 Thess. iii. 10. "If any will not work, neither

4. Εἰ δὲ οὐκ ἔχει τέχνην, κατὰ τὴν σύνεσιν ὑμῶν προνοήσατε, πῶς μὴ ἀργὸς μεθ' ὑμῶν ζήσεται χριστιανός.

5. Εἰ δ' οὐ θέλει οὕτω ποιεῖν, χριστέμπορός ἐστιν· προσέχετε ἀπὸ τῶν τοιούτων.

4. But if he has not handicraft (trade), provide according to your understanding that no Christian shall live idle among you.

5. And if he will not act thus he is a Christ-trafficker. Beware of such.

Κεφ. ιγ'.

1. Πᾶς δὲ προφήτης ἀληθινός, θέλων καθῆσθαι* πρὸς ὑμᾶς, ἄξιός ἐστι τῆς τροφῆς αὐτοῦ.

CHAP. XIII.

TREATMENT OF PROPHETS.

1. But every true Prophet who wishes to settle among you is worthy of his food (or, support).

---

*καθῆσαι, Br.; καθίσαι, Ha. Hi. Z.

let him eat." Paul set the noblest example of self-support, working at his own trade at night after preaching the gospel during the day. The early Christians were mostly of the lower classes, artisans, freedmen, slaves. Society, like a house, is built and regenerated from the bottom upwards, not from the top downwards. Ha.: " *Wie nachdrücklich wird die Pflicht der Arbeit eingeschärft, und zugleich die Solidarität aller Gemeindeglieder!* "

A Christian.] The name only once in the *Did.* It arose among the Gentiles in Antioch between 40 and 50, Acts xi. 26, and occurs again xxvi. 28, and 1 Pet iv. 16. The usual designations among the Christians were, "disciples," "believers," "brethren," "saints." The last is used in the same general sense in *Did.* IV. 2.

χριστέμπορος.] A *Christ-trafficker, Christ-monger, i. e.,* one who makes gain out of his Christian profession (comp. 1 Tim. vi. 5); a new word, but expressive and used afterwards by Pseudo-Ignatius and Pseudo-Clement. Barnabas (ch. x.) warns against selfish idlers who sponge upon Christian charity. Ignatius (*Ad Eph.* vii.) speaks of men "whose practice is to carry about the name (of Christ) in wicked guile," whom we must shun " as wild beasts." Polycarp (*Ad Phil.* vi.) warns the Philippians against those "who bear the name of the Lord in hypocrisy." Hermas (*Mand.* xi.) describes an itinerant charlatan who demands the first place in the assembly, lives in great luxury, and refuses to prophesy except for payment in advance. Lucian's Peregrinus Proteus is such an impostor who deceived the simple-hearted Christians. That race will never die out in this world.

NOTES TO CHAPTER XIII.

1. *Every Prophet who wishes to settle among you.*] There were two classes of Prophets, itinerant and stationary or local; while the Apostles were only itinerants (XI. 5).

Worthy of his food] or support, maintenance, no more and no less. The

2. Ὡσαύτως διδάσκαλος ἀ-
ληθινός ἐστιν ἄξιος καὶ αὐ-
τός ὥσπερ ὁ ἐργάτης τῆς τροφῆς αὐτοῦ·

3. Πᾶσαν οὖν ἀπαρχὴν
γεννημάτων ληνοῦ καὶ ἄλω-
νος βοῶν τε καὶ προβάτων
λαβὼν δώσεις [τὴν ἀπαρχὴν]*
τοῖς προφήταις· αὐτοὶ γάρ
εἰσιν οἱ ἀρχιερεῖς ὑμῶν.

2. Likewise a true Teacher is himself worthy, like the workman, of his food.ᵃ

3. Therefore thou shalt take and give all the first-fruit of the produce of the wine-press and threshing-floor, of oxen and sheep, to the Prophets; for they are your chief-priests.

---

* Omit τ. ἀπαρχ. Br. et al.   ᵃ Matt. x. 10.

---

principle and duty of ministerial support are laid down by Christ, Matt. x. 10 ; Luke x. 7, and by Paul 1 Cor. ix. 7, 9, 13, 14 ; 1 Tim. v. 18.

2. *Likewise a true Teacher.*] Prophets and Teachers are associated in Acts xiii. 1, distinguished in 1 Cor. xii. 28, 29; Eph. iv. 11. Paul calls himself "an Apostle and Teacher" of the Gentiles, 1 Tim. ii. 7; 2 Tim. i. 11. Rulers (ἡγούμενοι) and Teachers are identified in Heb. xiii. 7, 17. See the note of Ha., p. 50 sq.

3. *All the first-fruits.*] According to the provisions of the Mosaic law, Ex. xxii. 29; Num. xviii. 12 ; Deut. xviii. 3, 4 ; Ez. xliv. 30; Neh. x. 35–37. See Smith's or Schaff's *Bible Dict.* sub *First-fruits.* The law prescribed also tithes, *i. e.* the tenth of all produce, as well as of flocks and cattle; they belong to Jehovah and were paid to the Levites as the reward for their service, who were again ordered to devote a tenth of these receipts to the maintenance of the high-priest (Num. xviii. 21–28). The tithe is not mentioned in the *Did.*, but the Ap. Const. vii. 29 add after the first-fruits : "Thou shalt give the tenth of thy increase to the orphan, and to the widow, and to the poor and to the stranger."

Your chief priests.] Ap. Const. II. 25. In the N. T. ἀρχιερεύς is used (1) of the Jewish high-priest (הַכֹּהֵן הַגָּדוֹל, ὁ ἱερεὺς ὁ μέγας), Matt. xxvi. 3, 62, 63, 65, etc.; (2) of Christ, the true and eternal high-priest, in the Ep. to the Hebrews (ii. 17 ; iii. 1, etc.) ; (3) in the plural, of the members of the Sanhedrin, and of the heads of the twenty-four classes of priests (Matt. ii. 4, etc). The N. T. teaches the universal priesthood of all believers (2 Pet. ii. 9; Rev. i. 6), but not a special priesthood of ministers in distinction from the laity. This passage gives the first intimation of the sacerdotal view of the ministry, but the author confines it to the Prophets, and probably uses the word in a figurative or spiritual sense. The idea crept early and easily from the synagogue into the church, first by way of comparison and soon after in a realistic sense. About the same time (between A.D. 90 and 100) Bishop Clement of Rome (*Ad Cor.* ch. xl.) significantly *compared* the Christian ministry to the Aaronic priesthood and made a distinction between the

4. Ἐὰν δὲ μὴ ἔχητε προφήτην, δότε τοῖς πτωχοῖς·

5. Ἐὰν σιτίαν ποιῇς, τὴν ἀπαρχὴν λαβὼν δὸς κατὰ τὴν ἐντολήν·

6. Ὡσαύτως κεράμιον οἴνου ἢ ἐλαίου ἀνοίξας, τὴν ἀπαρχὴν λαβὼν δὸς τοῖς προφήταις.

7. Ἀργυρίου δὲ καὶ ἱματισμοῦ καὶ παντὸς κτήματος λαβὼν τὴν ἀπαρχὴν ὡς ἄν σοι δόξῃ, δὸς κατὰ τὴν ἐντολήν.

4. But if ye have no Prophet, give to the poor.

5. If thou preparest bread, take the first fruit and give according to the commandment.

6. Likewise when thou openest a jar of wine or of oil, take the first-fruit and give to the Prophets.

7. And of silver, and raiment, and every possession, take the first-fruit, as may seem good to thee, and give according to the commandment.

---

clergy and laity The passage has been declared an interpolation, but without any good reason. The next distinct trace of this idea we find in a letter of Polycrates, Bishop of Ephesus, about A.D. 190, to Victor, Bishop of Rome, as preserved by Eusebius (v. 24). Polycrates calls St. John "a priest who wore the sacerdotal plate" (ἱερεὺς τὸ πέταλον πεφορηκώς). Comp. *Church Hist.* ii. 216; and i. 431. After the close of the second century all the Bishops and Presbyters were called *priests* (ἱερεῖς, *sacerdotes*), and the Bishop sometimes *high-priest* (ἀρχιερεύς, *summus sacerdos, pontifex maximus*). Tertullian uses the terms (*De Bapt.* vi.; *De Pud.* i.; *De Exhort. Cast.*), but as a Montanist he protested against a priestly order and asserted the universal priesthood of all believers. Cyprian is the chief champion of sacerdotal episcopacy in the Ante-Nicene age. In the *Ap. Const.* the hierarchical and sacerdotal system is fully developed. I will only quote one passage (ii. 25): "The Bishops are your high-priests, as the Presbyters are your priests, and your present Deacons instead of your Levites; so are also your readers, your singers, your porters, your deaconesses, your widows, your virgins, and your orphans; but He who is above all these is the High Priest." The sacerdotal view prevailed in all Christendom till the time of the Reformation, which returned to the primitive idea of the universal priesthood of believers. See *Church Hist.* ii. 127, and 150 sq., and Lightfoot, Excurs. on the Christian Ministry in *Com. on Philippians*, p. 253 sqq.

4. *If ye have no Prophet.*] There were therefore congregations without Prophets, but not without Bishops and Deacons (XV. 1). In the absence of the former the latter were to teach. The *Did.* marks the transition period from the Apostles and Prophets who were passing away, to the Bishops and Presbyters who began to take their place.

σιτίαν.] σιτία means in Byzantine Greek *batch* or *baking of bread*. (See

Κεφ. ιδ'.

CHAP. XIV.

THE LORD'S DAY AND THE SACRIFICE.

1. Κατὰ κυριακὴν δὲ Κυρίου συναχθέντες κλάσατε ἄρτον καὶ εὐχαριστήσατε προσεξομολογησάμενοι* τὰ πα-

1. And on the Lord's Day of the Lord ᵃ come together, and break bread, and give thanks, having before con-

---

ᵃ Rev. i. 10.

* προεξομ. v. Gebhardt, Hi. Ha. [in the notes but not in the text] Z.

Sophocles, *Gr. Lex.*, p. 990.) In classical Greek σιτία is the plural of σιτίον, and means *grain* or *food*.

NOTES TO CHAPTER XIV.

This chapter interrupts the connection and should precede Ch. IX. But the writer, before proceeding to the local officers of the Church, inserts here a direction concerning the Lord's Day observance and public worship which is to be conducted chiefly by the Prophets (comp. X. 7). Perhaps the more immediate association in his mind was the priest (XIII. 3) and the sacrifice (XIV. 1); for the ideas of priest, altar, and sacrifice are inseparable, whether they be used in the realistic or in the figurative sense.

1. *On the Lord's Day of the Lord.*] The first use of κυριακή as a noun, but with the pleonastic addition τοῦ κυρίου. St. John (Rev. i. 10) uses it first as an adjective, κυριακὴ ἡμέρα, Dominica dies. The resurrection of Christ, his appearance to the disciples, and the pentecostal outpouring of the Holy Spirit, all of which took place on the first day of the week, are the basis of the Christian Sunday. Its observance in the Apostolic age may be inferred from Acts xx. 7; 1 Cor. xvi. 2; Rev. i. 10. The *Did.* gives us the first post-Apostolic testimony for Sunday as a day of public worship. Pliny (Letter to Trajan, x. 97) calls it "the stated day," on which the Christians in Bithynia assembled before daylight, to sing hymns to Christ as a God, and to bind themselves by a *sacramentum*. Barnabas (Ep. xv.) calls it "the eighth" day, in opposition to the Jewish Sabbath. Ignatius (*Ad Magnes.* ix.) calls it κυριακή, likewise in opposition to the Jewish observance (μηκέτι σαββατίζοντες, ἀλλὰ κατὰ κυριακὴν ζῶντες). Justin Martyr: "the day called Sunday" (ἡ τοῦ Ἡλίου λεγομένη ἡμέρα, Apol. i. lxvii.), on which the Christians hold their common assembly, because it is the first day of creation and the day on which Jesus Christ their Saviour rose from the dead.

Break bread and give thanks.] Designation of the Agape and Eucharist. Acts ii. 46; xx. 7, 11; 1 Cor. x. 16. This was the regular Lord's Day service, connected no doubt with Scripture reading, praying, singing, exhortation, according to Old Testament precedent. Ha.: "*Es ist von höchster Bedeutung für die Geschichte des Cultus, dass der Verfasser der Did. für den Sonntagsgottesdienst lediglich die Feier des Abendmahls nach vorhergegangener Exhomologese vorschreibt.*"

προσεξομολογησάμενοι] *having confessed in addition* to, or in connec-

ραπτώματα ὑμῶν, ὅπως κα- | fessed your transgressions,[a]
θαρὰ ἡ θυσία ἡμῶν ᾖ. | that your sacrifice may be pure.

2. Πᾶς δὲ ἔχων τὴν * ἀμφι- | 2. Let no one who has a
βολίαν μετὰ τοῦ ἑταίρου αὐ- | dispute with his fellow come
τοῦ μὴ συνελθέτω ὑμῖν ἕως | together with you until they

[a] Comp. James v. 16.

* τινά, von Gebhardt, Ha. Z.

tion with thanksgiving; but this verb occurs nowhere else and is probably a writing error for προεξομ, *having before confessed*. This emendation was suggested by von Geb. and is adopted by Ha. in the notes, though not in the text. First confession of sin, then thanksgiving. Confession is here enjoined as a regular part of public worship, and is also enforced IV. 14 (ἐν ἐκκλησίᾳ ἐξομολογήσῃ τὰ παραπτώματά σου). Comp. Jas. v. 16. In the Ap. Const. vii. 30 the confession of sin in connection with the Eucharist is omitted.

That your sacrifice may be pure.] θυσία (from θύω, *to kill and offer as sacrifice*) is often used tropically of spiritual sacrifices of praise and self-consecration, Rom. xii. 1 (θυσίαν ζῶσαν): 1 Pet. ii 5 (πνευματικὰς θυσίας); Phil. ii. 17 (θυσίᾳ καὶ λειτουργίᾳ τῆς πίστεως); Heb. xiii. 15 (ἀναφέρωμεν θυσίαν αἰνέσεως διαπαντὸς τῷ θεῷ.) The Eucharist, as the name indicates, was regarded as a feast of thanksgiving for all the mercies of God, temporal and spiritual, especially for the redemption, and as a sacrifice of renewed consecration of the whole congregation to Christ in return for his self-sacrifice for our sins. The elements of bread and wine were tokens and types of the gifts of nature and the gifts of grace with reference to the broken body and shed blood. They were presented as a thank-offering by the members of the congregation, and the remnants were given to the poor. In these gifts the Christian people yielded themselves as a priestly race to God, the giver of all good. Justin Martyr, *Dial. c. Tryph. Jud.* c. cxvii.: "Accordingly God, anticipating all the sacrifices which we offer through this name, and which Jesus the Christ enjoined us to offer, *i. e.*, in the Eucharist of the bread and the cup, and which are presented by Christians in all places throughout the world, bears witness that they are well-pleasing to Him." In his account of the celebration of the Eucharist, *Apol.* i. lxv., Justin M says: "When the President (the Bishop) has given thanks, and all the people have expressed their assent [by saying *Amen*], those who are called by us 'Deacons' give to each of those present to partake of the bread and wine mixed with water over which the thanksgiving was pronounced, and to those who are absent they carry away a portion (lxvi.). And this food is called among us 'Eucharist,' of which no one is allowed to partake but those who believe that the things we teach are true, and who have been washed with the washing for the remission of sins and who are living as Christ has enjoined."

2. *Until they are reconciled.*] According to the direction of Christ, Matt

οὐ διαλλαγῶσιν, ἵνα μὴ κοι- | are reconciled, that your sac-
νωϑῇ ἡ ϑυσία ἡμῶν *. | rifice may not be defiled.ᵃ
3. Αὕτη γάρ ἐστιν ἡ ῥηϑεῖ- | 3. For this is that which
σα ὑπὸ Κυρίου· Ἐν παντὶ | was spoken by the Lord: "In
τόπῳ καὶ χρόνῳ προσφέρειν | every place and time offer me

* ὑμῶν, Br. &c.   ᵃ Comp. Matt. v. 23, 24.

---

v. 23, 24. Reconciliation among men is a necessary prerequisite of a worthy communion which celebrates the reconciliation between God and man through the atoning sacrifice of Christ. This is implied here. Br. compares Irenæus, *Adv. Hær.* iv. 18, 1.

May not be defiled.] Br. quotes Matt. xv. 11-20; Mark vii. 15-23; Acts x. 15, 21, 28; Heb. ix. 13. Justin M. says (Apol. i. lxvi.): . . . "So we, who through the name of Jesus have believed as one man in God the Maker of all, have been stripped, through the name of his first-begotten Son, of the filthy garments, that is of our sins; and being vehemently inflamed by the word of his calling, we are the true high-priestly race of God, as even God himself bears witness, saying, that in every place among the Gentiles sacrifices are presented to Him well pleasing and pure (Mal. i. 10-12.) Now God receives sacrifices from no one, except through his priests."

3. *Spoken by the Lord.*] κύριος seems to refer to Christ, just mentioned in ver. 1, and implies that the writer believed in the pre-existence of Christ who spoke through the Prophets; comp. 1 Pet. i. 10, 11. (An argument against the charge of Ebionism.) The distinction made by Gordon that the *Did.* uses κύριος without the article of God, and ὁ κύριος of Christ is untenable; see the title διδαχὴ κυρίου.

In every place.] A free quotation of Mal. i. 11, 14 (Sept.). The only quotation from the canonical books of the O. T. except that in XVI. 7 from Zech. xiv. 5. See above, Ch. XXIV. 78 sqq.

The passage of Malachi was generally understood in the ancient church to be a prophecy of the eucharistic sacrifice. Justin M. refers to it frequently, *Apol.* i. lxvi.; *Dial. c. Tryph. Jud.* c. xxviii.; xli.; cxvi.; cxvii.; so also Irenæus *Adv. Hær.* iv. 17, 5, 6; 18, 1, 4; Clement of Alex. *Strom.* v. 14, 136; Tertullian, *Adv. Jud.* v.; *Adv. Marc.* iii. 22. The "Second Ordinances of the Apostles" (δεύτεραι τῶν Ἀποστ. διατάξεις) spoken of in the second Irenæus Fragment (ed. Stieren i. 854, and ed. Harvey ii. 500), probably refer to the Eucharistic sacrifice as the new sacrifice of the New Covenant (νέα προσφορά ἐν τῇ καινῇ διαϑήκῃ), in the place of the old sacrifices which ceased with the destruction of the Temple. Br. thinks it not unlikely (μηδὲν ἀπίϑανον) that these second Apostolic Ordinances are identical with our *Did.* This is at least far more probable than the opposite conjecture of Krawutzcky that the *Did.* was written in Ebionitic opposition to those Ordinances on account of the omission of νέα. See above p. 24, note. Bickell, on the contrary, finds here the germ of the Roman mass, and R. Catholic controversialists constantly appeal to the same passage of Malachi in proof of that institution. But the *Did.* plainly means only a thank-

μοι θυσίαν καθαράν· ὅτι βασιλεὺς μέγας εἰμί, λέγει Κύριος, καὶ τὸ ὄνομά μου θαυμαστὸν ἐν τοῖς ἔθνεσι.	a pure sacrifice, for I am a great King, saith the Lord, and my name is wonderful among the Gentiles."[a]
Κεφ. ιε΄.	CHAP. XV.
	BISHOPS AND DEACONS.
1. Χειροτονήσατε οὖν ἑαυτοῖς ἐπισκόπους καὶ διακόνους	1. Elect therefore for yourselves Bishops and Deacons

[a] Mal. i. 11, 14.

---

offering by the whole congregation. The idea of the Lord's Supper as an actual though unbloody repetition of the atoning sacrifice on the cross by the hands of the priest, came in later in the third century, at the time of Cyprian, in connection with the sacerdotal conception of the ministry, and the literal interpretation of the altar, Heb. xiii. 10. The truth underlying the Greek and Roman mass (for in this respect the two churches are entirely agreed) is the commemoration and renewed application of the one all-sufficient sacrifice on the cross in the Lord's Supper. On the gradual development of the idea of the Eucharistic sacrifice see *Church History*, vol. ii. 245 sq. and iii. 503 sqq.

NOTES TO CHAPTER XV.

This chapter treats of the local or stated and permanent ministers of the gospel. It is separated from the chapters on the Apostles and Prophets (XI.–XIII.), but connected with them by the eucharistic sacrifice on the Lord's Day as the chief part of Christian worship (XIV.). The congregations could not rely on the occasional services of these itinerant Teachers, who gradually passed away, together with the extraordinary gifts. Comp. above Ch. XII., p. 73 sqq.

1. χειροτονήσατε.] The Greek verb means in classical writers *to stretch out the hand* (χείρ), or *to vote for by show of hands*; then *to elect, to appoint*. So in Acts xiv. 23; 2 Cor. viii. 19; and here. Ignatius uses it in the same sense, *e. g.*, *Ad Philad.* x. 1 (ed. Zahn, p. 80: πρέπον ἐστίν ὑμῖν, ὡς ἐκκλησίᾳ θεοῦ, χειροτονῆσαι διάκονον εἰς τὸ πρεσβεῦσαι ἐκεῖ θεοῦ πρεσβείαν); comp. *Ad Smyrn.* xi. 2; *Ad Polyc.* vii. 2. The congregational officers, and even the Bishops and Popes were elected and supported by the people during the first centuries; but afterwards the Priests of the diocese monopolized the election of the Diocesan, and the college of Cardinals the election of the Pope. In later ecclesiastical Greek, χειροτονέω means *to ordain*, Ap. Const. viii. 4, 5, and Ap. Can. i.: "Let a Bishop be ordained (χειροτονείσθω) by two or three Bishops," and Ap. Can. ii.: "Let a Presbyter or Deacon, and the other Clergy, be ordained by one Bishop." Hence the Ap. Const. in the parallel passage vii. 31 substitute προχειρίσασθε for χειροτονήσατε.

ἐπισκόπους.] Used in the same sense as πρεσβύτεροι, who for this reason are omitted, as in the Pastoral Epistles (1 Tim. iii. 8–13), and Phil. i. 1.

ἀξίους τοῦ Κυρίου, ἄνδρας πραεῖς καὶ ἀφιλαργύρους καὶ ἀληθεῖς καὶ δεδοκιμασμένους· ὑμῖν γὰρ λειτουργοῦσι καὶ αὐτοὶ τὴν λειτουργίαν τῶν προφητῶν καὶ διδασκάλων.

2. Μὴ οὖν ὑπερίδητε αὐτούς· αὐτοὶ γάρ εἰσιν οἱ τετιμημένοι ὑμῶν μετὰ τῶν προφητῶν καὶ διδασκάλων.

3. Ἐλέγχετε δὲ ἀλλήλους μὴ ἐν ὀργῇ ἀλλ' ἐν εἰρήνῃ, ὡς ἔχετε ἐν τῷ εὐαγγελίῳ· καὶ παντὶ ἀστοχοῦντι κατὰ τοῦ ἑτέρου μηδεὶς λαλείτω μηδὲ παρ' ὑμῶν ἀκουέτω,* ἕως οὗ μετανοήσῃ.

worthy of the Lord, men meek, and not lovers of money, and truthful, and approved; for they too minister to you the ministry of the Prophets and Teachers.

2. Therefore despise them not, for they are those that are the honored [men] among you with the Prophets and Teachers.

3. And reprove one another not in wrath, but in peace, as ye have [it] in the gospel; and with every one that transgresses against another let no one speak, nor let him hear [a word] from you until he repents.

---

* ἀκουέσθω, Ili. Z.

The Didachographer and Clement of Rome furnish the last instances of the promiscuous use of these two terms which originally signified one and the same office. They wrote in the short period of transition from the Presbytero-Episcopate to the distinctive Episcopate. A few years later, in the Ignatian Epistles, the two officers are clearly distinct, although the Bishop of Ignatius is not yet a diocesan of a number of churches (as in Irenæus, Tertullian, and Cyprian), but simply the head of the college of Presbyters and Deacons of one congregation.

ἀφιλαργύρους] Comp. 1. Tim. iii. 4. Love of money and love of power were the besetting sins of the clergy from the beginning, in strong contrast with the example and teaching of the Apostles.

τὴν λειτουργίαν τῶν προφητῶν καὶ διδασκάλων.] The Apostles and Prophets were passing away or not always present, and the Bishops and Deacons gradually took their place. The qualifications and the duties are essentially the same (comp. XI. 11 ; XIII. 1, 2). Hence Paul requires the Bishop to be "apt to teach" (διδακτικός), 1 Tim. iii. 2 ; 2 Tim. ii. 24. This is inconsistent with the idea of a purely administrative and financial function of the primitive Bishops, as advocated by Hatch and Harnack.

2. This ver. likewise implies the gradual transition then going on from the extraordinary offices of inspired Apostles and Prophets to the ordinary Bishops and Presbyters who inherited the dignity of the former, but were liable at first to be despised as compared with the former. Hence the warning.

οἱ τετιμημένοι] used as a noun, *those held in honor.*

4. Τὰς δὲ εὐχὰς ὑμῶν καὶ τὰς ἐλεημοσύνας καὶ πάσας τὰς πράξεις οὕτως ποιήσατε ὡς ἔχετε ἐν τῷ εὐαγγελίῳ τοῦ Κυρίου ἡμῶν.

4. But so do your prayers and alms and all your actions as ye have [it] in the gospel of our Lord.

Κεφ. ιϛ'.

CHAP. XVI.
WATCHFULNESS AND THE COMING OF CHRIST.

1. Γρηγορεῖτε ὑπὲρ τῆς ζωῆς ὑμῶν· οἱ λύχνοι ὑμῶν μὴ σβεσθήτωσαν, καὶ αἱ ὀσφύες ὑμῶν μὴ ἐκλυέσθωσαν, ἀλλὰ γίνεσθε ἕτοιμοι· οὐ γὰρ οἴδατε τὴν ὥραν ἐν ᾗ ὁ Κύριος ἡμῶν ἔρχεται.

1. Watch over your life; let not your lamps be quenched and let not your loins be unloosed, but be ye ready; for ye know not the hour in which our Lord comes.[b]

[a] Luke xii. 35.   [b] Matt. xxv. 13.

NOTES TO CHAPTER XVI.

This chapter is a very proper conclusion of the Church Manual. It looks to the end of the present world and the glorious coming of Christ, and exhorts to watchfulness in view of that event for which Christians should always keep themselves in readiness whether it may happen sooner or later. The chapter is a summary of the eschatological discourses of our Lord in the Synoptical Gospels, especially Matt. xxiv. It might have been written before the destruction of the old theocracy but for the fact that all the specific references to Jerusalem and the Temple are omitted, as if that part of the Lord's prophecy had already been fulfilled. Comp. here Matt. xxiv. 42–44; Luke xii. 35; 1 Thess. iv. 15–18; 2 Thess. ii 1–12; 2 Tim. iii. 1–7; Jas. v. 7–11; 2 Pet. iii., Jude, and the Apocalypse.

Watch.] γρηγορέω is often used in the N. T. with reference to the second coming, Matt. xxiv. 42, 43; xxv. 13, etc. ὑπὲρ τῆς ζωῆς, comp. Heb. xiii. 17: "They watch in behalf of your souls as they that shall give account."

Let not your lamps be quenched, etc.] A reminiscence from Luke xii. 35: ἔστωσαν ὑμῶν αἱ ὀσφύες περιεζωσμέναι, καὶ οἱ λύχνοι (the plural occurs only in Luke, Matthew has λαμπάδες, xxv. 1, 3, 4, 7, 8) καιόμενοι. Comp. also Eph. vi. 14: "having girded your loins with truth."

For ye know not the hour.] From Matt. xxiv. 42, γρηγορεῖτε οὖν, ὅτι οὐκ οἴδατε ποίᾳ ἡμέρᾳ ὁ κύριος ὑμῶν ἔρχεται. Comp. Matt. xxv. 13: οὐκ οἴδατε τὴν ἡμέραν οὐδὲ τὴν ὥραν. Ha. notes a similar mixture of texts of Luke and Matthew in Tatian's *Diatessaron*. See Zahn's *Forschungen zur Gesch. des neutestam. Kanons*, i. (1881) p. 200.

2. Πυκνῶς δὲ συναχθήσεσ-
θε ζητοῦντες τὰ ἀνήκοντα
ταῖς ψυχαῖς ὑμῶν. οὐ γὰρ
ὠφελήσει ὑμᾶς ὁ πᾶς χρόνος
τῆς πίστεως ὑμῶν ἐὰν μὴ ἐν
τῷ ἐσχάτῳ καιρῷ τελειωθῆτε.

3. Ἐν γὰρ ταῖς ἐσχάταις
ἡμέραις πληθυνθήσονται οἱ
ψευδοπροφῆται καὶ οἱ φθο-
ρεῖς καὶ στραφήσονται τὰ
πρόβατα εἰς λύκους καὶ ἡ
ἀγάπη στραφήσεται εἰς μῖσος.

4. Αὐξανούσης γὰρ τῆς
ἀνομίας μισήσουσιν ἀλλήλους
καὶ διώξουσι καὶ παραδώ-
σουσι, καὶ τότε φανήσεται ὁ
κοσμοπλανὴς ὡς υἱὸς Θεοῦ καὶ

2. But be ye frequently gathered together, seeking the things that are profitable for your souls; for the whole time of your faith shall not profit you except in the last season ye be found perfect.

3. For in the last days the false prophets and destroyers shall be multiplied, and the sheep shall be turned into wolves, and love shall be turned into hate.

4. For when lawlessness increases, they shall hate and persecute, and deliver up one another; and then shall appear the 'world-deceiver as

---

2. *Be ye frequently gathered together.*] Barnabas ch. iv. 9: "Let us take heed (προσέχωμεν, as Ha. and Hi. read with the Lat. version) *in the last days,* for *the whole* (past) *time of our faith will profit us nothing* (οὐδὲν ὠφελήσει ὁ πᾶς χρόνος τῆς πίστεως ἡμῶν) unless now in this wicked time (ἐν τῷ ἀνόμῳ καιρῷ) we also withstand the coming scandals as becometh the sons of God." See other references in Br. and Ha.

3. *In the last days*] between the first and second coming of our Lord, between the αἰὼν οὗτος and the αἰὼν μέλλων. Among the Jews it meant the last days of the αἰὼν οὗτος, before the coming of the Messiah. The phrase is often used in the N. T., and is connected with the expectation of the speedy end of the world. ἐν ἐσχάταις ἡμέραις, Acts ii. 17. 2 Tim. iii. 1; Jas. v. 3; also ἐπ' ἐσχάτων (ἐσχάτου) τῶν ἡμερῶν, Heb. i. 1; 2 Pet. iii. 3; ἐν καιρῷ ἐσχάτῳ 1 Pet. i. 5; ἐν ἐσχάτῳ χρόνῳ, Jude 18; ἐπ' ἐσχάτων τῶν χρόνων, 1 Pet. i. 20; ἐσχάτη ἡμέρα, 1 John ii. 6, and τὰ τέλη τῶν αἰώνων, 1 Cor. x. 11. Barnabas iv. 9 uses ἐν ταῖς ἐσχάταις ἡμέραις.

3. *The false prophets.*] Matt. xxiv. 11: "many false Prophets shall rise and shall lead many astray." φθορεῖς, *destroyers, corrupters*, used in v. 2; comp. 2 Pet. ii. 12: "they shall in their destroying (ἐν τῇ φθορᾷ αὐτῶν) surely be destroyed (φθαρήσονται)."

The sheep shall be turned into wolves, etc.] Even some of the believers will fall away under the terrible temptations and trials of the last days.

4. *When lawlessness increases.*] Matt. xxiv. 12: "because lawlessness shall be multiplied the love of many shall wax cold."

ὁ κοσμοπλανής] This is the reading of the MS. for which Br. substitutes κοσμοπλάνος, *the world-deceiver, i. e.* the antichrist, "the man of ποιήσει σημεῖα καὶ τέρατα, καὶ ἡ γῆ παραδοθήσεται εἰς χεῖρας αὐτοῦ, καὶ ποιήσει ἀθέμιτα ἃ οὐδέποτε γέγονεν ἐξ αἰῶνος.

5. Τότε ἥξει ἡ κτίσις* τῶν ἀνθρώπων εἰς τὴν πύρωσιν τῆς δοκιμασίας καὶ σκανδαλισθήσονται πολλοὶ καὶ ἀπολοῦνται, οἱ δὲ ὑπομείναντες ἐν τῇ πίστει αὐτῶν σωθήσονται ὑπ'† αὐτοῦ τοῦ καταθέματος.

Son of God, and shall do signs and wonders,ᵃ and the earth shall be delivered into his hands, and he shall commit iniquities which have never yet come to pass from the beginning of the world.

5. And then shall the race of men come into the fire of trial, and many shall be offended and shall perish; but they who endure in their faith shall be saved under the curse itself [?].

ᵃ Comp. Matt. xxiv. 24.

* κρίσις, Hi. † ἀπ', Hi. Z.

sin, the son of perdition, he that opposeth and exalteth himself against all that is called God or that is worshipped; so that he sitteth in the temple of God, setting himself forth as God," 2 Thess. ii. 3, 4; "the lawless one," ver. 8. The word is new, but coined from Rev. xii. 9: ὁ πλανῶν τὴν οἰκουμένην, "the deceiver of the whole world" (said of Satan), and 2 John ver. 7: ὁ πλάνος καὶ ἀντίχριστος, "the deceiver and the antichrist." It occurs again in Ap. Const. vii. 32: καὶ τότε φανήσεται ὁ κοσμοπλάνος.

ὡς υἱὸς θεοῦ.] Ha.: *als wäre er Gottes Sohn*. Comp. 2 Thess. ii. 4: "he sitteth in the temple of God, setting himself forth as God" (ὅτι ἐστιν θεός). The expression implies, by contrast, that Christ is truly, what his antagonist pretends to be, the Son of God. Antichrist was regarded as the Christ of hell, as the devil is the god of hell.

5. *The fire of trial*] not purgatory in the future world, but a probatory fire of trial or testing in this world; for the writer speaks of men then living. Comp. 1 Pet. iv. 12: "Brethren, think it not strange concerning the fiery trial among you, which cometh upon you to prove you" (τῇ ἐν ὑμῖν πυρώσει πρὸς πειρασμὸν ὑμῖν γινομένῃ). 1 Cor. iii. 13: τὸ πῦρ δοκιμάσει.

They who have endured in their faith shall be saved.] Matt. x. 22: "he that endureth to the end the same shall be saved." Also Matt. xxiv. 13.

ὑπ' αὐτοῦ τοῦ καταθέματος.] The most difficult passage next to "the cosmic mystery" in XI. 11. κατάθεμα = καταναθεμα, *curse*. It is adopted by Tischendorf, W. and H., and the Revisers in Rev. xxii. 3 (with ℵ ᵃ A, B, P); comp. Zech. xiv. 13, Sept., οὐκ ἔσται ἀνάθεμα ἔτι. Various interpretations and renderings:

(1) *Under* (or, *from under*) *the curse itself*, namely the accursed world-de-

6. Καὶ τότε φανήσεται τὰ σημεῖα τῆς ἀληθείας· πρῶτον

6. And then shall appear the signs of the truth: first

---

ceiver; comp. Matt. xiii. 14, "the abomination of desolation" (τὸ βδέλυγμα τῆς ἐρημήσεως). The saints will suffer from the tyrannical persecution and temptation of Antichrist, but will be delivered at last from his power. This suits the context. The radical Homeric meaning of ὑπό is *under, from under*, especially after the verbs ἐρύεσθαι, ἁρπάζειν, ῥύεσθαι, rescuing *from under* another's power, or out of danger. See Liddell and Scott, sub ὑπό, No. I. Fa.: *under the very curse.* H. and N.: *from under the curse itself.* Harris: from the common curse of the destruction by fire (?).

(2) *By the curse himself*, *i. e.*, by Christ who is called a curse, or who is cursed by his enemies. So Br. (τὸν Χριστὸν ἴσως λέγει, ὃν καταναθεματίσουσιν οἱ σκανδαλισθησόμενοι ἐν αὐτῷ), and Ha. (*von dem Verfluchten selbst*), with reference to 1 Cor. xii. 3: "no man speaking in the Spirit of God saith, 'Jesus is anathema' (ἀνάθεμα Ἰησοῦς), and to the *maledicere Christo*, which Jews and heathen tried to extort from the Christians (Pliny's *Ep. ad Traj.*, and *Martyr. Polyc.* ix. 3: λοιδόρησον τὸν Χριστόν). So also St.: "*by* him *the curse*," and Spence: They will be saved "through Him whom they have been so sorely tempted to revile and curse, and who, in terrible irony is here called 'the very curse;'" but he translates, inconsistently: "*under* the very curse."

(3) ἐπ' αὐτοῦ τοῦ κάτω θέματος (ἤγουν ἐπὶ τῆς γῆς), a textual correction which Br. proposes in his notes as an alternative, but which he has given up in a letter to Ha. in favor of the first explanation (κατάθεμα λέγει . . . ἢ τὸν κοσμοπλάνον, ἢ τὴν θείαν καθόλου ἀράν).

(4) ἀπ' instead of ὑπ', *from the curse itself.* A conjecture of Hi. and Z.

(5) *From this curse.* This would require τούτου instead of αὐτοῦ. So H. and B. in the first ed., but in the second ed.: *from under even this curse*, which H. explains: "from under the curse just described, the riot of iniquity." B. M. and Sa. *de cette malédiction*.

(6) "They who endure in their faith *shall be preserved beneath the very curse*," that is, the trial when it is at its uttermost. So Prof. Orris (of Princeton) in the N. Y. "Independent" for May 7, 1885. But σωθήσονται must have the same meaning as in the parallel passages Matt. x. 22 and xxiv. 13.

(7) Krawutzcky (in his second essay, *l. c.* p. 582): "under the Temple Mount doomed to destruction. The Ebionites still turned in prayer towards the Temple." Very far-fetched.

6. *And then shall appear the signs of the truth.*] Matt. xxiv. 3: "what shall be the *sign* of thy presence (τὸ σημεῖον τῆς σῆς παρουσίας) and of the end of the world?" Ver. 30: "*Then shall appear the sign* of the Son of man in heaven." The "truth" is here either Christ himself (comp. John xiv. 6 (Ἐγώ εἰμι ἡ ἀλήθεια), or the truth as believed by the Christians concerning the second coming. The *three* signs are peculiar to the *Did.*, but were derived from Matt. xxiv. 30, 31.

σημεῖον ἐκπετάσεως * ἐν οὐ-ρανῷ, εἶτα σημεῖον φωνῆς σάλπιγγος, καὶ τὸ τρίτον ἀνάστασις νεκρῶν·

the sign of expansion in heaven; then the sign of the voice of the trumpet; and the third, the resurrection of the dead.

* ἐπιφάσεως, Potwin.

First the sign of expansion in heaven] ἐκπέτασις does not occur in the N. T., nor in the Sept., but in Plutarch, and means *a spreading* out, *an expansion* (from ἐκπετάννυμι, *to spread out*, e. g., a sail). So here. It is identical with " the *sign* of the Son of man in heaven," Matt. xxiv. 30, that is, a preparatory phenomenon in the skies which precedes the *personal* parousia of the Lord (ver. 8). It is probably the sign of the cross, for ἐκπέτασις is the patristic term for the attitude of the crucified, as Tertullian says: "*Homo expansis manibus imaginem crucis facit.*" See the passages quoted by John Wordsworth ("Guardian," March 26, 1884) and Harris (*The Teach. of the Ap. and the Sibylline Bks*, pp. 33–36). Other interpretations:

(1) The sign of an *opening* or an *unrolling* in heaven, as at the baptism of Christ (Matt. iii. 16, ἠνεώχθησαν), comp. Rev. xix. 11 (εἶδον τὸν οὐρανὸν ἀνεῳγμένον). So H. & B. (*an opening in heaven*), Sab. (*les cieux s'ouvriront*). But ἐκπέτασις cannot mean an *opening*.

(2) The sign of *the flying forth* (Fa.), or *a soaring forth* (Sp.). This rendering implies the derivation of ἐκπέτασις from ἐκπέτομαι or ἐκπέταμαι, *to fly out*, or, *away* (in Aristotle and Euripides). Br. and Fa. refer it to the ἁρπαγή of the then living saints "who shall be caught up in the clouds to meet the Lord in the air," 1 Thess. iv. 17. Fa.: "This seems to be the nearest approach to a quotation from St. Paul, though the order of events appears to be different" [?]. But in this case it would be better to understand here the *angels* who are sent out to gather the elect from one end of heaven to the other, Matt. xxiv. 31; comp. Rev. xiv. 6: "I saw another angel flying in mid heaven (πετόμενον ἐν μεσουρανήματι).

(3) Useless textual emendations by Potwin: ἐπιφάσεως (ἐπίφασις = ἐπιφάνεια, *a becoming visible*, *a display*); and by Hayman: ἐκπτώσεως (ἔκπτωσις, *a falling out, breaking forth*), with reference to the falling of the stars from heaven, Mark xiii. 25; Matt. xxiv. 29 (οἱ ἀστέρες πεσοῦνται ἀπὸ τοῦ οὐρανοῦ).

7. *The sign of the voice of the trumpet.*] Matt. xxiv. 31: "He shall send forth his angels μετὰ σάλπιγγος φωνῆς μεγάλης, with a great sound of a trumpet," or, "a trumpet of great sound" (W. and Hort put φωνῆς on the margin); 1 Cor. xv. 52: "in the twinkling of an eye, at the last trump (ἐν τῇ ἐσχάτῃ σάλπιγγι); for the trumpet shall sound (σαλπίσει γάρ), and the dead shall be raised incorruptible;" 1 Thess. iv. 16: "The Lord himself shall descend from heaven, with a shout (ἐν κελεύσματι), with the voice of the archangel, and with the trump of God (ἐν σάλπιγγι Θεοῦ)."

The resurrection of the dead.] The *Did.* seems to make the resurrection precede the parousia. This does not contradict Matt. xxiv. 30, 31. We

7. Οὐ πάντων δέ, ἀλλ' ὡς ἐρρέθη· "Ἥξει ὁ Κύριος καὶ πάντες οἱ ἅγιοι μετ' αὐτοῦ.

7. Not, however, of all, but as was said, ["The Lord shall come, and all the saints with him."][a]

8. Τότε ὄψεται ὁ κόσμος τὸν Κύριον ἐρχόμενον ἐπάνω τῶν νεφελῶν τοῦ οὐρανοῦ·

8. Then shall the world see the Lord coming upon the clouds of heaven.[b]

[a] Zech. xiv. 5.   [b] Matt. xxiv. 30.

must distinguish between the appearance of the *sign* of the Son of man, and of the *Son* of man himself. The resurrection occurs between the two. Paul presents the events of the parousia as simultaneous or nearly so, "in a moment," "in the twinkling of an eye," 1 Cor. xv. 52.

7. *Not, however, of all the dead.*] Comp. Rev. xx. 4–6: "This is the first resurrection." Paul teaches, 1 Thess. iv. 17, that "the dead in Christ shall rise first; then we that are alive, that are left, shall together with them be caught up in the clouds, to meet the Lord in the air;" 1 Cor. xv. 23: "Each in his own order: Christ the first-fruits; then they that are Christ's, at his coming: then cometh the end." He also teaches "a resurrection both of the just and the unjust," Acts xxiv. 15. So does Christ himself, John v. 29 (comp. Dan. xii. 2; Matt. xxv. 32, 33, 41, 46). Probably the *Did.* means a *first* resurrection preceding the millennium, to be followed by a *general* resurrection after the millennium; but as the writer says nothing of a second or general resurrection, we have no right to commit him to a particular theory; his silence might as well be construed in favor of the annihilation of the wicked. Barnabas, however, Papias, Justin Martyr, Irenæus and Tertullian were pronounced Chiliasts. See *Church History,* ii. 615 sqq. and Neander, i. 650-654 (Boston ed.).

The Lord will come and all the saints with him.] Literal Scripture quotation (ὡς ἐρρέθη) from Zech. xiv. 5. The application implies the divinity of Christ.

Then shall the world see the Lord.] Matt. xxiv. 30: ὄψονται τὸν υἱὸν τοῦ ἀνθρώπου ἐπὶ τῶν νεφελῶν τοῦ οὐρανοῦ. Comp. xvi. 27; xxvi. 64 (ἐρχόμενον ἐπὶ τῶν νεφελῶν τοῦ οὐρανοῦ). Justin M., *Dial. c. Tryph.* cxx. uses ἐπάνω, like the *Did.*: προσδοκᾶται πάλιν παρέσθαι ἐπάνω τῶν νεφελῶν Ἰησοῦς

Here the curtain falls, the world ends, eternity begins.

DOCUMENT II.

A Latin Fragment of the Doctrina Apostolorum.

This fragment was discovered by Dr. Oscar von Gebhardt, and published in Harnack's book, p. 277 sq. The Codex containing it is described by Funk in the "Theol. Quartalschrift," 1886, 650-655. It is a Homiliarium of the Epistle lessons for a part of the year, but contains no more of the *Doctr. Apost.* than this fragment. We give it with the references to the *Didache*, Barnabas, and Hermas on the margin.

DOCTRINA APOSTOLORUM.

Viæ duæ sunt in seculo, vitæ et mortis, lucis et tenebrarum.

In his constituti sunt Angeli duo, unus æquitatis, alter iniquitatis.

Distantia autem magna est duarum viarum.

Via ergo vitæ hæc est: Primò diliges Deum æternum, qui te fecit. Secundò proximum tuum, ut te ipsum. Omne autem, quod tibi non vis fieri, alii ne feceris.

Interpretatio autem horum verborum hæc est: non mœchaberis, non homicidium facies, non falsum testimonium dices, non puerum violaveris, non fornicaveris* . . . *non medicamenta mala facies: non occides filium in abortum, nec natum succides. Non concupisces quidquam de re proximi tui. Non perjurabis.*

DOCTRINE OF THE APOSTLES.

There are two ways in the [*Did.* I. 1.]
world, (one) *of life and* (one) [Ep. Bar. xviii.]
of death, (one) *of light and* (one) *of darkness.*

In them two angels are [Hermas, *Mand.* VI.]
stationed, the one of equity, the other of iniquity.

But there is a great difference [*Did.* I. 1.]
between the two ways.

Now the way of life is this: [I. 2.]
First, thou shalt love the eternal God who made thee. Secondly, thy neighbour as thyself. But all things whatsoever thou wouldest not should be done to thee, do not thou to another.

Now the interpretation of these [I. 3.]
words is this: thou shalt not com- [II. 2.]
mit adultery, thou shalt not com-
mit homicide, thou shalt not bear [II. 3.]
false witness, thou shalt not [II. 2.]
corrupt boys, thou shalt not com-
mit fornication . . . *thou shalt not mix poisons: thou shalt not kill children by abortion, nor those just born. Thou shalt not* [II. 3.]

---
* According to Dr. Funk the Cod. has no lacuna after *fornicaveris*.

[L. 4.]
[I. 5.]
[II. 6.]

Non malè loqueris. Non eris memor malorum factorum. Non eris duplex in consilium dandum, neque bilinguis; tendiculum enim mortis est lingua. Non erit verbum tuum vacuum nec mendax. Non eris cupidus nec avarus, nec rapax, nec adulator,* nec. . . .

covet anything of thy neighbour's goods. Thou shalt not forswear thyself. Thou shalt not revile. Thou shalt not cherish the memory of evil deeds. Thou shalt not be false in giving counsel, nor double-tongued; for such a tongue is a snare of death. Thou shalt not be vain nor false in thy speech. Thou shalt not be covetous, nor extortionate, nor rapacious, nor servile, nor. . . .

Cætera in Codice desiderantur.

(The rest in the MS. is wanting.)

A Critical Estimate of this Latin Fragment.

[The Rev. Dr. B. B. WARFIELD, Professor in the Western Theological Seminary, Allegheny, Penn., kindly places at my disposal the following critical discussion of this Latin *Didache* Fragment. He arrives independently at conclusions somewhat similar to those advocated by Dr. Holtzmann. I give the essay in full, and let it speak for itself.—P. S.]

THE very modest way in which Dr. von Gebhardt expresses himself when pointing out the value of the fragment of a Latin translation of the *Didache* which he discovered, has perhaps prevented its real importance from being noted. "It is at once clear," he says, "that an old Latin translation must be of high value not only for the text criticism of the $\Delta\iota\delta\alpha\chi\eta$, but also for the discussion of the integrity of that form of it which has been transmitted by the Constantinopolitan MS. But that it may be successfully turned to account, the translation should be complete, or, at least, should cover the greater part of the work. A fragment of such narrow extent as the one that we have ought to be used only with great circumspection."† He immediately adds that, nevertheless, it is impossible not to draw certain general conclusions from it. Among these general conclusions is one, perfectly simple in itself, while the corollaries that flow from it are such as to constitute this little fragment the key of the whole question of the origin, antiquity and value of the text of the *Didache* as given to us in the Constantinopolitan Codex. I shall try to point out very briefly how this happens.

It has been plain to every one from the beginning that the central problem concerning the *Didache* is its relation to the Epistle of Barnabas. Scholars have been all along divided on the question as to whether Barnabas originated the matter which was afterwards worked up into so neatly

---

* According to Funk the Cod. reads *adolator* for *adulator*.
† Harnack, p. 278.

ordered a treatise, or blunderingly borrowed it from the *Didache*. Only a few of the most discerning spirits—Drs. Lightfoot and Holtzmann, especially—saw that on the one hand Barnabas bears all the marks of a copier, and on the other the *Didache* fails to furnish the matter which he borrowed; and therefore felt bound to assume that they both borrowed their common matter from a third source. In this state of the controversy the Latin fragment comes in and lays before us a recension of the *Didache* text, of the type of the matter in Barnabas. Only two theories are possible with regard to it: it may be a copy of the Bryennios *Didache* conformed to Barnabas; or it may be the representative of that form of the *Didache* from which Barnabas' quotations are taken.

The first of these theories appears to me exceedingly unlikely. All the proof (which seems not only adequate, but irresistible) that Barnabas is not here its own original is against it. There is no appearance of reworking visible in the fragment itself. There are several indications that Barnabas has borrowed from just such a text as this presents—one instance of which (of equal significance with the one that "E. L. H." gives from II. 4) must suffice for an illustration here: The Latin fragment reads near the beginning: "In his constituti sunt Angeli duo, unus aequitatis, alter iniquitatis." Barnabas, quite after his fashion elsewhere, develops this into the long statement that "over one way are stationed light-bringing angels of God, over the other the angels of Satan; and he indeed is Lord from eternities even to eternities, but the other, prince of the present time of iniquity." It is very difficult to believe that the Latin phrase could have been made from this; but it is quite after Barnabas' habit to multiply the angels, describe their character by their masters, and then off at the end of an awkwardly added sentence drop a hint of the neglected '*iniquitatis*.' More important, however, than any of these considerations is the fact that the most characteristic point in the old Latin fragment—the omission of the passage from I. 3 ($εὐλογεῖτε$) through II. 1—is common not only to it and Barnabas, but also to the Apostolical Canons, and, indeed, in part, to all the documents representing the *Didache*, except the Bryennios MS. That this omission, moreover, was not a conscious one with the framer of the Canons is clear from the sequence of the apostolic names. As it is certain, then, that the Canons are here simply following their copy there is no reason to doubt that Barnabas is doing so too, and equally none that the Latin fragment is doing so too. Apart from this reasoning, it would be very unlikely that a copyist or translator, reproducing a text like that of Bryennios' MS., and adding to it here and there from Barnabas, should *omit* a long passage merely because it was not found in such a fragmentary compound as that given in Barnabas. It becomes, then, very highly probable that the Latin fragment is a representative of the type of *Didache* text from which Barnabas borrowed. [The following collation probably includes all the variations which may be attributed to the Greek text that underlay the Latin version:

Title: Latin omits $ΔΩΔΕΚΑ$ with Eusebius, Athanasius, Anastasius, Nicephorus, and all known witnesses.

Latin omits the second title.

I. 1. Latin inserts *in seculo* against all known authorities. Cf., however, Lactantius, *Epist. div. instit.* c. lix. "Duas esse *humanæ vitæ vias;*" also *Divin. Instit.* vi. 8. "Duæ sunt viæ . . . . per quas *humanam vitam* progredi necesse est."

Latin apparently omits μία before τῆς and before τοῦ. If so, it is against all witnesses.

Latin inserts "*lucis et tenebrarum*" with Barnabas, cf. Lactantius (Harnack, p. 286); against Constitutions and Canons.

Latin inserts a long sentence beginning, "*In his—*" with Barnabas and Hermas, cf. Lactantius (do. p. 285); against Constitutions and Canons.

Latin apparently omits μεταξύ with Barnabas; against Canons.

I. 2. Latin inserts *æternum* after "Deum ;" against all known witnesses.

I. 3 sq. Latin omits from εὐλογεῖτε to II. 1, inclusive with Barnabas, Canons, and partly Constitutions; against (in part) Hermas, Clems. Alex. and Constitutions. Lactantius (do. p. 285.) also apparently omits. Note: all witnesses apparently omit latter part of I. 5.

II. 2. Latin transposes οὐ φονεύσεις and οὐ μοιχεύσεις against all witnesses.

Latin misplaces οὐ ψευδομαρτυρήσεις of II. 3, against all.

II. 5. Latin reverses order of ψευδής and κενός with all witnesses extant (Constitutions, Canons).

Latin omits ἀλλὰ μεμεστωμένος πράξει with all (Constitutions, Canons).

II. 6. Latin inserts *cupidus* (cf. iii. 3) against all.

In estimating the meaning of this collation, it is important to remember that the Latin is a *version*, and may present more variations than the underlying Greek would. Furthermore, we must neglect all obvious clerical errors that may have affected but a single document.]

A careful examination of all the various readings between the old Latin fragment and the corresponding parts of Bryennios' codex not only confirms this conclusion, but enables us to state it more broadly, thus: We have two well-marked recensions of the *Didache* text,—the one represented by the old Latin, Barnabas, and the Canons, and the other by the Bryennios MS. and the Apostolical Constitutions. We need no longer ask doubtingly with Bishop Lightfoot: "May not both Barnabas and the *Doctrine* derive the matter which they have in common from a third source?" Recognizing them as representing variant recensions of a common work, we simply seek the original text of that work.

We proceed but a single step when we affirm, next, that the recension represented by the Latin translation is probably the older form of the *Didache* text. This is *a priori* likely: if the Latin represents a form of text which was already used by Barnabas,—the date of which can scarcely be brought lower than A.D. 106,—it is only barely possible to put another Christian text still behind it; and not at all likely that such a text as that represented in the Bryennios recension could be back of it. The meagre historical hints that are in our hands point to the same conclusion: the Latin form of text was already in circulation when Barnabas was written (A D. 106), while the other recension is first met with in Hermas, which, notwithstanding Zahn's and Salmon's able arguments, must be placed in the second half of the second century. There is more of importance in this historical argument than appears at first sight. For Hermas apparently quotes not from a text wholly like that of the Bryennios MS., but from one intermediate between the two recensions. At *Mandate* vi. 2, the angel clause at the opening of the *Didache* (which is peculiar to the Latin recension) is quoted: while at *Mandate* ii. 4–6 the alms-giving clause in *Didache* I. 5 (which is peculiar to the Bryennios recension) is quoted. We apparently see here the Bryennios recension in the act of formation. There is even reason to suspect that the actual Bryennios text is later in form than that which underlies any of the ancient reworkings—even than that used in the Apostolical Constitutions. Clement of Alexandria (*Frag. ex Nicetæ. Catena in Mat.* v. 42. Cf. also *Paed.* iii. 12) may have used either the transitional form that Hermas used, or the more settled form extracted by the Apostolical Constitutions, which presents still some variations from that of the Bryennios MS. Some instances of these Harnack gives at p. 210,—where the Constitutions and Canons agree against Bryennios; a marked instance (see v. Gebhardt in Harnack, p. 280) concerns this early portion in which the Latin is preserved. These readings prove either that the Constitutions used the Canons, or that they were founded on a text of the *Didache* slightly differing from that of Bryennios, in the direction of the Canons. The latter appears more probable; and if this be so we again actually see the *Didache* text growing from the form represented by the recension given in the Latin, Barnabas, and the Canons, through that which underlies Hermas, to that which underlies the Constitutions on to that which is given in the Bryennios MS. It must be observed that this does not prove that the type of *Didache* given in the Constantinople MS. is later than the Apostolical Constitutions themselves. It only suggests that the MS. of the *Didache* used by the compiler of these Constitutions was of a somewhat earlier type than that which the scribe Leon copied. The recension to which both belong, on the testimony of Clement of Alexandria and Hermas, must be as old as the first decade or two of the second half of the second century.

It will be observed that we are thus far in substantial agreement with Dr. Holtzmann, who writes: "It seems to me that Barnabas and the *Didache* should be coördinated, Barnabas as the older but more carelessly and arbitrarily made, the *Didache* as the probably later but at all events much more exact recension of the allegory of the two ways" (p. 155). I differ with Holtzmann only in considering the type of text that underlies Barnabas not only the older, but also quite as exact a representation of the *Didache*— *i. e.*, the original text from which the Bryennios type of text was developed. Whereas he says, "Among the still unknown and unnamed must the common root of Barnabas and the *Didache* be sought" (p. 159), I think that it is found, by the aid of the Latin fragment, in the recension that underlies Barnabas, the Canons, and it may be added Lactantius. This is in itself a reasonable supposition: when two types of one text are discoverable, and one appears older than the other, the natural supposition is that they are genealogically connected. There are no valid internal objections to this supposition: so far as the Latin text carries us, the most marked difference between the two recensions consists in additions in the Bryennios type to the title, and especially a long addition in the body of the document. Dr. v. Gebhardt suggests that this passage may have been accidentally omitted from the *exemplar* of the Latin translation: and points out that it may have been about two pages long, and thus may have been all on one leaf. But he himself points out also that it is not likely to have been all on one leaf. And in the course of this paper I have pointed out reasons for supposing it was inserted rather by the other recension. It may be added that Dr. v. Gebhardt's explanation becomes still more unlikely if we suppose that I. 6 was a still later insertion.

There are some internal hints in the Bryennios document itself that these additions are additions to the original form of that text; *e. g.*, II. 1 is very awkward; both of the commandments given in I. 2, concerning our duty to God and our neighbor, had been developed in the immediately succeeding context. Must we not suspect that the passage from $εὐλογεῖτε$, I. 3, having been inserted, a new start was needed, and this ill-fitting phrase was invented to take the place at the head of the list of prohibitions in II. 2 sq, which the opening sentence of I. 3 originally occupied? Again, if the development of the Bryennios text through Hermas and the Apostolical Constitutions, traced above, is judged to be rightly read, the genealogical affiliation of this text to the Latin type is proved. The fact that the Latin text is fuller in I. 1 than that of the Constantinopolitan Codex is not fatal to this finding: the general rule that this type of the text is the more original, is not without exceptions.

If on these grounds we assume that the original *Didache* is represented by the Latin version, we may trace its propagation through a twofold transmission. One appears in Barnabas, and later in the Canons, the author of which knew also Barnabas (the opening sentence is taken from the opening sentence of Barnabas; and an occasional reading, such as the insertion of $καὶ δοξάσεις τὸν λυτρωσάμενόν σε ἐκ θανάτου$ in I. 2 is common to Barnabas and the Canons against Bryennios and the Latin) and still later in Lactantius,—gathering something, no doubt, to itself on the way. It may be called the Gentile recension, and seems to have been in circulation chiefly in Egypt and the West. The other appears half-formed in Hermas, in Clement of Alexandria, in the Apostolical Constitutions, and is preserved in the Constantinopolitan Manuscript, and may be called the Jewish-Christian recension. Its origin (which like some other Jewish-Christian books, notably the Gospel according to the Hebrews, presupposes and is based on a Catholic original) belongs to the middle of the second century, and its complete development, as we have it in our *Didache*, to a time probably anterior to Clement of Alexandria. A great deal of its almost Ebionitic tone may have been acquired in this process of growth: as its completion cannot be placed earlier than Hermas, its last interpolator may have engrafted some Montanistic traits. I am anxious, however, that what I have just said shall not be misunderstood: the differences between the two recensions are wholly *textual*,—and the latest form, as given in the Bryennios MS., is not much further removed from the original than say Codex D of the Gospels from

Codex B The scope of the original is preserved intact through the whole transmission; as is shown by the two facts, (1) that Barnabas (iv. 9) already knows the end as well as the beginning, and (2) the disposition of the matter is artistic and neat. But though the *Didache* is never so altered as to cease to be substantially the *Didache*, it appears in two well-marked textual forms.

Some support may be gained for this from the fact that the Church writers who mention the *Didache* sometimes mention it in the plural. This is true of Eusebius, Anastasius of Sinai, and Nicephorus Callistus. The significance of this is increased by the coupling by Anastasius of Περίοδοι and Διδαχαὶ τῶν ἀποστόλων. We all know what the plural περίοδοι imports. It is barely possible that the Syriac "*Teaching of the Apostles*," published by Cureton, may also be included in this plural.*

The reconstruction of the Egyptian text of the *Didache* is comparatively easy for the short section where we have the Latin version. We have only to correct it by the preponderance of the other documents of its class: *e.g.*, omit *in seculo* in I. 1 and *æternum* in I. 2, correct the order of prohibitions in II. 2 sq., insert the appropriate words omitted in its *lacuna*, and omit *cupidus* at the end. When it fails us, we are in more difficulty. All words found in both recensions may be accepted as certainly parts of the original. This will give us the kernel; but not the whole document. And this was Krawutzcky's error in 1882. It is the same error that leads some students of the Synoptic Gospels to lay stress on the Triple Tradition as the whole original tradition. We can indeed be sure that this common matter was part of the original; but we can be equally sure that it was not all. So far as the matter extracted in Barnabas, the Canons, and Lactantius, goes, we are justified in using it as a fair representation of the Egyptian text. The affiliations of the Latin fragment teach us this. When it fails, there is nothing for us but to provisionally accept the Syrian Recension as a corrupt but substantial text. Here, too, we must keep in mind that the differences between the recensions scarcely rise above the ground of textual criticism; and it is only a question of purity of text that we are dealing with. We have the *Didache* competently exact in the latest text.

The bearing of this discussion on the value of the document given to us by Bryennios is obvious. It lowers its value for those who believed that it was in this exact form the basis of Barnabas' quotations. It immensely raises its value for those—perhaps the majority of critics—who believed it to have been made out of Barnabas. It prevents us from using it as it lies in the Constantinopolitan Codex as a purely first-century document, and warns us that it has elements and details that have crept in during the second century, possibly even somewhat late in it. But it vindicates for its general substance a first-century origin, and enables us to reconstruct the first-century form of text in a not inconsiderable portion.

---

* Concerning this book, see Gordon in the "Modern Review," July, 1884.

DOCUMENT III.

BARNABAS.

The Greek text of the Epistle of Barnabas has an appendix of four chapters not found in the old Latin version, and regarded by some as spurious. Three of these chapters (XVIII.-XX.) contain similar sentences to those found in the first five chapters of the *Didache*. They were either unskilfully and illogically compiled from it, or drawn from a still older common source, but cannot be original. Besides, there is a brief eschatological passage in Ch. IV. which resembles one in the sixteenth chapter of the *Didache*.

The Epistle of Barnabas was probably written by a Hellenistic Jew of Alexandria, belonging to the school of St. Paul, at the end of the first or early in the second century. See *Church History*, ii. 671 sqq., and the books there quoted.

In the Greek text I have compared Hilgenfeld (*Barnabæ Epistula integrum Græce iterum edidit, ed. altera emendata*, Lips. 1877), Funk (*Opera Patr. Ap.*, Tubing. vol. i. 1878), and the second ed. of von Gebhardt and Harnack (Lips. 1873). They have all used the readings of the Sinaitic MS. discovered by Tischendorf (1859, published 1862), and of the Jerusalem MS. discovered by Bryennios, 1875, and furnished by him to Hilgenfeld. The references to the *Didache* are marked on the outside margin, and the corresponding words are spaced in the Greek, and italicized in the English column.

IV. Διὸ προσέχωμεν ἐν ταῖς ἐσχάταις ἡμέραις. οὐδὲν γὰρ ὠφελήσει ἡμᾶς ὁ πᾶς χρόνος τῆς ζωῆς ἡμῶν καὶ τῆς πίστεως, ἐὰν μὴ νῦν ἐν τῷ ἀνόμῳ καιρῷ καὶ τοῖς μέλλουσι σκανδάλοις, ὡς πρέπει υἱοῖς Θεοῦ, ἀντιστῶμεν.

Ch. iv.—Wherefore let us give heed *in the last days: for the whole time of* our life and *faith will profit* us *nothing if* now *in the* lawless *time*, and impending offences we do not resist as befitteth sons of God.

[*Didache* XVI. 3.]

[XVI. 2.]

XVIII. Μεταβῶμεν δὲ καὶ

Ch. xviii.—But let us pass

ἐπὶ ἑτέραν γνῶσιν καὶ δι-
[I. 1.] δαχήν· Ὁδοὶ δύο εἰσὶ διδαχῆς καὶ ἐξουσίας· ἥ τε τοῦ
φωτὸς καὶ ἡ τοῦ σκότους.
[I. 1.] διαφορὰ δὲ πολλὴ τῶν
δύο ὁδῶν· ἐφ' ἧς μὲν γὰρ
εἰσι τεταγμένοι φωταγωγοὶ
ἄγγελοι τοῦ θεοῦ, ἐφ' ἧς δὲ
ἄγγελοι τοῦ σατανᾶ· (2) καὶ ὁ
μέν ἐστι κύριος ἀπ' αἰώνων
καὶ εἰς τοὺς αἰῶνας, ὁ δὲ ἄρ-
χων καιροῦ τοῦ νῦν τῆς ἀνομίας.

[I. 2.] XIX. Ἡ οὖν ὁδὸς τοῦ
φωτός ἐστιν αὕτη· ἐάν
τις θέλων ὁδὸν ὁδεύειν ἐπὶ τὸν
ὡρισμένον τόπον σκεύσῃ τοῖς
ἔργοις αὐτοῦ. ἔστιν οὖν ἡ
δοθεῖσα ἡμῖν γνῶσις τοῦ πε-
ριπατεῖν ἐν αὐτῇ τοιαύτη.(2)
Ἀγαπήσεις τόν σε ποι-
ήσαντα, φοβηθήσῃ τόν σε
πλάσαντα, δοξάσεις τόν σε
λυτρωσάμενον ἐκ θανάτου.

ἔσῃ ἁπλοῦς τῇ καρδίᾳ καὶ
πλούσιος τῷ πνεύματι, οὐ
κολληθήσῃ μετὰ τῶν πορευο-
[I. 1.] μένων ἐν ὁδῷ θανάτου.
[IV. 12.] μισήσεις πᾶν ὃ οὐκ
ἔστιν ἀρεστὸν τῷ θεῷ,
μισήσεις πᾶσαν ὑπό-
[IV. 13.] κρισιν· οὐ μὴ ἐγκαταλίπῃς ἐντολὰς κυ-
[III. 9.] ρίου. (3) οὐχ ὑψώσεις
σεαυτόν, ἔσῃ δὲ ταπεινό-
φρων κατὰ πάντα, οὐκ ἀρεῖς
[II. 6.] ἐπὶ σεαυτὸν δόξαν. οὐ λήψῃ βουλὴν πονηρὰν

over to another knowledge and teaching. *There are two ways* of teaching and of authority, one of light and one of darkness. *And there is a great difference between the two ways.* For over one are set light-bearing angels of God, but over the other, angels of Satan. And the one is Lord from eternity and to eternity, but the other is prince of the present time of lawlessness.

Ch. xix.—*The way of* light, then, is this: if any one desires to go to the appointed place, let him be zealous in his works. The knowledge then which is given to us in walking in this (way) is such as this: *Thou shalt love* him *who made thee,* thou shalt fear him who fashioned thee, thou shalt glorify him that ransomed thee from death.

Thou shalt be simple in heart and rich in spirit; thou shalt not cleave to those that walk *in (the) way of death. Thou shalt hate everything which is not pleasing to God, thou shalt hate every hypocrisy; thou shalt by no means forsake the Lord's commandments. Thou shalt not exalt thyself,* but shalt be humble in all things; thou shalt not take glory to thyself. *Thou shalt not take evil counsel*

κατὰ τοῦ πλησίον σου. οὐ δώσεις τῇ ψυχῇ σου θράσος.

(4) οὐ πορνεύσεις, οὐ μοιχεύσεις, οὐ παιδοφθορήσεις. οὐ μή σου ὁ λόγος τοῦ θεοῦ ἐξέλθῃ ἐν ἀκαθαρσίᾳ τινῶν.

οὐ λήψη πρόσωπον ἐλέγξαι τινὰ ἐπὶ παραπτώματι. ἔσῃ πραΰς, ἔσῃ ἡσύχιος, ἔσῃ τρέμων τοὺς λόγους, οὓς ἤκουσας. οὐ μνησικακήσεις τῷ ἀδελφῷ σου. (5) οὐ μὴ διψυχήσεις, πότερον ἔσται ἢ οὔ. οὐ μὴ λάβῃς ἐπὶ ματαίῳ τὸ ὄνομα κυρίου. ἀγαπήσεις τὸν πλησίον σου ὑπὲρ τὴν ψυχήν σου.

οὐ φονεύσεις τέκνον σου ἐν φθορᾷ, οὐδὲ πάλιν γεννηθὲν ἀνελεῖς. οὐ μὴ ἄρῃς τὴν χεῖρά σου ἀπὸ τοῦ υἱοῦ σου ἢ ἀπὸ τῆς θυγατρός σου, ἀλλὰ ἀπὸ τῆς νεότητος διδάξεις φόβον κυρίου. (6) οὐ μὴ γένῃ ἐπιθυμῶν τὰ τοῦ πλησίον σου, οὐ μὴ γένῃ πλεονέκτης, οὐδὲ κολληθήσῃ ἐκ ψυχῆς σου μετὰ ὑψηλῶν, ἀλλὰ μετὰ ταπεινῶν καὶ δικαίων

against thy neighbor; thou [III. 9.] shall not permit overboldness to thy soul.

Thou shalt not commit for- [II. 2.] nication; thou shalt not commit adultery; thou shalt not corrupt boys. Not from thee shall the word of God go forth with the impurity of some.

Thou shalt not respect per- [IV. 3.] sons in convicting any one for a transgression. Thou [III. 7, 8.] shalt be meek, thou shalt be gentle, thou shalt tremble at the words which thou hast heard. Thou shalt not be re- [II. 3.] vengeful against thy brother. Thou shalt not hesitate [IV. 4.] whether it shall be or not. Thou shalt not take in vain the name of the Lord. Thou [II. 7.] shalt love thy neighbor above thy life (or, soul.)

Thou shalt not slay a child [II. 2.] by abortion, nor again shalt thou destroy the new-born child. Thou shalt by no [IV. 9.] means take off thy hand from thy son, or from thy daughter, but from youth thou shalt teach (them) the fear of the Lord.

Thou shalt by no means be [II. 2.] lusting after the things of thy neighbor, thou shalt by [II. 6.] no means be rapacious, nor [III. 9.] shalt thou from thy soul cleave to (the) high, but with the lowly and righteous shalt

[III. 10.] ἀναστραφήσῃ. τὰ συμβαίνοντά σου ἐνεργή-
ματα ὡς ἀγαθὰ προσ-
δέξῃ, εἰδὼς ὅτι ἄνευ
θεοῦ οὐδὲν γίνεται. (7)
[II. 4.] οὐκ ἔσῃ διγνώμων οὐδὲ δίγλωσσος· παγὶς
γὰρ θανάτου ἐστὶν ἡ
[IV. 11.] διγλωσσία. ὑποταγή-
σῃ κυρίοις ὡς τύπῳ θε-
οῦ ἐν αἰσχύνῃ καὶ φό-
[IV. 10.] βῳ· οὐ μὴ ἐπιτάξῃς
δούλῳ σου ἢ παιδίσκῃ
σου ἐν πικρίᾳ τοῖς ἐπὶ
τὸν αὐτὸν θεὸν ἐλπί-
ζουσι, μήποτε οὐ φο-
βηθῶσι τὸν ἐπ' ἀμφο-
τέροις θεόν· ὅτι ἦλθεν
οὐ κατὰ πρόσωπον κα-
λέσαι, ἀλλ' ἐφ' οὓς τὸ
πνεῦμα ἡτοίμασε.

[IV. 8.] (8) κοινωνήσεις ἐν
πᾶσι τῷ πλησίον σου καὶ
οὐκ ἐρεῖς ἴδια εἶναι·
εἰ γὰρ ἐν τῷ ἀφθάρτῳ
κοινωνοί ἐστε, πόσῳ
μᾶλλον ἐν τοῖς φθαρ-
τοῖς. οὐκ ἔσῃ πρόγλωσσος·
παγὶς γὰρ στόμα θανάτου.
ὅσον δύνασαι ὑπὲρ τῆς ψυχῆς
[IV. 5.] σου ἁγνεύσεις. (9) μὴ γίνου πρὸς μὲν τὸ λα-
βεῖν ἐκτείνων τὰς χεῖ-
ρας, πρὸς δὲ τὸ δοῦναι
συσπῶν.

ἀγαπήσεις ὡς κόρην τοῦ
[IV. 1.] ὀφθαλμοῦ σου πάντα τὸν
λαλοῦντά σοι τὸν λό-
γον τοῦ κυρίου. (10)

thou consort. The events that
befall thee shalt thou accept
as good, knowing that nothing
occurs without the will of
God.

Thou shalt not be double-
minded nor double-tongued,
for a snare of death is the
double tongue. Thou shalt
obey rulers as an image of
God in modesty and fear.
Thou shalt by no means lay
thy hand in bitterness upon
thy bondman or bondmaid,
who hope in the same God,
lest they perchance shall not
fear the God who is over
(you) both; because he came
not to call men according to
appearance, but those whom
the Spirit made ready.

Thou shalt share in all
things with thy neighbor, and
shalt not say they are thine
own; for if ye are partners
in that which is incorruptible, how much more in the
corruptible (things)? Thou
shalt not be hasty of tongue,
for (the) mouth is a snare of
death. As much as thou
canst thou shalt make purifi-
cation for thy soul. Be not
one who stretches out his
hands for receiving, but draws
them in for giving.

Thou shalt love as the apple
of thine eye every one that
speaketh to thee the word of
the Lord. Thou shalt re-

μνησθήση ἡμέραν κρίσεως ἡμέρας καὶ νυκτὸς καὶ ἐκζητήσεις, καθ᾽ ἑκάστην ἡμέραν τὰ πρόσωπα τῶν ἁγίων. ἢ διὰ λόγου κοπιῶν καὶ πορευόμενος εἰς τὸ παρακαλέσαι καὶ μελετῶν εἰς τὸ σῶσαι ψυχὴν τῷ λόγῳ, ἢ διὰ τῶν χειρῶν σου ἐργάσῃ εἰς λύτρον ἁμαρτιῶν σου. (11) οὐ διστάσεις δοῦναι, οὐδὲ διδοὺς γογγύσεις· γνώσῃ δέ, τίς ὁ τοῦ μισθοῦ καλὸς ἀνταποδότης. φυλάξεις ἃ παρέλαβες, μήτε προστιθεὶς μήτε ἀφαιρῶν. εἰς τέλος μισήσεις τὸν πονηρόν.* κρινεῖς δικαίως. (12). οὐ ποιήσεις σχίσμα· εἰρηνεύσεις δὲ μαχομένους συναγαγών.

ἐξομολογήσῃ ἐπὶ ἁμαρτίᾳ σου. οὐ προσήξεις ἐπὶ προσευχὴν ἐν συνειδήσει πονηρᾷ.

αὕτη ἐστὶν ἡ ὁδὸς τοῦ φωτός.

XX. Ἡ δὲ τοῦ μέλανος ὁδός σκολιά ἐστι καὶ κατάρας μεστή. ὁδὸς γάρ ἐστι θανάτου αἰωνίου μετὰ τιμωρίας, ἐν ᾗ ἐστὶ τὰ ἀπολλύντα τὴν ψυχὴν αὐτῶν· εἰδωλολατρεία, θρασύτης, ὕψος δυνά-

member the day of judgment night and day, and *thou shalt* [IV. 2.] *seek out every day the faces of the saints*, either by word laboring, and going for the purpose of exhorting, and meditating how to save (thy) soul by the word, or *with thy* [IV. 6.] *hands thou shalt work for a ransom for thy sins. Thou* [IV. 7.] *shalt not hesitate to give, nor when giving shalt thou murmur; but thou shalt know who is the good recompenser of the reward. Thou shalt* [IV. 13.] *keep what thou hast received, neither adding to it nor taking from it.* To the end thou shalt hate the evil one (the evil). *Thou shalt judge righteously.*

Thou shalt not make di- [IV. 3.] *vision, but shalt make peace,* bringing together *those at strife.*

Thou shalt make confession [IV. 14.] *of thy sins. Thou shalt not come to prayer with an evil conscience.*

This is the way of light.

Ch. xx.—*But the way of* [V. 1.] darkness *is* crooked and *full of curse.* For it is a way of eternal death, with punishment, in which are the things which destroy their (men's) soul; *idolatry, overboldness, haughtiness* of power, *hy-*

---

* Probably a false reading for τὸ πονηρόν. A conjecture of Dr. C. Taylor.

μεως, ὑπόκρισις, δι- πλοκαρδία, μοιχεία, φόνος, ἁρπαγή, ὑπερη- φανία, παράβασις, δό- λος, κακία, αὐθάδεια, φαρμακεία, μαγεία, πλεονεξία, ἀφοβία θεοῦ· [V. 2.] (2) διῶκται τῶν ἀγα- θῶν, μισοῦντες ἀλή- θειαν, ἀγαπῶντες ψεῦ- δος, οὐ γινώσκοντες μισθὸν δικαιοσύνης, οὐ κολλώμενοι ἀγαθῷ, οὐ κρίσει δικαίᾳ, χήρᾳ καὶ ὀρφανῷ οὐ προσέχοντες, ἀγρυπνοῦντες οὐκ εἰς φόβον θεοῦ, ἀλλ' ἐπὶ τὸ πονηρόν, ὧν μακρὰν καὶ πόρρω πραΰτης καὶ ὑπομονή, ἀγαπῶντες μάταια, διώκοντες ἀνταπόδομα, οὐκ ἐλε- οῦντες πτωχόν, οὐ πονοῦντες ἐπὶ κατα- πονουμένῳ, εὐχερεῖς ἐπὶ καταλαλιᾷ, οὐ γινώσκον- τες τὸν ποιήσαντα αὐ- τούς, φονεῖς τέκνων, φθορεῖς πλάσματος θεοῦ, ἀποστρεφόμε- νοι τὸν ἐνδεόμενον, καταπονοῦντες τὸν θλιβόμενον, πλουσίων παράκλητοι, πενήτων ἄνομοι κριταί, παν- θαμάρτητοι.

pocrisy, duplicity, adultery, murder, robbery, arrogance, transgression, *craft, vice, self-will, sorcery, magic, greed,* no fear of God; *persecutors of (the) good, hating truth, loving falsehoods, not knowing the reward of righteousness, not cleaving to (that which is) good (and) not to righteous judgment,* not giving heed to widow and orphan, *on the watch not for fear of God, but for evil; far and distant from whom are meekness and patience; loving vanities, pursuing revenge, having no pity on the poor, not laboring for one in distress;* expert in evil speaking; *not knowing him that made them, murderers of children, destroyers of God's image, turning away from the needy, oppressing the afflicted, advocates of the rich, lawless judges of the poor, wholly sinful.*

DOCUMENT IV.

HERMAS.

"THE Shepherd of Hermas" (ὁ Ποιμήν, Hermæ Pastor) is a guide of Christian morality in the shape of an allegory or romance, and was once exceedingly popular in the Church, but is to most modern readers tedious and insipid. It is divided into *Visions, Mandates* or *Commandments*, and *Similitudes*.

The book presents two parallels to the first and second chapters of the *Didache*, with some features resembling Barnabas.

The date of Hermas is between 100 and 150, at all events later than that of the *Didache*, and Barnabas, especially if he used Theodotion's Version of Daniel,* which belongs to the first half of the second century, but may be older. See Dr. Salmon's note on Hermas and Theodotion at the close of his *Introduction to the N. Test.*, London, 1885.

The Greek text is taken from von Gebhardt and Harnack's *Patr. Ap.* iii. 72 sq. and 98; compared with Funk (*Patr. Ap.* i. 390 and 412), and Hilgenfeld (*Pastor Hermæ*, ed. ii. 1881).

---

* Prof. J. Rendel Harris, of Johns Hopkins University, Baltimore, in a note "On the angelology of Hermas" in the *University Circular*, April, 1884, p. 75, observed a connection between the obscure passage of Hermas, *Vision* iv. 2, 4, and Dan. vi. 22 (23); whereupon Dr. Hort, of Cambridge, in the same *Circular*, Dec 1884, p. 23, showed that Hermas in the passage referred to followed not the Septuagint but Theodotion's version of Daniel, as may be seen from the following comparison:

Hermas, *Vis.* iv. 2, 4.	Theodotion, Dan. vi. 22.	LXX. Dan. vi. 22.
Διὰ τοῦτο ὁ κύριος ἀπέστειλεν τὸν ἄγγελον αὐτοῦ τὸν ἐπὶ τῶν θηρίων ὄντα, οὗ τὸ ὄνομά ἐστιν Θεγρί, [emend. Harris Σεγρί] καὶ ἐνέφραξεν τὸ στόμα αὐτοῦ, ἵνα μή σε λυμάνῃ.	ὁ θεός μου ἀπέστειλεν τὸν ἄγγελον αὐτοῦ καὶ ἐνέφραξεν τὰ στόματα τῶν λεόντων καὶ οὐκ ἐλυμήναντό με.	σέσωκέν με ὁ θεὸς ἀπὸ τῶν λεόντων.

See Harnack's notice in the "Theolog. Literaturzeitung," 1885, No. VI., col. 146.

[Didache I. 5.]

Ἐντολὴ β'. Ἐργάζου τὸ ἀγαθὸν καὶ ἐκ τῶν κόπων σου ὧν ὁ θεὸς δίδωσίν σοι, πᾶσιν ὑστερουμένοις δίδου ἁπλῶς, μὴ διστάζων, τίνι δῷς ἢ τίνι μὴ δῷς. Πᾶσιν δίδου· πᾶσιν γὰρ ὁ θεὸς δίδοσθαι θέλει ἐκ τῶν ἰδίων δωρημάτων. 5. Οἱ οὖν λαμβάνοντες ἀποδώσουσιν λόγον τῷ θεῷ διατί ἔλαβον καὶ εἰς τί· οἱ μὲν γὰρ λαμβάνοντες θλιβόμενοι οὐ δικασθήσονται, οἱ δὲ ἐν ὑποκρίσει λαμβάνοντες τίσουσιν δίκην. 6. Ὁ οὖν διδοὺς ἀθῷός ἐστιν· ὡς γὰρ ἔλαβεν παρὰ τοῦ κυρίου τὴν διακονίαν τελέσαι, ἁπλῶς αὐτὴν ἐτέλεσεν, μηδὲν διακρίνων, τίνι δῷ ἢ μὴ δῷ.

COMMANDMENT II. 4–6.— Do good, and from thy labors, which God giveth thee, give in simplicity to all that are in need, not doubting to whom thou shouldst give and to whom thou shouldst not give. Give to all; *for God wills that* things should be *given to all from his own* gifts. 5. Those then, that receive shall give an account to God, why they received and for what purpose; for those that receive in distress shall not be condemned; but those who receive in hypocrisy shall pay a penalty.

6. *He then that giveth is guiltless;* for as he received from the Lord the ministry to fulfil, so he fulfilled it in simplicity, making no distinction to whom he should give or not give.

[II. 2 sq.]
[V. 1.]

Ἐντολὴ ή. Ποταπαί, φημί, κύριε, εἰσὶν αἱ πονηρίαι ἀφ' ὧν δεῖ με ἐγκρατεύεσθαι; Ἄκουε, φησίν, ἀπὸ μοιχείας καὶ πορνείας, ἀπὸ μεθύσματος ἀνομίας [Lat.: a potu iniquo], ἀπὸ τρυφῆς πονηρᾶς, ἀπὸ ἐδεσμάτων πολλῶν καὶ πολυτελείας πλούτου καὶ καυχήσεως καὶ ὑψηλοφροσύνης καὶ ὑπερηφανίας, καὶ ἀπὸ ψεύσματος καὶ καταλαλίας καὶ ὑποκρίσεως, μνησικακίας καὶ πάσης βλασφημίας.

Commandment VIII. 3–5.— "How many, O Master," I said, "are the sins from which we should abstain?" "Listen," he said; "from adultery and fornication, from lawlessness of drunkenness, from evil luxuriousness, from many meats, from extravagance of wealth, and boasting, and haughtiness, and arrogance, and falsehood, and evil-speaking, and hypocrisy, from revengefulness and every blasphemy.

4. Ταῦτα τὰ ἔργα πάντων πονηρότατά εἰσιν ἐν τῇ ζωῇ τῶν ἀνθρώπων. Ἀπὸ τούτων οὖν τῶν ἔργων δεῖ ἐγκρατεύεσθαι τὸν δοῦλον τοῦ θεοῦ· ὁ γὰρ μὴ ἐγκρατευόμενος ἀπὸ τούτων οὐ δύναται ζῆσαι τῷ θεῷ. Ἄκουε οὖν καὶ τὰ ἀκόλουθα τούτων. 5. Ἔτι γάρ, φημί, κύριε, πονηρὰ ἔργα ἐστί; Καί γε πολλά, φησίν, ἔστιν, ἀφ' ὧν δεῖ τὸν δοῦλον τοῦ θεοῦ ἐγκρατεύεσθαι· κλέμμα, ψεῦδος, ἀποστέρησις, ψευδομαρτυρία, πλεονεξία, ἐπιθυμία πονηρά, ἀπάτη, κενοδοξία, ἀλαζονεία καὶ ὅσα τούτοις ὅμοιά εἰσιν.

4. "These deeds are the worst of all in the life of man. From these deeds, then, the servant of God must abstain. For he who abstaineth not from these things, cannot live unto God. Hear now, also, the things that attend these."
5. "Are there then, Master," said I, "other evil deeds?" "Yea, truly," said he, "many there are from which the servant of God must refrain: theft, lying, fraud, false-witness, *covetousness,* [*Did.* 7. 1.] *evil desires, deceit,* vainglory, *pretence,* and whatever things are like these."

DOCUMENT V.

THE APOSTOLICAL CHURCH ORDER,

OR

THE ECCLESIASTICAL CANONS OF THE HOLY APOSTLES.

Comp. Ch. XXX.

This document must not be confounded with the *Apostolical Constitutions* (see Doc. VII.), nor with the *Apostolical Canons* appended to them, although it is closely related to both. It is the Apostolical Constitution or Canon Law of the Christians of Egypt, and is still in use among them. We give it here as an interesting link between the *Teaching of the Twelve Apostles* and the Pseudo-Clementine *Apostolical Constitutions*.

The Greek text is taken from the latest edition by Harnack (pp. 225–237), who adopts Lagarde's division into 30 canons derived from the Thebaic MS. The older editions have 20 canons. I have compared the texts of Joh. Wilhelm Bickell (*Geschichte des Kirchenrechts*, Giessen, 1843, Erster Band, pp. 107–132, from the Vienna MS., with a German translation under the title *Apostolische Kirchenordnung*), and of Adolf Hilgenfeld (*Novum Testamentum extra canonem receptum, ed. altera et emendata*, Lipsiæ, 1884, Fasc. iv. 111–120, under the title αἱ διαταγαὶ αἱ διὰ Κλήμεντος καὶ κανόνες ἐκκλησιαστικοὶ τῶν ἁγίων ἀποστόλων, *The Ordinances through Clement and the Ecclesiastical Canons of the Holy Apostles*, which he identifies with the *Duæ Viæ vel Judicium Petri*). I have given the principal variations in foot-notes, and added a number of explanatory remarks. The editions of Lagarde (*Reliquiæ juris ecclesiastici antiquissimæ*, 1856), and of Cardinal Pitra (*Juris ecclesiastici hist. monumenta*, Tom. i. Romæ, 1864) have been used by Harnack and Hilgenfeld.

The title in the Latin translation of the Æthiopic text by Ludolf (*Comm. in Hist. Aeth.* p. 314, as quoted by Bickell and Hilgenfeld) reads: "*Isti (sunt) canones patrum apostolorum quos constituerunt ad ordinandam ecclesiam christianam.*" In the Cod. Ottobon. sæc. xiv. first compared by Pitra, the document is abridged and called ἐπιτομὴ ὅρων τῶν ἁγίων ἀποστόλων καθολικῆς παραδόσεως, *Epitome of the Definitions of the Holy Apostles.* In the defective Moscow MS. discovered by O. von Gebhardt and published in the second edition of his and Harnack's Ep. of Barnabas (1878, p. xxix. sq.) the title reads: διατάξεις τῶν ἁγίων ἀποστόλων, *Ordinances of the Holy Apostles.*

The Egyptian text of the document was made known first by Tattam (in the Memphitic dialect of Lower Egypt), London, 1844, and then by Lagarde (in the Thebaic dialect of Upper Egypt) in his "*Ægyptiaca,*" Gottingæ, 1883. The Æthiopic version, edited in Æthiopic and Latin by W. Fell, Lips. 1881, seems to have been made from the Thebaic. The next document gives the Egyptian version from Tattam.

ΚΑΝΟΝΕΣ ΈΚΚΛΗΣΙΑΣΤΙΚΟΙ ΤΩΝ ΆΓΙΩΝ ΑΠΟΣΤΟΛΩΝ.

THE ECCLESIASTICAL CANONS OF THE HOLY APOSTLES.

Χαίρετε, υἱοὶ καὶ θυγατέρες, ἐν ὀνόματι κυρίου Ἰησοῦ Χριστοῦ, Ἰωάννης καὶ Ματθαῖος καὶ Πέτρος καὶ Ἀνδρέας καὶ Φίλιππος καὶ Σίμων καὶ Ἰάκωβος καὶ Ναθαναὴλ καὶ Θωμᾶς καὶ Κηφᾶς καὶ Βαρθολομαῖος καὶ Ἰούδας Ἰακώβου.

Greeting, sons and daughters, in the name of the Lord Jesus Christ. John and Matthew and Peter and Andrew and Philip, and Simon and James and Nathanael and Thomas and Cephas[1] and Bartholomew[2] and Judas of James.[3]

---

[1] Falsely distinguished from Peter, who is mentioned as the third Apostle. Clement of Alex. (in Eusebius, *H. Eccl.* i. 12) distinguishes the Cephas of Gal. ii. 11 from Peter, but counts him among the Seventy Disciples.

[2] Falsely distinguished from Nathanael (John, i. 46; xxi. 2), mentioned before.

[3] Judas *the brother* of James, see Luke, vi. 16; Acts, i. 13. Only one James is mentioned, and no distinction is made between the brother of John and the son of Alphæus. Matthias, who was elected in the place of the Traitor, is omitted. Paul is ignored. But owing to the imaginary Cephas and Bartholomew there are twelve Apostles. This erroneous and incomplete list was perhaps afterwards added.

1. Κατὰ κέλευσιν τοῦ κυρίου ἡμῶν Ἰησοῦ Χριστοῦ τοῦ σωτῆρος συναθροισθέντων ἡμῶν, καθὼς διέταξεν—πρὸ * τοῦ· Μέλλετε κληροῦσθαι τὰς ἐπαρχίας καταλογίσασθαι τόπον ἀριθμούς, ἐπισκόπων ἀξίας, πρεσβυτέρων ἕδρας, διακόνων παρεδρείας, ἀναγνωστῶν νουνεχίας, χηρῶν ἀνεγκλησίας καὶ ὅσα δέοι πρὸς θεμελίωσιν ἐκκλησίας, ἵνα τύπον τῶν ἐπουρανίων εἰδότες φυλάσσωνται ἀπὸ παντὸς ἀστοχήματος, εἰδότες ὅτι λόγον ὑφέξουσιν ἐν τῇ μεγάλῃ ἡμέρᾳ τῆς κρίσεως περὶ ὧν ἀκούσαντες οὐκ ἐφύλαξαν—καὶ ἐκέλευσεν ἡμᾶς ἐκπέμψασθαι τοὺς λόγους εἰς ὅλην τὴν οἰκουμένην·

1. Since we have assembled at a command of our Lord Jesus Christ the Saviour, according as he appointed—before the [injunction]: Ye are to assign districts,[1] to determine the numbers of places, the dignities of bishops, the seats of presbyters, the attendance (or, assistance) of deacons, the office (discretion) of readers, the blamelessness of widows,[2] and whatever be needful for founding a church, in order that, knowing the type of the heavenly [order],[3] they may keep themselves from every fault, knowing that they must render account at the great day of judgment for the things which they heard and did not keep—and as he commanded us to send forth the words into all the world.

---

[1] κληρόω, to appoint to an office by lot, to allot, assign. In ecclesiastical usage also to ordain. ἐπαρχία, the government of an ἔπαρχος (præfectus) or the district governed by him, the Roman provincia. The provinces were subdivided chiefly for fiscal, commercial and judicial purposes into smaller districts, called conventus, jurisdictiones.

[2] Bickell reads ἀνεκκλησίας, and translates: "die Entfernung der Wittwen von kirchlichen Verrichtungen." ἀνεκκλησία is not mentioned in the dictionaries, but the adjective is ἀνεκκλησίαστος, excluded from the church. Suicer, Thes. i. 332, explains it ἀλλότριος τῆς ἐκκλησίας, alienus ab ecclesia. I followed the reading of Lag. Ha. Hlg. ἀνεγκλησία, blamelessness. Pitra suggests παρακλήσεις.

[3] The ecclesiastical or terrestrial hierarchy was regarded as a reflection and copy of the celestial hierarchy of angelic orders,—an idea carried out most fully in the writings of Pseudo-Dionysius Areopagita and adopted by Thomas Aquinas and the mediæval schoolmen. See Church History, vol. iv. 597 sqq.

* Hilgenfeld puts πρὸ * * * ἐφύλαξαν in parentheses.

2. ἔδοξεν οὖν ἡμῖν πρὸς ὑπόμνησιν τῆς ἀδελφότητος καὶ νουθεσίαν ἑκάστῳ ὡς ὁ κύριος ἀπεκάλυψε κατὰ τὸ θέλημα τοῦ θεοῦ διὰ πνεύματος ἁγίου μνησθεῖσι λόγου ἐντείλασθαι ὑμῖν.

3. Ἰωάννης εἶπεν· ἄνδρες ἀδελφοί, εἰδότες ὅτι λόγον ὑφέξομεν περὶ τῶν διατεταγμένων ἡμῖν εἰς ἑνὸς πρόσωπον μὴ λαμβάνωμεν, ἀλλ᾽ ἐάν τις δοκῇ τι * ἀσύμφερον λέγειν,† ἀντιλεγέσθω αὐτῷ.

ἔδοξε δὲ πᾶσι πρῶτον Ἰωάννην εἰπεῖν.

[Didache I. 1, 2.]

4. Ἰωάννης εἶπεν· ὁδοὶ δύο εἰσί, μία τῆς ζωῆς, καὶ μία τοῦ θανάτου, διαφορὰ δὲ πολλὴ μεταξὺ τῶν δύο ὁδῶν· ἡ μὲν οὖν ‡ ὁδὸς τῆς ζωῆς ἐστιν αὕτη· πρῶτον· ἀγαπήσεις τὸν θεὸν τὸν ποιήσαντά σε ἐξ ὅλης τῆς καρδίας σου καὶ δοξάσεις τὸν λυτρωσάμενόν σε ἐκ θανάτου, ἥτις ἐστὶν ἐν- [2.] τολὴ πρώτη. δεύτερον· § ἀγαπήσεις τὸν πλησίον σου ὡς ἑαυτόν, ἥτις ἐστὶν ἐντολὴ δευτέρα, ἐν οἷς ὅλος ὁ

2. Therefore it seemed good to us, for a reminding of the brotherhood and a warning to each, as the Lord revealed it according to the will of God through the Holy Spirit, remembering the word [the command of the Lord] to enjoin it upon you.

3. John said: My brethren, knowing that we shall render account for the things assigned to us, let us each not regard the person of any one (not be partial to any one), but if any think it fitting to gainsay let him gainsay.[1]

Now it seemed good to all that John should speak first.

4. John said: *There are two ways, one of life and one of death, but there is a great difference between the two ways; for the way of life is this: First, thou shalt love the God who made thee*, with all thy heart, and shalt glorify him that ransomed thee from death, which is (the) first commandment. *Secondly, thou shalt love thy neighbor as thyself*, which is (the) second commandment: upon which hang all the law, and the prophets.

---

[1] Ludolf: *Et si quis dixerit quod non decet (dicere), objurget cum eo quod dixit id quod bonum non est.*

* Hlg. omits τι. † Bickell (B.), Hlg. συμφέρον ἀντιλέγειν.
‡ B. Hlg. γάρ.   § B. δευτέρα.

νόμος κρέμαται καὶ οἱ προφῆται.

5. Ματθαῖος εἶπεν· πάντα
ὅσα ἂν* μὴ θέλῃς† σοι
γίνεσθαι,‡ μηδὲ σὺ§
ἄλλῳ ποιήσῃς.∥ τού-
των δὲ τῶν λόγων τὴν
διδαχὴν εἰπέ, ἀδελφὲ
Πέτρε,

6. Πέτρος εἶπεν· οὐ φο-
νεύσεις, οὐ μοιχεύ-
σεις, οὐ πορνεύσεις,
οὐ¶ παιδοφθορήσεις,
οὐ κλέψεις, οὐ μαγεύ-
σεις, οὐ φαρμακεύσεις,
οὐ φονεύσεις τέκνον ἐν
φθορᾷ οὐδὲ** γεννη-
θὲν†† ἀποκτενεῖς, οὐκ‡‡
ἐπιθυμήσεις τὰ τοῦ
πλησίον· οὐκ ἐπιορκή-
σεις, οὐ ψευδομαρτυ-
ρήσεις, οὐ κακολογή-
σεις, οὐδὲ μνησικακή-
σεις, οὐκ ἔσῃ δίγνωμος
οὐδὲ δίγλωσσος· παγὶς
γὰρ θανάτου ἐστὶν ἡ
διγλωσσία. οὐκ ἔσται
ὁ λόγος σου κενός, οὐδὲ
ψευδής· οὐκ ἔσῃ πλεο-
νέκτης οὐδὲ ἅρπαξ
οὐδὲ ὑποκριτὴς οὐδὲ
κακοήθης οὐδὲ ὑπερή-
φανος, οὐ§§ λήψῃ βου-
λὴν πονηρὰν κατὰ τοῦ
πλησίον σου· οὐ μισή-

5. Matthew said: *All* [2.]
*things whatsoever thou wilt
not have befall thee, thou to
another shalt not do. Now
of these words* tell *the teaching,* brother Peter.

6. Peter said: *Thou shalt* [II. 2.]
*not kill; thou shalt not com-
mit adultery; thou shalt not
commit fornication; thou
shalt not pollute a youth; thou
shalt not steal; thou shalt not
be a sorcerer; thou shalt not
use enchantments; thou shalt
not slay a child by abortion,
nor kill what is born; thou
shalt not covet any thing that
is thy neighbor's; thou shalt
not forswear thyself; thou
shalt not bear false witness;
thou shalt not speak evil;* [3.]
*thou shalt not bear malice;
thou shalt not be double-* [4.]
*minded nor double-tongued,
for a snare of death is duplicity of tongue. Thy speech* [5.]
*shall not be empty, nor false;
thou shalt not be covetous,* [6.]
*nor rapacious, nor a hypo-
crite, nor malicious, nor
haughty, nor take evil counsel
against thy neighbor; thou*

---

* B. Hlg. omit. † Hlg. θέλεις.
‡ B. Hlg. γενέσθαι. § B. οὐ μηδὲ.
∥ B. Hlg. ποιήσεις. ¶ B. Hlg. omit clauses οὐ * * * μαγεύσεις.
** B. οὐ. †† B. γεννηθὲν * * * ἀποκτενεῖς.
‡‡ B. Hlg. omit clauses ουκ * * * ἐπιορκήσεις. §§ B. Hlg. οὐδὲ.

σεις πάντα ἄνθρωπον,
ἀλλ' οὓς μὲν ἐλέγξεις,
οὓς δὲ ἐλεήσεις, περὶ ὧν δὲ
προσεύξῃ, οὓς δὲ ἀγα-
πήσεις ὑπὲρ τὴν ψυχήν
σου.

[III. 1.] 7. Ἀνδρέας εἶπεν· τέκνον
μου, φεῦγε ἀπὸ παν-
τὸς πονηροῦ καὶ ἀπὸ
παντὸς ὁμοίου αὐτοῦ.
[2.] μὴ γίνου ὀργίλος· ὁδηγεῖ γὰρ ἡ ὀργὴ πρὸς
τὸν* φόνον· ἔστι γὰρ
δαιμόνιον ἀρρενικὸν ὁ θυμός.
[2.] μὴ γίνου ζηλωτὴς μηδὲ
ἐριστικὸς μηδὲ θυμώ-
δης†· ἐκ γὰρ τούτων
φόνος γεννᾶται.

[3.] 8. Φίλιππος εἶπεν· τέκνον
μου, ‡ μὴ γίνου ἐπιθυ-
μητής· ὁδηγεῖ γὰρ ἡ
ἐπιθυμία πρὸς τὴν πορ-
νείαν καὶ ἕλκει τοὺς ἀνθρώ-
πους πρὸς ἑαυτήν. ἔστι γὰρ
θηλυκὸν δαιμόνιον ἡ ἐπιθυμία,§ καὶ ὁ μὲν μετ' ὀργῆς, ὃ
δὲ μεθ' ἡδονῆς ἀπόλλυσι τοὺς
εἰσερχομένους ‖ εἰς¶ αὐτήν.**
ὁδὸς δὲ πονηροῦ πνεύματος
ἁμαρτία ψυχῆς, καὶ ὅταν
βραχείαν εἴσδυσιν σχῇ ἐν
αὐτῷ, πλατύνει αὐτὴν καὶ
ἄγει ἐπὶ πάντα τὰ κακὰ τὴν

shalt not hate any man, but some thou shalt reprove, and some thou shalt pity; and for some thou shalt pray, and some thou shalt love more than thine own soul.

7. Andrew said: *My child, flee from all evil, and from everything like it. Be not inclined to anger, for anger leads to murder;* for wrath is a male demon.[1] *Become not a zealot, nor contentious, nor passionate; for from these things murder is engendered.*

8. Philip said: *My child, be not lustful; for lust leadeth to fornication,* and draweth men to herself. *For lust is a female demon,* and the one ruins with anger, the other with lust, those that receive them.[2] Now (the) way of an evil spirit is the sin of the soul; and if it (the evil spirit) has only a narrow entrance within him, it widens the way and leads that soul to all bad things, and does not permit the man

---

[1] Lud.: *instar cacadæmonis.* Bickell: *ein männlicher Dämon.*
[2] Lud.: *Cacodæmon seductor est. Nam cum diabolus iram cum libidine conjungit, interitus æternus sequitur eum qui illud admittit.*

* B. Hlg. omit.
‡ B. Hlg. omit.
‖ B. Hlg. εἰσδεχομένους.
** B. Hlg. αἱτα.
† B. Hlg. θυμαντικός.
§ B. Hlg. τῆς ἐπιθυμίας.
¶ B. Hlg. omit.

ψυχὴν ἐκείνην καὶ οὐκ ἐᾷ διαβλέψαι τὸν ἄνθρωπον καὶ ἰδεῖν τὴν ἀλήθειαν. ὁ θυμὸς ὑμῶν μέτρον ἐχέτω καὶ ἐν βραχεῖ διαστήματι αὐτὸν ἡνιοχεῖτε καὶ ἀνακρούετε, ἵνα μὴ ἐμβάλλῃ ὑμᾶς εἰς ἔργον πονηρόν. θυμὸς γὰρ καὶ ἡδονὴ πονηρὰ ἐπὶ πολὺ* παραμένοντα κατὰ ἐπίτασιν δαιμόνια γίνεται, καὶ ὅταν ἐπιτρέψῃ αὐτοῖς ὁ ἄνθρωπος, οἰδαίνουσιν ἐν τῇ ψυχῇ αὐτοῦ καὶ γίνονται μείζονες καὶ ἀπάγουσιν αὐτὸν εἰς ἔργα ἄδικα καὶ ἐπιγελῶσιν αὐτῷ καὶ† ἥδονται ἐπὶ τῇ ἀπωλείᾳ τοῦ ἀνθρώπου.‡

to look clearly and see the truth. Let your wrath be restrained, and after a short interval, bridle and check it, that it may not hurl you into evil deeds. For wrath and evil desire, if they be suffered long to remain, become demons by reinforcement. And whenever man yields himself to them, they swell up in his soul and grow larger and lead him into unrighteous deeds, and deride him, and rejoice at the destruction of men.

9. Σίμων εἶπεν· τέκνον, μὴ γίνου αἰσχρολόγος μηδὲ ὑψηλόφθαλμος. ἐκ γὰρ τούτων μοιχεία§ γεννᾶται.∥

9. Simon said: *Child, be not foul-mouthed, nor lofty-eyed; for of these things come adulteries.* [3.]

10. Ἰάκωβος εἶπεν. τέκνον μου,¶ μὴ γίνου οἰωνοσκόπος, ἐπειδὴ** ὁδηγεῖ εἰς†† τὴν εἰδωλολατρείαν, μηδὲ ἐπαοιδὸς μηδὲ μαθηματικὸς μηδὲ περικαθαίρων μηδὲ θέλε αὐτὰ‡‡ ἰδεῖν μηδὲ ἀκούειν.§§ ἐκ

10. James said: *Child, be not an omen-watcher, since it leadeth to idolatry, nor a charmer, nor an astrologer, nor a purifier, nor be willing to look upon nor hear these things; for from all these idolatries are begotten.* [4.]

---

[1] The Coptic Constitution: "He (the demon) will take with him all other evil spirits; he will go to that soul and will not leave the man to meditate at all, lest he should see the truth."

* B. Hlg. ἐπιπολύ.
‡ B. Hlg. τῶν ἀνθρώπων.
∥ B. Hlg. γίνονται.
** B. ἐπεὶ δή.
‡‡ B. αὐτάς.

† Hlg. omits.
§ B. Hlg. μοιχεῖαι.
¶ B. Hlg. omit.
†† B. Hlg. πρός.
§§ B. Hlg. εἰδέναι.

γὰρ τούτων ἁπάντων
εἰδωλολατρεῖαι γεν
νῶνται.

[5.] 11. Ναθαναὴλ εἶπεν· τέκνον, μὴ γίνου ψεύστης, ἐπειδὴ ὁδηγεῖ τὸ ψεῦσμα ἐπὶ τὴν κλοπήν, μηδὲ φιλάργυρος μηδὲ κενόδοξος. ἐκ γὰρ τούτων ἁπάντων κλοπαὶ γεννῶνται.*

[6.] τέκνον, μὴ γίνου γόγγυσος, ἐπειδὴ ἄγει πρὸς τὴν βλασφημίαν, μηδὲ αὐθάδης μηδὲ πονηρόφρων. ἐκ γὰρ τούτων ἁπάντων βλασφη

[7.] μίαι γεννῶνται. ἴσθι δὲ πραΰς, ἐπεὶ† πραεῖς κληρονομήσουσι‡ τὴν

[8.] βασιλείαν τῶν οὐρανῶν. γίνου μακρόθυμος, ἐλεήμων, εἰρηνοποιός, καθαρὸς τῇ καρδίᾳ ἀπὸ παντὸς κακοῦ, ἄκακος καὶ ἡσύχιος, ἀγαθὸς καὶ φυλάσσων καὶ τρέμων τοὺς λόγους οὓς ἤκουσας·

[9.] οὐχ ὑψώσεις σεαυτὸν οὐδὲ δώσεις τὴν ψυχήν§ σου‖ μετὰ ὑψηλῶν, ἀλλὰ μετὰ δικαίων καὶ ταπεινῶν ἀναστραφήσῃ. τὰ δὲ συμ

11. Nathaniel said: *Child, be not a liar, since lying leads to theft, nor avaricious, nor vainglorious; for of all these things thefts are begotten.*

[Judas said] : *Child, be not a murmurer, since it leadeth to blasphemy, nor self-willed, nor evil-minded; for of all these things blasphemies are begotten. But be meek, since the meek shall inherit the kingdom of heaven. Be long-suffering, merciful, peace-making, pure in heart from every evil, guileless and gentle, good, and keeping and trembling at the words which thou hast heard; thou shalt not exalt thyself, nor permit over-boldness to thy soul, nor cleave with thy soul to (the) high, but with (the) righteous and lowly thou shalt consort.*

---

* Hlg. inserts Ἰούδας εἶπε. B. observes that these words were unquestionably omitted in the original Greek MS. merely by accident, and so he inserts "Judas sprach" in his translation.

† Hlg. ἐπειδή.

‡ B. Hlg. κληρονομοῦσι.

§ Hlg. τῇ ψυχῇ.

‖ Hlg. inserts θράσος οὐδὲ κολληθήσῃ τῇ ψυχῇ σου.

βαίνοντά σοι ἐνεργήματα ὡς ἀγαθὰ προσδέξῃ, εἰδὼς ὅτι ἄτερ Θεοῦ οὐδὲν γίνεται.

12. Θωμᾶς εἶπεν· τέκνον, τὸν λαλοῦντά σοι τὸν λόγον τοῦ Θεοῦ καὶ παραίτιόν σοι γινόμενον τῆς ζωῆς καὶ δόντα σοι τὴν ἐν κυρίῳ σφραγῖδα ἀγαπήσεις ὡς κόρην ὀφθαλμοῦ σου, μνησθήσῃ δὲ αὐτοῦ νύκτα καὶ ἡμέραν, τιμήσεις αὐτὸν ὡς τὸν κύριον. ὅθεν γὰρ ἡ κυριότης λαλεῖται, ἐκεῖ κύριός ἐστιν. ἐκζητήσεις δὲ τὸ πρόσωπον αὐτοῦ καθ' ἡμέραν καὶ τοὺς λοιποὺς ἁγίους, ἵνα ἐπαναπαύσῃ τοῖς λόγοις αὐτῶν· κολλώμενος* γὰρ ἁγίοις ἁγιασθήσῃ. τιμήσεις δὲ † αὐτόν, καθ' ὃ δυνατὸς εἶ, ἐκ τοῦ ἱδρῶτός σου καὶ ἐκ τοῦ πόνου τῶν χειρῶν σου. εἰ γὰρ ὁ κύριος δι' αὐτοῦ ἠξίωσέν σοι δοθῆναι πνευματικὴν τροφὴν καὶ ποτὸν καὶ ζωὴν αἰώνιον, σὺ ὀφείλεις πολὺ μᾶλλον τὴν φθαρτὴν καὶ πρόσκαιρον προσφέρειν τροφήν· ἄξιος γὰρ ὁ ἐργάτης τοῦ μισθοῦ αὐ-

The events that befall thee [10.] thou shalt accept as good, knowing that without God nothing occurs.

12. Thomas said: *Child,* [IV. 1.] *him that speaketh to thee the word of God,* and becometh to thee an author of life, and hath given thee the seal in the Lord, thou shalt love as the apple of thine eye, and *thou shalt remember him night and day, thou shalt honor him as the Lord; for where the Lordship (of Christ) is spoken of,*[1] *there is the Lord. And thou shalt seek* out [2.] his face *daily* and the rest of *the saints, that thou mayest be refreshed by their words:* for by cleaving to saints thou shalt be sanctified. Thou shall honor him, as far as thou art able,—from thy sweat and from the labor of thy hands. For if the Lord through him saw fit that *spiritual food and drink and eternal life be given thee,* thou oughtest much more the *perishable and transient food; for the laborer is worthy of his hire,* and *a threshing ox thou shalt not muzzle,* and *no one planteth a vine and eateth not its fruit.*

---

[1] Ludolph: *ubi memorant divinitatem.* Bickell: *woher die Sache des Herrn verkündigt wird.*

* B. inserts ὡς ἅγιος.   † B. omits δέ.

τοῦ, καὶ βοῦν ἀλοῶντα οὐ
φιμώσεις, καὶ οὐδεὶς φυτεύει
ἀμπελῶνα καὶ ἐκ τοῦ καρποῦ
αὐτοῦ οὐκ ἐσθίει.

[3] 13. Κηφᾶς εἶπεν·* οὐ ποιήσεις σχίσματα. εἰρηνεύσεις δὲ μαχομένους. κρινεῖς δικαίως. οὐ λήψῃ πρόσωπον† ἐλέγξαι‡ τινὰ§ ἐπὶ παραπτώματι. οὐ γὰρ ἰσχύει πλοῦτος παρὰ κυρίῳ· οὐ γὰρ ἀξία∥ προκρίνει οὐδὲ κάλλος ὠφελεῖ, ἀλλ' ἰσότης ἐστὶ πάντων παρ' [4.] αὐτῷ. ἐν προσευχῇ σου μὴ διψυχήσῃς πότερον ἔσ- [5.] ται ἢ οὔ. μὴ γίνου πρὸς μὲν τὸ λαβεῖν ἐκτείνων τὰς χεῖρας, πρὸς δὲ τὸ δοῦναι συσ- [6.] πῶν. ἐὰν ἔχῃς¶ διὰ τῶν χειρῶν σου, δώσεις λύτρωσιν τῶν [7.] ἁμαρτιῶν σου. οὐ διστάσεις δοῦναι** οὐδὲ διδοὺς γογγύσεις· γνώσῃ γὰρ τίς ἐστιν ὁ τοῦ μισθοῦ καλὸς [8.] ἀνταποδότης. οὐκ ἀποστραφήσῃ ἐνδεόμενον, συγκοινωνήσεις†† δὲ πάντα‡‡ τῷ ἀδελφῷ σου καὶ οὐκ ἐρεῖς ἴδια εἶναι· εἰ

13. Cephas said: *Thou shalt not make divisions, but shall make peace between those who contend; thou shalt judge justly; thou shalt not respect persons in reproving for a transgression. For wealth does not avail with the Lord; for dignity does not predispose, nor beauty aid, but there is equality of all with him. In thy prayer thou shalt not hesitate, whether it shall be or not; be not (one who) for receiving stretches out the hands, but for giving draws them in. If thou hast (anything) by thy hands thou shalt give ransom for thy sins; thou shalt not hesitate to give, nor when giving shalt thou murmur; for thou shalt know, who is the good dispenser of the recompense. Thou shalt not turn away from a needy one, but thou shalt share in all things with thy brother, and shall not say they are thine own; for if ye are partners in that which is imperishable, how*

---

* Ha. εἴπειν (a typogr. error).
† B. Hlg. insert τινά.
‡ B. ἐλέγξας.
§ B. Hlg. omit.
∥ B. ἀξίας.
¶ B. ἔχεις.
** B. Hlg. διδόναι.
†† B. Hlg. omit σύγ.
‡‡ B. Hlg. ἁπάντων.

γὰρ ἐν τῷ ἀθανάτῳ κοινωνοί ἐστε, πόσῳ* μᾶλλον ἐν τοῖς θνητοῖς.†   much more in the corruptible things.¹

---

¹ This last clause "for if," etc., is not found in the *Apostolical Constitutions*, but in Barnabas, xix. 8. Here the parallel ceases between the *Did.* and the *Apostolical Church Order*. The remaining 17 sections of the Doc. are therefore omitted. But as a curiosity the strange scene described in chaps. xxix.-xxxi. is here inserted:

xxix. John said: Ye have forgotten, brethren, that when the Master asked for the bread and the wine and blessed them and said: "This is my body and my blood," he did not allow these (women) to meet with us.

xxx. Martha said: On Mary's account, because he saw her smile.

xxxi. Mary said: I did not laugh. For he said to us formerly as he was teaching, that the weak should be strengthened through the strong.

The meaning of the speech of the women is, that Martha supposed Mary to be smiling because John's words might imply that women were to be kept from all participation in the Lord's Supper, whereas he really meant merely to deny their right to dispense the elements, which right had been claimed for deaconesses.

* B. πόσον   † B. Πlg φθαρτοῖς.

DOCUMENT VI.

THE COPTIC CHURCH ORDER.

From *The Apostolical Constitutions, or Canons of the Apostles in Coptic. With an English translation by Henry Tattam, LL.D., D.D., F.R.S., Archdeacon of Bedford.* London: Printed for the Oriental Translation Fund of Great Britain and Ireland. 1848. 214 and xv. pages.

The work is called, in Coptic and Arabic, The "Canons of our Holy Fathers the Apostles," and is divided into seven books. It is derived from the same sources as the Apostolical Constitutions, but is probably older. The MS. of the Coptic and Arabic text is a beautifully written quarto volume, and was procured by the Duke of Northumberland. It is said to be the only copy known in Egypt. The Coptic text is in the Memphitic or Bahiric dialect of Lower Egypt. It is not made directly from the Greek, but from an older version in the Thebaic or Sahidic dialect of Upper Egypt. Tattam purchased a copy of the greater part of the Sahidic original in Egypt, and collated it with the Memphitic, "with which it perfectly agrees." (Preface, p. xiv.) He lent it to Lagarde, who gave a full account of it in his *Reliquiæ juris eccles. ant.*, p. ix. sq. This Sahidic MS. is now in the British Museum, where its class mark is *Orient.* 440. Another Sahidic MS. written A.D. 1006, has recently been acquired from Sir C. A. Murray's collection by the British Museum, and is marked *Orient.* 1320.

The two versions are compared by Lightfoot, *Appendix to S. Clement of Rome*, 1877, pp. 278 (note), and 466 sqq. See also his remarks on the dialects of Egypt in Scrivener's *Introduction to the Criticism of the N. T.*, p. 335 sqq. (3d ed.).

The Coptic Constitutions contain the Pseudo-Clementine Ordinances concerning the ordination of Bishops, Presbyters, Deacons, the appointment of Readers, Subdeacons, Widows, Virgins, the administration of the Sacraments, the First-fruits and Tithes, etc. I give here only the first Book, which corresponds to the Greek "Apostolic Church Order."

THE APOSTOLICAL CONSTITUTIONS.

These are the Canons of our Fathers the Holy Apostles of our Lord Jesus Christ, which they appointed in the Churches.

Rejoice, O our sons and daughters, in the name of our Lord Jesus Christ, said John and Matthew, and Peter, and Andrew, Philip and Simon, James and Nathanael, Thomas and Cephas, Bartholomew, and Judas the brother of James.

1. According to the command of our Lord Jesus Christ, our Saviour,* that we should assemble together, he enjoined us, saying (whereas we had not yet divided the countries among us), Ye shall divide them among you so that each one may take his place according to your number.

Appoint the orders for Bishops, stations for Presbyters, and continual service for Deacons : prudent persons for readers, and blameless for widows ; † and appoint all other things by which it is meet the foundation of the Church should be established, that by them may be known the type of the things in heaven, that they may keep themselves from every spot. And they should know that they shall give account to God in the great day of judgment for all the things which they have heard and have not kept.

And He commanded us to make known these words in all the world.

2. It also appeared to us, that each one of us should speak as the Lord hath given him grace, according to the will of God the Father, by the Holy Spirit, making remembrance of His words, that we may command them to you. They will be remembered, and the fraternal teaching.

3. John said, "Men and brethren, we know that we shall give account for those things which we hear, and for those things which have been commanded us. Let not any one of us accept the person of his friend. But if any one should hear

---

* *Our Saviour*, in the Sahidic, which corrects the Memphitic.

† " Let not a widow be taken into the number under threescore years old —well-reported of for good works ; if she have brought up children, if she have lodged strangers, if she have washed the saints' feet, if she have relieved the afflicted, if she have diligently followed every good work."—1 Tim. v. 9, 10.

his friend speak of those things which are not profitable, let him restrain him, saying, "what thou sayest is not good." It therefore pleased them that John should speak first.

4. John said, "There are two ways, one is the way of life, and the other is the way of death; and there is much difference in these two ways. But the way of life is this, Thou shalt love * the Lord thy God with all thy heart, who created thee, and thou shalt glorify him who redeemed thee from death; for this is the first commandment.

"But the second is this, Thou shalt love thy neighbour as thyself. On these two commandments hang the law and the Prophets."

5. Matthew said, "Every thing that thou wouldest not should be done to thee, that do not thou also to another; that is, what thou hatest do not to another. But thou, O Peter my brother, teach them these things."

6. Peter said, "Thou shalt not kill; thou shalt not commit adultery; thou shalt not commit fornication; thou shalt not pollute a youth; thou shalt not steal; thou shalt not be a sorcerer; thou shalt not use divination; thou shalt not cause a woman to miscarry, neither if she hath brought forth a child shalt thou kill it. Thou shalt not covet any thing that is thy neighbour's: thou shalt not bear false witness: thou shalt not speak evil of any one, neither shalt thou think evil. Thou shalt not be double-minded, neither shalt thou be double-tongued, for a double tongue is a snare of death. Thy speech shall not be vain, neither tending to a lie. Thou shalt not be covetous, neither rapacious; nor a hypocrite, nor of an evil heart, nor proud. Thou shalt not speak an evil word against thy neighbour. Thou shalt not hate any man, but thou shalt reprove some, and shalt have mercy upon others. Thou shalt pray for some, and shalt love others as thy own soul."

7. Andrew said, "My son, flee from all evil, and hate all evil. Be not angry, because anger leads to murder, for anger is an evil demon. Be not emulous, neither be contentious, nor quarrelsome, for envy proceeds from these."

8. Philip said, "My son, be not of unlawful desires, because desire leads to fornication, drawing men to it involuntarily: for lust is a demon. † For if the evil spirit of anger is united with

---

* The Sahidic is correct, *thou shalt love*. † Arabic, *Satan*.

that of sensuality, they destroy those who shall receive them. And the way of the evil spirit is the sin of the soul. For when he sees a little quiet entering in he will make the way broad; and he will take with him all other evil spirits : he will go to that soul, and will not leave the man to meditate at all, lest he should see the truth. Let a restraint be put to your anger, and curb it with not a little care, that you may cast it behind you, lest it should precipitate you into some evil deed. For wrath and evil desire, if they are suffered always remaining, are demons. And when they have dominion over a man they change him in soul, that he may be prepared for a great deed : and when they have led him into unrighteous acts, they deride him, and will rejoice in the destruction of that man."

9. Simon said, "My son, be not the utterer of an evil expression, nor of obscenity, neither be thou haughty, for of these things come adulteries."

10. James said, "My son, be not a diviner, for divination leads to idolatry ; neither be thou an enchanter, nor an astrologer, nor a magician, nor an idolater;* neither teach them nor hear them ; for from these things proceeds idolatry."

11. Nathanael said, "My son, be not a liar, because a falsehood leads to blasphemy. Neither be thou a lover of silver nor a lover of vain glory, for from these thefts arise."

"My son, be not a murmurer, because repining leads a man to blasphemy. Be thou not harsh, nor a thinker of evil, for of all these things contentions are begotten. But be thou meek, for the meek shall inherit the earth. And be thou also merciful, peaceable, compassionate, cleansed in thy heart from all evil. Be thou sincere, gentle, good ; trembling at the words of God which thou hast heard, and do thou keep them. Do not exalt thyself, neither shalt thou give thy heart to pride, but thou shalt increase more and more with the just and humble. Every evil which cometh upon thee receive as good, knowing that nothing shall come upon thee but from God."

12. Thomas said, "My son, he who declares to thee the words of God, and hath been the cause of life to thee, and hath given the holy seal to thee which is in the Lord, thou shalt love him as the apple of thine eyes, and remember him by night and

---

* The Sahidic has, *one that bewitcheth.*

day: thou shalt honour him as of the Lord: for in that place in which the word of power is, there is the Lord; and thou shalt seek his face daily; him, and those who remain of the saints, that thou mayest rest thee on their words: for he who is united to the saints shall be holy. Thou shalt honour him according to thy power, by the sweat* of thy brow, and by the labour of thy hands: for if the Lord hath made thee meet that he might impart to thee spiritual food, and spiritual drink, and eternal life, by him; it becomes thee also the more, that thou shouldest impart to him the food which perishes and is temporal; for the labourer is worthy of his hire. For it is written, Thou shalt not muzzle the ox treading out the corn: neither does any one plant a vineyard and not eat of the fruit thereof."

13. Cephas said, "Thou shalt not make schisms: thou shalt reconcile in peace those who contend with one another. Judge in righteousness without accepting of persons. Reprove him who hath sinned, for his sin. Suffer not wealth to prevail before God, neither justify the unworthy, for beauty profiteth not; but righteous judgment before all. Doubt not† in thy prayer, thinking whether what thou hast asked of him will be or not. Let it not indeed be that when thou receivest thou stretchest out thine hand, but when thou shouldest give thou drawest thy hand to thee. But if thou hast at hand‡ thou shalt give for the redemption of thy sins. Thou shalt not doubt, thou shalt give; neither when thou hast given shalt thou murmur, knowing this reward is of God. Thou shalt not turn away from the needy, but shalt communicate with the needy in all things: Thou shalt not say these things are mine alone. If ye communicate with one another of those things which are incorruptible, how much rather should ye not do it in those things which are corruptible?"

14. Bartholomew said, "I beseech you, my Brethren, while you have time, and he who asks remains with you, (and) you are able to do good to them, do not fail in any thing to any one, which you have the power to do.

"For the day of the Lord draweth nigh, in which every thing

---

* Coptic is literally, *thy sweat*.

† Literally, *be not of a double heart*.

‡ Literally, *of thy hands*, or *from the labours of thy hands*.

that is seen shall be dissolved, and the wicked shall be destroyed with it, for the Lord cometh, and his reward is with him.

"Be ye lawgivers to your own selves; be ye teachers to yourselves alone, as God hath taught you. Thou shalt keep those things which thou hast received, thou shalt not take from them, neither shalt thou add to them."

15. Peter said, "Men and brethren, all the remaining precepts of the holy scriptures are sufficient to teach you; but let us declare them to those to whom we have been commanded." Then it pleased them all that Peter should speak.

16. Peter said, "If there should be a place having a few faithful men in it, before the multitude increase, who shall be able to make a dedication to pious uses for the Bishop to the extent of twelve men, let them write to the churches round about them, *informing them of* the place in which the multitude of the faithful (assemble and) are established.

"That three chosen men in that place may come, that they may examine with diligence him who is worthy of this grade. If one of the people who hath a good reputation, being guiltless, without anger, a lover of the poor, prudent, wise, not given to wine, not a fornicator, not covetous,* not a contemner, not partial,† and the like of these things.

"If he have not a wife it is a good thing; but if he have married a wife, having children, let him abide with her, continuing stedfast in every doctrine, able to explain the Scriptures well; but if he be ignorant of literature let him be meek: let him abound in love towards every man, lest they should accuse the Bishop in any affair, and he should be at all culpable."

17. John said, "If the Bishop whom they shall appoint hath attended to the knowledge and patience of the love of God with those with him, let him ordain two Presbyters when he has examined them."

18. And all answered, not two, but three, because there are twenty-four Presbyters—twelve on the right hand, and twelve on the left.‡

---

* Literally, *not a lover of the larger portion.*

† Literally, *not an accepter of persons.*

‡ Rev. iv. 4.—*Καὶ κυκλόθεν τοῦ θρόνου θρόνοι εἴκοσι καὶ τέσσαρες· καὶ ἐπὶ τοὺς θρόνους εἶδον τοὺς εἴκοσι καὶ τέσσαρας πρεσβυτέρους καθημένους, περιβεβλημένους ἐν ἱματίοις λευκοῖς· καὶ ἔσχον ἐπὶ τὰς κεφαλὰς αὐτῶν στεφάνους χρυσοῦς.*

THE COPTIC CHURCH ORDER.   255

John said, "You have rightly recalled these things to remembrance, O my brethren ; for when those on the right hand have received the censers from the hands of the angels, they present them before the Lord.* But those on the left hand shall be sustained by the multitude of angels.† But it behoves the Presbyters that they should be in the world, after the manner of old men, removing far off, that they should not touch a woman, being charitable (and) lovers of the brethren : that they should not accept persons, being partakers of the holy mysteries with the Bishop, assisting in all things, collecting the multitude together, that they may love their Shepherd. And the Presbyters on the right hand have the care of those who labour at the altar, that they should honour those who are worthy of all honour, and rebuke those who merit their rebuke. The Presbyters on the left hand shall have the care of the people, that they may be upright, that no one may be disturbed. And they shall instruct them that they should be in all subjection. But when they have instructed one, answering contumaciously, ‡ those within the altar should be of one heart, and one mind, that they may receive the reward of that honour according to its desert. And all the rest shall fear lest they should deviate, and one of them should become changed like one wasting away,§ and all should be brought into captivity."

19. James said, "The Reader shall be appointed after he has been fully proved ; ‖ bridling his tongue, not a drunkard, not a derider in his speech, but decorous in his appearance ; obedient, being the first to congregate on the Lord's-day ; a servant knowing what is meet for him, that he may fulfil the work of publishing the Gospel. For he who fills the ears of others with his doctrines, it becomes him the more that he should be a faithful workman before God."

20. Matthew said, "Let the Deacons be appointed by three testifying to their life. For it is written, 'By the mouth of

---

* Rev. v. 8.—Καὶ οἱ εἰκοσιτέσσαρες πρεσβύτεροι ἔπεσον ἐνώπιον τοῦ ἀρνίου, ἔχοντες ἕκαστος . . . . φιάλας χρυσᾶς, γεμούσας θυμιαμάτων, αἵ εἰσιν αἱ προσευχαὶ τῶν ἁγίων.

† This passage is obscure.

‡ The Coptic words are rendered in Arabic by, *with modesty, respect.*

§ Or, *and one of them should become a hypocrite like one wasting away with a gangrene.*

‖ Or, *after he has been proved by a great trial.*

two or three witnesses shall every word be established.' Let them be proved in every service, all the people bearing witness to them, that they have resided with one wife, have brought up their children well, being humble, prudent, meek, sober, quiet;* not vehement, nor murmurers; not double-tongued, nor wrathful, for wrath destroyeth the wise; nor hypocrites. They shall not afflict the poor, neither shall they accept the person of the rich; they shall not be drinkers of much wine, being ready to act in every good service in secret. Cheerful in their habitations, constraining the brethren who have, that they should open their hand to give. And they also being givers, the goods being in common, that the people may honour them with all honour, and all fear, beseeching with great earnestness those who walk in dissimulation. And some they should teach, and some they should rebuke, but the rest they should prohibit. But let those who despise, and the contumelious, be cast out, knowing that all men who are vehement, or slanderers, fight against Christ."

21. Cephas said, "Let three widows be appointed; two, that they may give their whole attention to prayer for every one who is in temptations, and that they may render thanks to him whom they follow. But the other one should be left constantly with the women who are tried in sickness, ministering well; watching and telling to the Presbyters the things which take place. Not a lover of filthy lucre; not given to drink; that she may be able to watch, that she may minister in the night. And if another one desires to help to do good works, let her do so according to the pleasure of her heart; for these are the good things which the Lord first commanded."

22. Andrew said, "Let the Deacons be doers of good works, drawing near by day and night in every place. They must not exalt themselves above the poor; neither must they accept the persons of the rich. They shall know the afflicted, that they may give to him out of their store of provisions; constraining those who are able for good works to gather them in, attending to the words of our master, 'I was an hungered, and ye gave me meat.' For those who have ministered without sin, gain for themselves much confidence."

23. Philip said, "Let the laymen obey the decrees which have been delivered to them for the laity, being in subjection to those

---

* Is rendered by the Arabic, *guides*.

who serve at the altar. Let every one please God in the place to which he hath been appointed. They should not love hostility to one another. They should not envy for the situation which is appointed for each one ; but let every one abide in the calling to which he hath been called of God. Let not any one inquire after the offence of his neighbour,* in his course on which he has entered, for the angels exceed not the command of the Lord."

24. Andrew said, "It is a good thing to appoint women to be made Deaconesses."

25. Peter said, "We have first to appoint this concerning the Eucharist, and the body and blood of the Lord : we will (then) make known the thing diligently."

26. John said, "Have you forgotten, O my brethren, in the day that our Master took the bread and the cup he blessed them, saying, ' This is my body and my blood ?' You have seen that he gave no place for the women, that they might help with them. (Martha answered for Mary because he saw her laughing : Mary said, ' I laughed not.') For he said to us, teaching, that the weak shall be liberated by the strong."

27. Cephas said, "Some say it becomes the women to pray standing, and that they should not cast themselves down upon the earth."

28. James said, "We shall be able to appoint women for a service, besides this service only, that they assist the indigent."

29. Philip said, "Brethren, concerning the gift, he who labours gathers for himself a good treasure ; but he who collects for himself a good treasure, collects riches for himself in the kingdom of heaven. He shall be reputed a workman of God, continuing for ever."

30. Peter said, "Brethren, the authority is not of one, by constraint, but as we were commanded by the Lord.

"I pray you that you keep the commandments of God, not taking any thing from them, nor adding to them ; in the name of our Lord Jesus Christ, whose is the glory for ever. Amen.

The first book of the Canons of our Fathers the Apostles is finished, which are in the hands of Clemens ; and this is the second book, in the peace of God. Amen.

---

* The margin has by a later hand, instead of *his friend, his neighbour,* according to the Sahidic.

DOCUMENT VII.

THE SEVENTH BOOK OF THE APOSTOLICAL CONSTITUTIONS.

The Seventh Book of the Apostolical Constitutions of Pseudo-Clement of Rome, Chs. I.–XXXII., is an enlargement of the *Didache*, adapted to the state of the Eastern Church in the first half of the fourth century. The Greek text is from the edition of GUIL. UELTZEN (*Constitutiones Apostolicæ*, Suerini et Rostochii, 1853, p. 160–178), which is also reprinted by Bryennios (in his Proleg. p. λβ'–ν'). I compared with it the edition of P. A. DE LAGARDE (*Const. Apost.*, Lips. et Londini, 1862, p. 197–212), and marked his readings in brackets and in foot-notes. The translation is by Whiston, revised by James Donaldson, LL.D. (in Clark's "Ante-Nicene Library," vol. XVII., 1870), and slightly changed here. I have noted the passages borrowed from the *Didache* on the margin, and distinguished them by spaced type in the Greek column, by italics in the English column.

CAP. I.—Τοῦ νομοθέτου Μωσέως εἰρηκότος τοῖς Ἰσραηλίταις Ἰδοὺ, δέδωκα πρὸ προσώπου ὑμῶν τὴν ὁδὸν τῆς ζωῆς καὶ τὴν ὁδὸν τοῦ θανάτου, καὶ ἐπιφέροντος "Ἔκλεξαι τὴν ζωήν, ἵνα ζήσῃς (Deut. xxx. 19)· καὶ τοῦ προφήτου Ἡλία λέγοντος τῷ λαῷ Ἕως πότε χωλανεῖτε ἐπ' ἀμφοτέραις ταῖς ἰγνύαις ὑμῶν; εἰ Θεός ἐστι Κύριος, πορεύεσθε ὀπίσω αὐτοῦ (1 Reg. xviii. 21)· εἰκότως ἔλεγε καὶ ὁ Κύριος Ἰησοῦς Οὐδεὶς δύναται δυσὶ κυρίοις δουλεύειν· ἢ γὰρ τὸν ἕνα μισήσει καὶ τὸν ἕτερον ἀγαπήσει, ἢ ἑνὸς ἀνθέξεται

CH. I.—The lawgiver Moses said to the Israelites, "Behold, I have set before your face the way of life and the way of death;"[1] and added, "*Choose life, that thou mayest live.*"[2] Elijah the prophet also said to the people: "How long will you halt on both your legs? If the Lord be God, follow Him."[3] The Lord Jesus also said justly: "*No one can serve two masters: for either he will hate the one, and love the other; or else he will hold to the one, and despise the other.*"[4] We also, following

---

[1] Deut. xxx. 15. [2] Deut. xxx. 19. [3] 1 Kings xviii. 21. [4] Matt. vi. 24.

καὶ τοῦ ἑτέρου καταφρονήσει (Matt. vi. 24)· ἀναγκαίως καὶ ἡμεῖς, ἑπόμενοι τῷ διδασκάλῳ Χριστῷ, ὅς ἐστι σωτὴρ πάντων, ἀνθρώπων, μάλιστα πιστῶν, φαμὲν ὡς δύο ὁδοὶ εἰσί, μία τῆς ζωῆς, καὶ μία τοῦ θανάτου. Οὐδεμίαν δὲ σύγκρισιν ἔχουσι πρὸς ἑαυτάς (πολὺ γὰρ τὸ διάφορον), μᾶλλον δὲ πάντη κεχωρισμέναι τυγχάνουσι· καὶ φυσικὴ μέν ἐστιν ἡ τῆς ζωῆς ὁδός, ἐπείσακτος δὲ ἡ τοῦ θανάτου, οὐ τοῦ κατὰ γνώμην Θεοῦ ὑπάρξαντος, ἀλλὰ τοῦ ἐξ ἐπιβουλῆς τοῦ ἀλλοτρίου.

[Did. I. 1.]

CAP. II.— Πρώτη οὖν τυγχάνει ἡ ὁδὸς τῆς ζωῆς· καὶ ἔστιν αὕτη, ἣν καὶ ὁ νόμος διαγορεύει (Deut. vi.), ἀγαπᾶν Κύριον τὸν Θεὸν ἐξ ὅλης τῆς διανοίας* καὶ ἐξ ὅλης τῆς ψυχῆς τὸν ἕνα καὶ μόνον, παρ' ὃν ἄλλος οὐκ ἔστιν, καὶ τὸν πλησίον ὡς ἑαυτόν. Καὶ πᾶν, ὃ μὴ θέλεις γενέσθαι σοι, καὶ σὺ τοῦτο ἄλλῳ οὐ ποιήσεις (cf. Luc. vi. 31)·† εὐλογεῖτε τοὺς κατα-

[I. 2.]

[I. 2.]

[I. 3.]

our teacher Christ, "who is the Saviour of all men, especially of those that believe,"[1] are obliged to say that *there are two ways—the one of life, the other of death;* but there is no comparison between the two, for they are *very different,* or rather entirely separate; and the way of life is that of nature, but the way of death was afterwards introduced,—it not being according to the mind of God, but from the snares of the adversary.[2]

CH. II.—*Now the first way is that of life; and is this,* which the law also does appoint: "*To love the Lord God* with all thy mind, and with all thy soul, who is the one and only God, besides whom there is no other;"[3] "*and thy neighbour as thyself.*"[4] "*And whatsoever thou wouldest not should be done to thee, that do not thou to another.*"[5] "*Bless them that curse you; pray for them that despitefully use*

---

[1] 1 Tim. iv. 10.
[2] The Greek words properly mean: "Introduced was the way of death; not of that death which exists according to the mind of God, but that which has arisen from the plots of the adversary."
[3] Deut. vi. 5; Mark xii. 32.   [4] Lev. xix. 18.   [5] Tob. iv. 16.

* Lagarde omits τῆς διανοίας.
† Lagarde adds: τοῦτ' ἔστιν Ὅ σὺ μισεῖς, ἄλλῳ οὐ ποιήσεις.

SEVENTH BOOK OF THE APOSTOLICAL CONSTITUTIONS. 261

ρωμένους ὑμᾶς, προσεύχεσθε ὑπὲρ τῶν ἐπηρεαζόντων ὑμᾶς, ἀγαπᾶτε τοὺς ἐχθροὺς ὑμῶν. Ποία γὰρ ὑμῖν χάρις, ἐὰν φιλεῖτε* τοὺς φιλοῦντας ὑμᾶς; καὶ γὰρ [καὶ] οἱ ἐθνικοὶ τοῦτο ποιοῦσιν· ὑμεῖς δὲ φιλεῖτε τοὺς μισοῦντας ὑμᾶς καὶ ἐχθρὸν οὐχ ἕξετε· Οὐ μισήσεις γάρ, φησί, πάντα ἄνθρωπον, οὐκ Αἰγύπτιον, οὐκ Ἰδουμαῖον (cf. Deut. xxiii. 7), ἅπαντες γάρ εἰσι τοῦ Θεοῦ ἔργα. Φεύγετε δὲ οὐ τὰς φύσεις, ἀλλὰ τὰς γνώμας τῶν πονηρῶν.† Ἀπέχου τῶν σαρκικῶν καὶ κοσμικῶν ἐπιθυμιῶν. Ἐάν τίς σοι δῷ ῥάπισμα [εἰς τὴν δεξιὰν σιαγόνα], στρέψον αὐτῷ καὶ τὴν ἄλλην· οὐ φαύλης οὔσης τῆς ἀμύνης, ἀλλὰ τιμιωτέρας τῆς ἀνεξικακίας· λέγει γὰρ ὁ Δαβίδ Εἰ ἀνταπέδωκα τοῖς ἀνταποδιδοῦσί μοι κακά (Ps. vii. 5). Ἐὰν ἀγγαρεύσῃ σέ τις μίλιον [ἕν], ὕπαγε μετ' αὐτοῦ δύο, καὶ τῷ θέλοντί σοι κριθῆναι καὶ τὸν χιτῶνά σου λαβεῖν, ἄφες αὐτῷ καὶ

you."[1] "Love your enemies; *for what thanks is it if ye love those that love you? for even the Gentiles do the same.*"[2] "But do ye love those that hate you, and ye shall have no enemy." For says He, "*Thou shalt not hate any man;* no, not an Egyptian, nor an Edomite;"[3] for they are all the workmanship of God. Avoid not the persons, but the sentiments, of the wicked. "*Abstain from fleshly and worldly lusts.*"[4] "*If any one gives thee a stroke on thy right cheek, turn to him the other also.*"[5] Not that revenge is evil, but that patience is more honourable. For David says, "If I have made returns to them that repaid me evil."[6] "*If any one impress thee to go one mile, go with him twain.*"[7] And, "*He that will sue thee at the law, and take away thy coat, let him have thy cloak also.*"[8] "*And from him that taketh thy goods, require them not again.*"[9] "*Give to him that asketh thee,* and from him that would borrow of thee do not

[II. 7.]

[I. 4.]

[I. 4.]

[I. 5.]

---

[1] Matt. v. 44.   [2] Luke vi. 32; Matt. v. 47.   [3] Deut. xxiii. 7.
[4] 1 Pet. ii. 11.   [5] Matt v. 39.   [6] Ps. viii. 5.
[7] Matt. v. 41.   [8] Matt. v. 40.   [9] Luke vi. 30.

* Lagarde: φιλῆτε.   † Lagarde: τῶν κακῶν.

τὸ ἱμάτιον, καὶ ἀπὸ τοῦ αἴροντος τὰ σὰ μὴ ἀπαίτει. Τῷ αἰτοῦντί σε δίδου, καὶ ἀπὸ τοῦ θέλοντος δανείσασθαι παρὰ σοῦ μὴ [αποστραφεὶς] ἀποκλείσῃς τὴν χεῖρα, δίκαιος γὰρ ἀνὴρ οἰκτείρει καὶ κιχρᾷ· πᾶσι γὰρ θέλει δίδοσθαι ὁ πατὴρ ὁ τὸν ἥλιον αὑτοῦ ἀνατέλλων ἐπὶ πονηροὺς καὶ ἀγαθοὺς, καὶ τὸν ὑετὸν αὐτοῦ βρέχων ἐπὶ δικαίους καὶ ἀδίκους. Πᾶσιν οὖν δίκαιον διδόναι ἐξ οἰκείων πόνων· Τίμα γὰρ, φησί, τὸν Κύριον ἀπὸ σῶν δικαίων πόνων (Prov. iii. 9)· προτιμητέον δὲ τοὺς ἁγίους. — Οὐ φονεύσεις, τοῦτ᾽ ἔστιν οὐ φθερεῖς τὸν ὅμοιόν σοι ἄνθρωπον, διαλύεις γὰρ τὰ καλῶς γινόμενα· οὐχ ὡς παντὸς φόνου φαύλου τυγχάνοντος, ἀλλὰ μόνου τοῦ ἀθώου, τοῦ δ᾽ ἐνδίκου ἄρχουσι μόνοις ἀφωρισμένου.—Οὐ μοιχεύσεις, διαιρεῖς γὰρ τὴν μίαν σάρκα εἰς δύο· Ἔσονται γὰρ, φησίν, οἱ δύο εἰς σάρκα μίαν (Gen. ii.24)· ἓν γὰρ εἰσιν ἀνὴρ καὶ γυνὴ τῇ φύσει, τῇ συμπνοίᾳ, τῇ ἑνώσει, τῇ διαθέσει, τῷ βίῳ, τῷ τρόπῳ, κεχωρισμένοι δέ εἰσι τῷ σχήματι καὶ τῷ ἀριθμῷ.— Οὐ παιδοφθορήσεις· παρὰ φύσιν γὰρ τὸ κακὸν ἐκ

shut thy hand."[1] For "the righteous man is pitiful, and lendeth."[2] *For your Father would have you give to all*, who Himself "maketh His sun to rise on the evil and on the good, and sendeth His rain on the just and on the unjust."[3] *It is therefore reasonable to give to all* out of thine own labours;" for says He, "Honour the Lord out of thy righteous labours,"[4] but so that the saints be preferred.[5] "*Thou shalt not kill;*" that is, thou shalt not destroy a man like thyself: for thou dissolvest what was well made. Not as if all killing were wicked, but only that of the innocent: but the killing which is just is reserved to the magistrates alone. "*Thou shalt not commit adultery:*" for thou dividest one flesh into two. "They two shall be one flesh:"[6] for the husband and wife are one in nature, in consent, in union, in disposition, and the conduct of life; but they are separated in sex and number. "*Thou shalt not corrupt boys:*"[7] for this wickedness is contrary to nature, and arose

---

[1] Matt. v. 42. [2] Ps. cxii. 5. [3] Matt. v. 45. [4] Prov. iii. 9; Ex. xx., etc.
[5] Gal. vi. 10. [6] Gen. ii. 24. [7] Lev. xviii. 20.

Σοδόμων φυὲν, ἥτις πυρὸς θεηλάτου παρανάλωμα γέγονεν· ἐπικατάρατος δὲ ὁ τοιοῦτος καὶ ἐρεῖ πᾶς ὁ λαός Γένοιτο.—Οὐ πορνεύσεις· Οὐκ ἔσται γάρ, φησί, πορνεύων ἐν υἱοῖς Ἰσραηλ (Deut. xxiii. 17).—Οὐ κλέψεις· Ἄχαρ γὰρ κλέψας ἐν τῷ Ἰσραὴλ ἐν Ἱεριχὼ λίθοις βληθεὶς τοῦ ζῆν ὑπεξῆλθε, καὶ Γιεζεῖ κλέψας καὶ ψευσάμενος ἐκληρονόμησε τοῦ Νεεμὰν τὴν λέπραν, καὶ Ἰούδας κλέπτων τὰ τῶν πενήτων τὸν Κύριον τῆς δόξης παρέδωκεν Ἰουδαίοις, καὶ μεταμεληθεὶς ἀπήγξατο καὶ ἐλάκησε μέσος καὶ ἐξεχύθη πάντα τὰ σπλάγχνα αὐτοῦ, καὶ Ἀνανίας καὶ Σαπφείρα ἡ τούτου γυνή, κλέψαντες τὰ ἴδια καὶ πειράσαντες τὸ πνεῦμα Κυρίου, παραχρῆμα ἀποφάσει Πέτρου τοῦ συναποστόλου ἡμῶν ἐθανατώθησαν.—

CAP. III.—Οὐ μαγεύσεις, οὐ φαρμακεύσεις· Φαρμακοὺς γάρ, φησίν, οὐ περιβιώσετε (Exod. xxii. 18). —Οὐ φονεύσεις τέκνον σου ἐν φθορᾷ, οὐδὲ τὸ

from Sodom, which was therefore entirely consumed with fire sent from God.[1] "Let such an one be accursed: and all the people shall say, So be it."[2] "Thou [II. 2.] shalt not commit fornication:" for says He, "There shall not be a fornicator among the children of Israel."[3] "Thou shalt not [II. 2.] steal:" for Achan, when he had stolen in Israel at Jericho, was stoned to death;[4] and Gehazi, who stole, and told a lie, inherited the leprosy of Naaman;[5] and Judas, who stole the poor's money, betrayed the Lord of glory to the Jews,[6] and repented, and hanged himself, and burst asunder in the midst, and all his bowels gushed out;[7] and Ananias, and Sapphira his wife, who stole their own goods, and "tempted the Spirit of the Lord," were immediately, at the sentence of Peter our fellow-apostle,[8] struck dead.[9]

CH. III.—*Thou shalt not* [II. 2.] *use magic. Thou shalt not use witchcraft;* for He says, "Ye shall not suffer a witch to live."[10] *Thou shalt not* [II. 2.] *slay thy child by causing*

---

[1] Gen. xix. [2] Deut. xxvii. [3] Deut. xxiii. 17. [4] Josh. vii.
[5] 2 Kings v. [6] John xii. 6; Matt. xxvii. 5. [7] Acts i. 18.
[8] The Apostles are assumed to be speaking in the Apostolical Constitutions.
[9] Acts v. 5, 10, [10] Ex. xxii. 18.

γεννηθὲν ἀποκτενεῖς. πᾶν γὰρ τὸ ἐξεικονισμένον, ψυχὴν λαβὸν παρὰ Θεοῦ, φονευθὲν ἐκδικηθήσεται, ἀδίκως ἀναιρεθέν (cf. Exod. xxi. 23 graece). — Οὐκ ἐπιθυμήσεις τὰ τοῦ πλησίον σου, οἷον τὴν γυναῖκα ἢ τὸν παῖδα ἢ τὸν βοῦν ἢ τὸν ἀγρόν. — Οὐκ ἐπιορκήσεις· ἐρρήθη γὰρ μὴ ὀμόσαι ὅλως· εἰ δὲ μηγε, κἂν εὐορκήσῃς, ὅτι ἐπαινεθήσεται πᾶς ὁ ὀμνύων ἐν αὐτῷ (Ps. lxiii. 11). — Οὐ ψευδομαρτυρήσεις, ὅτι ὁ συκοφαντῶν πένητα παροξύνει τὸν ποιήσαντα αὐτόν (Prov. xiv. 31).

Cap. IV. — Οὐ κακολογήσεις· Μὴ ἀγάπα γάρ, φησί, κακολογεῖν, ἵνα μὴ ἐξαρθῇς (Prov. xx. 13) · οὐδὲ μνησικακήσεις, ὁδοὶ γὰρ μνησικάκων εἰς θάνατον (Prov. xii. 28 graece). — Οὐκ ἔσῃ δίγνωμος, οὐδὲ δίγλωσσος· παγὶς γὰρ ἰσχυρὰ ἀνδρὶ τὰ ἴδια χείλη, καὶ ἀνὴρ γλωσσώδης οὐ κατευθυνθήσεται ἐπὶ τῆς γῆς (Prov. vi. 2; Ps. cxl. 11) · οὐκ ἔσται ὁ λόγος σου κε-

abortion, nor kill that which is begotten; for "everything that is shaped, and has received a soul from God, if it be slain, shall be avenged, as being unjustly destroyed."[1] "Thou shalt not covet the things that belong to thy neighbour, as his wife, or his servant, or his ox, or his field." "Thou shalt not forswear thyself;" for it is said, "Thou shalt not swear at all."[2] But if that cannot be avoided, thou shalt swear truly; for "every one that swears by Him shall be commended."[3] "Thou shalt not bear false witness;" for "he that falsely accuses the needy provokes to anger Him that made him."[4]

Ch. IV. — Thou shalt not speak evil; for says He, "Love not to speak evil, lest thou be taken away." Nor shalt thou be mindful of injuries; for "the ways of those that remember injuries are unto death."[5] Thou shalt not be double-minded nor double-tongued; for "a man's own lips are a strong snare to him,"[6] and "a talkative person shall not be prospered upon earth."[7]

---

[1] Ex. xxi. 23, LXX.   [2] Matt. v. 34.   [3] Ps. lxiii. 12.
[4] Prov. xiv. 31.   [5] Prov. xii. 28.   [6] Prov. vi. 2.
[7] Ps. cxl. 11.

νός, περὶ παντὸς γὰρ λόγου ἀργοῦ δώσετε λόγον (Matt. xii. 36)· οὐ ψεύσῃ· Ἀπολεῖς γὰρ, φησί, πάντας τοὺς λαλοῦντας τὸ ψεῦδος (Ps. v. 7). — Οὐκ ἔσῃ πλεονέκτης, οὐδὲ ἅρπαξ· Οὐαὶ γὰρ, φησίν, ὁ πλεονεκτῶν τὸν πλησίον πλεονεξίαν κακήν (cf. Hab. ii. 9). — Οὐκ ἔσῃ ὑποκριτής, ἵνα μὴ τὸ μέρος σου μετ' αὐτῶν θῇς (cf. Matt. xxiv. 51). —

Cap. V. — Οὐκ ἔσῃ κακοήθης, οὐδὲ ὑπερήφανος· ὑπερηφάνοις γὰρ ὁ Θεὸς ἀντιτάσσεται (Prov. iii. 34 graece). — Οὐ λήψῃ πρόσωπον* ἐν κρίσει, ὅτι τοῦ Κυρίου ἡ κρίσις (Deut. i. 17). — Οὐ μισήσεις πάντα ἄνθρωπον. Ἐλεγμῷ ἐλέγξεις τὸν ἀδελφόν σου καὶ οὐ λήψῃ, δι' αὐτὸν ἁμαρτίαν (Lev. xix. 17), καὶ ἔλεγχε σοφὸν καὶ ἀγαπήσει σε Prov. ix. 8). — Φεῦγε ἀπὸ παντὸς κακοῦ καὶ ἀπὸ παντὸς ὁμοίου αὐτῷ· Ἄπεχε γὰρ, φησίν, ἀπὸ ἀδίκου, καὶ τρόμος οὐκ ἐγγιεῖ σοι (Is. liv. 14). — Μὴ γίνου ὀργίλος, μηδὲ βάσκανος, μηδὲ ζηλωτής, μηδὲ μα-

Thy speech shall not be vain: for "ye shall give an account of every idle word."[1] *Thou* [II. 5.] *shalt not tell lies;* for says He, "Thou shalt destroy all those that speak lies."[2] *Thou shalt not be covetous* [II. 6.] *nor rapacious:* for says He, "Woe to him that is covetous towards his neighbour with an evil covetousness."[3] *Thou shalt not be a hypocrite,* lest thy "portion be with them."[4]

Ch. V. — *Thou shalt not* [II. 6.] *be ill-natured nor proud:* for "God resisteth the proud."[5] "Thou shalt not accept persons in judgment; for the judgment is the Lord's." *Thou shalt not* [II. 7.] *hate any man; thou shalt surely reprove thy brother,* and not become guilty on his account;"[6] and, "Reprove a wise man, and he will love thee."[7] *Eschew* [III. 1.] *all evil and all that is like it:* for says He, "Abstain from injustice, and trembling shall not come nigh thee."[8] *Be not soon an-* [III. 2.] *gry, nor spiteful, nor passionate, nor furious, nor daring,* lest thou undergo the

---

[1] Matt. xii. 36 ; Lev. xix. 11. [2] Ps. v. 6. [3] Hab. ii. 9.
[4] Matt. xxiv. 51. [5] 1 Pet. v. 5. [6] Deut. i. 17 ; Lev. xix. 17.
[7] Prov. ix. 8. [8] Isa. liv. 14.

* Lagarde adds δυνάστου.

νικὸς, μηδὲ θρασύς, [ἵνα] μὴ πάθῃς τὰ τοῦ Καῒν καὶ τὰ τοῦ Σαοὺλ καὶ τὰ τοῦ Ἰωάβ· ὅτι ὃς μὲν ἀπέκτεινε τὸν ἀδελφὸν αὑτοῦ τὸν Ἄβελ διὰ τὸ πρόκριτον αὐτὸν εὑρεθῆναι παρὰ Θεῷ καὶ διὰ τὸ προκριθῆναι* τὴν θυσίαν αὐτοῦ· ὃς δὲ τὸν ὅσιον Δαβὶδ ἐδίωκε νικήσαντα [τὸν] Γολιὰδ τὸν Φιλιστιαῖον, ζηλώσας ἐπὶ τῇ τῶν χορευτριῶν εὐφημίᾳ· ὃς δὲ τοὺς δύο στρατάρχας† ἀνεῖλε, τὸν Ἀβεννὴρ τὸν τοῦ Ἰσραὴλ καὶ Ἀμεσσὰ τὸν τοῦ Ἰούδα —

[III. 4.] CAP. VI. — Μὴ γίνου οἰωνοσκόπος, ὅτι ὁδηγεῖ πρὸς εἰδωλολατρείαν· Οἰώνισμα δὲ, φησὶν ὁ Σαμουήλ, ἁμαρτία ἐστί (1 Sam. xv. 23), καὶ Οὐκ ἔσται οἰωνισμὸς ἐν Ἰακώβ, οὐδὲ μαντεία ἐν Ἰσραὴλ (Num. xxiii.

[III. 4.] 23)· οὐκ ἔσῃ ἐπᾴδων ἢ περικαθαίρων τὸν υἱόν σου, οὐ κληδονιεῖς, οὐδὲ οἰωνισθήσῃ, οὐδὲ ὀρνεοσκοπήσεις, οὐδὲ μαθήσῃ μαθήματα πομηρά·‡ ταῦτα γὰρ ἅπαντα καὶ ὁ νόμος ἀπεῖπε (Lev. xix.; Deut. xviii.). — Μὴ γίνου ἐπιθυμητὴς κακῶν, ὁδηγηθήσῃ γὰρ εἰς ἀμετρίαν ἁμαρτημά-

[III. 3.] των. — Οὐκ ἔσῃ αἰσχρολόγος, οὐδὲ ῥιψόφθαλμος, οὐδὲ μέθυσος· ἐκ γὰρ

fate of Cain, and of Saul, and of Joab: for the first of these slew his brother Abel, because Abel was found to be preferred before him with God, and because Abel's sacrifice was preferred;[1] the second persecuted holy David, who had slain Goliah the Philistine, being envious of the praises of the women who danced;[2] the third slew two generals of armies —Abner of Israel, and Amasa of Judah.[3]

CH. VI.—*Be not a diviner, for that leads to idolatry;* for says Samuel, "Divination is sin;"[4] and, "There shall be no divination in Jacob, nor soothsaying in Israel."[5] *Thou shalt not use enchantments or purgations* for thy child. Thou shall not be a soothsayer nor a diviner by great or little birds. Nor shalt thou learn wicked arts; for all these things has the law forbidden.[6] Be not one that wishes for evil, for thou wilt be led into intolerable sins.[7] *Thou shalt not speak obscenely, nor cast wanton glances, nor be a drunkard; for from such causes arise whoredoms*

---

[1] Gen. iv. [2] 1 Sam. xvii. xviii. [3] 2 Sam. iii., xx. [4] 1 Sam. xv. 23.
[5] Num. xxiii. 23. [6] Deut. xviii. 10, 11. [7] Lev. xix. 26, 31.

* Lagarde: προσδεχθῆναι. † Lagarde: στρατηλάτας.
‡ Lagarde: μάθημα πονηρόν.

τούτων πορνεῖαι καὶ μοιχεῖαι γίνονται.— Μὴ γίνου φιλάργυρος, ἵνα μὴ ἀντὶ Θεοῦ δουλεύσῃς τῷ μαμονᾷ.— Μὴ γίνου κενόδοξος, μηδὲ μετέωρος, μηδὲ ὑψηλόφρων, ἐκ γὰρ τούτων ἁπάντων ἀλαζονίαι γίνονται·* μνήσθητι τοῦ εἰπόντος Κύριε, οὐχ ὑψώθη ἡ καρδία μου, οὐδὲ ἐμετεωρίσθησαν οἱ ὀφθαλμοί μου, οὐδὲ ἐπορεύθην ἐν μεγάλοις οὐδὲ ἐν θαυμασίοις ὑπὲρ ἐμέ, εἰ μὴ ἐταπεινοφρόνουν (Ps. cxxxi. 1, 2).

CAP. VII.— Μὴ γίνου γόγγυσος, μνησθεὶς τῆς τιμωρίας ἧς ὑπέστησαν οἱ καταγογγύσαντες κατὰ Μωσέως.— Μὴ ἔσο αὐθάδης, μηδὲ πονηρόφρων, μηδὲ σκληροκάρδιος, μηδὲ θυμώδης, μηδὲ μικρόψυχος, πάντα γὰρ ταῦτα ὁδηγεῖ πρὸς βλασφημίαν· ἴσθι δὲ πρᾶος ὡς Μωυσῆς καὶ Δαβίδ, ἐπεὶ οἱ πραεῖς κληρονομήσουσι γῆν (Matt. v. 5).—

CAP. VIII.— Γίνου μακρόθυμος· ὁ γὰρ τοιοῦτος πολὺς ἐν φρονήσει, ἐπείπερ ὀλιγόψυχος ἰσχυρῶς† ἄφρων (Prov. xiv. 29 graece). — Γίνου ἐλεήμων· μακάριοι γὰρ οἱ ἐλεήμονες, ὅτι αὐτοὶ ἐλεηθή-

and adulteries. Be not a [III. 5.] lover of money, lest thou "serve mammon instead of God." [1] Be not vainglorious, nor haughty, nor high-minded. For from all these things, arrogance [Did. thefts] does spring. Remember him who said: "Lord, my heart is not haughty, nor mine eyes lofty: I have not exercised myself in great matters, nor in things too high for me; but I was humble." [2]

CH. VII.—Be not a mur- [III. 6.] murer, remembering the punishment which those underwent who murmured against Moses. Be not self-willed, be not malicious, be not hard-hearted, be not passionate, be not mean-spirited; for all these things lead to blasphemy. But be meek, [III. 7.] as were Moses and David, [3] since the meek shall inherit the earth." [4]

CH. VIII.—Be slow to [III. 8.] wrath; for such an one is very prudent, since "he that is hasty of spirit is a very fool." [5] Be merciful; for "blessed are the merciful: for they shall obtain

---

[1] Matt. vi. 24. [2] Ps. cxxxi. 1. [3] Num. xii. 3; Ps. cxxxi. 1.
[4] Matt. v. 5. [5] Prov. xiv. 29.

* Lagarde: γεννῶνται. † Lagarde: ἰσχυρός.

[III. 8.] σονται (Matt. v. 7).—Ἔσο ἄκακος, ἥσυχος, ἀγαθός, τρέμων τοὺς λόγους τοῦ Θεοῦ.— Οὐχ ὑψώσεις σεαυτὸν ὡς ὁ φαρισαῖος· ὅτι πᾶς ὁ ὑψῶν ἑαυτὸν ταπεινωθήσεται, καὶ τὸ ὑψηλὸν ἐν ἀνθρώποις βδέλυγμα παρὰ τῷ Θεῷ (Luc. xviii.
[III. 9.] 14; xvi. 15).— Οὐ δώσεις τῇ ψυχῇ σου θράσος, ὅτι θρασὺς ἀνὴρ ἐμπεσεῖται εἰς κακά (cf. Prov. xiii.17 graece). —Οὐ συμπορεύσῃ μετὰ ἀφρόνων, ἀλλὰ μετὰ σοφῶν καὶ δικαίων· [ὁ συμπορευόμενος γὰρ σοφοῖς σοφὸς ἔσται, ὁ δὲ συμπορευόμενος ἄφροσι γνω-
[III. 10.] σθήσεται (Prov. xiii.20).]—Τὰ συμβαίνοντά σοι πάθη εὐμενῶς δέχου καὶ τὰς περιστάσεις ἀλύπως, εἰδὼς ὅτι μισθὸς παρὰ Θεοῦ σοι δοθήσεται ὡς τῷ Ἰὼβ καὶ τῷ Λαζάρῳ.

[IV. 1.] CAP. IX.— Τὸν λαλοῦντά σοι τὸν λόγον τοῦ Θεοῦ δοξάσεις, μνησθήσῃ δὲ αὐτοῦ ἡμέρας καὶ νυκτός, τιμήσεις δὲ αὐτὸν οὐχ ὡς γενέσεως αἴτιον, ἀλλ' ὡς τοῦ εὖ εἶναί σοι πρόξενον γινόμενον·

mercy."[1] *Be sincere, quiet, good, "trembling at the word of God."*[2] Thou shalt not exalt thyself, as did the Pharisee; for "every one that exalteth himself shall be abased,"[3] and "that which is of high esteem with men is abomination with God."[4] *Thou shalt not entertain confidence in thy soul;* for "a confident man shall fall into mischief."[5] Thou shalt not go along with the foolish, but with the wise and righteous; for "he that walketh[6] with wise men shall be wise, but he that walketh with the foolish shall be known."[7] Receive the afflictions *that fall upon thee* with an even mind, and the chances of life without sorrow, knowing that a reward shall be given to thee by God, as was given to Job and to Lazarus.[8]

CH. IX.—*Thou shalt honor him that speaks to thee the word of God, and be mindful of him day and night; and thou shalt reverence him,* not as the author of thy birth, but as one that is made the occasion of thy

---

[1] Matt. v. 7.   [2] Isa. lxvi. 2.   [3] Luke xviii. 14.
[4] Luke xvi. 15.   [5] Prov. xiii. 17, LXX.
[6] The words from "for he that walketh" to "be known" are omitted in one MS., and by Lagarde.   [7] Prov. xiii. 20.   [8] Job xlii.; Luke xvi.

ὅπου γὰρ ἡ περὶ Θεοῦ διδασκαλία, ἐκεῖ ὁ Θεός πάρεστιν.—Ἐκζητήσεις καθ' ἡμέραν τὸ πρόσωπον τῶν ἁγίων, ἵν' ἐπαναπαύῃ τοῖς λόγοις αὐτῶν.—

CAP. X.— Οὐ ποιήσεις σχίσματα πρὸς τοὺς ἁγίους, μνησθεὶς τῶν Κορειτῶν.—Εἰρηνεύσεις μαχομένους ὡς Μωσῆς, συναλλάσσων εἰς φιλίαν.—Κρινεῖς δικαίως· τοῦ γὰρ Κυρίου ἡ κρίσις (Deut. i. 17).—Οὐ λήψῃ πρόσωπον ἐλέγξαι ἐπὶ παραπτώματι, ὡς Ἠλίας καὶ Μιχαίας τὸν Ἀχαάβ, καὶ Ἀβδεμέλεχ ὁ Αἰθίοψ τὸν Σεδεκίαν, καὶ Νάθαν τὸν Δαβὶδ, καὶ Ἰωάννης τὸν Ἡρώδην.—

CAP. XI.— Μὴ γίνου δίψυχος ἐν προσευχῇ σου, εἰ ἔσται ἢ οὔ· λέγει γὰρ ὁ Κύριος ἐμοὶ Πέτρῳ ἐπὶ τῆς θαλάσσης Ὀλιγόπιστε, εἰς τί ἐδίστασας (Matt. xiv. 31);—Μὴ γίνου πρὸς μὲν τὸ λαβεῖν ἐκτείνων τὴν χεῖρα, πρὸς δὲ τὸ δοῦναι συστέλλων·

CAP. XII.— ἐὰν ἔχεις,

well-being. *For where the* [IV. 1, 2.] *doctrine concerning God is, there God is present. Thou shalt every day seek the face of the saints, that thou mayest acquiesce in their words.*

CH. X.—*Thou shalt not* [IV. 3.] *make schisms* among the saints, but be mindful of the followers of Corah.[1] *Thou shalt make peace be-* [IV. 3.] *tween those that are at variance,* as Moses did when he persuaded them to be friends.[2] *Thou shalt judge* [IV. 3.] *righteously;* for "the judgment is the Lord's."[3] *Thou* [IV. 3.] *shalt not have respect of persons when thou reprovest for sins;* but do as Elijah and Micaiah did to Ahab, and Ebedmelech the Ethiopian to Zedechiah, and Nathan to David, and John to Herod.[4]

CH. XI.—*Be not of a* [IV. 4.] *doubtful mind* in thy prayer, whether it shall be granted or no. For the Lord said to me, Peter, upon the sea: "O thou of little faith, wherefore didst thou doubt?"[5] "*Be not thou ready to stretch* [IV. 5.] *out thy hand to receive, and to shut it when thou shouldst give.*"[6]

CH. XII.—*If thou hast by* [IV. 6.]

---

[1] Num. xvi. [2] Ex. ii. 13. [3] Deut. i. 17.
[4] 1 Kings xviii. xxi. xxii.; 2 Sam. xii.; Matt. xiv.
[5] Matt. xiv. 31. [6] Ecclus. iv. 31.

διὰ τῶν χειρῶν σου δός, ἵνα ἐργάσῃ εἰς λύτρωσιν ἁμαρτιῶν σου· ἐλεημοσύναις γὰρ καὶ πίστεσιν ἀποκαθαίρονται ἁμαρτίαι (Prov. xvi. 6). [IV.7.] Οὐ διστάσεις δοῦναι πτωχῷ, οὐδὲ διδοὺς γογγύσεις, γνώσῃ γὰρ τίς ἐστιν ὁ τοῦ μισθοῦ ἀνταποδότης· Ὁ ἐλεῶν γάρ, φησί, πτωχὸν Κυρίῳ δανείζει, κατὰ δὲ τὸ δόμα αὐτοῦ, οὕτως ἀνταποδοθήσεται αὐτῷ (Prov. xix. 17). [IV.8.] Οὐκ ἀποστραφήσῃ ἐνδεόμενον·* Ὃς φράσσει γάρ, φησί, τὰ ὦτα αὐτοῦ μὴ εἰσακοῦσαι τοῦ δεομένου,† καὶ αὐτὸς ἐπικαλέσεται καὶ οὐκ ἔσται ὁ εἰσακούων αὐτοῦ (Prov. xxi. 13). [IV.8.] Κοινωνήσεις εἰς πάντα τῷ ἀδελφῷ σου καὶ οὐκ ἐρεῖς ἴδια εἶναι, κοινὴ γὰρ ἡ μετάληψις παρὰ Θεοῦ πᾶσιν ἀνθρώποις παρεσκευάσθη. [IV.9.] — Οὐκ ἀρεῖς τὴν χεῖρά σου ἀπὸ τοῦ υἱοῦ σου ἢ ἀπὸ τῆς θυγατρός σου, ἀλλὰ ἀπὸ νεότητος διδάξεις αὐτοὺς τὸν φόβον τοῦ Θεοῦ. Παίδευε γάρ, φησί, τὸν υἱόν σου, οὕτω γὰρ ἔσται σοι εὔελπις (Prov. xix. 18).—

the work of thy hands, give, that thou mayest labor for *the redemption of thy sins;* for "by alms and acts of faith sins are purged away."[1] *Thou shalt not grudge to give* to the poor, *nor when thou hast given shalt thou murmur; for thou shalt know who will repay thee thy reward.* For says he: "He that hath mercy on the poor man lendeth to the Lord; according to his gift, so shall it be repaid him again."[2] *Thou shalt not turn away from him that is needy;* for says he: "He that stoppeth his ears, that he may not hear the cry of the needy, himself also shall call, and there shall be none to hear him."[3] *Thou shalt communicate in all things to thy brother, and shalt not say* [thy goods] *are thine own;* for the common participation of the necessaries of life is appointed to all men by God. *Thou shalt not take off thine hand from thy son or from thy daughter, but shalt teach* them *the fear of God from their youth;* for says he: "Cor-

---

[1] Prov. xv. 27; xvi. 6.   [2] Prov. xix. 17.   [3] Prov. xxi. 13.

* Lagarde: ἐνδεούμενον.
† Lagarde: ἀκοῦσαι ἐνδεουμένου for εἰσακοῦσαι τοῦ δεομένου.

Cap. XIII.—Οὐκ ἐπιτάξεις δούλῳ σου ἢ παιδίσκῃ τοῖς ἐπὶ τὸν αὐτὸν Θεὸν πεποιθόσιν ἐν πικρίᾳ ψυχῆς, μή ποτε στενάξωσιν ἐπὶ σοὶ καὶ ἔσται σοι ὀργὴ παρὰ Θεοῦ· καὶ ὑμεῖς, οἱ δοῦλοι, ὑποτάγητε τοῖς κυρίοις ὑμῶν ὡς τύποις* Θεοῦ ἐν προσοχῇ† καὶ φόβῳ, ὡς τῷ‡ Κυρίῳ καὶ οὐκ ἀνθρώποις.—

Cap. XIV.—Μισήσεις πᾶσαν ὑπόκρισιν, καὶ πᾶν, ὃ ἐὰν ᾖ ἀρεστὸν Κυρίῳ, ποιήσεις· οὐ μὴ ἐγκαταλίπῃς ἐντολὰς Κυρίου, φυλάξεις δὲ ἃ παρέλαβες παρ' αὐτοῦ, μήτε προστιθεὶς ἐπ' αὐτοῖς μήτε ἀφαιρῶν ἀπ' αὐτῶν· οὐ προσθήσεις γὰρ τοῖς λόγοις αὐτοῦ, ἵνα μὴ ἐλέγξῃ σε καὶ ψευδὴς γένῃ (Prov. xxx. 6).—Ἐξομολογήσῃ ᾗ Κυρίῳ τῷ Θεῷ σου τὰ ἁμαρτήματά σου καὶ οὐκ ἔτι προσθήσεις ἐπ' αὐτοῖς, ἵνα εὖ σοι γένηται παρὰ Κυρίῳ τῷ Θεῷ σου, ὃς οὐ βούλεται τὸν θάνατον τοῦ ἁμαρτωλοῦ, ἀλλὰ τὴν μετάνοιαν.

Ch. XIII.—*Thou shalt not command thy man-servant, or thy maid-servant, who trust in the same God, with bitterness of soul, lest they groan against thee, and wrath be upon thee from God. And, ye servants,* [IV. 10.] [IV. 11.] *"be subject to your masters,"* [2] *as to the representatives of God, with attention and fear, "as to the Lord, and not to men."* [3]

Ch. XIV.—*Thou shalt hate* [IV. 12, 13.] *all hypocrisy; and whatsoever is pleasing to the Lord, that shalt thou do. By no means forsake the commands of the Lord. But thou shalt observe what things thou hast received from Him, neither adding to them nor taking away from them. "For thou shalt not add unto His words, lest He convict thee, and thou becomest a liar."* [4] *Thou shalt con* [IV. 14.] *fess thy sins unto the Lord thy God; and thou shalt not add unto them, that it may be well with thee from the Lord thy God, who willeth not the death of a sinner, but his repentance.*

---

[1] Prov. xix. 18. [2] Eph. vi. 5. [3] Eph. vi. 7. [4] Prov. xxx. 6.
* Lagarde: τύπῳ. So in *Did.*   † Lagarde: αἰσχύνῃ. So in *Did.*
‡ Lagarde omits τῷ.

Cap. XV.— *Τὸν πατέρα σου καὶ τὴν μητέρα θεραπεύσεις ὡς αἰτίους σοι γενέσεως, ἵνα γένῃ μακροχρόνιος ἐπὶ τῆς γῆς ἧς Κύριος ὁ Θεός σου δίδωσί σοι* (Exod. xx. 12) · *τοὺς ἀδελφούς σου καὶ τοὺς συγγενεῖς σου μὴ ὑπερίδῃς· τοὺς γὰρ οἰκείους τοῦ σπέρματός σου οὐχ ὑπερόψει* (Is. lviii. 7) —

Cap. XVI. — *Τὸν βασιλέα φοβηθήσῃ, εἰδὼς ὅτι τοῦ Κυρίου ἐστὶν ἡ χειροτονία· τοὺς ἄρχοντας αὐτοῦ τιμήσεις ὡς λειτουργοὺς Θεοῦ, ἔκδικοι γάρ εἰσι πάσης ἀδικίας· οἷς ἀποτίσατε τέλος, φόρον καὶ πᾶσαν εἰσφορὰν εὐγνωμόνως.—*

[IV. 14.] Cap. XVII. — *Οὐ προσελεύσῃ ἐπὶ προσευχήν σου ἐν ἡμέρᾳ πονηρίας σου, πρὶν ἂν λύσῃς τὴν πικρίαν σου.—Αὕτη ἐστὶν ἡ ὁδὸς τῆς ζωῆς, ἧς γένοιτο ἐντὸς ὑμᾶς εὑρεθῆναι διὰ Ἰησοῦ Χριστοῦ τοῦ Κυρίου ἡμῶν.*

[V. 1.] Cap. XVIII. — *Ἡ δὲ ὁδὸς τοῦ θανάτου ἐστὶν ἐν πράξεσι πονηραῖς θεωρουμένη· ἐν αὐτῇ γὰρ ἄγνοια* * *Θεοῦ, καὶ πολλῶν κακῶν*† *καὶ δολῶν καὶ ταραχῶν ἐπει-* [V. 1.] *σαγωγή, δι' ὧν φόνοι, μοιχεῖαι, πορνεῖαι, ἐπιορκίαι, ἐπιθυμίαι παρά-*

Ch. XV.—Thou shalt be observant to thy father and mother as the causes of thy being born, that thou mayest live long on the earth which the Lord thy God giveth thee. Do not overlook thy brethren or thy kinsfolk; for "thou shalt not overlook those nearly related to thee."[1]

Ch. XVI.—Thou shalt fear the king, knowing that his appointment is of the Lord. His rulers thou shalt honor as the ministers of God, for they are the revengers of all unrighteousness; to whom pay taxes, tribute, and every oblation with a willing mind.

Ch. XVII.—*Thou shalt not proceed to thy prayer in the day of thy wickedness,* before thou hast laid aside thy bitterness. *This is the way of life,* in which may ye be found, through Jesus Christ our Lord.

Ch. XVIII.—*But the way of death is* known by its wicked practices: for therein is the ignorance of God, and the introduction of many evils, and disorders, and disturbances; whereby come *murders, adulteries, fornications,* perjuries, un-

---

[1] Isa. lviii. 7.

* Lagarde inserts τοῦ.

† Lagarde reads merely πολλῶν θεῶν, and omits κακῶν....ταραχῶν.

νομοι, κλοπαὶ, εἰδωλολατρεῖαι, μαγίαι, φαρμακεῖαι, ἁρπαγαὶ, ψευδομαρτυρίαι, ὑποκρίσεις, διπλοκαρδίαι, δόλος, ὑπερηφανία, κακία, αὐθάδεια, πλεονεξία, αἰσχρολογία, ζηλοτυπία, θρασύτης, ὑψηλοφροσύνη, ἀλαζονεία, ἀφοβία, διωγμὸς ἀγαθῶν, ἀληθείας ἔχθρα, ψεύδους ἀγάπη, ἄγνοια δικαιοσύνης. Οἱ γὰρ τούτων ποιηταὶ οὐ κολλῶνται ἀγαθῷ, οὐδὲ κρίσει δικαίῳ.* ἀγρυπνοῦσιν οὐκ εἰς τὸ ἀγαθόν, ἀλλ' εἰς τὸ πονηρόν· ὧν μακρὰν πραότης καὶ ὑπομονή· μάταια ἀγαπῶντες, διώκοντες ἀνταπόδομα, οὐκ ἐλεοῦντες πτωχόν, οὐ πονοῦντες ἐπὶ καταπονουμένῳ, οὐ γινώσκοντες τὸν ποιήσαντα αὐτούς, φονεῖς τέκνων, φθορεῖς πλάσματος Θεοῦ, ἀποστρεφόμενοι ἐνδεόμενον,† καταπονοῦντες θλιβόμενον, πλουσίων παράκλητοι, πενήτων ὑπερόπται, πανθαμάρτητοι. Ῥυσθείητε, τέκ-

lawful *lusts, thefts, idolatries, magic arts, witchcrafts, rapines, false-witnesses, hypocrisies, double-heartedness, deceit, pride, malice, insolence, covetousness, obscene talk, jealousy, confidence, haughtiness, arrogance, impudence, persecution of the good, enmity to truth, love of lies, ignorance of righteousness. For they who do such things do not adhere to good-* [V. 2.] *ness, or to righteous judgment: they watch not for good, but for evil; from whom meekness and patience are far off, who love vain things, pursuing after reward, having no pity on the poor, not labouring for him that is in misery, nor knowing Him that made them; murderers of infants, destroyers of the workmanship of God, that turn away from the needy, adding affliction to the afflicted, the flatterers of the rich, the despisers of the poor, full of sin. May you, children, be delivered from all these.*

---

* Lagarde: δικαία.
† Lagarde omits next two words.

να, ἀπὸ τούτων ἁπάντων.*

[VI. 1.] CAP. XIX.—Ὅρα μή τίς σε πλανήσῃ ἀπὸ τῆς εὐσεβείας· Οὐκ ἐκκλινεῖς γάρ, φησίν, ἀπ' αὐτῆς δεξιὰ ἢ εὐώνυμα† (Deut. v. 32), ἵνα συνῇς ἐν πᾶσιν οἷς ἐὰν πράσσῃς· οὐ γάρ, ἐὰν μὴ ἐκτραπῇς ἔξω τῆς εὐθείας ὁδοῦ, δυσσεβήσεις.

[VI. 3.] CAP. XX.—Περὶ δὲ βρωμάτων λέγει σοι ὁ Κύριος Τὰ ἀγαθὰ τῆς γῆς φάγεσθε καὶ πᾶν κρέας ἔδεσθε ὡς λάχανα χλόης (Is. i. 19; Gen. ix. 3), τὸ δὲ αἷμα ἐκχεεῖς (Deut. xv. 23)· οὐ γὰρ τὰ εἰσερχόμενα εἰς τὸ στόμα κοινοῖ τὸν ἄνθρωπον, ἀλλὰ τὰ ἐκπορευόμενα, λέγω δὴ βλασφημίαι, καταλαλιαὶ καὶ εἴ τι τοιοῦτον. Σὺ δὲ φάγῃ τὸν μυελὸν τῆς γῆς μετὰ δικαιοσύνης· ὅτι εἴ τι καλόν, αὐτοῦ, καὶ εἴ τι ἀγαθόν, αὐτοῦ· σῖτος νεανίσκοις καὶ οἶνος εὐωδιάζων παρθένοις (Zach. ix. 17)· τίς γὰρ φάγεται ἢ τίς πίεται παρὲξ αὐτοῦ ‡ (Eccl. ii. 25 graece); Παραινεῖ δέ σοι καὶ ὁ σοφὸς Ἔσδρας λέγων Πορεύεσθε καὶ φάγετε λιπάσματα καὶ πίετε

CH. XIX.—*See that no one seduce thee* from piety; for says He: "Thou mayst not turn aside from it to the right hand, or to the left, that thou mayst have understanding in all that thou doest."[1] For if thou dost not turn out of the right way, thou wilt not be ungodly.

CH. XX.—*Now concerning the several sorts of food*, the Lord says to thee, "Ye shall eat the good things of the earth;"[2] and, "All sorts of flesh shall ye eat, as the green herb;"[3] but, "Thou shalt pour out the blood."[4] For "not those things that go into the mouth, but those that come out of it, defile a man;"[5] I mean blasphemies, evil-speaking, and if there be any other thing of the like nature.[6] But "do thou eat the fat of the land with righteousness."[7] For "if there be anything pleasant, it is His; and if there be anything good, it is His. Wheat for the young men, and wine to cheer the

---

[1] Deut. v. 32. [2] Isa. i. 19. [3] Gen. ix. 3. [4] Deut. xv. 23.
[5] Matt. xv. 11. [6] Mark vii. 22. [7] Zech. ix. 17.

* Lagarde: πάντων. † Lagarde: ἀριστερά.
‡ Lagarde omits from here to end of chapter.

γλυκάσματα καὶ μὴ λυπεῖσθε
(Neh. viii. 10).

CAP. XXI.—Ἀπὸ δὲ τῶν εἰδωλοθύτων φεύγετε, ἐπὶ τιμῇ γὰρ δαιμόνων θύουσι ταῦτα,* ἐφ' ὕβρει δηλαδὴ τοῦ μόνου Θεοῦ· ὅπως μὴ γένησθε κοινωνοὶ δαιμόνων.

CAP. XXII.—Περὶ δὲ βαπτίσματος, ὦ ἐπίσκοπε ἢ πρεσβύτερε, ἤδη μὲν καὶ πρότερον διεταξάμεθα, καὶ νῦν δέ φαμεν ὅτι οὕτω βαπτίσεις, ὡς ὁ Κύριος διετάξατο ἡμῖν λέγων Πορευθέντες μαθητεύσατε πάντα τὰ ἔθνη, βαπτίζοντες αὐτοὺς εἰς τὸ ὄνομα τοῦ Πατρὸς καὶ τοῦ Υἱοῦ καὶ τοῦ ἁγίου Πνεύματος, διδάσκοντες αὐτοὺς τηρεῖν πάντα ὅσα ἐνετειλάμην ὑμῖν (Matt. xxviii. 19)· τοῦ ἀποστείλαντος Πατρός, τοῦ ἐλθόντος Χριστοῦ, τοῦ μαρτυρήσαντος Παρακλήτου. Χρίσεις δὲ πρῶτον ἐλαίῳ ἁγίῳ, ἔπειτα βαπτίσεις ὕδατι καὶ [τὸ] τελευταῖον σφραγίσεις μύρῳ· ἵνα τὸ μὲν

maids." For "who shall eat or who shall drink without Him?"[1] Wise Ezra[2] does also admonish thee, and say: "Go your way, and eat the fat, and drink the sweet, and be not sorrowful."[3]

CH. XXI.—*But do ye abstain from things offered to idols;*[4] for they offer them in honor of demons, that is, to the dishonor of the one God, that ye may not become partners with demons. [VI. 3.]

CH. XXII.—*Now concerning Baptism*, O Bishop, or Presbyter, we have already given direction, and we now say, that *thou shalt so baptize* as the Lord commanded us, saying: "Go ye, and teach all nations, *baptizing them into the name of the Father, and of the Son, and of the Holy Ghost*, teaching them to observe all things whatsoever I have commanded you:"[5] of the Father who sent; of Christ who came, of the Comforter who testified. But thou shalt beforehand anoint the person with holy oil, and afterward *baptize him with water,* and in the conclusion shalt seal him with the ointment; that the [VII. 1.]

---
[1] Eccles. ii. 25, LXX.
[2] The words from "Wise Ezra" to "sorrowful" are omitted by Lagarde.
[3] Neh. viii. 10.   [4] 1 Cor. x. 20.   [5] Matt. xxviii. 19.

* Lagarde: αἰτᾶ.

276 SEVENTH BOOK OF THE APOSTOLICAL CONSTITUTIONS.

χρῖσμα μετοχὴ ᾖ τοῦ ἁγίου πνεύματος, τὸ δὲ ὕδωρ σύμβολον τοῦ θανάτου τὸ δὲ μύρον σφραγὶς τῶν συνθηκῶν. Εἰ δὲ μήτε ἔλαιον ᾖ μήτε μύρον, ἀρκεῖ* ὕδωρ καὶ πρὸς χρῖσιν καὶ πρὸς σφραγῖδα καὶ πρὸς ὁμολογίαν τοῦ ἀποθανόντος ἤτοι συναποθνήσκοντος. [VII. 4.] Πρὸ δὲ τοῦ βαπτίσματος νηστευσάτω ὁ βαπτιζόμενος· καὶ γὰρ ὁ Κύριος πρῶτον βαπτισθεὶς ὑπὸ Ἰωάννου καὶ εἰς τὴν ἔρημον αὐλισθεὶς, μετέπειτα ἐνήστευσε τεσσαράκοντα ἡμέρας καὶ τεσσαράκοντα νύκτας. Ἐβαπτίσθη δὲ καὶ ἐνήστευσεν οὐκ αὐτὸς ἀπορυπώσεως ἢ νηστείας χρείαν ἔχων ἢ καθάρσεως ὁ τῇ φύσει καθαρὸς καὶ ἅγιος, ἀλλ' ἵνα καὶ Ἰωάννῃ ἀλήθειαν προσμαρτυρήσῃ καὶ ἡμῖν ὑπογραμμὸν παράσχηται. Οὐκοῦν ὁ μὲν Κύριος οὐκ εἰς ἑαυτοῦ πάθος ἐβαπτίσατο ἢ θάνατον ἢ ἀνάστασιν (οὐδέπω γὰρ οὐδὲν τούτων ἐγεγόνει), ἀλλ' εἰς διάταξιν ἑτέραν, διὸ καὶ ἀπ' ἐξουσίας μετὰ τὸ βάπτισμα νηστεύει ὡς Κύριος Ἰωάννου· ὁ δὲ εἰς τὸν αὐτοῦ θάνατον μυούμενος πρότερον ὀφείλει νηστεῦσαι καὶ τότε βαπτίσασθαι† (οὐ γὰρ δίκαιον τὸν συνταφέντα καὶ συνανα-

anointing with oil may be the participation of the Holy Spirit, and the water the symbol of the death [of Christ], and the ointment the seal of the covenants. But if there be neither oil nor ointment, water is sufficient both for the anointing, and for the seal, and for the confession of Him that is dead, or indeed is dying together [with Christ]. *But before Baptism, let him that is baptized fast;* for even the Lord, when He was first baptized by John, and abode in the wilderness, did afterward fast forty days and forty nights.[1] But He was baptized, and then fasted, not having Himself any need of cleansing, or of fasting, or of purgation, who was by nature pure and holy; but that He might testify the truth to John, and afford an example to us. Wherefore our Lord was not baptized into His own passion, or death, or resurrection—for none of those things had then happened—but for another purpose. Wherefore He by His own authority fasted after His Baptism, as being the Lord of John. But he who is to be initiated into His

---

[1] Matt. iii. iv.   * Lagarde: τό.   † Lagarde: βαπτισθῆναι.

στάντα παρ᾽ αὐτὴν τὴν ἀνάστασιν κατηφεῖν), οὐ γὰρ κύριος ὁ ἄνθρωπος τῆς διατά-
ξεως τῆς τοῦ σωτῆρος· ἐπείπερ ὁ μὲν δεσπότης, ὁ δὲ ὑπή-
κοος.

death ought first to fast, and then to be baptized. For it is not reasonable that he who has been buried [with Christ], and is risen again with Him, should appear dejected at His very resurrection. For man is not lord of our Saviour's constitution, since one is the Master and the other the servant.

CAP. XXIII.— Αἱ δὲ νη-
στεῖαι ὑμῶν μὴ ἔστω-
σαν μετὰ τῶν ὑπο-
κριτῶν, νηστεύουσι
γὰρ δευτέρᾳ σαββά-
των καὶ πέμπτῃ.
Ὑμεῖς δὲ ἢ τὰς πέντε
νηστεύσατε ἡμέρας, ἢ τε-
τράδα καὶ παρασκευήν·
ὅτι τῇ μὲν τετράδι ἡ κρίσις
ἐξῆλθεν ἡ κατὰ τοῦ Κυρίου,
Ἰούδα χρήμασιν ἐπαγγειλα-
μένου τὴν προδοσίαν· τὴν δὲ
παρασκευήν, ὅτι ἔπαθεν ὁ Κύριος ἐν αὐτῇ πάθος τὸ διὰ
σταυροῦ ὑπὸ Ποντίου Πιλά-
του. Τὸ σάββατον μέντοι καὶ
τὴν κυριακὴν ἑορτάζετε, ὅτι
τὸ μὲν δημιουργίας ἐστὶν ὑπό-
μνημα, ἡ δὲ ἀναστάσεως. Ἐν
δὲ μόνον σάββατον ὑμῖν φυ-
λακτέον ἐν ὅλῳ τῷ ἐνιαυτῷ,
τὸ τῆς τοῦ Κυρίου ταφῆς, ὅπερ
νηστεύειν προσῆκεν, ἀλλ᾽ οὐχ
ἑορτάζειν· ἐν ὅσῳ γὰρ ὁ δημιουργὸς ὑπὸ γῆν τυγχάνει,
ἰσχυρότερον τὸ περὶ αὐτοῦ
πένθος τῆς κατὰ τὴν δημιουρ-
γίαν χαρᾶς, ὅτι ὁ δημιουργὸς

CH. XXIII.—*But let not* [VIII. 1.] *your fasts be with the hypocrites ; for they fast on the second and fifth days of the week.* But do ye either fast the entire five days, or *on the fourth* day of the week, and *on the day of the preparation*, because on the fourth day the condemnation went out against the Lord, Judas then promising to betray Him for money ; and you must fast on the day of the preparation, because on that day the Lord suffered the death of the cross under Pontius Pilate. But keep the Sabbath, and the Lord's day festival ; because the former is the memorial of the creation, and the latter of the resurrection. But there is one only Sabbath to be observed by you in the whole year, which is that of our Lord's burial, on which men ought to keep a fast, but not a festival. For inasmuch as τῶν ἑαυτοῦ δημιουργημάτων φύσει τε καὶ ἀξίᾳ τιμιώτερος.

the Creator was then under the earth, the sorrow for Him is more forcible than the joy for the creation; for the Creator is more honorable by nature and dignity than His own creatures.

[VIII. 2.] CAP. XXIV.—Ὅταν δὲ προσεύχησθε, μὴ γίνεσθε ὡς οἱ ὑποκριταί, ἀλλ' ὡς ὁ Κύριος ἡμῖν ἐν τῷ εὐαγγελίῳ διετάξατο, οὕτω προσεύχεσθε "Πάτερ ἡμῶν ὁ ἐν τοῖς οὐρανοῖς, ἁγιασθήτω τὸ ὄνομά σου· ἐλθέτω ἡ βασιλεία σου· γενηθήτω τὸ θέλημά σου ὡς ἐν οὐρανῷ καὶ ἐπὶ τῆς γῆς· τὸν ἄρτον ἡμῶν τὸν ἐπιούσιον δὸς ἡμῖν σήμερον· καὶ ἄφες ἡμῖν τὰ ὀφειλήματα ἡμῶν, ὡς καὶ ἡμεῖς ἀφίεμεν τοῖς ὀφειλέταις ἡμῶν· καὶ μὴ εἰσενέγκῃς ἡμᾶς εἰς πειρασμόν, ἀλλὰ ῥῦσαι ἡμᾶς ἀπὸ τοῦ πονηροῦ· ὅτι σοῦ ἐστιν ἡ βασιλεία* εἰς τοὺς αἰῶνας· ἀμήν" (Matt. vi. 9 sqq.).

[VIII. 3.] Τρὶς τῆς ἡμέρας οὕτω προσεύχεσθε, προπαρασκευάζοντες ἑαυτοὺς ἀξίους τῆς υἱοθεσίας τοῦ πατρός, ἵνα μή, ἀναξίως ὑμῶν αὐτὸν πατέρα καλούντων, ὀνειδισθῆτε

Cπ. XXIV.—Now, "when ye pray, be not ye as the hypocrites;"[1] but as the Lord has appointed us in the Gospel, so pray ye: "Our Father who art in Heaven, hallowed be Thy name; Thy kingdom come; Thy will be done, as in Heaven, so on earth; give us this day our daily bread [Did. debt], as we forgive our debtors; and lead us not into temptation, but deliver us from evil [or the evil One, i.e., the Devil]; for Thine is the kingdom for ever. Amen."[2] Pray thus thrice in a day, preparing yourselves beforehand, that ye may be worthy of the adoption of the Father; lest, when you call Him Father unworthily, you be reproached by Him, as Israel once His first-born son was told: "If I be a Father, where is my glory? And if I be a Lord, where is my fear?"[3] For the glory of fathers is the holiness of

---

[1] Matt. vi. 5.   [2] Matt. vi. 9, etc.   [3] Mal. i. 6.

* Lagarde: καὶ ἡ δύναμις καὶ ἡ δόξα.

ὑπ' αὐτοῦ, ὡς καὶ ὁ Ἰσραὴλ ὅ ποτε πρωτότοκος υἱὸς ἤκουσεν ὅτι Εἰ πατήρ εἰμι ἐγώ, ποῦ ἔστιν ἡ δόξα μου; καὶ εἰ Κύριός εἰμι, ποῦ ἐστιν ὁ φόβος μου (Mal. i. 6); δόξα γὰρ πατέρων ὁσιότης παίδων καὶ τιμὴ δεσποτῶν οἰκετῶν φόβος, ὥσπερ οὖν τὸ ἐναντίον ἀδοξία καὶ ἀναρχία· Δι' ὑμᾶς γάρ, φησί,* τὸ ὄνομά μου βλασφημεῖται ἐν τοῖς ἔθνεσι (Is. lii. 5).

their children, and the honor of masters is the fear of their servants, as the contrary is dishonor and confusion. For says He: "Through you my name is blasphemed among the Gentiles."[1]

CAP. XXV.— Γίνεσθε δὲ πάντοτε εὐχάριστοι, ὡς πιστοὶ καὶ εὐγνώμονες δοῦλοι· περὶ μὲν τῆς εὐχαριστίας οὕτω λέγοντες "Εὐχαριστοῦμέν σοι, πάτερ ἡμῶν, ὑπὲρ ζωῆς ἧς ἐγνώρισας ἡμῖν διὰ Ἰησοῦ τοῦ παιδός σου, δι' οὗ καὶ τὰ πάντα ἐποίησας καὶ τῶν ὅλων προνοεῖς, ὃν καὶ ἀπέστειλας ἐπὶ σωτηρίᾳ τῇ ἡμετέρᾳ γενέσθαι ἄνθρωπον, ὃν καὶ συνεχώρησας παθεῖν καὶ ἀποθανεῖν, ὃν καὶ ἀναστήσας εὐδόκησας δοξάσαι καὶ ἐκάθισας ἐκ δεξιῶν σου, δι' οὗ καὶ ἐπηγγείλω ἡμῖν τὴν ἀνάστασιν τῶν νεκρῶν. Σὺ δέσποτα παντοκράτορ Θεὲ αἰώνιε, ὥσπερ ἦν τοῦτο διεσκορπισμένον καὶ συναχθὲν ἐγένετο εἰς ἄρτος, οὕτω συναγαγέ σου τὴν ἐκ-

CH. XXV.—Be ye always thankful, as faithful and honest servants; and concerning the eucharistic thanksgiving say thus: We thank Thee, our Father, for that life which Thou hast made known to us by Jesus Thy Son, by whom Thou madest all things, and takest care of the whole world; whom Thou didst send to become man for our salvation; whom Thou hast permitted to suffer and to die; whom Thou hast raised up, and been pleased to glorify, and hast set Him down on Thy right hand; by whom Thou hast promised us the resurrection of the dead. Do Thou, O Lord Almighty, everlasting God, so gather together Thy church from the ends of the earth into Thy kingdom, as [IX. 1, 3.] [IX. 4.]

---

[1] Isa. lii. 5.

* Lagarde omits.

κλησίαν ἀπὸ τῶν περάτων τῆς γῆς εἰς* σὴν βασιλείαν. Ἔτι εὐχαριστοῦμεν, πάτερ ἡμῶν, ὑπὲρ τοῦ τιμίου αἵματος Ἰησοῦ Χριστοῦ τοῦ ἐκχυθέντος ὑπὲρ ἡμῶν καὶ τοῦ τιμίου σώματος, οὗ καὶ ἀντίτυπα ταῦτα ἐπιτελοῦμεν, αὐτοῦ διαταξαμένου ἡμῖν καταγγέλλειν τὸν αὐτοῦ θάνατον· δι' αὐτοῦ γάρ σοι καὶ ἡ δόξα εἰς τοὺς αἰῶνας· ἀμήν."

[IX. 5.] Μηδεὶς δὲ ἐσθιέτω ἐξ αὐτῶν τῶν ἀμυήτων, ἀλλὰ μόνοι οἱ βεβαπτισμένοι εἰς τὸν τοῦ Κυρίου† θάνατον. Εἰ δέ τις ἀμύητος κρύψας ἑαυτὸν μεταλάβῃ, κρίμα αἰώνιον φάγεται, ὅτι μὴ ὢν τῆς εἰς Χριστὸν πίστεως μετέλαβεν ὧν οὐ θέμις, εἰς τιμωρίαν ἑαυτοῦ· εἰ δέ τις κατὰ ἄγνοιαν μεταλάβοι, τοῦτον τάχιον στοιχειώσαντες μυήσατε, ὅπως μὴ καταφρονητὴς ἐξέλθοι.

[X. 1.] CAP. XXVI. — Μετὰ δὲ τὴν μετάληψιν οὕτως εὐχαριστήσατε "Εὐχαριστοῦμέν σοι, ὁ Θεὸς καὶ πατὴρ Ἰησοῦ τοῦ σωτῆρος

this [corn] was once scattered, and is now become one loaf. We also, our Father, thank Thee for the precious blood of Jesus Christ, which was shed for us, and for His precious body, whereof we celebrate this representation, as Himself appointed us, "to show forth His death."[1] For through Him *glory* is to be given to Thee *for ever*. Amen.

Let no one eat of these things that is not initiated; *but those only who have been baptized* into the death of the Lord. But if any one that is not initiated conceal himself, and partake of the same, he eats eternal judgment;[2] because, being not of the faith of Christ, he has partaken of such things as it is not lawful for him to partake of, to his own punishment. But if any one is a partaker through ignorance, instruct him quickly, and initiate him, that he may not go out and despise you.

CH. XXVI.—*After* the participation, *give thanks in this manner: We thank thee,* O God, and *Father* of Jesus our Saviour, *for Thy holy*

---

[1] 1 Cor. xi. 26.

* Lagarde inserts τὴν.

[2] 1 Cor. xi. 29.

† Lagarde inserts χριστοῦ.

ἡμῶν, ὑπὲρ τοῦ ἁγίου [ὀνόματός σου, om. by Ueltzen, but in nearly all other eds.*] οὗ κατεσκήνωσας ἐν ἡμῖν, καὶ ὑπὲρ τῆς γνώσεως καὶ πίστεως καὶ ἀγάπης καὶ ἀθανασίας ἧς ἔδωκας ἡμῖν διὰ Ἰησοῦ τοῦ παιδός σου. Σὺ δέσποτα παντοκράτορ, ὁ Θεὸς τῶν ὅλων, ὁ κτίσας τὸν κόσμον καὶ τὰ ἐν αὐτῷ δι' αὐτοῦ, καὶ νόμον κατεφύτευσας ἐν † ταῖς ψυχαῖς ἡμῶν καὶ τὰ πρὸς μετάληψιν προευτρέπισας ἀνθρώποις· ὁ Θεὸς τῶν ἁγίων καὶ ἀμέμπτων πατέρων ἡμῶν, Ἀβραὰμ καὶ Ἰσαὰκ καὶ Ἰακὼβ, τῶν πιστῶν δούλων σου· ὁ δυνατὸς Θεός, ὁ πιστὸς καὶ ἀληθινὸς καὶ ἀψευδὴς ἐν ταῖς ἐπαγγελίαις· ὁ ἀποστείλας ἐπὶ γῆς Ἰησοῦν τὸν Χριστόν σου ἀνθρώποις συναναστραφῆναι ὡς ἄνθρωπον, Θεὸν ὄντα λόγον καὶ ἄνθρωπον, καὶ τὴν πλάνην πρόρριζον ἀνελεῖν· αὐτὸς καὶ νῦν δι' αὐτοῦ μνήσθητι τῆς ἁγίας σου ἐκκλησίας ταύτης, ἣν περιεποιήσω τῷ τιμίῳ αἵματι τοῦ Χριστοῦ σου, καὶ ῥῦσαι αὐτὴν ἀπὸ παντὸς πονηροῦ καὶ τελείωσον αὐτὴν ἐν τῇ ἀγάπῃ σου καὶ τῇ ἀληθείᾳ σου, καὶ συνάγαγε

name, *which Thou hast made to inhabit among us; and that knowledge, faith,* love, *and immortality* which Thou hast given *us through Thy Son Jesus. Thou, O Almighty Lord,* the God of the universe, *hast created the World, and the things that are therein,* by Him; and hast planted a law in our souls, *and beforehand didst prepare things for the convenience of men.* O God of our holy and blameless fathers, Abraham, and Isaac, and Jacob, Thy faithful servants; Thou, O God, who art powerful, faithful, and true, and without deceit in Thy promises; who didst send upon earth Jesus Thy Christ to live with men, as a man, when He was God the Word, and man, to take away error by the roots: do Thou even now, through Him, *be mind-* [X. 5.] *ful of this Thy holy church,* which Thou hast purchased with the precious blood of Thy Christ, *and deliver it from all evil, and perfect it in Thy love* and Thy truth, *and gather us all together into Thy kingdom which Thou hast prepared. Maranatha. "Hosanna to the Son of David.* Blessed be He that cometh in the name

---

* Lagarde omits σου.   † Lagarde omits.

πάντας ἡμᾶς εἰς τὴν σὴν βασιλείαν, ἣν ἡτοίμασας αὐτήν [αὐτῇ].

[X. 6.] Μαρανα θά· ὡσαννὰ τῷ υἱῷ [Did. θεῷ], Δαβίδ, εὐλογημένος ὁ ἐρχόμενος ἐν ὀνόματι Κυρίου, Θεὸς Κύριος ὁ ἐπιφανεὶς ἡμῖν ἐν σαρκί."

[X. 6.] Εἴ τις ἅγιος, προσερχέσθω· εἰ δέ τις οὐκ ἔστι, γινέσθω διὰ μετα-

[X. 7.] νοίας. Ἐπιτρέπετε δὲ καὶ τοῖς πρεσβυτέροις [Did. προφήταις] ὑμῶν εὐχαριστεῖν.

CAP. XXVII.— Περὶ δὲ τοῦ μύρου οὕτως εὐχαριστήσατε "Εὐχαριστοῦμέν σοι, Θεὲ δημιουργὲ τῶν ὅλων, καὶ ὑπὲρ τῆς εὐωδίας τοῦ μύρου, καὶ ὑπὲρ τοῦ ἀθανάτου αἰῶνος οὗ ἐγνώρισας ἡμῖν διὰ Ἰησοῦ τοῦ παιδός σου· ὅτι σοῦ ἐστιν ἡ δόξα καὶ ἡ δύναμις εἰς τοὺς αἰῶνας· ἀμήν."

[XI. 1.] "Ὃς ἐὰν ἐλθὼν οὕτως εὐχαριστῇ, προσδέξασθαι αὐτὸν ὡς Χριστοῦ μαθητήν· ἐὰν δὲ ἄλλην διδαχὴν κηρύσσῃ παρ' ἣν ὑμῖν παρέδωκεν ὁ Χριστὸς δι' ἡμῶν, τῷ τοιούτῳ μὴ συγχωρεῖτε εὐχαριστεῖν· ὑβρίζει γὰρ ὁ τοιοῦτος τὸν Θεόν, ἤπερ δοξάζει.

[XII. 1.] CAP. XXVIII.— Πᾶς δὲ ὁ

of the Lord"[1]—God the Lord, who was manifested to us in the flesh. *If any one be holy, let him draw near; but if any one be not such, let him become such by repentance. Permit* also to your presbyters [*Did.* to your prophets], *to give thanks.*

CH. XXVII.—Concerning the ointment give thanks in this manner: We give Thee thanks, O God, the Creator of the whole world, both for the fragrancy of the ointment, and for the immortality which thou hast made known to us by Thy Son Jesus. For Thine is the glory and the power for ever. Amen. *Whosoever comes to you,* and gives thanks *in this manner, receive him* as a disciple of Christ. But if he preach another doctrine, different from that which Christ by us has delivered to you, such an one you must not permit to give thanks; for such an one rather affronts God than glorifies Him.

CH. XXVIII.—*But who-*

---
[1] 1 Cor. xvi. 22; Matt. xxi. 9; Mark xi. 10.

ἐρχόμενος πρὸς ὑμᾶς, δοκιμασθείς, οὕτω δεχέσθω· σύνεσιν γὰρ ἔχετε, καὶ δύνασθε γνῶναι* δεξιὰν ἢ ἀριστερὰν καὶ διακρῖναι ψευδοδιδασκάλους διδασκάλων. Ἐλθόντι μέν τοι τῷ διδασκάλῳ ἐκ ψυχῆς ἐπιχορηγήσατε τὰ δέοντα· τῷ δὲ ψευδοδιδασκάλῳ δώσετε μὲν τὰ † πρὸς χρείαν, οὐ παραδέξεσθε δὲ αὐτοῦ τὴν πλάνην, οὔτε μὴν συμπροσεύξησθε αὐτῷ, ἵνα μὴ συμμιανθῆτε αὐτῷ. Πᾶς προφήτης ἀληθινὸς ἢ διδάσκαλος ἐρχόμενος πρὸς ὑμᾶς ἄξιός ἐστι τῆς τροφῆς ὡς ἐργάτης λόγου δικαιοσύνης.

soever comes to you, let him be first examined, and then received; for ye have understanding, and are able to know the right hand from the left, and to distinguish false teachers from true teachers. But when a teacher comes to you, supply him with what he wants with all readiness. And even when a false teacher comes, you shall give him for his necessity, but shall not receive his error. Nor indeed may ye pray together with him, lest ye be polluted as well as he. *Every true Prophet or Teacher* that comes to you *is worthy of his maintenance, as being a labourer* in the word of righteousness.[1] [XIII. 1, 2.]

CAP. XXIX.—Πᾶσαν ἀπαρχὴν γεννημάτων ληνοῦ, ἅλωνος βοῶν τε καὶ προβάτων δώσεις τοῖς ἱερεῦσιν, ἵνα εὐλογηθῶσιν αἱ ἀποθῆκαι τῶν ταμείων σου καὶ τὰ ἐκφόρια τῆς γῆς σου, καὶ στηριχθῇς σίτῳ καὶ οἴνῳ καὶ ἐλαίῳ, καὶ αὐξηθῇ τὰ βουκόλια τῶν βοῶν σου καὶ τὰ ποίμνια τῶν προβάτων σου· πᾶσαν δεκάτην δώσεις τῷ ὀρφανῷ καὶ τῇ χήρᾳ, τῷ πτωχῷ καὶ τῷ προσηλύτῳ. Πᾶσαν ἀπαρχὴν ἄρτων

CH. XXIX.—*All the first-fruits of the winepress, the threshing-floor, the oxen, and the sheep*, shalt thou give to the priests,[2] that thy storehouses and garners and the products of thy land may be blessed, and thou mayst be strengthened with corn and wine and oil, and the herds of thy cattle and flocks of thy sheep may be increased. Thou shalt give the tenth of thy increase to the orphan, and to the widow, and to the [XIII. 3.]

---

[1] Matt. x. 41.   [2] Num. xviii.
* Lagarde: διαγνῶναι.   † Lagarde inserts δέοντα.

[XIII. 5, 6.] θερμῶν, κεραμίου οἴνου ἢ ἐλαίου ἢ μέλιτος ἢ ἀκροδρύων, σταφυλῆς ἢ τῶν ἄλλων τὴν ἀπαρχὴν δώ- [XIII. 7.] σεις τοῖς ἱερεῦσιν· ἀργυρίου δὲ καὶ* ἱματισμοῦ καὶ παντὸς κτήματος τῷ ὀρφανῷ καὶ τῇ χήρᾳ.

[XIV. 1.] CAP. XXX.—Τὴν ἀναστάσιμον τοῦ Κυρίου ἡμέραν, τὴν κυριακὴν φαμὲν, συνέρχεσθε ἀδιαλείπτως, εὐχαριστοῦντες τῷ Θεῷ καὶ ἐξομολογούμενοι ἐφ᾽ οἷς εὐηργέτησεν ἡμᾶς ὁ† Θεὸς διὰ Χριστοῦ ῥυσάμενος ἀγνοίας, πλάνης, δεσμῶν· ὅπως ἄμεμπτος ᾖ ἡ θυσία ὑμῶν καὶ εὐανάφορος Θεῷ, τῷ εἰπόντι περὶ τῆς οἰκουμενικῆς αὐτοῦ ἐκκλησίας ὅτι Ἐν παντὶ τόπῳ μοι προσενεχθήσεται θυμίαμα καὶ θυσία καθαρά· ὅτι βασιλεὺς μέγας ἐγώ εἰμι, λέγει Κύριος παντοκράτωρ, καὶ τὸ ὄνομά μου θαυμαστὸν ἐν τοῖς ἔθνεσι (Mal. i. 11, 14.)

[XV. 1.] CAP. XXXI.—Προχειρίσασθε δὲ ἐπισκόπους ἀξίους τοῦ Κυρίου καὶ πρεσβυτέρους καὶ διακό-

poor, and to the stranger. *All the first-fruits of thy hot bread, of thy barrels of wine, or oil,* or honey, or nuts, or grapes, or *the first-fruits* of other things, *shalt thou give to the priests; but those of silver and of garments, and of all sort of possessions, to the orphan and to the widow.*

CH. XXX.—On the day of the resurrection *of the Lord,* that is, *the Lord's day, assemble yourselves together, without fail, giving thanks to God,* and praising Him for those mercies God has bestowed upon you through Christ, and has delivered you from ignorance, error, and bondage, *that your sacrifice may be* unspotted, and acceptable to God, *who has* said concerning His universal church: " *In every place shall* incense and *a pure sacrifice be offered unto me;* for *I am a great* King, *saith the Lord* Almighty, *and my name is wonderful among the Gentiles."* [1]

CH. XXXI.—Do you first ordain *Bishops worthy of the Lord,* and Presbyters *and Deacons,* pious men, right-

---

[1] Mal. i. 11, 14.

* Lagarde : ἤ.

† Lagarde omits.

νους, ἄνδρας εὐλαβεῖς, δικαίους, πραεῖς, ἀφιλαργύρους, φιλαληθεῖς, δεδοκιμασμένους, ὁσίους, ἀπροσωπολήπτους, δυναμένους διδάσκειν τὸν λόγον τῆς εὐσεβείας, ὀρθοτομοῦντας ἐν τοῖς τοῦ Κυρίου δόγμασιν. Ὑμεῖς δὲ τιμᾶτε τούτους ὡς πατέρας, ὡς κυρίους, ὡς εὐεργέτας, ὡς τοῦ εὖ εἶναι αἰτίους.

Ἐλέγχετε δὲ ἀλλήλους, μὴ ἐν ὀργῇ, ἀλλ' ἐν μακροθυμίᾳ μετὰ χρηστότητος καὶ εἰρήνης. Πάντα τὰ προστεταγμένα ὑμῖν ὑπὸ τοῦ Κυρίου φυλάξατε. Γρηγορεῖτε ὑπὲρ τῆς ζωῆς ὑμῶν. Ἔστωσαν αἱ ὀσφύες ὑμῶν περιεζωσμέναι καὶ οἱ λύχνοι καιόμενοι, καὶ ὑμεῖς ὅμοιοι ἀνθρώποις προσδεχομένοις τὸν κύριον ἑαυτῶν πότε ἥξει, ἑσπέρας ἢ πρωὶ ἢ ἀλεκτοροφωνίας ἢ μεσονυκτίου· ᾗ γὰρ ὥρᾳ οὐ προσδοκῶσιν, ἐλεύσεται ὁ Κύριος, καὶ ἐὰν αὐτῷ ἀνοίξωσι, μακάριοι οἱ δοῦλοι ἐκεῖνοι, ὅτι εὑρέθησαν γρηγοροῦντες· ὅτι περιζώσεται καὶ ἀνακλινεῖ αὐτοὺς καὶ παρελθὼν διακονήσει αὐτοῖς. Νήφετε οὖν καὶ προσεύχεσθε μὴ ὑπνῶσαι εἰς θάνατον· οὐ γὰρ ὀνήσει ὑμᾶς τὰ πρότερα κατορθώματα [Did. ὁ πᾶς χρό-

ous, meek, free from the love of money, lovers of truth, approved, holy, not acceptors of persons, who are able to teach the word of piety, and rightly dividing the doctrines of the Lord.[1] *And* [XV. 2.] do ye honor such as your fathers, as your lords, as your benefactors, as the causes of your well-being. *Reprove* [XV. 3.] ye one another, not in anger, but in mildness, with kindness and *peace*. Observe all things that are commanded you by the Lord. *Be watch-* [XVI. 1.] *ful for your life.* "Let your loins be girded about, and your lights burning, and ye like unto men who wait for their Lord, when He will come, at even, or in the morning, or at cockcrowing, or at midnight. For at what hour they think not, the Lord will come; and if they open to Him, blessed are those servants, because they were found watching. For He will gird Himself, and will make them to sit down to meat, and will come forth and serve them."[1] Watch therefore, and pray, that ye do not sleep unto death. *For* your [XVI. 2.] former good deeds [*Did.* the whole time of your faith], *will not profit you*, if at the

---

[1] Tim. ii. 15.   [2] Luke xii. 35; Mark xiii. 35.

νος τῆς πίστεως ὑμῶν], ἐὰν εἰς τὰ ἔσχατα ὑμῶν ἀποπλανηθῆτε τῆς πίστεως τῆς ἀληθοῦς.

[XVI. 3.] CAP. XXXII. — Ἐν γὰρ ταῖς ἐσχάταις ἡμέραις πληθυνθήσονται οἱ ψευδοπροφῆται καὶ οἱ φθορεῖς τοῦ λόγου, καὶ στραφήσονται τὰ πρόβατα εἰς λύκους καὶ ἡ ἀγάπη εἰς μῖσος· πληθυνθείσης γὰρ τῆς [XVI. 4.] ἀνομίας, ψυγήσεται ἡ ἀγάπη τῶν πολλῶν, μισήσουσι γὰρ ἀλλήλους οἱ ἄνθρωποι καὶ διώξουσι καὶ προδώσουσι. Καὶ τότε φανήσεται ὁ κοσμοπλάνος, ὁ τῆς ἀληθείας ἐχθρὸς, ὁ τοῦ ψεύδους προστάτης, ὃν ὁ Κύριος Ἰησοῦς* ἀνελεῖ τῷ πνεύματι τοῦ στόματος αὐτοῦ ὁ διὰ χειλέων [XVI. 5.] ἀναιρῶν ἀσεβῆ· καὶ πολλοὶ σκανδαλισθήσονται ἐπ' αὐτῷ, οἱ† δὲ ὑπομείναντες εἰς τέλος, οὗτοι‡ [XVI. 6.] σωθήσονται. Καὶ τότε φανήσεται τὸ§ σημεῖον τοῦ υἱοῦ τοῦ ἀνθρώπου ἐν τῷ οὐρανῷ, εἶτα φωνὴ σάλπιγγος ἔσται δι' ἀρχαγγέλου καὶ μεταξὺ ἀναβίωσις τῶν κεκοιμημένων· καὶ τότε ἥξει [XVI. 7, 8.] ὁ Κύριος καὶ πάντες οἱ

CH. XXXII.—*For in the last days false prophets shall be multiplied, and such as corrupt* the word ; *and the sheep shall be changed into wolves, and love into hatred : for through the abounding of lawlessness* the love of many shall wax cold. *For men shall hate, and persecute, and betray one another. And then shall appear the deceiver of the world, the enemy of the truth, the prince of lies,*[1] whom the Lord Jesus " shall destroy with the spirit of His mouth, who takes away the wicked with his lips ; *and many shall be offended at Him. But they that endure to the* end, the same *shall be saved. And then shall appear the sign of the Son of man in heaven;* "[2] *and afterwards shall be the voice of a trumpet by the archangel ;*[3] *and in that interval shall be the revival of those that were asleep.* And then *shall the Lord come, and all the saints with Him,* with a great concussion *above the clouds,*

---

[1] 2 Thess. ii.   [2] Isa. xi. 4 ; Matt. xxiv.   [3] 1 Thess. iv. 16.

* Lagarde omits.   † Lagarde : ὁ δὲ ὑπομείνας.
‡ Lagarde : οὗτος.   § Lagarde reads ὁ υἱός.

ἅγιοι μετ' αὐτοῦ ἐν συσσεισμῷ ἐπάνω τῶν νεφελῶν μετ' ἀγγέλων δυνάμεως αὐτοῦ ἐπὶ θρόνου βασιλείας, κατακρῖναι τὸν κοσμοπλάνον διάβολον καὶ ἀποδοῦναι ἑκάστῳ κατὰ τὴν πρᾶξιν αὐτοῦ. Τότε ἀπελεύσονται οἱ μὲν πονηροὶ εἰς αἰώνιον κόλασιν, οἱ δὲ δίκαιοι πορεύσονται εἰς ζωὴν αἰώνιον, κληρονομοῦντες ἐκεῖνα, ἃ ὀφθαλμὸς οὐκ εἶδε καὶ οὖς οὐκ ἤκουσε καὶ ἐπὶ καρδίαν ἀνθρώπου οὐκ ἀνέβη, ἃ ἡτοίμασεν ὁ Θεὸς τοῖς ἀγαπῶσιν αὐτόν (1 Cor. ii. 9)· καὶ χαρήσονται ἐν τῇ βασιλείᾳ τοῦ Θεοῦ τῇ ἐν Χριστῷ Ἰησοῦ.

with the angels of His power, in the throne of His kingdom,[1] to condemn [the devil], the deceiver of the world, and to render to every one according to his deeds. "Then shall the wicked go away into eternal punishment, but the righteous shall go into eternal life,"[2] to inherit those things "which eye hath not seen, nor ear heard, nor have entered into the heart of man, such things as God hath prepared for them that love Him;"[3] and they shall rejoice in the kingdom of God, which is in Christ Jesus.

The remainder of the Seventh Book from ch. 33–49 has no bearing on the *Didache* and contains mostly prayers.

---

[1] Matt. xvi. 27.
[2] Matt. xxv. 46.
[3] 1 Cor. ii. 9.

A LETTER AND COMMUNICATION FROM METROPOLITAN BRYENNIOS.

[AFTER the sketch of the discoverer of the *Didache* was printed (Ch. III., pp. 8 and 9), I received from him an autobiographical sketch and letter which I here add, with the translation of my friend, Rev. Dr. Howard Crosby, an expert in modern as well as ancient Greek.]

PHILOTHEOS BRYENNIOS, Metropolitan of Nicomedia, born in 1833 at Constantinople of very poor parents, was educated in his primary learning in the schools of Tataūla. Tataūla or Tataula is a suburb of Constantinople, inhabited by ten or twelve thousand orthodox Greeks.

Being poor and lacking the necessary means for an education, he provided these by leading the music and by singing in the sacred temple of Saint Demetrius in that quarter, until, meeting with preferment and assistance from the then Metropolitan of Cyzicus (but afterward Patriarch of Constantinople) Joachim, he was admitted into the patriarchal seminary, situated not far from Byzantium in the small island of Chalce, and now still in a flourishing condition. The seminary is known as "The Theological School in Chalce of the Great Church of Christ." Here, after the conclusion of his studies, he was ordained deacon, and, having been created "Teacher of the Orthodox Theology" by the said school, he, through the preferment again of the Metropolitan of Cyzicus, and at the expense of the Greek banker in Constantinople, George Zariphe, was sent to Germany at the close of 1856 for a more complete training in his studies. He attended chiefly theological and philosophical lectures in the Universities of Leipzig, Berlin, and Munich.

In the beginning of 1861 he was summoned to Constantinople by his superior, Joachim II., who had then lately been transferred from the metropolitan see of Cyzicus to the patriarchal throne of Constantinople, and was introduced into the Theological School of Chalce as Professor of Ecclesiastical History, Exegesis, and other studies. In 1863, having been ordained a presbyter and having been honored with the honorary title of "Archimandrite of the œcumenical throne of Constantinople," he succeeded, in the mastership and direction of the said school, his own teacher, Constantine Typaldus, who resigned the mastership on account of old age. But not long afterward, when Joachim II. was removed from the patriarchal throne, he also resigned the mastership, but retained the chair of the before-mentioned theological studies.

In the patriarchate of Gregory VI., he was called to Constantinople and settled in December of 1867 as master and professor of the other great patriarchal school there in the Phanar— "The Great School of the Nation," which is the superior Greek gymnasium in Constantinople, which was restored shortly after the capture of the city under the Patriarch Gennadius Scholarius in the year 1457, and was from that date organized more and more perfectly from time to time, and has produced much fruit and comfort to the distressed Greek race throughout the East. Over this school Bryennios presided seven full years, having under him about six hundred youths, who by him and twelve other professors were taught sacred learning, Greek literature, rhetoric, the elements of philosophy, experimental physics, chemistry and natural history, general history, mathematics, and the Latin, French and Turkish languages.

In August, 1875, he went a second time to Germany, sent by the Holy Synod of Metropolitans and Patriarch, and was present at the conference of Old Catholics then being held at Bonn, having with him the archimandrite John, professor then in the Theological School of Chalce, but now Metropolitan of Cæsarea in Cappadocia.* In Bonn, where he became acquainted with many learned Englishmen and with the leaders of the Old Catholics, patriarchal letters brought the news to him that

---

[* That remarkable Conference of Old Catholics, Greek and Russian Catholics, and Anglo-Catholics, was held at Bonn, August 10-16, 1875, under the presiding genius and learning of the aged Dr. Döllinger of Munich, to adjust, if possible, the *Filioque* controversy, and agreed on six Theses on the eternal procession of the Holy Spirit from the Father alone through the Son, in essential harmony with the teaching of St. John of Damascus. See the Theses in Schaff, *Creeds of Christendom*, vol. ii., 552-554.]

he had been chosen Metropolitan of Serrae in Macedonia, and ordered him forthwith to join the assembly in Constantinople. So, returning home through Paris and Vienna, and being ordained Metropolitan Bishop of Serrae, he departed for Serrae in December, 1875.

In 1877 he was transferred to the Metropolitan see of Nicomedia, and continued from October, 1877, to October, 1884, a regular member of the patriarchal Synod in Constantinople, taking part in its more important questions and affairs.

In 1880 he went to Bucharest, as Commissioner of the Eastern Orthodox Patriarchal and other independent churches, for the settlement of the question which had long before arisen between the Roumanian Government and the aforesaid churches concerning the Greek monasteries that had been plundered under the rule of Kouza in Moldavia and Wallachia. And in the same year he was created Doctor of Theology, by the National University of Greece in Athens, and in 1884 the University of Edinburgh conferred upon him this honorary title.

Bryennios became known to the West by the publication of two remarkable memorials of Christian antiquity:

(1) "The two Epistles to the Corinthians of our holy father Clement, bishop of Rome, from a MS. of the Constantinopolitan Phanariot library of the most holy Sepulchre, now first edited entire with prolegomena and notes by Philotheos Bryennios, Metropolitan of Serrae. Constantinople, 1875."

(2) "The Teaching of the Twelve Apostles, from the Jerusalem MS., now first edited with prolegomena and notes, in which is a comparison and unpublished portion from the same MS. of the synopsis of the Old Testament by John Chrysostom, by Philotheos Bryennios, Metropolitan of Nicomedia. Constantinople, 1883."

In 1882 he was instructed by the Holy Synod of Metropolitans in Constantinople and the Patriarch Joachim III. to answer the Encyclical Letter of Pope Leo XIII. concerning Methodius and Cyrillus, the Apostles of the Slaves, which also he did by writing a series of articles in the theological periodical "Ecclesiastical Truth," published in Constantinople. These articles were afterwards published with the approbation and at the expense of the Holy Synod, and in a separate pamphlet bearing the title, "A Refutation of the Encyclical Letter of Pope Leo XIIL, by Philotheos Bryennios, Metropolitan of Nicomedia, first published in the 'Ecclesiastical Truth,' but now revised and with some additions republished with the approbation and at the expense of the Holy Synod of the Great Church of Christ. Constantinople, 1882." Large octavo, pp. 1–174.

He has also written in different periodicals and in the journals of Constantinople many other shorter essays, letters and discourses delivered by him at different times.

There was separately published his "Statement of the Condition of the Great School of the Nation, 1867–1875, by Philotheos Bryennios, Archimandrite and Master of the school. Constantinople."

There still remains unpublished the MS. of his Ecclesiastical History, used continually in many copies by his numerous pupils.

LEARNED SIR:

I gladly received your bundle of letters and read all with pleasure. In the within you have connectedly what you desired. Perhaps the items noted are many; but you can accept whatever is worth mention and useful among them, and mark out and omit whatever is superfluous and of no use.

NICOMED. PHILOTHEOS.

NICOMEDIA *Feby.* ⅙, 1885.

Rev. Dr. PHILIP SCHAFF, New York.

Φιλόθεος Βρυέννιος, μητροπολίτης Νικομηδείας, γεννηθεὶς τὸ 1833 ἐν Κωνσταντινουπόλει ἐκ γονέων πτωχοτάτων, ἐξεπαιδεύθη τὴν πρώτην ἐγκύκλιον παίδευσιν ἐν τοῖς διδασκαλείοις Ταταούλων—ἔστι δὲ τὰ Τατάουλα ἢ Ταταῦλα προάστειον τῆς Κωνσταντινουπόλεως ὑπὸ 10—12 χιλιάδων ὀρθοδόξων ἑλλήνων οἰκούμενον. Πτωχὸς ὢν καὶ τῶν πρὸς ἐκπαίδευσιν ἀναγκαίων ὑστερούμενος ἐπορίζετο ταῦτα κανοναρχῶν καὶ ψάλλων ἐν τῷ αὐτόθι ἱερῷ ναῷ τοῦ ἁγίου Δημητρίου, ἕως οὗ τυχὼν τῆς προστασίας καὶ βοηθείας τοῦ τότε μητροπολίτου Κυζίκου, ὕστερον δὲ πατριάρχου Κωνσταντινουπόλεως, Ἰωακείμ, εἰσήχθη εἰς τὸ οὐ μακρὰν τοῦ Βυζαντίου ἐπὶ τῆς μικρᾶς νήσου Χάλκης κείμενον. καὶ νῦν ἔτι ἀκμάζον πατριαρχικὸν Σεμινάριον—"Ἡ ἐν Χάλκῃ Θεολογικὴ Σχολὴ τῆς τοῦ Χριστοῦ Μεγάλης ἐκκλησίας". Ἐνταῦθα διάκονος μετὰ τὸ πέρας τῶν μαθημάτων ἐχειροτονήθη, καὶ "διδάσκαλος τῆς ὀρθοδόξου θεολογίας" ὑπὸ τῆς εἰρημένης Σχολῆς ἀναγορευθείς, τῇ προστασίᾳ καὶ αὖθις τοῦ μητροπολίτου Κυζίκου, ἀναλώμασι δὲ τοῦ ἐν Κωνσταντινουπόλει ἕλληνος τραπεζίτου Γεωργίου Ζαρίβη εἰς Γερμανίαν ἀπεστάλη τελευτῶντος τοῦ 1856 πρὸς τελειοτέραν ἐν τοῖς μαθήμασι κατάρτισιν. Διήκουσε δὲ θεολογικῶν μάλιστα καὶ φιλοσοφικῶν μαθημάτων ἐν τοῖς πανεπιστημίοις Λειψίας, Βερολίνου καὶ Μονάχου (München). Ἀρχομένου δὲ τοῦ 1861 προσεκλήθη εἰς Κωνσταντινούπολιν ὑπὸ τοῦ προστάτου αὐτοῦ Ἰωακεὶμ τοῦ Β', ἀρτίως τότε ἀπὸ τῆς μητροπόλεως Κυζίκου εἰς τὸν πατριαρχικὸν θρόνον Κωνσταντινουπόλεως μετατεθέντος, καὶ εἰς τὴν ἐν Χάλκῃ θεολογικὴν Σχολὴν εἰσάγεται ὡς καθηγητὴς τῆς ἐκκλησιαστικῆς ἱστορίας, τῆς ἐξηγητικῆς καὶ ἄλλων μαθημάτων. Τὸ 1863 χειροτονηθεὶς πρεσβύτερος καὶ τῷ τιμητικῷ τίτλῳ τοῦ ἀρχιμανδρίτου τοῦ οἰκουμενικοῦ θρόνου Κωνσταντινουπόλεως τιμηθείς, διαδέχεται ἐν τῇ σχολαρχίᾳ καὶ διευθύνσει τῆς ῥηθείσης Σχολῆς τὸν ἑαυτοῦ διδάσκαλον Κωνσταντῖνον τὸν Τυπάλδον παραιτησάμενον τὴν σχολαρχίαν γήρως ἕνεκεν. Ἀλλὰ μετ' οὐ πολὺ ἐκβληθέντος τοῦ πατριαρχικοῦ θρόνου Ἰωακεὶμ τοῦ Β', παρητήσατο καὶ αὐτὸς τὴν σχολαρχίαν, οὐ μὴν δὲ καὶ τὴν ἕδραν τῶν εἰρημένων θεολογικῶν μαθημάτων. Ἐπὶ πατριάρχου Γρηγορίου τοῦ ς' προσκληθεὶς εἰς Κωνσταντινούπολιν κατεστάθη κατὰ τὸν Δεκέμβριον τοῦ 1867 σχολάρχης καὶ καθηγητὴς τῆς αὐτόθι ἐν Φαναρίῳ εὑρισκομένης ἑτέρας μεγάλης πατριαρχικῆς Σχολῆς—"Μεγάλη τοῦ Γένους Σχολή"—, ἥτις ἐστὶ τὸ τελειότερον ἐν Κωνσταντινουπόλει ἑλληνικὸν γυμνάσιον, ἀνακαινισθεῖσα μικρὸν μετὰ τὴν ἅλωσιν ἐπὶ πατριάρχου Γενναδίου τοῦ Σχολαρίου ἐν ἔτει 1457, καὶ ἔκτοτε ἐπὶ τὸ τελειότερον ἑκάστοτε συγκροτουμένη καὶ πολλὰ τῷ ταλαιπώρῳ τῶν ἑλλήνων ἔθνει κατὰ τὴν Ἀνατολὴν καρποφοροῦσα καὶ παραμυθουμένη. Τῆς Σχολῆς ταύτης προέστη ὁ Βρυέννιος ἑπτὰ ὅλα ἔτη, ἔχων ὑπ' αὐτῷ περὶ τοὺς 600 νέους διδασκομένους ὑπ' αυτοῦ τε καὶ ἑτέρων 12 καθηγητῶν τὰ ἱερὰ μαθήματα, τὰ ἑλληνικά, τὴν ῥητορικήν, στοιχεῖα φιλοσοφίας, πειραματικῆς φυσικῆς, χημείας καὶ φυσικῆς ἱστορίας, γενικὴν ἱστορίαν, μαθηματικὰ καὶ τὰς γλώσσας λατινικήν, γαλλικὴν καὶ τουρκικήν.

Κατὰ τὸν Αὔγουστον τοῦ 1875 ἀνέβη τὸ δεύτερον εἰς Γερμανίαν ἀποσταλεὶς ὑπὸ τῆς ἐν Κωνσταντινουπόλει περὶ τὸν πατριάρχην ἱερᾶς Συνόδου τῶν μητροπολιτῶν, καὶ παρέστη τῇ τηνικαῦτα ἐν Βόνῃ γενομένῃ Conference τῶν Παλαιοκαθολικῶν, ἔχων μεθ' ἑαυτοῦ τὸν ἀρχιμανδρίτην Ἰωάννην, καθηγητὴν τότε τῆς Θεολογικῆς Σχολῆς τῆς Χάλκης, νῦν δὲ μητροπολίτην Καισαρείας Καππαδοκίας. Ἐν Βόνῃ, ἔνθα γνώριμος ἐγένετο πολλοῖς τῶν λογίων ἄγγλων καὶ τοῖς ἡγουμένοις τῶν Παλαιοκαθολικῶν, γράμματα πατριαρχικὰ τὴν ἀγγελίαν ἐκόμισαν αὐτῷ ὅτι μητροπολίτης ἐξελέγη Σερρῶν (ἐν Μακεδονίᾳ) καὶ παρεκελεύοντο ἀνυπερθέτως ἅψασθαι τῆς εἰς Κωνσταντινούπολιν ἀγούσης· ὅθεν καὶ διὰ Παρισίων καὶ Βιέννης εἰς τὰ ἴδια ἐπανακάμψας καὶ ἐπίσκοπος μητροπολίτης Σερρῶν χειροτονηθείς, εἰς Σέρρας ἀπῆρεν τὸν Δεκεμβρ. τοῦ 1875.

Τὸ 1877 μετετέθη εἰς τὴν μητρόπολιν Νικομηδείας καὶ διετέλεσεν ἀπὸ τοῦ Ὀκτωβρίου τοῦ 1877—τοῦ Ὀκτωβρίου τοῦ 1884 μέλος τακτικὸν τῆς ἐν Κωνσταντινουπόλει πατριαρχικῆς Συνόδου, μετασχὼν τῶν σπουδαιοτέρων ζητημάτων καὶ ὑποθέσεων αὐτῆς. Τὸ 1880 ἦλθεν εἰς Βουκορέστιον ὡς ἐπίτροπος τῶν ἐν Ἀνατολῇ ὀρθοδόξων πατριαρχικῶν καὶ λοιπῶν αὐτοκεφάλων ἐκκλησιῶν πρὸς διευθέτησιν τοῦ μεταξὺ τῆς ρουμουνικῆς Κυβερνήσεως καὶ τῶν εἰρημένων ἐκκλησιῶν πρὸ πολλοῦ ἀναφυέντος ζητήματος περὶ τῶν ἐπὶ ἡγεμόνος Κούζα κατὰ τὴν Μολδαβίαν καὶ Βλαχίαν διαρπαγέντων ἑλληνικῶν μοναστηρίων. Κατὰ τὸ αὐτὸ δὲ ἔτος ἀνηγορεύθη ὑπὸ τοῦ ἐν Ἀθήναις ἐθνικοῦ τῆς Ἑλλάδος πανεπιστημίου διδάκτωρ τῆς θεολογίας, τὸ δὲ 1884 ἀπένειμεν αὐτῷ τιμητικῶς τὸν τίτλον τοῦτον καὶ τὸ ἐν Ἐδιμβούργῳ πανεπιστήμιον.

Ὁ Βρυέννιος ἐγένετο γνωστὸς τῇ Δύσει διὰ τῆς ἐκδόσεως δύο ἀξιολογωτάτων μνημείων τῆς χριστιανικῆς ἀρχαιότητος, ἅπερ εἰσὶ 1) "Τοῦ ἐν ἁγίοις πατρὸς ἡμῶν Κλήμεντος ἐπισκόπου Ῥώμης αἱ δύο πρὸς Κορινθίους ἐπιστολαί, ἐκ χειρογράφου τῆς ἐν Φαναρίῳ Κωνσταντινουπόλεως βιβλιοθήκης τοῦ παναγίου Τάφου, νῦν πρῶτον ἐκδιδόμεναι πλήρεις μετὰ προλεγομένων καὶ σημειώσεων ὑπὸ Φιλοθέου Βρυεννίου μητροπολίτου Σερρῶν. Ἐν Κωνσταντινουπόλει 1875." 2) "Διδαχὴ τῶν δώδεκα ἀποστόλων ἐκ τοῦ ἱεροσολυμιτικοῦ χειρογράφου νῦν πρῶτον ἐκδιδομένη μετὰ προλεγομένων καὶ σημειώσεων, ἐν οἷς καὶ τῆς Συνόψεως τῆς Π. Δ., τῆς ὑπὸ Ἰωάννου τοῦ Χρυσοστόμου, σύγκρισις καὶ μέρος ἀνέκδοτον ἀπὸ τοῦ αὐτοῦ χειρογράφου, ὑπὸ Φιλοθέου Βρυεννίου μητροπολίτου Νικομηδείας. Ἐν Κωνσταντινουπόλει 1883."—Τὸ 1882 ἀνετέθη αὐτῷ ὑπὸ τῆς ἐν Κωνσταντινουπόλει ἱερᾶς Συνόδου τῶν μητροπολιτῶν καὶ τοῦ τότε πατριάρχου Ἰωακείμ τοῦ Γ΄ ἀπαντῆσαι πρὸς τὴν ἐγκύκλιον τοῦ πάπα Λέοντος τοῦ ΙΓ΄ περὶ Μεθοδίου καὶ Κυρίλλου τῶν ἀποστόλων τῶν Σλαύων, ὃ καὶ ἐποίησε γράψας σειρὰν ἄρθρων ἐν τῷ ἐν Κωνσταντινουπόλει ἐκδιδομένῳ θεολογικῷ περιοδικῷ συγγράμματι "Ἐκκλησιαστικὴ Ἀλήθεια." Τὰ ἄρθρα ταῦτα ἐξεδόθησαν ὕστερον ἐγκρίσει καὶ δαπάνῃ τῆς ἱερᾶς Συνόδου καὶ ἐν ἰδίῳ φυλλαδίῳ φέροντι ἐπιγραφὴν "Πάπα Λέοντος ΙΓ΄ ἐγκυκλίου ἐπιστολῆς ἔλεγχος ὑπὸ Φιλοθέου Βρυεννίου μητροπολίτου Νικομηδείας, δημοσιευθεὶς τὸ πρῶτον ἐν τῇ "Ἐκκλ. Ἀληθείᾳ," νῦν δὲ ἀναθεωρηθεὶς καὶ ἐν μέρει διασκευασθεὶς ὑπ᾽ αὐτοῦ ἐκδίδοται αὖθις ἐγκρίσει καὶ δαπάνῃ τῆς ἱερᾶς Συνόδου τῆς τοῦ Χριστοῦ Μεγάλης ἐκκλησίας. Ἐν Κωνσταντινουπόλει 1882." εἰς μέγ. ὄγδοον σελ. 1-174.

Ὁ αὐτὸς ἔγραψεν ἐν διαφόροις περιοδικοῖς καὶ ἐν ἐφημερίσι τῆς Κωνσταντινουπόλεως καὶ πολλὰς ἄλλας βραχυτέρας διατριβάς, ἐπιστολὰς καὶ λόγους ἐκφωνηθέντας ὑπ᾽ αὐτοῦ κατὰ διαφόρους καιρούς. Ἰδίᾳ ἐξεδόθησαν αἱ τούτου "ἐκθέσεις περὶ τῆς καταστάσεως τῆς Μεγάλης τοῦ Γένους Σχολῆς 1867-1875, ὑπὸ Φιλοθέου Βρυεννίου ἀρχιμανδρίτου καὶ σχολάρχου. Ἐν Κωνσταντινουπόλει." Ἀνέκδοτον μένει εἰσέτι τὸ χειρόγραφον τῆς ἐκκλησιαστικῆς αὐτοῦ ἱστορίας, φερόμενον καὶ νῦν ἔτι ἐν χερσὶ τῶν πολυαρίθμων αὐτοῦ μαθητῶν ἐν πολλοῖς ἀντιγράφοις.—

Ἐλλόγιμε ἄνερ,

Ἄσμενος ἐκομισάμην τῶν σῶν γραμμάτων τὸ θάτερον καὶ εὐγνωμόνως ἀνέγνων ταῦτα. Ἐν τῷδε συνημμένως ἔχεις τὸ ζητηθέν. Ἴσως πολλὰ τὰ σημειωθέντα· ἀλλὰ οὐ ὅτι μὲν λόγου ἄξιον καὶ χρήσιμον ἐν τούτοις δέξαι, εἰ ἡ δὲ περιττὸν καὶ ἄχρηστον ἐξουδενώσας ἄφες.

Ἐν Νικομηδείᾳ
10/22 φεβρ. 1885

[signature]

Rev. D. Philip Schaff
New-York

FIRST APPENDIX.

ADDITIONS TO THE LITERATURE ON THE DIDACHE,

From May, 1885, till March, 1886, alphabetically arranged.

(Comp. Ch. XXXIII.)

BINNIE, WILLIAM, D.D. (Prof. of Church History in the Free Church College of Aberdeen), "in The British and Foreign Evangelical Review." London and Edinburgh, Oct. 1885, pp. 640–660.
The following is a brief summary. The *Did.* is "the most valuable treatise in the collection of the Apostolic Fathers, with the single exception of Clement's Ep. to the Romans." It dates from the same period, *i. e.* the close of the first century, if not earlier, probably from Egypt (?). The purely ethical character of the first part does not prove an ignorance of dogmatic teaching, but the latter part assumes in "Church members a familiar acquaintance with the gospel history and with such central verities as the Divinity of Christ." The author was perfectly familiar with Matthew and Luke but not with the Epistles, and proves (against Baur) the existence of orthodox Christianity independent of the Apostle Paul. The Church was already an organized body, not a mere concourse of individual believers. It was served by ministers called to their office by inward impulse and the choice and election of their brethren. Some were travelling preachers, like Paul and Barnabas, or Wesley and Whitfield, others resident pastors of one particular flock. The rest of the article is taken up with a discussion of the constitution of the Church, the assumed identity of presbyters and bishops, the itinerant ministry and the settled and salaried pastorate. Dr. B. finds in the *Did.* the essential elements of Presbyterian church polity. But where are the Apostles and Prophets?

BORNEMANN, W. (Privatdocent in Göttingen), in the "Theol. Literaturzeitung," ed. by Harnack & Schürer, Leipzig, 1885, No. 17 fol. 413, directs attention to a passage of ORIGEN, *Hom.* vi. *in Librum Judicum* preserved only in a Latin translation (*Opera*, ed. Lommatsch xi. 258, Migne's ed. ii. f. 975), which betrays acquaintance with the *Didache*. Origen says:

"*Antequam panis coelestis consequamur annonam et carnibus Agni immolati satiemur, antequam* VERÆ VITIS QUÆ ASCENDIT DE RADICE DAVID, *sanguine inebriemur, donec parvuli sumus et lacte alimur, et initiorum Christi sermonem tenemus, tamquam, parvuli sub procuratoribus agimus et actoribus angelis.*" The *vera vitis de radice David*, is undoubtedly the $\dot{\alpha}\gamma \iota \alpha$ $\overset{"}{\alpha}\mu\pi\epsilon\lambda o\varsigma$ $\varDelta\alpha\beta\iota\delta$ of the eucharistic prayer in the *Didache* (IX. 2). The term was used also by Clement of Alexandria, as quoted p. 191. It confirms the interpretation there given that it is probably a mystic name of Christ with reference to the parable of the Vine, John xv. 1, and the eucharistic blood.

Bornemann derives from the passage an argument for the Egyptian origin of the *Did.* as advocated by Harnack. But Ch. IX. 4, points to a hilly country (see p. 192, compared with the Egyptian prayer of Pseudo-Athanasius, p. 194).

For another possible reference of Origen to the *Did.* see POTWIN below.

DELITZSCH, FRANZ (Doctor and Prof. of Theology in Leipzig) published an interesting note on the "Holy Vine of David" in his tract *Die Bibel und der Wein, ein Thirza-Vortrag*, Leipzig 1885, and in "The Expositor" (London and New York) for Jan. 1886, pp. 68 and 69. He holds the *Didache* to be "an ancient and beyond doubt *Jewish-Christian Church Order*," and conjectures that the "Holy Vine of David" was a name of the Messiah. He bases his view on Ps. lxxx. 15, 16 as rendered in the Aramaic Targum: "Elohim Zebaoth, oh ! turn now again, look from heaven and see, and remember in mercy *this vine* [Israel]; and *the vine-shoot* which Thy right hand hath planted, and the *King Messiah (Malka Meshicha)*, whom Thou hast established for Thyself." The Hebrew reads : . . . "visit *this vine*. And protect *him* whom Thy right hand hath planted, and *the son* whom Thou hast firmly bound to Thee." Delitzsch quotes also a passage from the Talmud (*Berachoth*, 57a): "He who sees a choice vine in a dream, may look for the Messiah, for it is written (Gen. xlix. 11), 'He bindeth to the vine his foal, and to the choice vine his ass's colt.'" He adds: "The two references to the source of the figure (Vine = Messiah) in the newly discovered document of the early Church mutually supplement each other."

GEBHARDT, Dr. OSCAR VON (the discoverer of the Latin fragment of the *Didache*), in a letter from Berlin Sept. 28, 1885, intended for publication, says:

"The especial merit of your book on the *Didache* (of which I already expressed my grateful acknowledgment) seems to me to consist chiefly in this fact : that upon all the far-branching questions which this highly important monument of the ancient Church has raised, it gives us the proper orientation for a full understanding by its comprehensive contents, and its use of the best, yet often very remote and inaccessible helps. And such a comprehensive and exhaustive work was a necessity, since the *Didache*, although so small, as far as the number of its pages goes, had called forth a considerable literature. This particularly difficult labor, however, required a scholar who, by reason of his own study in the sources, was master in numerous departments ; and such men are very rare in our times. It is only the recognition of a fact, which no one acquainted with your works will deny, when I expressly claim such a qualification for you.

"You will receive especial thanks in many circles for your linking the doctrines and practices of the ancient Church as they are expressed in the *Didache*, with the many controversial questions of the modern Church.

"I have in mind especially that section of your book where you treat of the sacrament of baptism. The pertinent passage in the *Didache* (Ch. VII.) is truly of the greatest interest, because up to this time we did not possess so old and so unmistakable a testimony for the facultative (optional and exceptional) validity of baptism by aspersion. But you correctly lay stress upon the fact that, in regard to the matter itself, we learn nothing new ; that the *Didache* rather confirms what has been, according to all known sources, the practice of the Church of the olden time.

"If I remember correctly, you remark, in this connection, that there are not wanting those who consider the *Didache*, as we have it in the Constantinopolitan MS., to be a forgery of a later date. In regard to this assertion I may be allowed to say that, quite apart from the contents of the writing, the external appearance of the MS. itself bears quite irrefutable testimony to its genuineness. An idea of it one can derive from the specimen pages you give on pp. 4 and 6 of your work. One must, indeed, understand little of Greek palæography to be, even for a moment, in any doubt. Whoever would maintain the hypothesis of forgery must set the document high up in antiquity ; for not even the wildest fancy would assign it to any of the centuries immediately preceding the eleventh, in which the MS. was written (1056).

"The external appearance of your *Oldest Church Manual* speaks for itself, and does not require any praise on my part."

HARRIS, J. RENDEL, Fellow of Clare College, Cambridge (for some time Associate Professor of New Testament Greek and Palæography in Johns Hopkins University, Baltimore, returned to England, 1885 ; see pp. 151 and 153): *The Teaching of the Apostles and the Sibylline Books*. Cambridge (H. W. Wallis). 1885. 36 pp. The learned author says (p. 3): "Bryennios' little tract is increasing in recognized importance, almost from day to day. It is no longer a question of mere identification between a lost book and a found book by means of the number of lines in a MS. and the record of a stichometric table of the middle ages : *non numerandi sed ponderandi sunt versus ;* and being weighed, they require for a counterpoise the largest stones which the Ecclesiastical historian can find in his bag. In fact, the $\Delta\iota\delta\alpha\chi\dot{\eta}$ $\tau\tilde{\omega}\nu$ $\mathrm{'}A\pi\omicron\sigma\tau\acute{\omicron}\lambda\omega\nu$ is the keystone of Church history, whether we include under that term the New Testament records or those of the first four centuries of the Faith ; and, if we widen our conception of Church history so as to include the Semitic origins of Christianity, it is the bridge that spans the gulf between the Church and the Synagogue from which it was so early divided. It is surprising that so small a book should have so much to say." He thinks that "we are a long way yet from the place where we can assert that the last word has been said either on the text or its interpretation." The *Doctrina Petri* forms a companion volume to the *Did.* and "may even have a nexus internal and external with it."

Prof. Harris points out a number of interesting coincidences between the *Didache* and the so-called *Sibylline Oracles*[*]—a collection of prophecies and religious teachings in Greek hexameter under the assumed authority and inspiration of a Sibyl, partly of Jewish and Gentile, partly of Jewish-Christian origin, best edited in Greek and German by Dr. Friedlieb,

---

[*] Sabatier (*La Didachè*, p. 51) had previously pointed to this resemblance : "*Les conclusions de l'auteur de la Did. sont très voisins de celles du Pseudo-Phocylide, qui écrivit vers le milieu du premier siècle un manuel de morale juive, simplifié pour les paiens. Voir : Bernays, Ueber das phokyl. Gedicht*, p. 130-150." Comp. p. 79-80.

of Breslau (*Die Sibyllinischen Weissagungen vollständig gesammelt*, etc. Leipzig, 1852, 229 and cxxiii. pp.). This curious book was freely quoted by the early Christian Apologists along-side with the Old Testament prophecy as an argument for Christianity, and the Sibyl is mentioned with David in the famous *Dies Iræ* as a witness of the day of judgment ("*teste David cum Sibylla*"). Harris maintains that parts of the *Did.* have been versified by the Sibyllist or Pseudo-Phocylides in the first or second century.

The coincidences occur in the teaching of Two Ways, the Way of Life and the Way of Death (*Orac. Sib.* vi. 9; viii. 399; *Did.* I. 1); in several moral precepts concerning love to our neighbor and alms-giving; in the allusion to the custom of baptism by immersion in running water (*Did.* VII. 1, ἐν ὕδατι ζῶντι,, *O. Sib.* iv. 164: ἐν ποταμοῖς λούσασθε ὅλον δέμας ἀενάοισι, translated by Friedlieb: "*Und in schwellenden Strömen waschet die ganze Gestalt ab*"); and in the teaching on the Second Advent, which is to be preceded by the triple signs, and by Belial or Beliar, *i. e.*, Antichrist and his false miracles (*O. Sib.* ii. 167; iii., 52, 86; comp. the κοσμοπλάνος in *Did.* XVI. 4). Harris explains the ἐκπέτασις in heaven (*Did.* XVI. 7) of the sign of the cross, and quotes besides patristic passages three parallel passages from *O. Sib.* viii. 303 (ἐκπετάσει χέρας, of the crucifixion); viii. 251; I. 372 (ἐκπετάσει χεῖρας καὶ πάντα μετρήσῃ).

I may add a passage of the Sibyl on the final fate of the wicked (ii. 2, 53 sqq.) which Friedlieb thus renders:

"*Und es werden dann Alle hindurch durch den brennenden Strom gehn,*
Und durch die Flamme, die nimmer erlischt. Jedoch die Gerechten
Werden alle gerettet hierbei. Die Gottlosen aber
Gehen auf ewig zu Grund (ὀλοῦντα εἰς αἰῶνας ὅλους)."

The description which follows shows that the author means by destruction not annihilation, but everlasting punishment; for he says, "the wicked will desire death as a good, but it will flee from them" (v. 208, 209).

JESSUP, Rev. Dr. HENRY H. (American Presbyt. missionary at Beirut, Syria), in reply to a letter of inquiry, Jan. 4, 1886, corrected an error in a quotation from another book concerning the Syrian modes of Baptism. The quotation has been omitted in this revised edition. Dr. Jessup's letter was published in full in the New York "Independent" for Feb. 18, 1886. Dr. Jessup confirms our view on the mode of Baptism in the East.

KRAWUTZCKY, Dr. (Prof. at Breslau), whose two remarkable papers on the *Didache* are noticed on pp. 23, 137 and 145, desires me, in a private letter of Aug. 5, 1885, to state in a second edition that he does not mean to charge the *Didache* with Ebionism proper, but only with a leaning towards it (*ebionitisirende Richtung*), which the author had *before* the revival of Ebionism in the second half of the second century. "*Die Zwölfapostellehre war seine* ERSTLINGSCHRIFT *und noch vor seiner Verbindung mit Montanus sowie erst recht vor seinem Auftreten als ebionitischen Sectenstifters entstanden.*" He adds: "*Ich finde Ihre Arbeit ebenso interessant und schätzenswert als inhaltreich, wie weit immer auch die beiderseitigen Auffassungen der Vorlage auseinander gehen. Der weitere Fortschritt der Forschungen dürfte leicht hier noch eine grössere Annäherung herbeiführen.*" A wish which I heartily reciprocate.

LECHLER. DR. GOTTHARD VICTOR (Prof. of Theol. in Leipzig): *Das Apostolische und Nachapostolische Zeitalter. . . Dritte vollständig neu bearbeitete Aufl.* Karlsruhe und Leipzig, 1885. In this thorough reconstruction of a work which appeared first in 1851 as a prize essay of the Teyler Theol. Soc. of Haarlem, the venerable author does full justice to the *Didache* and its importance for the history of the post-apostolic age, pp. 553–558, and 568–593. His views independently agree with those expressed in this book, except that he assigns it (with Harnack) to *Gentile* Christianity (p. 592) on account of the inscription τοῖς ἔθνεσιν (which, however, no more proves this than the μαθητεύσατε πάντα τὰ ἔθνη in Matt. xxviii. 19).

He maintains (against Bryennios, Harnack, and Krawutzcky) the priority of the *Didache* over the Ep. of Barnabas, and traces the former to the very border of the Apostolic Age (though not as far back as Sabatier). The *Did.* (III. 10) uses the poetic and rare ἄτερ θεοῦ, which Barn. in the parallel passage (xix. 6) changes into the more usual ἄνευ θεοῦ. The *Did.* adheres to biblical simplicity, while Barn. is artificial and overwrought. The former speaks of the "Teaching of the Apostles," the latter adds a mysterious "*Gnosis* to the Teaching;" the "Way of Life," and the "Way of Death" in the *Did.* became in Barn. a "Way of Light," and a "Way of Darkness" or of "Satan." The *Did.* quotes from Matthew simply as "gospel," Barn. as "Scripture" (ὡς γέγραπται), which implies ecclesiastical reception into the canon. The *Did.* is also older than Hermas.

The *Did.* shows the great stress laid by the Apostolic Church on practical Christianity and pure, even ascetic, morality in contrast with surrounding heathen corruption.

Lechler finds in the *Did.* a recognition of the divinity of Christ, because the baptismal formula (VII. 1, 3) implies it, and because it declares him to be the author of eternal life (IX. 2; X. 1, 2), which is meant also in the "Way of Life," and calls him "the Lord," and "our Lord" in the sense of Jehovah; for it applies to him (XIV. 5) the prophetic passage, Zech. xiv. 5, ἥξει κύριος ὁ θεός, and identifies the coming of Christ on the clouds of heaven with the coming of *God* himself (XVI. 6). The term κυριότης (IV. 1) signifies "*die göttliche Herrscherwürde Christi.*" The fact that the κοσμοπλάνος shall appear *as if he were* the son of God (ὡς υἱὸς θεοῦ, XVI. 4), implies that Christ is *really* the Son of God. Lechler finds also an allusion to the blood of Christ in the designation "the holy vine of David" (IX. 2). He understands the conclusion of Ch. XVI. in the premillennarian sense of a glorious reign of Christ on earth before the *general* resurrection and judgment.

LIGHTFOOT, Dr. J. B. (Bishop of Durham), in his great work on *S. Ignatius and S. Polycarp*, London, 1885, vol. i., 739, has a brief note on the *Didache*, in which he reaffirms his former opinion (see p. 149) about the antiquity and church organization, but changes his view about the Egyptian origin of the *Did.* (in both respects confirming our own views). I give the passage in full:

"After the portion relating to the ministry was printed off, the remarkable document entitled Διδαχή τῶν δώδεκα ἀποστόλων was given to the world by Bryennios (1884). It seems to me to confirm very strongly the historical views put forward by me in the essay, 'On the Christian Ministry,' to which I have here referred.* Nor does it necessitate any modification of what I have written in this discussion on the genuineness of the Epistles of Ignatius. As I stated briefly in a paper read at the Carlisle Church Congress (1884), the indications in the Διδαχή seem to me to point to a very early age. Among those who maintain the opposite view, the most thorough and learned discussion is that of Harnack (*Texte u. Untersuchungen*, II. ii., p. 63 sq.), who places it between A.D. 135 (A.D. 140) and A.D. 165 (p. 159). Yet it seems not a little strange to assign to a document, of which he himself says (p. 101) that the ecclesiastical organization more closely resembles that of S. Paul in the Epistle to the Corinthians than that ' of the author of the Epistle to the Ephesians,' a date bordering close upon the age of Irenæus. The First Epistle to the Corinthians was written A.D. 57, *i. e*, nearly a century before the medium date (A.D. 150) between the limits, which he allows to the Διδαχή. The great work of Irenæus was written during the episcopate of Eleutherus (A.D. 175-189), and therefore forty years later at the outside. On what conceivable grounds of reason or experience can we suppose that the development of the Church was so very slow during that preceding century, and so exceptionally fast during these succeeding decades? It still appears to me that the indications in the Διδαχή point to the later decades of the first century, though a little more latitude may be allowed, if it emanated from Egypt, where the progress of ecclesiastical organization was apparently slower than elsewhere. The passage, however (p. ix), which speaks of the corn, from which the eucharistic bread is made, as having 'been scattered *on the mountains*,' seems fatal to Egypt as its locality.† I find that Sabatier (*La Didache*, p. 165, Paris, 1885) places it even earlier than I had ventured to do, and dates it about the middle of the first century, before the great missionary journeys of Paul.'"

In the course of private correspondence, Bishop Lightfoot directed my attention to his note on Col. ii. 12, for his view on the Baptismal question as presented by Paul (in confirmation of my exposition of the *Didache*, Ch. VII.). It is as follows (*St. Paul's Epistles to the Colossians and Philemon*, p. 250):

"Baptism is the grave of the old man, and the birth of the new. As he sinks beneath the Baptismal waters, the believer buries there all his corrupt

---

* Especially the identity of bishops and presbyters, concerning which Bishop Lightfoot says, in his *Com. on Philippians*, p. 93: "It is a fact now generally recognized by theologians of all shades of opinion, that in the language of the New Testament the same office in the Church is called indifferently 'bishop' (ἐπίσκοπος) and 'elder' or 'presbyter' (πρεσβύτερος)." The question is discussed in this book, p. 73-75. Since then two books have appeared which take the same ground on the episcopal question: Ernst Kühl, *Die Gemeindeverfassung in den Pastoralbriefen*, Berlin, 1885, and Joh. Müller, *Die Verfassung der christlichen Kirche in den ersten beiden Jahrhunderten und die Beziehung derselben zu der Kritik der Pastoralbriefe*, Leipzig, 1885. Comp. also Harnack's elaborate review of Bp. Lightfoot's *Ignatius* in the "Expositor," London, for Jan., 1886.

† See above, pp. 124, 192, 194.

affections and past sins ; as he emerges thence, he rises regenerate, quickened to new hopes and a new life. This it is, because it is not only the crowning act of his own faith, but also the seal of God's adoption and the earnest of God's Spirit. Thus Baptism is an image of his participation both in the death and in the resurrection of Christ. See *Apost. Const.* iii. 17, ἡ κατάδυσις τὸ συναποϑανεῖν, ἡ ἀνάδυσις τὸ συναναστῆναι. For this twofold image, as it presents itself to St. Paul, see especially Rom. vi. 3 sq." Lightfoot also observes on βαπτισμός : " A distinction seems to be observed elsewhere in the N. T. between βάπτισμα, ' baptism' properly so called, and βαπτισμός, ' lustration ' or ' washing ' of divers kinds, *e. g.*, of vessels (Mark, vii. 4, [8,] Heb. ix. 10). Even Heb. vi. 2, βαπτισμῶν διδαχῆς, which at first sight might seem to be an exception to this rule, is perhaps not really so (Bleek *ad loc.*). Here, however, where the various readings βαπτισμῷ and βαπτίσματι appear in competition, the preference ought probably to be given to βαπτισμῷ as being highly supported by itself and as the less usual word in this sense . . . In the Latin version *baptisma* and *baptismus* are used indiscriminately ; and this is the case also with the Latin fathers. . . . So far as the two words have any inherent difference of meaning, βαπτισμός denotes rather the act in process, and βάπτισμα the result."

MEYBOOM, H. U. (Dr., of Assen): *De leer der Twaalf Apostelen*, two articles in the " Theologisch Tijdschrift " (published at Leiden), xix. Sept. 1885, pp. 531–551, and November, 1885, pp. 596–632. The most elaborate Dutch study on the *Didache* as yet published. The author is familiar with the Continental literature on the *Didache*, but less so with the English and American.

The first article consists of a Dutch translation of the treatise with a few opening and closing words and many catena-like notes, drawn from the copious literature of the subject. The second is a *historia litteraria*, and gives in turn, and very fully, the views of Bryennios (596–602), Krawutzcky (603–606), Hilgenfeld (606–607, cf. also 625 sq.), and Harnack (607–619). At this point the method changes, and opinions are then collected on the date of the treatise (619–622), its relation to Hermas and Barnabas (622–625) and its unity (625–628). The author's own conclusions are briefly indicated on pp. 628–632. He holds that as yet everything is unsettled and uncertain. " As regards time, place and manner of its origin, about as good as nothing can be as yet settled with certainty." In date he would be inclined to follow Harnack, and say 140–165, save that the unity of the book is too problematical. The value of the piece, thus, consists in its full presentations of the opinions thus far published by the scholars of Germany and France. Few English studies are known at first hand : probably only Spence and Gordon. Of American studies only Potwin (from the " Bibliotheca Sacra," 1884) is known at first hand. Yet through these and Sabatier he quotes Farrar, Orris, Hitchcock and Brown, and other early American publications.

The outlines of the early history of the Dutch discussions may be gathered from him as follows : the first announcement of the discovery was made in Holland in the *Nieuwe Rotterdammer Courant*, Feb. 19, 1884 ; the sole edition as yet is that of Prins, mentioned on p. 155 of this book ; the chief discussions as yet published are (besides Meyboom's own) the three following: W. C. *van Manen* in the "Bijblad van de Hervorming," 1884, No. 6; *M. A. N. Rovers* in his "Biblioth. van Mod. Theol." v., p. 810 sq.; and *Prof. M. A Gooszen* (of the National Church's supplementary professors at Leiden) in "Geloof en Vrijheid," 1885, pp. 459–506. The Dutch have certainly lagged behind the rest of Protestant Christendom in serious study of this treatise of old Christianity.

This notice was kindly furnished to me by Dr. Warfield, and I have verified it by a reference to Dr. Meyboom's article in the Dutch periodical.

POTWIN, THOMAS S. (of Hartford, Conn.), has discovered a second allusion to the *Didache* in Origen, and published it in "The Independent," of New York, for Jan. 21, 1886. It is found in *De Principiis*, iii. 2, 7. [Migne's ed. of Origen, vol. iii. 313]: "*Propterea docet nos* SCRIPTURA DIVINÀ, *omnia* QUÆ ACCIDUNT *nobis tumquam a Deo illata* SUSCIPERE, *scientes* QUOD SINE DEO NIHIL FIT. *Quod autem hæc ita sint, id est,* QUOD SINE DEO NIHIL FIAT, *quomodo possumus dubitare, Domino et Salvatore pronunciante et docente, 'Nonne passeres,'*" etc. Matt. x. 29. ("Therefore, *Holy Scripture* teaches us to receive all *that happens* as sent by God, knowing that *without God nothing happens.* For how can we doubt that such is the case, namely, that *without God nothing happens,* when our Saviour himself declares, 'Are not two sparrows sold for a farthing? and not one of them shall fall on the ground without your Father who is in heaven?'")

The Latin in the translation of Rufinus closely corresponds to a passage in the *Didache*, III. 10: "The events that befall thee thou shalt accept as good, for without God nothing happens." There is no such passage in the Bible, though the thought is entirely Scriptural (comp. Matt. x. 29; Heb. xii. 7–11; Sirach ii. 4).

That Origen, like his teacher, Clement of Alexandria, should quote the *Didache* as inspired Scripture, need not surprise us, as they had a very elastic view of inspiration and the canon. But the quotation of Origen may as well have been taken from the Epistle of Barnabas, in which the same passage occurs, and which is quoted by Origen in the same chapter.

VOLKMAR, GUSTAV (D.D., Prof. of Theol. in Zürich, a follower of Dr. Baur and the Tübingen School): *Urchristliches Andachtsbuch. Die neu entdeckte urchristliche Schrift Lehre der zwölf Apostel an die Völker. Deutsch herausgegeben und in der Kürze erklärt.* Leipzig und Zürich, 1885 (47 pages).

Volkmar speaks extravagantly of the importance of the *Didache*, calling it a material supplement to our New Testament and a precious devotional manual of primitive Christianity for the people. He gives a German translation of the text with a few notes, and refers for the critical questions to Bryennios and Harnack, promising a further discussion in the "Theolog. Zeitschrift aus der Schweiz" (which I have not seen). He translates the vexed passage Ch. XI. 11 ($\pi o\iota\tilde{\omega}\nu$ $\varepsilon\iota\varsigma$ $\mu\upsilon\sigma\tau\eta\rho\iota o\nu$ $\varkappa o\sigma\mu\iota\varkappa\grave{o}\nu$ $\grave{\varepsilon}\varkappa\varkappa\lambda\eta\sigma\iota\alpha\varsigma$), "*wenn er nach dem weltlichen Sinnbild der Gemeinde handelt,*" and agrees with the (wrong) interpretation of Harnack, namely, that it refers to clerical celibacy, or rather abstinence in marriage, which the *Did.* is supposed to allow, but not to command (p. 29, note). He interprets $\dot{\upsilon}\pi'$ $\alpha\dot{\upsilon}\tau o\tilde{\upsilon}$ $\tau o\tilde{\upsilon}$ $\varkappa\alpha\tau\alpha\vartheta\acute{\varepsilon}\mu\alpha\tau o\varsigma$,

XVI. 5: "*durch den der am Kreuz ein Fluch geworden.*" He assigns (p. 88 sq.) the composition of the *Did.* to a Jewish Christian, probably at Pella in Perea, in the period of the Jewish rebellion against Hadrian between 132 and 135, and identifies "the world-deceiver" in Ch. XVI. with the Pseudo-Messiah *Bar Cochba*, who cruelly persecuted the Christians unless they renounced and blasphemed Jesus (Justin Mart. *Apol.* i. 31). But the hypothesis is sufficiently refuted by the fact that the *Did.* represents the coming of the world-deceiver as future, and not as past or present.

WARFIELD, BENJAMIN B., D.D. (Professor in the Western Theolog. Seminary, Allegheny, Penn.): *Text, Sources, and Contents of " The Two Ways,"* *or First Section of the Didache*, in "The Bibliotheca Sacra," Oberlin, Ohio, for January, 1886, pp. 100-161. An elaborate critical analysis of Chs. I.-VI. of the *Didache* in extension and partial correction of the author's essay inserted in this book, pp. 220-225.

Dr. W. compares the various forms of the " Two Ways " in 1.) the Constantinopolitan MS. (publ. by Bryennios, 1883); 2.) the Latin Fragment (recovered by Dr. O. von Gebhardt, 1884); 3.) the reworking in chs. xviii.-xx. of the Ep. of Barnabas; 4.) the Ecclesiastical Canons (third century or early in the fourth); 5.) the Apostolical Constitutions (fourth century); and 6.) the silent quotations from the *Did.* by Hermas, Clement of Alex., the Sibylline Oracles, Pseudo-Cyprian, and Lactantius. He maintains the priority of the *Didache*, but reconstructs its text according to the agreements of the several documents that contain it. He illustrates the relation of these several forms by the following table:

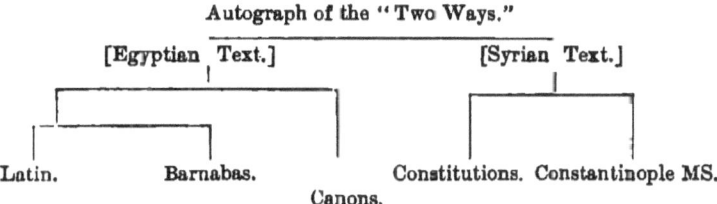

Dr. Warfield thinks that the "Two Ways" is orthodox as far as it goes, that it belongs to the same Jewish-Christian type as the Epistle of St. James and the Testaments of the XII Patriarchs, and that it dates from A.D. 100 or a little earlier.

Dr. W. has also written a review of Schaff's book, in the "Presbyt. Review" for Jan., 1886, pp. 173-176, and of several other works on the *Did.* in the "Andover Review" for December, 1885, pp. 593-599. Comp. also "The Expositor" (London), for February, 1886, pp. 156-159, and "The Independent," New York, March 4, 1886 (on 'An interpolation in the *Didache*').

I may briefly refer to some of the more lengthy and scholarly notices of the first edition of this work in "The Churchman," London, Oct., 1885 (by Dr Plummer, of Durham); "The Baptist Quarterly Review," N. York, July, 1885 (by Prof. Lincoln); Zarncke's "Lit. Centralblatt," Leipzig, Aug.

15, 1885; Messner's "Neue Evang. Kirchenzeitung," Berlin, Aug. 1, 1885; "The British Quarterly," for Oct., 1885 (Dr. Allon); "The Athenæum," London, Oct. 24, 1885; "The Church Quarterly Review," London, Jan., 1886; the "Theol. Literaturzeitung," Leipzig, 1886, No. 12 (by Harnack); Luthardt's "Theol. Literaturblatt," 1886, No. 45 (by N. Bonwetsch, of Dorpat); Harnack's *Die Apostellehre und die jüd. beiden Wege*, Leipzig, 1886, p. 40.

SECOND APPENDIX.

THE DIDACHE LITERATURE FROM 1886 TO 1888.

BALTZER, EDUARD (Pastor emeritus): *Die wiedergefundene Zwölfapostellehre. Mit Bemerkungen.* Rudolstadt i. Thür. (Hartung und Sohn), 1886. 14 pages.

A translation based upon Harnack's, accompanied by a few notes.

BEHM, in an article entitled *Bemerkungen zu Did.*, ix. 2, in the "Zeitschrift für kirchliche Wissenschaft und kirchliches Leben," Nov. 1886, pp. 575–578, explains the word $ἄμπελος$ from Justin Martyr's *Dial. c. Tryph.*, c. 110. He says: "Dieselbe ($ἄμπελος$) ist gemeint als Sinnbild der messianischen Reichsgründung Gottes."

BONWETSCH, G. N. (see p. 143), in Luthardt's "Theol. Literaturblatt," Leipzig, Nov. 12, 1886. A favorable notice of Schaff's *Manual*. The *Did.* is independent of Barnabas, and is of Jewish Christian origin. The prayer (Chap. X.) precedes the communion, which is purposely omitted.

BRATKE, E. (Lic. Dr. Prof. in Breslau): *Ueber die Einheitlichkeit der Didache*, in the "Jahrbücher für Protest. Theologie," 1886, ii., pp. 302–311.

He starts from Holtzmann's view and undertakes to prove, first, that the various writings on the "Two Ways" have not borrowed from one another, but were derived from a common source; and secondly, that this common source was most closely represented by the Latin version made known in the fragment published by Dr. von Gebhardt. The original "Two Ways" was written in Egypt before Barnabas, and afterwards enriched by the addition of a church order (chs. vii.–xvi.). This addition was made in Syria before Clement of Alexandria. The view of Bratke somewhat resembles those of Warfield and McGiffert.

BROWNE, C. GORDON: *An Essay on the "Teaching of the Twelve Apostles," read before the Burnham and Maidenhead Clerical Society, October* 13, 1887. Parkstone, 1887, 22 pp. Of the nature of a popular lecture, containing a general account of the discovery of the *Didache* and of the opinions of scholars as to its date and nature, and as to the interpretation of certain difficult passages. The author closes by quoting a passage from the *Church Quarterly Review*, in which the mention of Apostles, prophets and teachers, the conclusion is drawn that the *Didache* represents a stage of development later than the first epistle to the Corinthians, but earlier than Ephesians. Since it originated, however, probably in Syria or Palestine, "from some remote half isolated district, perhaps beyond the Jordan," it is allowed that it may have been written as late as 90 A.D., but no later.

BRUCE, ALEXANDER BALMAIN, D.D. (Prof. of Apologetics and N. T. Exegesis in Free Church College, Glasgow), discusses the *Didache* in his *The*

Miraculous Element in the Gospels, N. York, 1886, pp. 112–114, to show its inferiority to the Gospels. "It is the body of apostolic teaching without the soul, the letter without the spirit, its pure morality, but untouched by its evangelic tone, the gospel conspicuous by its absence, Christianity already reduced to a neo-legalism."

CHIAPPELLI (Prof. of the Hist. of Philos. in the Univ. of Naples): *Studi d'Antica Letteratura Christiana,* pp. 21–148.

FUNK, FRANCISCUS XAVERIUS (Prof. in the Rom. Cath. Theol. Faculty of Tübingen): *Doctrina Duodecim Apostolorum, Canones Apostolici ac Reliquæ Doctrinæ de Duabus Viis Expositiones Veteres.* Tubingæ, 1887. lxvii and 113.

Dr. Funk, the successor of Bishop Hefele in the chair of Church History at Tübingen, has assigned the *Didache* the first place among the works of the Apostolic Fathers, before Barnabas, Clement of Rome, Polycarp and Ignatius, and issued it in a new edition of the first volume of his *Opera Patrum Apostolicorum.* The Prolegomena discuss the origin, genuineness, time and place, contents, editions, and versions of the *Didache* and its relation to cognate documents. He puts it in the closing years of the first century, prior to the Epistle of Barnabas (which he assigns to the reign of Nerva). He finds, with Zahn, traces of it in Justin Martyr (in *Apol.* I. 15–18; comp. with *Did.* 1, 3–5; perhaps also in *Apol.* 1, 61), and in Tatian's *Diatessaron,* which borrowed the combination of the texts of Matthew and Luke from *Did.* I. 4. He denies the Egyptian origin and leaves the choice between Syria and Palestine. The text is accompanied with Latin notes. Besides he gives all the other cognate documents like this edition, which it very strongly resembles in order and completeness, and to which he frequently refers as the *editio post Harnackianam priorem completissima* (p. l).

Dr. Funk has also published a special discussion of the *Apostellehre und apostolische Kirchenordnung,* in the Tübingen "Theol. Quartalschrift," 1887, pp. 276–306 and 355–374, with reference to Schaff's *The Oldest Church Manual* (2d ed. 1886), and Harnack's *Die Apostellehre und die jüdischen beiden Wege* (1886). He says of the former that it contains "*die eingehendste Untersuchung, die vollständigste Zusammenstellung der einschlägigen Texte und Dokumente, annähernd vollständiges Litteraturverzeichniss und zwar so, dass bei den wichtigeren Schriften die entscheidenden Punkte kurz angegeben werden, und bei der Umsicht und Gründlichkeit, mit der es ausgearbeitet ist, wird es nicht blos jenseits, sondern auch diesseits des Ozeans seine Dienste leisten.*" Harnack's second work Dr. F. characterizes very properly as a "*bündige Zusammenfassung der Hauptfragen zur schnellen Orientirung,*" but he dissents from the new position even more than from his former view. He maintains against Harnack the priority of the *Did.* over Barnabas, and tries to refute his recent view, adopted from Dr. Taylor, that the "Two Ways," or the first six chapters, were originally a catechism for Jewish proselytes from the first century, which passed through several Christian transformations (1. Barnabas; 2. Latin fragment and Church Order; 3. Didache and Apost. Constitutions). He argues for the *Christian* origin of the "Two Ways" from the close connection of the love of God and love to our neighbor (as in Matt. 22: 38, 39), to which there is no Jewish parallel, the acquaintance of the *Did.* with the gospel in 1: 3–2: 1; 3: 1; 5: 1; as also with Paul's Epistles (6), and the command, Thou shalt not hate any man (2: 7), which is anti-Jewish. He also contends against Bratke and Warfield, for the genuineness of 1: 3–2: 1, which they regard as an interpolation.

HARNACK, ADOLF (Prof. at Marburg, formerly at Giessen. Comp. above p. 144) : *Die Apostellehre und die jüdischen beiden Wege. Erweiterter Abdruck aus der Realencyklopädie für protestantische Theologie und Kirche nebst Texten.* Leipzig, 1886. 59 pages. Printed in a somewhat briefer form and without texts in the second ed. of Herzog's "Realencycl.," Vol. XVII., pp. 656–675 (condensed translation in the revised ed. of Schaff-Herzog's "Encycl.," Vol. I., pp. 637b–640b). Comp. also his *Die Quellen der sogen. Apost. Kirchenordnung nebst einer Untersuchung über den Ursprung des Lectorats und der anderen niederen Weihen* in "Texte und Untersuchungen," ed. by O. von Gebhardt and A. Harnack, Bd. II., Heft. 5. Leipzig, 1886, 106 pages.

Die Apostellehre und die jüdischen beiden Wege is published instead of a second edition of Harnack's large work. The most important questions connected with the composition and character of the *Didache* are discussed, and the conclusions agree in the main with those reached in the earlier work (for instance the Jewish Christian authorship is still denied ; but to understand Harnack's position on this question, his view in regard to the significance of Jewish and heathen Christianity in general must be remembered). In one very important particular the author has entirely changed his position. Barnabas is no longer made one of the sources of the *Didache*, but a common source is assumed for the two, and this is held to be a pre-Christian, Jewish work, the "Two Ways." He admits further that the passage I: 3–II: 1, was wanting in the original, and that III: 1–6, was perhaps wanting in many copies of it. He formulates the history of the "Two Ways" as follows : an unknown Christian edited the "Two Ways" as the "Teaching of the Apostles" by adding to it C. VII.–XVI., in which he betrays a knowledge of the Epistle of Barnabas. This edition has disappeared. If we still possessed the Greek original of the Latin version complete, or the copy of the *Didache* used by the author of the Canons we should probably have the original form of the Christian "Teaching," for the Latin and the Canons exhibit an older text than the Constantinople manuscript. This recension was augmented by the addition of I: 3–II: 1, and a few minor changes being made, the form of the *Didache* which we possess and which was known to the author of the Apostolic Constitutions resulted. It is probable that still other recensions were in existence. The passage I : 3–II : 1, was added for the sake of providing the "Teaching of the Apostles" with specifically evangelical matter, the lack of which was felt. This passage being an interpolation, the original form of the Christian "Teaching" may be put considerably earlier than our present recension. The author gives the following table :

SECOND APPENDIX.

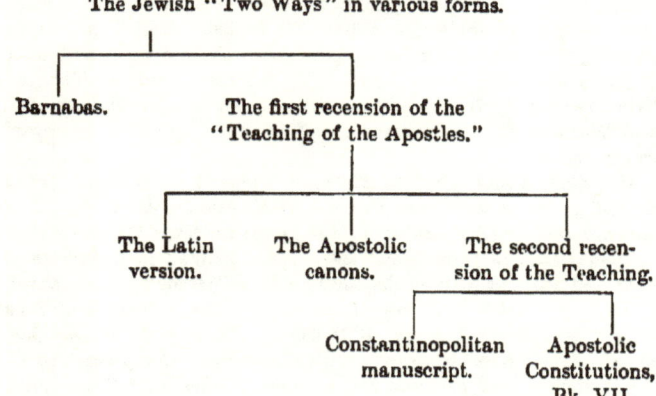

The pamphlet contains at the close the Greek text of the *Didache* and an attempted reconstruction of the Jewish "Two Ways."

Comp. also the author's three articles "*Zur Lehre der Zwölf Apostel*" in the "Theol. Literaturzeitung" (Leipzig), 1886, No. 12 and 15, and 1887, No. 2, in which he reviews the current literature upon the *Didache*.

HARRIS, J. RENDEL: *The Teaching of the Apostles (ΔΙΔΑΧΗ ΤΩΝ ΑΠΟΣΤΟΛΩΝ), newly edited, with fac-simile text and a commentary, for the Johns Hopkins University, Baltimore, from the MS. of the Holy Sepulchre (Convent of the Greek Church), Jerusalem.* Baltimore and London, 1887. Pp. viii, 107, with ten autotype plates.

A magnificent fac-simile edition of the *Didache* which puts the student practically in possession of the manuscript itself. The autotype plates are superb, the whole book worthy of them. Beside the fac-simile reproduction, a careful transcription of the text is given, and the remainder of the volume is filled with prolegomena and notes. The plates offer us very little that is new in regard to the text, and confirm Bryennios's accuracy in a remarkable manner. The only important change to be made is in xii:3 and xiii:1 where the MS. reads καθήσθαι not καθήσαι. The prolegomena contain a very complete list of the known authorities for the text of which twenty-seven (doubtful and certain) are given and discussed at length. The epistle of Jude (verses 22 and 23) is enumerated among the writings which quote from the Teaching.

The most obscure passages are illuminated with a great wealth of illustration and the correctness of the received text maintained. The Hebraisms of the document receive especial attention, and much original work is done in connection with the list of vices. The author concludes: "There is ground for suspicion that the Vidui of the Day of Atonement, the catalogue of vices in the Teaching, and the catalogue in the first chapter of Romans, are all derived from a lost alphabetical catalogue of sins." The opinion that the first five (six) chapters of the Teaching formed originally a separate document of Jewish origin is rejected; the view that I: 3–II: 1 is an interpolation is accepted with some hesitation. The prolegomena conclude with numerous notes upon various passages, some of them quite suggestive, especially in illustration of the decidedly Jewish character of the Teaching. —See good notices of this book in the "Bibliotheca Sacra" (Oberlin, Ohio) for April, 1888, pp. 372–377; by Harnack in the "Theol. Literaturzeitung" (Leipzig), 1888, No. 5; and by Warfield in the "Presbyt. Review," July, 1888.

The same author in his work, "The Teaching of the Apostles and the Sibylline Books" (see above, p. 299) points out parallels between the *Didache* and the Pseudo-Athanasian Σύνταγμα διδασκαλίας πρὸς μονάζοντας (Migne, xxviii., col. 835 sq.), which has been shown by Eichhorn (*Athanasii de vita ascetica testimonia collecta*, 1886) to be a genuine work of Athanasius. The first part of the Σύνταγμα is a working over of the *Didache* like the Apostolic Canons and the seventh book of the Apost. Const. Comp. Harnack's notice in the "Theol. Literaturzeitung," 1887, No. 2. "Therefore," says Harnack, "Athanasius himself has used the *Did.* in the instruction of Catechumens, and has made it available for monks. He has used not only ch. 1–6, but has reproduced also chap. 8 with additions." Comp. also Warfield's articles in the "Journal of the Exegetical Society," pp. 86–98 (see p. 317 below).

HERON, Rev. JAMES: *The Church of the Sub-Apostolic Age: its life, worship, and organization, in the light of the " Teaching of the Twelve Apostles."* London, 1888, pp. xi, 300.

Eighty-six pages are devoted to the *Didache* itself, the remainder of the book to church questions illustrated by it. The existence of an original independent "Two Ways" is denied, but the author believes that "prior to Barnabas, Hermas, Justin Martyr, and the rest, there was an original Christian *Didache* not very different from our *Didache*, but whose text may have had some additions made to it somewhat later from the traditional oral teaching which no doubt accompanied and supplemented it." As to its date, it is concluded that "the *Didache* assumed the form with which Bryennios has made us familiar not later than the opening of the second century, and it may have been a good deal earlier."

Among the church questions discussed in the second part of the book, the chief are the New Testament Canon and Church Organization. To the latter are devoted more than a hundred pages, in which Hatch's, Harnack's and Lightfoot's views as to the origin of episcopacy are examined in detail and all rejected, the traditional non-episcopal view being accepted over against the theory of the last named.

HILGENFELD, Dr. ADOLF (see p. 144), in "Zeitschrift für wissenschaftliche Theologie," Leipzig, 1887, Vol. XXX., 114-121. A critical notice of the works of Schaff, Warfield, Taylor, and Harnack (II) on the *Didache*. He finds the progress of research chiefly in America. "*Die Forschung finde ich namentlich in Nordamerika gefördert. Der Deutschamerikaner Phil. Schaff hat eine prachtvolle, überaus vollständige und sorgfältige Ausgabe geboten.*" "*Sehr lehrreich ist des Amerikaners B. B. Warfield Abhandlung*" [in Bibliotheca Sacra," Jan. 1886; see above, p. 305]. He is glad to find that W. agrees with him in regarding I. 3–II. 2 (εὐλογεῖτε—διδαχῆς) as an interpolation, that he and Harnack (in his second work, reprinted from Herzog's "Encycl.") separate I. 1–VI. 2 as an older work on the "Two Ways" from the rest. But he rejects the Jewish origin of the first six chs., since a Jew would not begin with the two great commandments, nor say, "Thou shalt hate no one" (II. 4), but rather, "Thou shalt love thy neighbor and hate thine enemy" (comp. Matt. 5: 43). He still holds to his former view that the *Did.* in its present shape dates from a Montanist after the middle of the second century.

KURTZ, Dr. JOH. H., in the 10th ed. of his *Kirchengeschichte*, Leipz., 1887, I., 97 *sq.*, devotes two pages to the *Did.*, giving a summary of its contents.

LECHLER, GOTTHARD VICTOR (see above, p. 301), in his pamphlet "Urkundenfunde zur Geschichte des Christlichen Altertums," Leipz., 1886. pp. 63–75, gives an account of the *Didache* and a brief discussion of it. The positions taken are in general the same as in the work mentioned on p. 301. He emphasizes more clearly than there his belief that Barnabas did not draw from the *Didache*. nor the *Didache* from Barnabas, nor the two from a common written source, but that "gewisse Grundsätze apostolischer Verkündigung, noch vor ihrer schriftlichen Aufzeichnung, allmählich eine Art stereotyper Form angenommen hatten, deren literarischen Niederschlag wir in der *Didache* einerseits, andererseits in dem Barnabasbrief und Hermas, zu erkennen hätten." While holding, as in the previous work, that the *Didache* was intended for heathen Christians, he yet emphasizes in the present case its *Jewish Christian origin.* In regard to the place of composition, he contents himself with a *non liquet.*

LINCOLN, HEMAN, D.D., in "Bibliotheca Sacra," Oberlin, O., July, 1884, pp. 590–594, discusses the merits of the *Did.* It is more interesting for its antiquity than its doctrinal worth. The author was a Jewish Christian who had not yet penetrated into the deeper spirit of Christianity, but had a lofty ideal of Christian life. The breadth and force of ethical teaching increase the surprise at the absence of doctrine. The book is orthodox, not because it affirms the cardinal truths of the Gospel, but only because it does not deny them. [Supplement to p. 152.]

LÜDEMANN, H. (Prof. of Church History in Bern), in the "Theol. Jahresbericht," ed. by Lipsius, Vol. IV., Leipzig, 1885, pp. 99–108, Vol. V., 1886, pp. 130–137 and Vol. VI., 1887, pp. 121–124.

Comprehensive and critical reviews of the principal *Did.* literature for three successive years. The writer sides with Warfield *against* the Jewish origin of the "Two Ways."

MCGIFFERT. Rev. ARTHUR C., in "The Andover Review," Vol. V., April, 1886, pp. 430–442. He ably discusses *The Didache viewed in its Relations to Other Writings*, and sums up his conclusions as follows : "We hold that an earlier and as yet undiscovered source underlies the common matter of our parallel documents ; that this source had its origin in Egypt ; was used in the composition of Barnabas, and formed the basis of the Latin translation; was augmented somewhat and afterward quoted by Clement; was used by the Canons and referred to by Athanasius. As thus augmented it was carried to Syria, and became the basis of the first five chapters of our present *Didache*, the compilation of which was the work of a Syrian or Palestinian writer.

"Finally, we believe that the first five chapters of the Bryennios *Didache*, with the omission of the sections I. 3–II. 1 and III. 1–6, are, though not indeed an exact, yet the best known representative of the original source."

I add Mr. McGiffert's own statement (made to me privately, at my request,) of the relation of his view to that of Dr. Warfield.

"Prof. Warfield, in his article in the 'Andover Review,' for July, 1886, agrees fully with the main points of the theories both of Bratke and of myself, summing up the matter as follows: 'We are at one in seeing that the *Didache* has behind it a very important textual history; in finding its birthplace in Egypt; in assigning the Latin version and Barnabas and the Canons to this Egyptian form; in perceiving that it was perfected to its present form in Syria; in seeing that the chief distinction between the Egyptian and Syrian form resides in the absence or presence of I. 3 $εὐλογεῖτε$-II. 1; and in recognising that the text of our present *Didache*, after the omissions that are necessary have been made, gives us, in its earliest chapters, a substantially accurate representation of the original "Two Ways." That is to say, we are at one in all that is of the real substance of the theory.' In examining my theory in detail, he contends that Barnabas and the Latin drew independently from an already corrupted source, and that the Latin did not draw directly from Barnabas as assumed by me. I admit that Warfield seems to me to be quite right in this contention, and in going beyond my position to have made a decided advance. He contends further that the passage III. 1–6 formed a part of the original source and was not a later interpolation as originally held by me. In this matter, too, I see my error, which was caused, as Warfield says, by my mistaking, as he and Bratke had done before me, the oldest attestation for the oldest text. I am still of the opinion that the source from which Barnabas drew did not contain the passage in question, but, as Warfield shows, that does not involve the omission in the original 'Two Ways'—an omission which he is right in saying cannot be allowed in the face of so much external testimony to the contrary. Finally, Prof. Warfield differs with both Dr. Bratke and myself in expressing grave doubts as to the separate circulation of the 'Two Ways.' His grounds for doubting are strong, and have been only increased by the discovery of more parallels to the last half of the *Did.* in quarters where only the first part could formerly be proved to be known. That a Christian 'Two Ways,' or 'Teaching,' without the chapters on church order, so circulated I now believe to be very improbable. But that there did exist such an independent *Jewish* 'Two Ways' seems to me to be sufficiently proved. That it was made part of a church order, such as our completed *Didache*, at the same time that it was Christianized appears at least highly probable."

MAJOCCHI, RUDOLFO: *La Dottrina dei Dodici Apostoli. Documento del primo secolo della chiesa, pubblicato nel suo testo originale con versione e commenti. Edizione seconda corretta ed ampliata.* Modena, 288 pp.

Eighty-eight pages are devoted to prolegomena, the remainder of the work to the text, Latin version and commentary. The author of the *Didache* is held to be a Jewish Christian, probably one of the early leaders of the school of Alexandria. The work is assigned to the apostolic age, the second half of the first century. The various introductory questions which have most absorbed the attention of scholars, such as the integrity of the "Teaching," its sources and its relations to other works, are not touched upon. The commentary is very full, but contains nothing of particular note. In the sixteenth chapter σημεῖον ἐκπετάσεως is translated *signum aperitionis*. An index of the most important words and phrases of the *Didache* is added.

MÜNCHEN, KARL (Soc. of Jesus): "*Die Lehre der 12 Apostel,*" *eine Schrift des 1. Jahrhunderts*, in the "Zeitschrift für Kath. Theologie," Innsbruck, 1886; No. IV., pp. 629–677. A learned and able essay on the age and origin of the *Did.* The author shows that it must have been written between A.D. 70 and 100, nearer 70, if not before, and refutes at length the arguments of Harnack for a later date. It originated in Jerusalem, and represents a catechetical system and church order which, in its essential features, was prepared by the apostles, and verbally transmitted and variously adapted to different churches before it was written down. The *Did.* is the oldest Jerusalem type, and in no way dependent on the Alexandrian Barnabas or the Roman Hermas. The Gospel referred to is the Gospel of Matthew and no other. " *Der Hauptpunkt unserer Hypothese ist der, dass schon die Apostel einen Sittenspiegel und eine Kirchenordnung entworfen haben* " (p. 662).

The author promises another article on the doctrinal character of the book and its relation to the Roman hierarchy.

ORRIS, S. STANHOPE, in an article *The Pseudo-Athanasius and the Teaching* in "The Independent" (Apr. 15, 1886), has pointed out the close connection of the Pseudo-Athanasian *Fides Nicaena* (Migne xxviii., col. 1635 sq.) with the *Didache*. Comp. Harnack's notice in the " Theol. Literaturzeitung," 1887, No. 2, and the notice of Harris's "Teaching of the Apostles and the Sibylline Books," in this appendix, p. 311, as well as the articles of Warfield mentioned there.

POTWIN, THOS. S. (see p. 304), in the "Andover Review" for April, 1886, pp. 443 sq., illustrates the last chapter of the *Didache* from passages in Justin Martyr (*Apol.* II., 7), Irenæus (v. 28), Hippolytus (*Christ and Antichrist*, c. 6 and 49), Origen (*De Princ.*, praef. 7); Commodian (*Instr.* 41, 42), Methodius (*De Resurr.*, 8), and Lactantius (*Div. Inst.*, vii. 17), who teach likewise that Antichrist is not an apostate church, nor an infidel power, but a counterfeit of Christ, calling himself the Son of God, deceiving the world, drawing men to an idolatrous worship of himself, subjecting believers to a fiery ordeal, until he should be destroyed with his followers at the second appearance of the real Christ, and that the end of the world will come as a destruction of the race because of its wickedness (not as a cyclical winding up of nature).

RANKE, LEOPOLD VON. His judgment on the *Didache* is given in a pamphlet which appeared after his death (May 23, 1886) under the title *Zu Leopold von Ranke's Heimgang. Als MS. gedruckt.* Leipzig, 1886, p. 9.

A few days before his death on May 3, Ranke spoke to his son Otto von Ranke of his last studies, the *Didache:* "Mit grosser Freude erzählte er von seinen letzten Studien. Sie betrafen die von Bryennios uns Licht gezogene Διδαχή των δώδεκα αποστόλων. 'Sie ist unzweifelhaft ächt, sie ist älter als der Hermas. Für den dritten Band meiner Weltgeschichte, der in neuer Auflage erscheint, habe ich eine Bemerkung gemacht. Die Διδαχή bestätigt ja nur im wesentlichen meine Auffassung.'"

RIDDLE, M. B., D.D. (Prof. of N. T. Exegesis in the Western Theol. Seminary, at Allegheny, Penn.), in the American edition of the "Ante-Nicene Library," Vol. VII., pp. 372–383 (Buffalo, N. Y., 1886).

A preliminary discussion, English translation and brief notes. No positive opinion is expressed upon the disputed questions, but the writer thinks it very probable that the resemblances between Barnabas and the *Didache* are to be accounted for by their use of a common source, and if they had this common source (the *Duae Viae*) it may have belonged to Egypt and the completed *Didache* to Syria (in agreement with the view of Bracke, Warfield and McGiffert). The version is that of Hall and Napier, published originally in the "Sunday-School Times" (Philadelphia), April 12, 1884, only a few slight changes being made.

SALMON, GEORGE, D.D., in Smith and Wace's "Dictionary of Christian Biography," Vol. IV., pp. 806–815 (London, 1887).

The article contains an excellent analysis and outline of the *Didache*, and a most important discussion of the various questions respecting its origin and its relations to other works. The author assumes an ancient Jewish "Two Ways" as the original source of the parallel sections, and thinks that Barnabas drew directly from this, and was not acquainted with the *Didache* itself. The coincidences between Barnabas and the *Didache* outside of the "Two Ways" sections are to be explained by supposing the final editor of the *Didache* to have been acquainted with Barnabas. The writers of the Eccles. Canons and the Latin version were also acquainted only with the "Two Ways," not with the *Didache*. The author traces three stages in the growth of the *Didache:* (1). Barnabas represents the original Jewish manual, probably not quoting from any written document, but from his recollection of the instruction he had possibly himself received. This original may have contained directions for baptism, and some other things found in a Christianized form in the later chapters of our *Didache*.

(2). "In the Church Ordinances [Eccles. Canons] and in the Latin *Doctrina* we have the manual as it was modified for use in a Christian community." "We are without evidence whether this manual contained more than the 'Two Ways,' though we think it probable that it did." (3). "In the *Didache* published by Bryennios we have the manual enlarged by further Christian additions; the precepts in the original manual being expanded, others added from the New Testament, and besides some wholly new sections."

The author claims that the Eucharist proper is not treated of before the fourteenth chapter. The prayers of Chaps. IX. and X. are not eucharistic prayers, but are the thanksgivings to be used before and after the joint solemn meal, the Eucharist accompanying the Agape or Love Feast. In his Introduction, mentioned just below, the author in connection with these prayers expresses the belief that "in the corresponding place of the original Jewish manual, the proselyte was taught as the concluding piece of his instruction forms of benediction to be used before and after solemn meals. These forms, I take it, the compiler of the *Didache* adapted for Christian use, leaving it free, however, to persons endowed with prophetical gifts to use different forms if they chose. These forms might be used in the Christian Love Feasts."

The *Didache* is assigned a date as early as 120 A.D. It is supposed to have emanated from the Christian Jews living east of the Jordan. The author concludes : "The antiquity of the document gives it great interest ; but since we believe that it never obtained any wide circulation or influence, and since the diversities between the Jewish Christians from whom it emanated and the rest of the Christian world soon were perceived to be so great, that the former came to be regarded as a heretical sect, we cannot look on the *Didache* as an authority, making known to us the practice of Gentile churches at any time, however early."

With this article is to be compared a chapter upon the "Teaching" by the same author in his *Introduction to the New Testament* (2d ed., London, 1886), pp. 600–618, in which the same general views are expressed. In discussing the relation of Barnabas to the "Two Ways" he remarks, "Barnabas, merely in giving practical exhortation, interwove, as his memory furnished them, precepts from a manual with which he had formerly been familiar," and this leads him to add in a note, "I now suspect that he had been a Gentile proselyte to Judaism, and had thus become acquainted with the 'Two Ways.'"

TAYLOR, C.: *The Teaching of the Twelve Apostles with illustrations from the Talmud. Two Lectures on an ancient church manual discovered at Constantinople; given at the Royal Institution of Great Britain on May 29 and June 6*, 1885. Cambridge, 1886, 136 pp.

The chief value of this work lies in the wealth of parallels brought to illustrate the *Teaching* from Jewish sources. The first lecture is devoted to the first six chapters of the *Didache*, and the author concludes that an earlier manual of the "Two Ways" existed "upon which our chapters I.–VI. were framed and from which in their final form they differ mainly by the addition of the longer paragraphs of chapter I., and of some clauses perhaps in chapter IV." This manual was "of Jewish character and possibly pre-Christian in date." The author concludes also that the *Teaching* cannot have drawn from the epistle of Barnabas, but that Barnabas is the copyist ; his source being either the *Teaching* itself or a document of which it has preserved the original form.

Lecture II. is devoted to the illustration of Chaps. VII.–XVI. The author concludes : "There is also another use of such illustrations in a case like that of our newly discovered document. Everything which goes to confirm its Jewish character has a bearing on the question of its date. If it is derived immediately from Jewish sources, it must either have emanated from a mere sect which long preserved its Hebraic peculiarities, or it must have come down to us from the primitive age in which Christianity had but just separated itself from the parent stock of Judaism. The former alternative must be rejected if at an early date we find it quoted with profound respect beyond the pale of Judaism; and we are thus finally led to regard it, in whatever may be its original form, as a genuine fragment of the earliest tradition of the church."

The lectures are followed by an English translation of the *Teaching* accompanied with notes.

Comp. also the same author's articles, *The Didache and the Epistle of Barnabas*, in "The Expositor," 1886, Apr., pp. 316–317, and June, pp. 401–428.

In the first article the priority of the *Didache* is shown from a comparison of the "Way of Death," with the parallels in Barnabas. In the second the *Didache* and the Epistle are compared in their entirety, and the author concludes that Barnabas knew the whole of the former.

Comp. also the article of the same author, *The Didache and Justin Martyr. Traces of the so-called "Teaching of the Twelve Apostles," in the writings of Justin Martyr.* I. *Traces of the "Two Ways," in the writings of Justin,* in "The Expositor," Nov., 1887; pp. 359–371.

Numerous parallels are here pointed out between the "Two Ways" and Justin's writings, which lead the author to conclude that the latter was acquainted with the *Didache*, at least with the "Two Ways," as augmented by the Christian passage, I. 3–II. 1.

WARFIELD, B. B.: *Notes on the Didache,* in the "Journal of the Society of Biblical Literature and Exegesis" (Boston), 1886, June, pp. 86–98. I. *The Pseudo-Athanasius and the Didache* (pp. 86–91). II. *The Book of Jubilees and the Didache* (pp. 91–98).

The first is a notice of the Pseudo-Athanasian parallels discovered by Harris and Orris (see above, pp. 310 and 314). The two parallels are examined and found to draw from a common source which forms a new witness to the text of the *Didache* and the value of which is pointed out by Warfield (comp. Harnack's notice mentioned above, p. 311). In the second essay the author maintains that the original "Two Ways" was not Jewish but Jewish Christian. He points out also some parallels between the *Didache* and the "Testament of the XII. Patriarchs" as well as between the *Did.* and the "Book of Jubilees." He does not claim that the parallels are marked enough to warrant the conclusion that their authors knew the *Did.*, but considers the latter parallel as close as any which has been found in a Jewish writing, unless Tobit IV. be excepted.

Warfield also published an article in the "Andover Review" for July, 1886, pp. 81–97, entitled, *The Didache and its Kindred Forms (with especial reference to the paper of Dr. McGiffert).* Upon this see the remarks of Dr. McGiffert on p. 313 above.

WOHLENBERG, G.: *Die Lehre der zwölf Apostel in ihrem Verhältniss zum neutestamentlichen Schrifttum. Eine Untersuchung.* Erlangen, 1888. 96 pp.

The author finds in the *Didache* the earliest testimony to the existence of our Gospels of Matthew and Luke, and in its prayers a most weighty witness to the historical character of the Gospel of John. He finds traces of a knowledge of the Acts, Romans, Ephesians, I. and II. Thessalonians and possibly of Philippians, I. Timothy, Hebrews, I. Peter, and II. John. He concludes that the *Didache* presupposes a general circulation of the Gospel canon so far as it had been formed, and that some forty years after the composition of our synoptic Gospels two of them at least had gained normative and canonical significance in the church, but among the readers for whom the *Didache* was written (probably Egyptian) an extra-Gospel canon cannot be assumed.

ZAHN, TH., in his *Studien zu Justinus Martyr*, in Brieger's "Zeitschrift für Kirchengeschichte," Vol. VIII., pp. 66–85, makes it very plausible that Justin Martyr knew the *Didache*, which therefore must have been written before A.D. 140. The resemblance is found in the teaching on baptism.

Since the Second Appendix was in type, I have received some new publications on the *Didache*, which deserve a brief notice.

KNOOP, OTTO (Gymnasiallehrer in Posen, Prussia): *Der dogmatische Inhalt der Διδαχὴ τῶν δώδεκα ἀποστόλων. Beilage zum Programm des Königlichen Friedrich-Wilhelms-Gymnasiums in Posen.* Posen, 1888, 28 pages, 4to.

This gymnasial program discusses, as the title indicates, chiefly the doctrinal contents or the theology of the *Didache*, under the following heads: 1, time and place of composition; 2, contents of the *Didache;* 3, its object; 4, its relation to the sacred writings; 5, the doctrine concerning the triune God; 6, God the Father; 7, Sin; 8, Jesus Christ; 9, the Holy Spirit; 10, the Church; 11, Baptism; 12, the Eucharist; 13, Prayer; 14, Fasting; 15, the higher Christian perfection; 16, Eschatology; 17, the Christian Congregation; 18, the Christian teachers; 19, the officers of the Christian Congregation.

As regards the time and place of composition, Knoop agrees with the views of Harnack in his first treatise (he does not mention the second). In the section which treats of the relation of the *Didache* to the sacred writings, he says (p. 7): "The sources from which our author drew are the Words of the Lord, handed down orally and by writing; then, also, the Old Testament. That the author used Hermas appears improbable, and it is also doubtful whether he used the Epistle of Barnabas. We think it more probable that the writer of the Barnabas-Epistle made use of the *Didache*." There is no trace of a New Testament canon, and the allusions to the apostolic writings are given as the Word of the Lord through the Apostles. The words of the Prophets are also quoted as the Word of the Lord. The *Did.* follows no other authority but the Old Testament and the Gospel. The doctrine of the Trinity is implied in the baptismal formula twice stated in ch. VII. Sin and guilt are taught in the catechism, ch. V.; the need of redemption, in IV. 6, 14; XVI. 1. Christ spoke through the Prophets. He is pre-existent. His divinity is implied in the baptismal formula, and expressly stated in the designation "the God of David" (X. 6), according to the reading of the MS., which needs no correction into "the Son of David." River-baptism by immersion (*Immersionstaufe*) is enjoined in ch. VII., as the rule, but baptism in other water and by aspersion (*Aspersionstaufe*) is allowed in exceptional cases (*wenn der Gesundheitszustand es erfordert*, p. 13). The Eucharist gives spiritual nourishment to eternal life (X. 3), and therefore must be repeated every Lord's Day (XIV. 1), in connection with the Agape, to which the words μετὰ τὸ ἐμπλησθῆναι (X. 1) refer. Here Knoop agrees with Zahn. He finds in the *Did.* the distinction of a higher and lower morality, and understands the difficult passage ch. XI. 11 of voluntary celibacy (in agreement with Harnack), as a part of Christian perfection. The last chapter enjoins the duty of constant watchfulness in view of the coming of the Lord, which is near at hand, though Antichrist had not yet appeared.

The essay is a clear summary, but presents nothing new.

LUTHARDT, DR. CHR. ERNST (Prof. of Theol. at Leipzig; see. p. 146), in his *Geschichte der christlichen Ethik*, Leipzig, 1888, Part I., 93-98, devotes several pages to the moral section of the *Didache*. He sustains the views advocated in this book, that the *Didache* is of Jewish Christian origin, though intended for Gentiles (τοῖς ἔθνεσιν), and that it is the oldest church manual, dating from the first century, probably from Palestine or Syria (at least the eucharistic prayers, where the grain on the mountains is mentioned, cannot be from Egypt). He places the *Didache* correctly between the Apostles and the Apostolic Fathers. It is Jewish Christian without being anti-Pauline, and represents the cor sensus of the Apostles (p. 95). The moral section (chs. I.-VI.) shows "*den apostolischen Durchschnittscharacter, aber bereits mit Spuren judaistischer Gesetzlichkeit,*" *i.e.* the average ethical standard of the Apostles, but modified by elements of Jewish legalism. "In this form Christianity appealed to the nobler aspirations of Greek and Roman moralists, and achieved its victory over the heathen world."

GORE, CHARLES, M.A. (Principal of the Pusey House; Fellow of Trinity College, Oxford, etc.): *The Ministry of the Church*, London and New York (James Pott & Co.), 1889. The author discusses the *Did.* in Appended Notes, p. 411-419. He regards it as a primitive manual of church directions by a Jewish Christian of Palestine or Syria, probably of the East Jordanic district, remote from Pauline influences. "It belongs rather to the enlightened synagogue, than to the illuminated Church." The advice about "bearing the yoke" of Jewish observance only up to a man's power, "reveals an intensely Jewish atmosphere, and carries us back in its very language to the circumstances of the Apostolic Council (Acts XV. 10-28)." The eucharist is represented as a Jewish feast Christianized. The book points to the Jewish Christians of the Epistle to the Hebrews. It supposes a state of the Christian ministry which existed long anterior to Ignatius.

TAYLOR, C., D.D. (Master of St. John's College, Cambridge, see p. 316), in "The Classical Review" for Oct., 1388 (Vol. II., 262 sq.), has a suggestive note on the difficult passage ἱδρωτάτω, ch. I. 6, and modifies his former translation (*The Teaching*, etc., p. 123) thus: "Let thine alms *go on sweating* into thine hands until thou know to whom thou shouldest give." ἱδρωτάτω is the present imperative from a *hapax legomenon* ἱδρωτάω, and gives good sense. It need not be changed into ἱδρωσάτω, the aorist imperative from the known verb ἱδρόω, nor is it necessary to prefix the negative μή, as a correction of the sense. For the context implies a continued process, and there is no such contradiction between this and the preceding command, "Give to every one that asketh," as to require the negative for harmonizing the two sayings. The one is addressed to those that have to give of their means; the other to those who have to "sweat" for their living (Gen. III. 19), who have to "labor" that they may give alms (Eph. IV. 28).

Prof. Skeat directed Dr. Taylor's attention to the following remarkable parallel in *Piers Plowman* (B. VII. 73):

> "Catoun kenneth men thus, and the clerke of the stories,
> *Cui des videto*, is Catounes techinge.
> And in the stories he techeth to bistowe thyn almes;
> *Sit elemosina tua in manu tua, donec studes cui des*.
> Ac Gregori was a gode man, and bade us gyven alle
> That asketh for his love that usalle leneth."

Dr. Taylor is inclined to see in the sentence *Sit elemosina tua*, etc., a corruption of *Sudet elemosina tua in manus duas donec scias cui des*.

RICHARDSON, ERNEST C. (M.A., librarian of the Theological Seminary at Hartford, Connecticut), gives a carefully prepared list of the Didache-literature down to 1887, in his "Bibliographical Synopsis" of the Ante-Nicene Christian literature, which is part of the Index volume of the American edition of the *Ante-Nicene Fathers*, Buffalo (now New York), 1887, pp. 83-86.

ALPHABETICAL INDEX.

The Index covers pp. 1 to 158 and 297 to 318, but does not include the Greek words, which are arranged alphabetically in Chapter XXV. Neither the Commentary on the *Did.*, nor the Documents are indexed.

Addis, W. E., on editions of *Did.*, 147.
Advent of Christ, 75 sqq.
Affusion, Baptism by, 33, 41 sqq.; gradual substitute for immersion, 51.
Agape, 57 sqq.
Alexandria, as place of composition of *Did.* 123.
Allon, Dr., 306.
Almsgiving, 63 sq.
Anabaptists, 53.
Anthropology of the *Did.*, 25.
Antichrist, 75 sqq.
Antioch, as place of *Did.'s* composition, 124.
Apocrypha quoted in *Did.*, 81.
Apostles, 64 sq., 67 sq.
Apostolic Preaching, a lost treatise, 110.
Apostolic Sees, 66.
Apostolical Church Order, 12, 18, 19, 21, 127 sqq., and Docs. V. and VI.
Apostolical Canons. *See* above.
Apostolical Constitutions, 21, and Doc. VII.
Aquinas, Thomas, on Baptism, 44.
Arrangement of matter, 16.
Aspersion, Baptism by, 33, 41 sqq.
Athanasius, 116.
Augsburg, Confession, on Baptism, 53, note.

Baltzer, E., on the *Did.*, 307.
Bapheides on Baptism, 42; review of Bryennios' ed of *Did.*, 142; probable date of *Did.*, 142.
Baptism, in the *Didache*, 25, 29 sq.; formula of, 30; Infant, 31; not a clerical function, 35; in the Catacombs, 36 sqq.; in the Baptismal pictures, 37-40; in the Greek Church, 42; Syrian mode of, 43; in the Latin Church, 45; in the Anglican church, 45 sqq.; after the Reformation, 51 sqq.; summary of results of historical sketch of, 54 sqq.; how the controversy may be settled, 57. *See* Immersion and Affusion.

Baptist view, arguments for, 56.
Barnabas, Epistle of, 3, 12; date of, 121 sq.; Doc. III.
Barnabas and *Didache* compared, 19, 20, 21; on the canon, 78. *See* Doc. III.
Behm, explanation of the word ἄμπελος, 307.
Berggren, J. E., on *Did.*, 154.
Bestmann, H. J., on *Did.*, 123, 127, 143.
Bibliography, 140 sqq.
Bickell, Georg, on *Did.*, 129, 143.
Bickell, J. W., 11; on Apostolical Church Order, 128 sq.
Bielenstein, A., on *Did.*, 143.
Bingham, Joseph, on mode of baptism, 46.
Binnie, Wm., on *Did.*, 297.
Bishops, 64 sqq., 73 sqq.; word explained, 74.
Boase, notice of *Did.*, 151.
Bonaventura, on Baptism, 44.
Bonet-Maury, G., 63, 120, 123, 153.
Bonwetsch, 11, 143, 306.
Bornemann, W., on *Did.*, 297.
Bratke, E., on the *Did.*, 305 sq., 307.
Brown, Francis, 12; on the quotations, 88, 91; ed. of *Did.* with Dr. Hitchcock, 114, 121, 123, 151.
Browne, C. G., on the *Did.*, 307.
Bruce, A. B., an estimate of the *Did.*, 307 sq.
Bryennios, Philotheos, dedication to, III.; edition of the Clementine Epistles, 2, 4; his discovery of the Jerusalem MS., 8; biographical sketch of, 8, 9; on Baptism, 33; his edition of the *Did.*, 114, 116, 118, 121, 141 sq.; on date of *Did.*, 122; autobiographical sketch and letter, at the end.
"Bryennios Manuscript," three reproduced pages of, 151.

Calvin on Baptism, 52.
Camp, C. C., trans. of *Did.*, 151.
Canon, N. T., and *Did.*, 78.

Canons, Apostolical or Ecclesiastical. *See* Apostolical Church Order.
Caspari, C. P., 120, 122, 154.
Cassel, Paul, notice of *Did.*, 143.
Catacombs, Pictures of Baptism, illustrating the *Didache*, 36 sqq.
Chiappelli, 308.
Chiliasm of the *Did.*, 77.
Christ, baptism of, 36, 37, 38.
Christians, solidarity and hospitality of primitive, 63, 64.
Christology, of the *Didache*, 25.
Chrysostom, 3.
Church, prayers for, meaning of, 25.
Church government in *Did.*, 62 sqq.
Churton, 125.
Citations from the Scriptures, 80 sqq.
Clement of Alexandria, 114, 121.
Clement, Pseudo-, 24.
Clement of Rome Epistles of, 3, 67, 79.
Clinical Baptism, 33.
Codex, Jerusalem. *See* Jerusalem Manuscript.
Commandments and the *Did.*, the Ten., 81.
Constantine the Great, 32.
Constitutions, Apostolic, 12, 132 sqq.; seventh book of, Doc. VII.
Cote, 36, 38, 40.
Coxe, H. O., 8.
Craven, E. R., 151, Comments on *Did.*, 153.
Credner, 118.
Cup, at Eucharist, 57.
Cyprian, on clinical baptism, 33 sq.; on church orders, 66.
Cyprian, Pseudo-, 117.

David, holy vine of, 115 (*see* Com. on IX. 2).
Deaconesses, 73.
Deacons, 64 sqq., 73 sqq.
De Aleatoribus of Pseudo-Cyprian, 117.
De Romestin, H., 11, 17, 121, 123, 147.
De Rossi, on Catacomb pictures, 36, 39, 40.
Dexter, H. M., quoted, 53.
Didache (*see* Table of Contents at beginning), fac-similes of 4, 6, 7; publication of, 10-12; contradictory estimates of, 12-14; title of, 14; contents of, 16; doctrinal outline, 17; its relation to Epistle of Barnabas, 19, 20; to Shepherd of Hermas, 21; to the Apostolical Church Order, 21; to the Apostolical Constitutions, 21; its theology, 22; represents Christianity as a holy life, 22; draws from the Bible, 22; yet infinitely below it in tone, 22, 23; its doctrinal omissions mean little, 23; its teachings orthodox, 23; not Ebionitic, 23; chief doctrinal points 24; liturgical part, 26; the Christian week, 27 sq.; prescribes the Lord's Prayer, and fasts, 29; baptismal teaching, 29 sqq., 120; Eucharistic teachings, 57 sqq , 121; no separation between Agape and Eucharist, 60; on form of government and gospel ministers, 66 sqq., 120; and the Canon, 78 sqq.; style and vocabulary, 95 sqq.; authenticity of, 114 sqq.; passed into other books and out of sight, 118.; date, 119 sqq.; place, 123 sqq.; authorship, 125.
Doctrina Apostolorum, 118.
Doctrines in Teaching, 22 sqq.
Duæ Viæ, 18 sqq.
Duchesne, L., notice of *Did.*, 153.

Ebionitic origin of *Did.*, discussed, 23, 26, 120.
Edward VI. immersed, 51.
Elders, 64 sqq.
Elizabeth, Queen, immersed, 51.
Erasmus, quoted, 51.
Eschatology, 75 sqq., 121.
Eucharist, 25, 57 sqq.; prayers in *Did.*, 57, 58, 315 sq.; embraced primitively the Agape and the Communion proper, 58; no allusion to atonement in *Did.*'s prayers, 61.
Eusebius mentions *Did.*, 116.
Evangelists, 64.
Exorcism, 35.

Farrar, F. W., 11, 121, 123, 147.
Fasting, before Baptism, 34, 35; on Wednesdays and Fridays, 25, 29.
Fitzgerald, J., trans. of *Did.*, 151.
Friday, fasting enjoined on, 25, 28.
Friedberg, E, art. on *Did.*, 144.
Funk, F. X., 3, 4, 5, 11, 121, 123, 144, 308 sq.

Gardiner, F., trans. of *Did.*, 151.
Garrucci, on Catacomb pictures, 36, 37, 39, 40; on immersion, 44.
Gebhardt, O. von, 4, 11; designation of MS., 8; discovers Latin fragment of *Did.*, 119. *See* Doc. II.; letter on the *Did.*, 298.
Glossolalia not in *Did.*, 61, 120.

ALPHABETICAL INDEX. 323

Gnosticism not alluded to, 120.
God, 24; his providence, 25.
Gordon, Alexander, art. on *Did.*, 148.
Gore, Charles, 319.
Gospel acc. to the Egyptians, 23, 86.
Gospel acc. to the Hebrews, 86.
Gospels in *Did.*, 81 sqq.
Government, ecclesiastical, in *Did.*, 63.
Grabe, 117.
Gregory I., on immersion, 44.
Gregory, Caspar René, 10.

Hale, C. R., photographs of *Did.*, 151.
Hall, E. Edwin, art. on *Did.*, 151.
Hall, I. H., phraseology of *Did.* 95 ; trans. of *Did.*, 151; phraseology cf. 153.
Harnack, A., 10, 16, 17, 117, 119, 128 ; date of *Did.*, 123 ; designation of MS., 3, 4 ; on ancient mode of Baptism, 49 sqq.; ecclesiastical organization, 63; views on Gospels in *Did.*, 86 ; on the quotations, 86, 89; on authenticity, 114 ; puts Barnabas before *Did*, 121 ; edition of *Did.*, 144 ; second edition, 309 sq ; notice of Schaff's ed., 306.
Harris, J. R., 116, 142 ; place of *Did.*, ed. of three pages of MS., 151; source and value of *Did.*, 153 ; the *Did.* and the Sibylline books, 299 sq., 311; fac-simile edition of the *Did.*, 310 sq.; the *Did.* and the Σύνταγμα, 311.
Hatch, Edwin, 11.
Helveg, Fr., trans. of *Did.*, 155.
Hermas, Shepherd of, 12, Doc. IV.; parellels with *Did.*, 21 ; relation to *Did.*, 122 ; and the Canon, 79.
Heron, James, on the *Did.* and church organization, 311.
Hicks, E. L., arts. on *Did.*, 121, 140.
Hilgenfeld, A., 3, 11, 17, 18, 117 ; date of *Did.*, 120, 123; designation of MS., 3 ; Montanism in *Did.*, 72, 120; *Did.* after Barrnabas, 121; Ed. of *Did.*, 144; notice of other works, 311 sq.
Hitchcock, R. D., 12, 121, 123, 151.
Holtzmann, 11, 16, 17, 128 ; on *Did.*, 121, 145.
Holy Spirit, 25.
Hort, on Hermas, 122.
Hospitality, 63.

Ignatius, Epistles (so called), 5, 66, 122 ; and the Canon, 79.

Immersion, in living water, 30, 32 ; exceptions to the rule. 33 ; in the Catacombs and in the ancient church, 36 sqq.; and pouring, historical sketch of, 41 sqq.; not general among early Baptists, 53. *See* Baptism and Aspersion.
Infant Baptism, 31.
Irenæus, 66, 115, 116, 121.

James alluded to, 93.
Jerome, 87, 117.
Jerusalem as place of *Did.'s* composition, 124.
Jerusalem Monastery, 1 ; Library of, 2.
Jerusalem MS., appearance and contents, 2 sqq.; number, 3.
Jessup, H. H., on Syrian Baptism, 300.
John, Gospel of, and *Did.*, 91 sq.
Joseph and Mary, genealogy of, in Jerusalem, MS., 6, 7
Judgment, day of, 25.
Judicium secundum Petrum (or Petri), 12, 18, 117. *See* also Duæ Viæ.
Justin Martyr, 121 ; description of Baptism, 30 ; on fasting, 35 ; on the right to baptize, 35 ; and the Canon, 79.

Knoop, 318.
Krawutzcky, 11, 23 sq., 86, 89, 115, 116, 117, 121, 123, 128, 145, 300.
Kraus, on the Catacombs, 36.

Lagarde, 115, 129.
Langen on *Did.*, 121, 123, 145.
Language of *Did.*, 95 sqq.
Lay-Baptism, 35 note ‡.
Lechler, G. V., on the *Did.*, 301, 312.
Leon, the copyist of the Jerusalem MS., 5.
Lightfoot, J. B., 3, 4, 9, 11, 120, 121, 123 ; outline of opinions, 149 ; note on the *Did.* and the Christian ministry, and on baptism, 301 sq.
Lincoln, Heman, notice of *Did.*, 152, 305, 312.
Lipsius, 86, 89 ; on *Did.*, 121, 146.
Literature, 140 sq.
Long, J. C., art. or *Did.*, 152.
Lord's day, 25, 27, 28; Prayer, 25, 29.
Lord's supper. *See* Eucharist.
Lucian, 64, 69, 71.
Lüdemann, H., on the *Did.*, 312.
Luke, Gospel of, quoted, 88.
Luthardt, 146, 319.

21

McGiffert, A. C., on the *Did.* and on Warfield's views, 312 sq.
Majocchi, R., on the *Did.*, 313 sq.
Malachi, quoted, 80.
Marriott on mode of Baptism, 48.
Mary of Cassoboli, spurious epistle of, 4; spurious letter of Ignatius to, 5.
Massebieau, 16, 121, 123, 153.
Mathieau, S., art. on *Did.*, 154.
Matthew, Gospel of, quoted, 82.
Melk, Library of, 119.
Ménégoz, E., arts. on *Did.*, 154.
Messner, 306.
Meyboom, H. U., on the *Did.*, 304.
Millennium, calculations relating to fallacious, 76; view of *Did.*, 77.
Montfauçon, 3.
Montanism, not in *Did.*, 72, 120.
Most Holy Sepulchre, Monastery of, 1.
München, K., on the age and origin of the *Did.*, 314.
Muralt, E., de, art. on *Did.*, 154.

Napier, John T., trans. of *Did.*, 151.
Neale, John Mason, on Baptism, 42.
Neander, on ancient mode of Baptism, 49.
New Testament in *Did.*, 78 sqq.
Nicephorous mentions *Did.*, 118.
Nirschl, Josef, rev. Bryennios, 146.
Northcote and Brownlow, 36.
Novatianus, baptized by aspersion, 34.

Old Testament in *Did.*, 78 sqq.
Origen, 116, 174, 304.
Orris, S. S., text and transl., 152; the *Did.* and Pseudo-Athanasius, 314.

Papias and the Canon, 79.
Parker, J. H., 36.
Passover, Jewish, described, 58 sq., contrasted with the Christian Agape, 59.
Pastor Hermae. *See* Hermas.
Pastoral Epistles, 65.
Paul alluded to, 92 sq.
Paulssen, A. S., trans. of *Did.*, 155.
Peter Lombard on Baptism, 44.
Peter, St., alluded to, 93, 95.
Petersen, trans. of *Did.*, 146.
Pez, Bernhard, 119.
Pfaff, fragm. from Irenæus, 117.
Phanar, 1.
Phraseology of *Did.*, by I. H. Hall, 153.
Pitra, J. B., 129.
Place of composition of *Did.*, 123.
Plummer, A., 11, 89, 149, 305.

Polycarp, 72, 79.
Potwin, L. S., vocabulary of *Did.*, 95; on age, 121, 123, 152.
Potwin, Thos. S., the *Did.* and Origen, 304; the *Did.* and Justin Martyr, 314.
Pouring, in Baptism. *See* Affusion.
Prayer and Fasting, 29 sqq.
Prayer Book on Baptism, 51 sq.
Presbyter, 64 sqq.; name explained, 74.
Prins, J. J., ed. of *Did.*, 155.
Procter, quoted, 52.
Prophets, 64, 69; the ancient, 70 sq.; false, 69.
Pseudo-Cyprian, 117.
Pseudo-Ignatian Epistles, 5.

Quotations, Scripture, and allusions in the *Did.*, 94 sq.

Ranke, L. von, remarks on the *Did.*, 314 sq.
Ravenna, Council of, on mode of Baptism, 45.
Réville, Jean, art. on *Did.*, 154.
Riddle, M. B., on the *Did.*, 315.
Robertson, A., 11, 149.
Roller, on the Catacombs, 36; Baptismal pictures, 37; on mode of Baptism, 39, 40.
Roma Sotterranea, by De Rossi, Northcote and Brownlow, and Kraus, 36.
Rördam, T., art. on *Did.*, 155.
Rufinus mentions Duæ Vitæ, 18, 117.

Sabatier, Paul, ed. of *Did.*, 154.
Sabbath, 27.
Sacrifice, the Christian. *See* Eucharist.
Sadler, 123, 125.
Salmon, 122; on the *Did.*, 315 sq.
Schaff, P., ed. of *Did.*, 152.
Schultze, Victor, on Catacombs, 36, 38.
Scotch Confession, Second, on Baptism, 53.
Second coming of Christ, 75 sqq.
Second Ordinances of the Apostles, 115.
Septuagint, words common to *Did.* and, 105 sqq.
Shepherd of Hermas, 21.
Sirach quoted, 94.
Smyth, Egbert C., 12, 152; on the *Didache* and Baptismal pictures, 36.
Spence, Canon, 11, 121, 123, 127, 149.

Spirit, Holy, 25.
Stanley, Dean, on mode of Baptism, 47 sq.
Starbuck, C. C., 12, 152.
Sunday, 27.
Symeon of Jerusalem, conjectured as author of *Did.*, 127.

Taylor, C., lectures on the *Did.* and the Talmud, 149, 316 sq.; articles on the *Did.* and Barnabas, and on the *Did.* and Justin, 317; note on ἱδρωτάτω, 320.
Teachers, 64 sqq., 72 sq.
Teaching of the Twelve Apostles. *See* Didache.
Tertullian, on Infant Baptism, on mode of Baptism, 32, 33; on fasting, 35; on the right to baptize, 35, on church order, 66.
Thanksgiving, 56 sqq. *See* Eucharist.
Theology of *Did.*, 22 sqq.
Title of *Did.*, 15.
Tobit quoted, 94.
Trinity, 25.
Two Ways, 18; figure used in Talmud, 21, and in Xenophon, 21, 22; Rufinus on, 18.

V. [enables], E[dmund], 125, 150.
Varming, C., trans. of *Did.*, 155.
Vocabulary of *Did.*, 59 sqq.
Volkmar, G., on the *Did.*, 304.

Waldenses and the *Did.*, 119.

Wall, William on mode of baptism, 45, 51.
Warfield, B. B., 121. *See* essay on Doc. II.; notice of his critical discussion of the text of the "Two Ways," 305; on the *Did* and Pseudo-Athanasius, the *Did.* and Bk. of Jubilees, 317.
Watchfulness, 75.
Way of darkness, 19.
Way of death, 26.
Way of life, 26.
Way of light, 19.
Week, days of, 127.
Wednesday, fasting on, 25, 28.
Westminster Assembly, on Baptism, 52.
Wohlenberg, G., the *Did.* and the New Testament, 317 sq.
Words not in New Testament, 99 sqq.
Wordsworth, J., 11, 89, 128, 150.
World-deceiver, 76.
Worship, freedom of, in *Did.*, 61.
Wünsche, A., text and trans. 11, 146.

Zahn, Th., 11, 16; Barnabas, integrity of, later than *Did.*, 121; Hermas, date of, 122; date of, 123; ed. of *Did.*, 114, 117, 146; the *Did.* and Justin Martyr, 318.
Zarncke, 305.
Zechariah quoted, 81.
Zöckler, O., arts. on *Did.*, 147.
Zwingli on infant and heathen adult salvation, 53.

www.ingramcontent.com/pod-product-compliance
Lightning Source LLC
Chambersburg PA
CBHW030007240426
43672CB00007B/861